Edward Thompson

Mike Davis

Raymond Williams

Rudolf Bahro

Lucio Magri

Etienne Balibar

Roy and Zhores Medvedev

John Cox

Saburo Kugai

Marcus Raskin

Noam Chomsky

Alan Wolfe

Mary Kaldor

Fred Halliday

Exterminism
and Cold War

Edited by New Left Review

Verso

First published 1982
© foreword and collection, *New Left Review*
Copyright in individual contributions remains
with their respective authors

Verso Editions and NLB
15 Greek Street, London W1

Filmset in Garamond by
Preface Ltd
Salisbury, Wilts

Printed in Great Britain by
Thetford Press Ltd
Thetford, Norfolk

**British Library
Cataloguing in Publication Data**

Exterminism and cold war.
  1. Atomic warfare
  I. Thompson, E. P.
  355'.0355   UA646
  ISBN 0-86091-051-2
  ISBN 0-86091-746-0 Pbk

Contents

Foreword

The advent of the epoch of nuclear weapons, announced to the world at Hiroshima and Nagasaki, irreversibly changed the nature of warfare. Acceptance of this truth is virtually universal today, even if corresponding action has been minimal. But the new possibility of a global holocaust has altered the bases and terms of the prospect for socialism no less permanently, making it overwhelmingly more urgent, yet practically more difficult, than ever before. Only a planet freed from class division and imperial exploitation, in which liberty and equality were common international realities, could be a peaceful environment for the human race. But the very existence of huge military machines clustered around weapons of mass destruction lends a terrible inertia to present political and economic structures, impeding free development of the broad social movements necessary to bring a classless society nearer—movements whose very stirring may jeopardize the 'equilibrium' of terror on which the precarious and partial peace we still know appears to rest. This entirely unprecedented situation demands a reworking of the principal traditions of socialist thought. The idea of a military conflagration that could wipe out every form of human society never occurred to Owen or Fourier, Marx or Engels, Morris or Lenin. But it is impossible to imagine the basic structures of their thought remaining unaltered had this been historically conceivable in their time.

The threat of nuclear war has been with us now for more than three decades, yet socialist culture has scarcely started to take the measure of its consequences for the traditional visions of world history widely shared on the left. One of the reasons for the difficulty experienced in doing so lies in the very vocabulary of the socialist movement. The perspective that won overall hegemony by the turn of the century, providing the dominant idiom of the international labour movement to this day, was Marxist. The historical materialism of Marx and Engels, as of their successors in the era of Luxemburg and Lenin, conceived progress towards socialism as the fruit of unrelenting struggle of class against class, labour against capital, which could only be finally resolved by a revolutionary victory of the exploited over their exploiters, if necessary—and few of them doubted the necessity—by force of arms. Revolutionary socialism was thus impregnated from the start by the expectation and model of civil war—whose own military terminology it tended to assimilate into the ordinary language of militancy (battles, fronts, retreats, advances, tactics, strategy). The alternative experience of a reformism preaching collaboration rather than conflict between classes—or 'social peace'—and abandoning socialism for the mere administration of capitalism itself, could only confirm this fundamental stance. Marxism as a theory and vocabulary of class struggle has remained the essential language of most active socialists throughout the world.

The tension introduced into this inheritance by the coming of nuclear weapons is an obvious one. For the possibility of planetary destruction affects all classes, as it does all societies. It poses the question of a common humanity *before* the advent of the classless society that socialist thought has always insisted could alone realize it. A shared interest in human survival now unites exploiters and exploited—in 'the last historical resort', it is true, but that resort is now perpetually close at hand. Socialism has, of course, always promised an ultimate universalism—although its particular means was the victory of the working class, its goal was not to be the rule of that class, but the dissolution of all classes. The early Marx emphasized its future benefits even for the possessors, alienated like the dispossessed in the civilization of capital. But by and large this universalist horizon has never been centrally focused in the Marxist tradition. Utopian socialism related much more directly to it. Precisely because Owen, Saint-Simon and Fourier lacked either a materialist theory of historical change, or any conception of the particular transforming agency of labour, they could imagine socialism much more immediately as a general emancipation: hence, among other merits that have been rediscovered today, the much greater prominence they accorded to the liberation of women. The resources of that utopianism will need to be drawn upon and developed again, if socialism is to confront with any realism the universal threat of a military explosion that would annihilate every class. At the same time, however, the advance represented by what its founders called 'scientific' socialism cannot be rescinded: class struggle, from which the utopians looked away, has not been suspended or even reduced by the thermonuclear age—it has only been deformed and displaced. Socialism still needs, more than ever, a *historical* perspective for the transition beyond a world haunted by nuclear fear as well as divided by social misery and injustice, and such a perspective must indicate particular agencies and strategies for its realization, even if these will inevitably be more complex than those envisaged by Marx or Engels in their time. The long-separated traditions, which can as properly be called romantic and rational, of those who first developed socialism as an idea, need to be rejoined and crossed today, if the notions of peace and revolution are ever to be united without contradiction.

This task, involving as it does a rethinking of values as well as of analyses, has lain largely neglected these past years. *New Left Review* shared that neglect, perhaps in its case with more responsibility than others bore. For in the early sixties it was one of the principal intellectual participants in the debates over nuclear disarmament in Britain, as its two predecessors—*Universities and Left Review* and *The New Reasoner*—had been. The declining impetus of CND, after the Cuban missile crisis, took nuclear warfare off the agenda of mass politics in England for nearly two decades. NLR did nothing to reinstate the issue, its attention turning to other priorities in the following years. The arms race actually gathered speed during the period of 'detente', but the revival of nuclear disarmament as a demand mobilizing a vast popular movement had to wait till the eighties. The immediate political occasion was, of course, the NATO decision, taken at Brussels in December 1979, to install Cruise and Pershing II missiles in Europe—a potentially critical escalation of the arms race in an area already crammed with the greatest concentration of weapons of mass destruction on earth. In Britain, the prime intellectual stimulus for the revival was given by Edward Thompson, in an act of public service with few comparisons in the recent history of any country. Early in 1980, in the course of his many addresses and essays on the growing perils of the international situation, Thompson published in NLR one of his most far-reaching reflections: 'Notes on Exterminism, the Last Stage of Civilization'. Concluding these, he asked for readers' amendments, and action, in the common cause of peace. NLR resolved to organize as wide a discussion as it could of the questions raised, and the theses proposed, by 'Notes on Exterminism'. The result is the present volume.

Two features of the collection need some explanation. The first is the pattern of contributions to it. One of the relative weaknesses of the literature produced by CND as a movement in Britain, two decades ago, was its predominantly national focus. This was probably an inevitable limitation of a period in which strong movements against the dangers of nuclear war existed only in two major countries—the UK and Japan (where the public campaign has always been the broadest and most sustained in the world). But it was a major limitation nevertheless, since the issue of world peace is by definition an international one. Today, in contrast, the effort to move beyond purely national appeals is the hallmark of the peace movement in Britain—resulting, in April 1980, in the Appeal for European Nuclear Disarmament, and the organization that has since sought, with great energy and devotion, to give effect to it. In keeping with that spirit, the primary aim of the present book has been to promote a genuinely *international* debate on the issues of thermonuclear war and peace.

At the same time—and here too in awareness of past limitations—the principal focus of the volume is *political*. The bulk of the writing that galvanized the peace movement in the West in the late fifties was concerned mainly with a description of the untold devastation that a nuclear war would wreak on every form of life on earth, and—secondarily—with an account of the arms race that was leading in its direction. These two themes, taking the central scientific and military realities of nuclear war as their major emphases, continue to play a vital role today. Without them, there can be no imaginative mobilization of human energies of the sort that alone can halt the slide towards final disaster. They constitute the first condition of any significant peace literature, and there can be no more welcome sign than the remarkable success of current books such as *Overkill*, *Protest and Survive* or *The Fate of the Earth*. But there is a necessary complement to works of this kind, of which there was less in CND's first phase: that is, historical scrutiny of the nature of the Cold War, which has posed the greatest dangers of global conflict, and political analysis of the roots and distribution of contemporary militarism, and of the types of future society that could lift the nightmare of a suicidal end of history. Discussion of these questions must inevitably be more controversial. For that reason alone, an open collaborative form that would seek to confront different views without corralling the potential of any of them seemed the appropriate one.

The contributors to this symposium are all socialists, active in movements against the dangers of war in their own countries. Most—but not all—of them have a Marxist background. None of them presumes that the long-term answers to the issues before the peace movement are easy or obvious ones. Their essays were written at different times between the spring of 1980 and the winter of 1981—a period that saw the tumultuous growth of protest against the new spiral in the arms race, first in nearly all the nations of Western Europe and then in the United States itself, while the international situation continued to deteriorate, with the launching by the Reagan Administration of the largest military programme ever conceived, the imposition of martial law in Poland, the escalation of counter-revolution in Central America. All these find their reflection in the different essays assembled below. The order in which they are arranged is in part topical and in part geographical, by origin of the author. Edward Thompson's keynote essay, which starts the volume, is succeeded by the most extended direct response to its theses, that of Mike Davis. There then follow, in sequence, contributions from each of the main European countries—Raymond Williams from Britain, Rudolf Bahro from Germany, Lucio Magri from Italy, Etienne Balibar from France, and Roy and Zhores Medvedev from the USSR. This section concludes with John Cox's description of what even a 'limited' nuclear war would do to the fabric of civilization in Europe. Saburo Kugai and Marcus Raskin then extend the arena of debate to the two major powers outside Europe, Japan and the United States. After these nationally focused essays, there come four texts that deal more generally with the nature of the arms race and the character of the Cold War as a whole, by Noam Chomsky, Alan Wolfe, Mary Kaldor and Fred Halliday. Finally, Edward Thompson responds to some of the major arguments raised in the course of the discussion.

Editors and authors must be conscious, on completing a volume such as this one, of its imperfections. These can only be remedied by much wider and longer debate, which we all hope will continue in a sustained and comradely way over the years ahead. In the present book, four main recurrent questions, treated from different perspectives and with different answers, can be distinguished. The first is the social nature and basis of what Thompson has called 'exterminism'—the apparent drive of industrial civilization towards its own self-destruction in the post-war arms race. The second bears on the respective roles and responsibilities of the two great powers, the USA and USSR, in the onset and the perpetuation of the Cold War. The third concerns the relative importance of the distinct major theatres of the Cold War—the Far East, Europe, and the Third World. The fourth question, of course, comprises the whole nexus of problems posed by the quest for a realistic way out of the looming dangers of 'Exterminism and Cold War'. All of these involve large judgements about the shape of contemporary history. In his response to the discussion Edward Thompson doubts, as an historian himself, the possibility of arriving at any sure or satisfactory conclusions in this domain. The times that we ourselves live through, he suggests, are too close for us to be able to see the pattern of significance they will acquire for our posterity, if there be any. Proportions and meanings are likely to be drastically altered from the distance of any settled retrospect. The salutary force of this warning, against all presumption in trying to read the signs of the present or recent past, is one that all socialists should heed.

Yet great works of history have been written by contemporaries of, even participants in, the events they recounted. The birth of the discipline itself, after all, lies in just such a narrative—an account of a Greek war by one who fought in it. From Thucydides's *Peloponnesian War* to Clarendon's *History of the Rebellion* to Trotsky's *History of the Russian Revolution*, 'contemporary' history has furnished some of the masterpieces of historical understanding and imagination. The real difficulty, faced equally by leading actors and by lesser spectators, in the attempt to explore the nature and meaning of the Cold War, or the military conflicts that have accompanied it, is not position in time but scale in space. Contemporary history is here *world* history, that of a globe now integrated into one vast field of inter-related conflicts. This poses intellectual problems of a quite new kind, for any inquiry into the dangers of war or the prospects for peace. The immensity of the surface across which their fate is now decided can be encompassed only by interpretations and explanations of a truly extraordinary reach. Common sense and poetic intuition have their place in efforts to understand the shape of our time; but they will always themselves rest on a particular historical vision, avowed or not. All of these should be taken seriously among fellow-socialists, who can have no a priori certainty of the rightness or wrongness of any one of them in a given instance—be they the 'seven-league boots' of class struggle, of which Thompson speaks, or the moon-boots of ecology, or whatever may best serve those who explore the bonding of collective Selves against the Other in the official national hatreds of our age. Detailed evidence and argument alone can arbitrate among them. The most appropriate maxim here is a necessarily paradoxical one: all hypotheses concerning historical problems and directions as large as these should combine audacity of range with modesty of claim.

Historical interpretation on this scale always implies political recommendation. The international peace movement itself comprises a wide variety of opinions, among which the views of socialists are in a minority. Does the advocacy of socialism within its ranks harm the unity of the cause of peace? Does the assertion of perspectives from the 'left' render the movement less 'central'? We do not believe so, for one simple reason. War is a determinate activity—an old and frightful practice that has produced its own theories, from Clausewitz to the strategists of nuclear death today. Peace is not. It is the sheer absence of war, and as such intrinsically 'negative'. Surely this is part of the reason why it has been so difficult in the past to sustain lasting mobilizations for it. For these to be possible in future, peace must acquire a tangible social shape capable of inspiring the positive dreams and loyalties of millions. For all the tragedies that have befallen the ideal in this century, what could that shape be, if not socialist?

NLR

Contributors

Rudolf Bahro (b. 1935) was a member of the East German SED from 1954 to 1977, when he was imprisoned for having written and published *Die Alternative* (in English, *The Alternative in Eastern Europe*). Since his release in 1980 he has been active in the peace and 'green' movements in West Germany.

Etienne Balibar (b. 1942) teaches at the University of Paris I. He was a member of the French Communist Party from 1961 to 1981, when he was expelled for his opposition to the PCF's policy towards immigrants. He has been active in campaigns for French left unity since 1978. He is the co-author (with Louis Althusser) of *Reading Capital*.

Noam Chomsky (b. 1928) is a professor of linguistics at Massuchusetts Institute of Technology. He was active in the movement against the US war in Vietnam. His most recent publications include *The Political Economy of Human Rights* and *Towards a New Cold War*.

John Cox (b. 1935) is a consultant engineer in the field of safety and hazard study. He is a member of the Communist Party of Great Britain. Active in CND since 1961, he was chairman of the organization between 1971 and 1977 and is currently its vice-chairman. He is the author of *Overkill*.

Mike Davis (b. 1946) was an organizer of Students for a Democratic Society during the Vietnam War, and was subsequently active in the rank-and-file movement of the Teamsters Union. He is on the editorial committee of *New Left Review* and has published studies of the American working class.

Fred Halliday (b. 1946) is a fellow of the Transnational Institute and a member of the editorial committee of *New Left Review*. Active in solidarity work relating to the Arab world, he serves on the Middle East sub-committee of the Labour Party NEC. His recent publications include *Iran: Dictatorship and Development* and (with Maxine Molyneux) *The Ethiopian Revolution*.

Mary Kaldor (b. 1946) is a fellow of the Science Policy Research Unit and the Institute of Development Studies in the University of Sussex. She edits *END Notes* and is a member of the defence sub-committee of the Labour Party NEC. Her recent writings include *The Disintegrating West* and *The Baroque Arsenal*.

Saburo Kugai (b. 1926) was director of the Institute of American Studies, Tokyo, from 1963 to 1972. A long-time activist in anti-nuclear movements in Japan, since 1977 he has been chief organizer of the National Liaison Conference for Nuclear Disarmament. He is the author of *American Nuclear and Energy Strategy*.

Lucio Magri (b. 1932) was a member of the Italian Communist Party from 1957 to 1969, when he co-founded *Il Manifesto*. Since 1976 he has been leader, and a parliamentary deputy, of PDUP. His publications include *Considerazioni sui fatti di maggio*.

Roy Medvedev (b. 1925) was departmental head of the Institute of Vocational Education, the Soviet Academy of Pedagogical Sciences, between 1960 and 1970. He is active in the Russian opposition and is the author of *Let History Judge*, (with his brother Zhores) *Khrushchev—The Years in Power*, and *Leninism and Western Socialism*.

Zhores Medvedev (b. 1925) was laboratory head of the Institute of Medical Radiology, Obinsk, between 1963 and 1969. Since 1973 he has been attached to the National Institute of Medical Research in London. He has written *The Rise and Fall of T. D. Lysenko*, (with Roy) *Khrushchev—The Years in Power*, and *The Nuclear Disaster in the Urals*.

Marcus Raskin (b. 1934) was a member of the special staff of the National Security Council and of the US Disarmament Delegation between 1961 and 1963. He resigned from US government service in the latter year and co-founded the Institute for Policy Studies. He is currently associate chairman of the New Democratic Coalition; his publications include *Vietnam Reader*, *Being and Doing*, and *The Politics of National Security*.

Edward Thompson (b. 1924) is a historian. He was a member of the Communist Party of Great Britain from 1942 to 1956, and subsequently played a central role in the New Left and in CND. He is a founder of END and a member of the Labour Party. His publications include *William Morris: From Romantic to Revolutionary*, *The Making of the English Working Class*, *Writing by Candlelight*, *Protest and Survive* and *Zero Option*.

Raymond Williams (b. 1921) is professor of drama in the University of Cambridge. He was active in the New Left and CND in the late fifties and early sixties, and was a member of the Labour Party between 1961 and 1966. He edited the *May Day Manifesto*, and his many other publications include *The Long Revolution*, *The Country and the City*, *Politics and Letters*, and *Problems in Materialism and Culture*.

Alan Wolfe (b. 1942) is professor of sociology in Queen's College, New York. He is a member of the editorial board of *The Nation* and has written *The Limits of Legitimacy*, *The Rise and Fall of the 'Soviet Threat'*, and *America's Impasse*.

Notes on Exterminism, the Last Stage of Civilization

Edward Thompson

Comrades, we need a cogent theoretical and class analysis of the present war crisis.* Yes. But to structure an analysis in a consecutive rational manner may be, at the same time, to impose a consequential rationality[1] upon the object of analysis. What if the object is *ir*rational? What if events are being willed by no single causative historical logic ('the increasingly aggressive military posture of world imperialism', etc.)—a logic which then may be analysed in terms of origins, intentions or goals, contradictions or conjunctures—but are simply the product of a messy inertia? This inertia may have drifted down to us as a collocation of fragmented forces (political and military formations, ideological imperatives, weapons technologies): or, rather, as two antagonistic collocations of such fragments, interlocked by their oppositions? What we endure in the present is historically formed, and to that degree subject to rational analysis: but it exists now as a critical mass on the point of irrational detonation. Detonation might be triggered by accident, miscalculation, by the implacable upwards creep of weapons technology, or by a sudden hot flush of ideological passion.[2] If we drill all this in too tidy a logical formation we will be unprepared for the irrationality of the event. Twenty-one years ago, in the forerunner to this journal, Peter Sedgwick (addressing the arguments of a different moment) alerted us to this irrationality: 'A conspiracy theory was implicit in all analysis produced from within the Stalinist orbit. "The ruling circles of the United States" were "bending all their efforts to prepare a new war", "fresh plans of aggression" being constantly prepared by these very circles. A criminal foresight was thus ascribed to the enemy, in a manner both implausible and alien to Marxist categories. What Wright Mills calls "the drift and thrust towards World War Three" is indeed to be ascribed to the existence of oligarchic and military ruling classes (whose distribution over the continents of the globe is, incidentally, somewhat more widespread than the Partisans of Peace ever hinted). But the danger of war arises, not from conscious planning on the part of the elites . . . If this were so, we could all sleep safely, for the "ruling circles" would hardly be likely to plot their own annihilation . . . War is possible as the outcome of policies initiated by these irresponsible minorities, *as the final unforeseen link in a causal chain forged at each stage by the previous choice of some ruling class.* World War Three could burst out as "something that no one willed"; the resultant of competing configurations of social forces . . . If Man is ever obliterated from the earth by means of his own armaments, there will be no simple answer to the question: Did he fall, or was he pushed?'[3]

Twenty-one years on, and the immediacy of this question, as well as the political demands of the moment, break up the mind. I can offer no more than notes, fragments of an argument. Some fragments must take the form of questions, addressed to the immobilism of the Marxist left.

The Deep Structure of the Cold War

A swift caricature of whatever theory underlies this immobilism would run like this. It is in stance a priori: the increasingly expert literature on weaponry, militarism, and peace research remains unread.[4] It is informed by a subliminal teleology: history must move through its pre-programmed stages, do what men will, and we may refuse, with religiose optimism, Marx's grimmer option: 'the mutual ruin of the contending classes.' It confuses origins with consequences. And it confides in an anthropomorphic interpretation of political, economic and military formations, to which are attributed intentions and goals. Since the 'cause' of the Cold War is commonly ascribed solely to the evil will of 'imperialism', it then becomes possible to analyse events in terms of imperialism's supposed rationality (however malevolent these reasons) rather than in terms of the irrational outcome of colliding formations and wills.

In its story-line it goes something like this. The original, and also the replicating, cause of Cold War lies in the drives of world imperialism. These drives are then analysed, with attention to Africa, South-East Asia, Latin America, and with a peroration about the Middle East and oil. China is invoked as part of the revolutionary heritage: its inconvenient diplomatic and military postures are then forgotten.[5] Europe is passed over without analysis, except in its accessory role in world imperialism. State socialism, however 'deformed' (and here Marxists of different persuasions offer different grade-marks for deformity), has a military posture which is 'overwhelmingly defensive'. This can be confirmed by an a priori exercise, through a brief attention to differing modes of production and social systems: the capitalist mode is motivated by the drive for profit and for new fields of exploitation, whereas the arms race imposes an unwelcome burden upon socialist states (however deformed) by diverting resources from socialist construction.

As for the Bomb, that is a Thing, and a Thing cannot be a historical agent. Preoccupation with the horrors of an imaginary nuclear war is diversionary (did not the Vietcong call that bluff?), and it leads to hideous heresies, such as 'neutralism', 'pacifism', and to utter confusion in the class struggle. CND exemplified such capitulations to moralism and 'pacifism', which is why it 'failed'. Meanwhile, the anti-imperialist struggle prospers in the Third World (Vietnam, Angola, Iran, Nicaragua, Zimbabwe), and eventually it will be carried thence to the 'barbarians' in the capitalist heartlands.[6] The best that these barbarians can do, while they wait, is to engage in frontal class confrontation until the capitalist economies begin to buckle.

But there might be other ways to situate our analysis. We would examine, less origins, than the consequences of consequences. We would attend with care to military technology, strategy and formations. We would confront the possibility of war with a controlled pessimism of the intellect. We would read the immediate past as the irrational outcome of a collision of wills, and we would expect the immediate future to enlarge that irrationality.

I can only glimpse the story-line that this might give us. But it would, I think, replace Europe, and, at a short remove, China, at the centre of the story. It would start from the US–USSR polarization, and, by extension, the USSR–China–US triangle. What is known as the 'Cold War' is the central human fracture, the absolute pole of power, the fulcrum upon which power turns, in the world. This is the field-of-force which engenders armies, diplomacies and ideologies, which imposes client relationships upon lesser powers and exports arms and militarisms to the periphery.

On the periphery there is still political mobility, and the story-line already given is acceptable enough, although more distorted (and distorted into militarist forms) by the dull enforcement of the central poles than the story usually allows. In exceptional cases, where the polar antagonism is so acute that conventional military intervention would bring the immediate probability of US–USSR confrontation, the space for political mobility is actually enlarged: Iran and the Middle East are the obvious examples.[7] But along the central fracture, political mobility has been, for thirty years, congealed: at worst, it assumes degenerative forms. And here we must acknowledge not one but two imperial formations, however different their origin and character. For the Soviet Union, which extends from the Baltic states to Mongolia, includes within its strategic imperatives all that inflammable human material in Eastern Europe which must be held perpetually under political, military and ideological controls.

It must become clear already that 'imperialism' is an inadequate category to encompass more than a part of this situation of global contradiction and collision. It is a situation without precedent, and it becomes lost to view when we try to stuff it into inapposite categories. It is a situation both of antagonism and of reciprocity, for the increment of weaponry on both sides takes place in part according to a reciprocal logic, and is even regulated by elaborate agreed rules. The MX missile is a clever device to stretch to the limits without rupturing the games-plan of SALT II: each missile will chunter on tracks between a number of concealed firing-points, but inspection-covers will periodically be thrown open to Soviet satellite observation to reassure 'the enemy' that there is only one missile in each track-system.[8]

In this games-plan it matters less than may be supposed to define the military posture of the Soviet Union (or of 'the West') as 'basically defensive'. That is no more than a moralistic attribution of supposed intention. Both superpowers are mounted and armed for instant annihilating attack. Barbed wire, pillboxes, trenches, anti-tank guns—the accessories of a Maginot Line—might be categorized as 'defensive' weapons, but ICBMs may not.

The Bomb is, after all, something more than an inert Thing. First, it is, in its destructive yield and its programmed trajectory, a thing of menace. Second, it is a component in a weapons *system*: and producing, manning and supporting that system is a correspondent social system—a distinct organization of labour, research and operation, with distinctive hierarchies of command, rules of secrecy, prior access to resources and skills, and high levels of policing and discipline: a distinctive organization of production, which, while militarist in character, employs and is supported by great numbers of civilians (civil servants, scientists, academics) who are subordinated to its discipline and rules.[9]

It means rather little to peer into the entrails of two differing modes of production, searching for auguries as to the future, if we are so inattentive as to overlook what these modes produce. For, increasingly, what is being produced by both the United States and the USSR is the means of war, just as, increasingly, what is being exported, with competitive rivalry, by both powers to the Third World are war materials and attendant militarist systems, infrastructures and technologies.[10]

There is an internal dynamic and reciprocal logic here which requires a new category for its analysis. If 'the hand-mill gives you society with the feudal lord; the steam-mill, society with the industrial capitalist', what are we given by those Satanic mills which are now at work, grinding out the means of human extermination? I have reached this point of thought more than once before, but have turned my head away in despair. Now, when I look at it directly, I know that the category which we need is that of 'exterminism'.

The Logic of Nuclear Weapons Systems

Originism and anthropomorphism have no need to examine weaponry and strategy. Weapons are things, and strategies are instrumental plans for implementing policies which originate elsewhere. Thus what we must do is examine the ruling elites and their political intentions. All the rest can be taken as given.

This sounds like commonsense. But it is wrong. It is to foreclose analysis of self-generating independent variables before it has even commenced. Nuclear weapons (all weapons) are things: yet they, and their attendant support-systems, seem to grow of their own accord, as if possessed by an independent will. Here at least we should reach for that talisman, 'relative autonomy'.

This increment in the means of extermination is, of course, the outcome of someone's choice. But where do such choices originate? Are they political or technological choices? The answer is complex. One part of the answer is that, given the defences of official secrecy—defences almost impermeable in the Soviet Union—we do not know.

The rival arsenals of the USA and USSR stood at 6,500 substantial nuclear weapons in 1960: at 14,200 in 1979: and, even within the games-plan of SALT II, will arrive at some 24,000 *strategic* weapons by 1985.[11] Analysts used to explain this steady, and accelerating, increment according to a simple action–reaction model: 'Implicit in this view were the ideas that the decisions of leaders actually determined force structure and that leaders' orders were carried out by the military bureaucracy. . . . It implied that the leaders of each side reacted rationally to the behaviour of the other side.'[12]

This rationality is now challenged. Weapons innovation is self-generating. The impulse to 'modernize' and to experiment takes place independently of the ebb and flow of international diplomacy, although it is given an upward thrust by each crisis or by each innovation by 'the enemy'. Weapons research evolves according to long waves of planning, and the weapons for the year 2000 are now at the R & D (research and development) stage. Deborah Shapley defines this incremental pressure as 'technology creep', owing to its 'gradual, inconspicuous, bureaucratic character'. Its modes differ: US weapons increment is more active and innovative, USSR increment more reactive, imitative, and in the form of 'follow-on' modifications.

But in both powers there is a steady incremental pressure more inexorable than can be explained by recourse to notions of an 'arms lobby' or a military 'interest'. Shapley lists as factors, in the United States, 'the enthusiasm of scientists for advertising the potential of their work, the interest of program managers and design bureaus in testing improvements, and the armed services' wish to have the most up-to-date versions of their systems'. Alva Myrdal adds 'the interservice competition for shares of the military budgets, leading to an arms race within the arms race'—a competition evident in Britain now as service chiefs compete around the 'successor' to Polaris—and the 'mental virus' of the 'technological imperative'. Zuckerman identifies similar forces: 'the men in the laboratories', the 'alchemists of our times', who 'have succeeded in creating a world with an irrational foundation, on which a new set of political realities has in turn had to be built'. He implies ('working in secret ways which cannot be divulged') that official secrecy prevents him from further revealing their mode of operation and political impingement. [13]

This does not seem a sufficient explanation for a thrust which is absorbing a significant proportion of the world's GNP, and which is manifestly irrational even in military terms (weaponry for adequate mutual 'deterrence', or mutual assured destruction (MAD) already existed, in the absence of any effective anti-ballistic missile defences, some twenty years ago). What Shapley and Zuckerman do not emphasize, and what any socialist would insert into the argument, is the competitive drive of capitalist arms producers, a drive which has become more intense within the shadow of recession. We will return to this important component of exterminism in a moment.

Yet it is not clear to me that we have found a simple explanation for this incremental thrust in profit-taking (in the West) and in action–reaction (in the East). Weapons research, in both blocs, originates in bureaucratic decisions rather than out of the play of market forces. The state is always the customer: and, in market economies, the state guarantees the high—even arbitrary—profit return, which is passed on (often in hidden allocations) to the taxpayer. Arms manufacture may take place in the public or the private 'sector', but even where, as in the United States, there is acute competition between private enterprises for the state's tender, the number of competitors is diminishing, and covert agreements are normal between the great competitors to ensure a 'fair' division of the spoils. We do not need the profit motive to bring us to extermination, although it helps. Ideology and a general bureaucratic inertial thrust help more.

There is no profit motive in the Soviet Union: *ergo*, the 'fault' for the arms race lies only with 'the West'. How do we know this? Can states and bureaucracies not have motives for arming? The briefest survey of historical, as well as contemporary, evidence will tell us that they can. The decisive point for Soviet armament increment appears to date from around the time of the fall of Khruschev: from the mid-1960s, there has been a steady growth in nuclear weaponry, as well as development and modernization of the armed forces. In terms of differential growth, the pace of the Soviet armourers seemed to accelerate in the 1970s, during the 'quiet' years of detente; by a stupendous concentration of resources and scarce scientific skills, the Soviet armourers reached forward until nuclear weapons 'parity' with the United States seemed within their grasp. At the same time, the Soviet navy was deployed as an active world presence. Similar economic and technological decisions as in 'the West' (economies of scale, long production runs) have underwritten the entry of Soviet armourers as major salesmen in the markets of the Third World. Figures for all these matters are ideologically contaminated and in dispute: but socialists who refuse them any credence (as figments of CIA propaganda) are sadly ill-informed. The facts are of this order.[14]

Obviously, political decisions influenced this increment. The political elite in the Soviet Union 'decided' to pursue that infinitely receding objective of nuclear weapons 'parity', and at the same time to signal its world presence as a military and naval power. But then, *how* did the elite arrive at this decision? Under what pressures were its policies and ideology militarized?

Weapons, to be sure, are things. Their increment is not independent of political decisions. But politics itself may be militarized: and decisions about weaponry now impose the political choices of tomorrow. Weapons, it turns out, are political agents also.

Weapons, and weapons systems, are never politically neutral. When European settlers with muskets encountered Red Indian tribes with bows and arrows, the politics of the matter were determined by the barrels of their guns. If the settlers had only had bows and arrows, this would have imposed upon them the politics of the peace-pipe and the parley. As to 'the Bomb', the refinement of nuclear weaponry has been steadily eroding the interval in which any 'political' option might be made. The replacement of liquid by solid fuel means that rockets may now stand in their silos, instantly ready. The time of delivery has contracted: in the mid-1970s the time required for the interhemispheric delivery of nuclear bombs had shrunk to about ten minutes, and it is now perhaps less.[15] This hair-trigger situation, combined with the increasing accuracy of missiles and automated electronic reaction-systems, has encouraged fantasies that a war might actually be launched with advantage to the aggressor ('taking out' every one of the enemy's ICBMs in their case-hardened silos), or that a 'limited' war might be fought in which only selected targets were 'taken out'.

In such a hair-trigger situation, the very notion of 'political' options becomes increasingly incredible. The persons who decide will not be a harrassed President or First Secretary (perhaps not available at the moment of emergency) but a small group of military technicians, whose whole training and rationale is that of war, and who can, by no conceivable argument, be said to represent the rational interests of any economic or political formation. Very probably they will act without any 'political' mediation: already, in the Cuban missile crisis, American naval commanders engaged in the exceedingly hazardous tactic of forcing Soviet submarines to surface, in pursuance of standard operating procedures during a red alert and without the knowledge of the US President.

Today's hair-trigger military technology annihilates the very moment of 'politics'. One exterminist system confronts another, and the act will follow the logic of advantage within the parameters of exterminism.

The 'Theatre' of Apocalypse

In extremity this may be so. But, surely, there is a long political terrain to be travelled first, before we reach an unlikely extremity (from which it is best to avert our eyes)? And surely strategic decisions are no more than the projections upon the global map of prior political choices?

This is wrong again, or half-wrong. Military strategy is not politically non-aligned. NATO 'modernization' with Cruise missiles and Pershing IIs is a case in point.

Strategy imploded upon West European political life at Brussels on 12 December 1979, in a supposedly technological-strategic decision to 'modernize' NATO nuclear armoury. Ground-launched cruise missiles on European territory are the hardware designated by US strategists for a 'limited' or 'theatre' war. They are commended for their extreme accuracy, even if the claims for CEPs (Circular Error Probable) of only a few hundred feet may be empty brags.

They implode upon politics for two reasons. First, they translate the notion of 'theatre' war from fantasy to actuality. ICBMs carry such colossal destructive power that they do, in fact, deter. Even military strategists, while multiplying warheads, can see the irrationality of ICBM warfare. The militarists have unprecedented resources, which, however, they can never put to use. Hence extreme impatience builds up, most notably in the Pentagon, to design some new games-plan, which would advantage the power superior in nuclear technology. In this re-writing, Soviet strategists are unaccountably uncooperative: 'Recent moves in NATO have encouraged plans for selective, discrete strikes rather than all-out exchanges. . . . Unfortunately, the Soviet Union has shown little interest in Western ideas on limited nuclear war.'[16]

Even so, the Soviet hand might be forced: faced with a *fait accompli*—limited 'theatre' war ('taking out' selected targets in Russia as well as 'taking out' most of Europe) might be imposed upon the Soviet Union if the clear alternative was ICBM obliteration. This would then be a victory for 'the free West'.

The pressure rises upwards from the laboratories and the strategic war-games simulation rooms to NATO planning committees (co-opting on the way the compliant cowboys who inhabit the Institute for Strategic Studies[17] and the Royal Institute of International Affairs) to the United States Secretary for Defence and to the President's national security adviser (the prime architect of the Iranian helicopter fiasco), Zbigniew Brzezinski:

'*Brzezinski*: I think you see already the beginning of a serious review manifesting itself in the Secretary of Defence's defence posture statement, in being able to respond to nuclear threats in a flexible manner, in the serious thought being given to our nuclear targeting plans, in the much higher emphasis being placed on command and control capabilities.

'All of these reviews are designed to enhance our ability to bargain in the context of severe crisis, to avoid a situation in which the President would be put under irresistable pressure to preempt, to avoid leaving the United States only the options of yielding or engaging in a spasmodic and apocalyptic nuclear exchange. *Question*: Are you saying that you want the United States to be able to fight a "limited" nuclear war? *Brzezinski*: I am saying that the United States, in order to maintain effective deterrence, has to have choices which give us a wider range of options than either a spasmodic nuclear exchange or a limited conventional war.'[18]

The only unaccountable element in this whole operation is the fact that NATO politicians have eagerly endorsed a 'choice', by United States strategists, to designate their territories as the 'theatre' of apocalypse. What has happened is that an option of astonishing political dimensions has been imposed upon West Europe in the anodyne vocabulary of strategy and technology. In fact, in this case the strategy was invented long before the weapons. The embodiment of 'flexible-response' strategy was endorsed by NATO as early as 1967; was enforced by Schlesinger; and was a matter of open discussion among experts in the early 1970s. It was in 1975 that the American analyst, Herbert York, wrote with admirable candour: 'Today's Western Europeans have chosen to buy current political stability by placing awful risks . . . over their lives and their future. Perhaps their choice was inadvertent; perhaps they did not and even today still do not realize what they have done.'[19]

US strategy by then had already adopted the imperative that the United States should be the Sanctuary, and that nuclear war should be limited to external 'theatres': West Europe was designated (without the knowledge of its peoples) as the sacrificial proxy. That the peoples of West Europe did not 'know' of this new designation was the effect of official secrecy and the management of information; that intellectuals (and socialist intellectuals) did not know merits less excuse—Herbert York and Alva Myrdal were there for us to read.[20] The new generation of missiles to match this strategy was in advanced development by the mid-1970s. What has been presented in the West European media, and in debates in West European parliaments, in the last few months as a regrettable but necessary 'response' to the Soviet SS–20s was set in motion before the SS–20 had been heard of. It is difficult to know whether these politicians are plain liars, illiterates, or the victims of polluted civil service briefs.

The final act of 'decision' was registered, at Brussels, in a non-elective, quasi-political, quasi-military assembly: NATO. The fantasy was translated into fact in a series of elaborate bureaucratic planning steps, inscribed with runic acronyms: NATO's LTDP (Long-Term Defence Programme), NPG (Nuclear Planning Group), and HLG (High Level Group). From 1977 to 1979 the NPG and HLG scurried through secretive meetings at Los Alamos, Brussels, Fredrikshaven, Colorado Springs, Homestead Air Force Base (Florida), etc.[21] NATO then 'requests' the US government, in its generosity, to send this can of rattlesnakes across to the designated theatre, and, in the same instant, notifies European governments that they are to receive them.

One watches, spellbound, the bureaucratic forms of exterminism. I do not mean that 'strategy' or 'bureaucracy' did all this unaided. No one could have been more abject in their complicity than Mrs Thatcher and Mr Pym. I mean only to note that a prior condition for the extermination of European peoples is the extermination of open democratic process. And I am inviting readers to admire the style of the thing.

The second reason why this military hardware implodes upon our political life is this. Cruise missiles are, with finality, *committing*. Ground-launched, operated solely by US personnel (whatever evasive parliamentary provisos are made about 'consultation'), they commit this nation absolutely to strategic imperatives imposed by Sanctuary USA. In every crisis, someone else's finger will be upon 'our' trigger.

Cruise missiles are *committing*: strategically, but also politically. They place us, with finality, in the games-plan of the Pentagon. True, F-111s which, during the Iranian helicopter fiasco (and we know what 'consultation' went on then) were placed at Lakenheath on nuclear alert, are committing also. But the Cruise missiles have a new kind of political visibility, a manifest symbolism of subjection. That is why they must be repelled.

This is not—need one say this?—to urge a reversion to the old sloganry of 'national independence'—'Yankees Out'! The cause of European Nuclear Disarmament (END) is only one point of engagement in the international struggle for peace. The alert, generous and growing North American peace movements will understand this and will give us their support, just as (in quieter and more complex ways) opinion will bring its own pressures to bear in the Soviet Union also. For no 'theatre' war which reaches the point of nuclear exchanges will ever be contained within its theatre; it will be, at the most, a matter of days before the ICBMs launch off, and Washington and Moscow, Utah and West Siberia, are brought within the 'theatre'. END will provide a shield, just as other shields must be formed in the Pacific and the Middle East.

It is not the 'Yankees' but the exterminists who must be called out—and, first of all, our own. Two vignettes: returning through the US base at Upper Heyford, Oxfordshire, after the march against cruise missiles on 17 May 1979, one over-enthusiastic marcher was shouting abuse at the American personnel: he was promptly taken in custody, by the *British* police. One North American marcher politely engaged in conversation a black American airman who was on his way out of the base. Was it true, she asked, that this was a British base, or was it really an American one? The airman commenced to offer a courteous reply: he was promptly interrupted and taken off in custody, by the *American* military security police.

The Scope for Self-determination

There is a contradiction in the logic we have traced above. The diplomacy of ICBM annihilation increasingly polarizes the world into absolute antagonism. Yet, since the launching of these missiles is the final act, the room for the deployment of the lesser means of war becomes, except at the periphery, increasingly restricted and hazardous. The client states of each grand alliance are reduced to impotence: they surrender their fate into the keeping of the Great Stockpile.

Examine the possible sequence of events in Iran, if the helicopter operation had not providentially aborted. (1) US troops, with miscellaneous CIA auxiliaries, arrive in Teheran. (2) Bloody fighting, the release of a few hostages, and the slaughter of the rest. (3) The USA bombs Iranian installations or mounts a punitive expeditionary force, in revenge for the slaughter of hostages, and to save the Presidential face. (4) The Iranian government appeals to the Soviet Union for military aid. (5) Confrontation. The point is that, at each stage of this sequence, the client states of NATO would have remained wholly captive and without 'consultation'.

It is in the face of such sequences that Britain and France make their pitiful and expensive gestures at maintaining an 'independent deterrent'. Polaris and the French S3 are aimed, not at the Warsaw powers, but at the White House. If they can commit us, we must maintain at least a mini-bluff that we can commit them. Trident will be purchased for £5,000 million or more to buy a modicum of influence upon the Pentagon. As a 'deterrent' against the Soviet Union, Polaris, Trident and S3 are absurd: they are no more than our own pistols, and the right to determine the moment at which we will blow out our own brains.

But within this contradiction, little opportunities sometimes appear. The nations which resume mobility are those which detach themselves from either pole. Non-alignment brings an increment in real diplomatic influence. The superpowers must court stubborn Yugoslavia: captive Britain need not be noticed at all. European Nuclear Disarmament—the expulsion of weapons and bases, and detachment from bloc diplomacies—will be an act of self-determination, striking at the most sensitive points of power.

The Thrust of Exterminism

But that is a utopian vision. Let us return to the deep structure of the Cold War, or the thrust of exterminism.

Figures gesture only at process. Global figures are slippery digits. But by some calculations, the percentage of the world's GNP expended upon armaments has run, at any time since World War II, at between 6 per cent and 8 per cent, whereas in the run-up to the previous two world wars it was never higher than 3 per cent.[22] The current United States and NATO

powers commitment to an *annual* increment, in real terms, of 3 per cent
plus in arms budgeting (an increment which, no doubt, will be matched by
the Warsaw powers, and also by China) may well push this towards 10 per
cent in the next few years.

This may not appear as a fearsome figure until we appreciate three
things. First, this production is concentrated in the economies of the
advanced powers. The 'European-oriented alliances' (NATO and Warsaw
powers) were responsible, in the mid-1970s, 'for about four-fifths of the
total world military expenditure'.[23] This affects in radical ways the
structuring of advanced economies. Second, such figures (derived from
declared budgets) give only a partial view, since various support-systems
for militarism (scientific, ideological) are civilian in character and their cost
is masked.

Finally, this small figure (8 per cent) indicates the allocation of a surplus
withdrawn from circulation, services and consumption. It is this surplus
which we often take to be indicative of the priorities, the embodied
symbols of temporal authority or of spiritual aspiration, which mark the
character of a civilization. That surplus, worked up into artefacts, indicates
what holds men and women in thrall and what they worship: the great
tumuli, the megalithic circles, the temples, the pyramids, the great
medieval cathedrals, the giant rockets in their silos, the MX missile
system.

The MX missile project is noble in scope, greatly exceeding the
prospects of any prior civilization in its grandeur. It will occupy a
6,000-square-miles complex in Nevada and Utah; require 10,000 miles of
roadway; the missile-tracks will move, on 200 individual loops, between
4,600 case-hardened shelters. Security extensions and approach roads, with
ancillary installations, may increase the total occupied area to 20,000
square miles. It is a greater, and far more expensive, project than the
Panama Canal or the whole Alaskan pipeline system.

Undoubtedly, the MX missile-system will be the greatest single artefact
of any civilization. It will be the ultimate serpentine temple of
exterminism. The rockets in their shelters, like giant menhirs pointing to
the sky, will perform for 'the free West' not a military but a spiritual
function. They will keep evil spirits at bay, and summon worshippers to
the phallic rites of money. Within the aura of those gigantic nuclear
circles, the high priests of ideology will perform ritual sacrifices of taxes. In
distant outposts of the faith, at Westminster, Brussels, and the Hague,
druidical servitors will bow low to the West and incant missilic runes.

Many millennia afterwards, visiting archaeologists from another planet
will dig among the still radioactive embers and debate the function of the

great temple. The debate will be in vain. For the temple will be erected to celebrate the ultimate dysfunction of humanity: self-destruct.

Nuclear Economics

What both modes of production are now, increasingly, producing are nuclear weapons, tanks, submarines, small arms, nerve gas, etc.[24] Of course, some of this production is consumed: that is the privilege of the Third World, whose military expenditure has increased four-fold in the past two decades: from 10 per cent of the global total in 1960 to 24 per cent in 1978. The rate is accelerating. Over the same period Third World GNP was calculated to increase by a factor of 2.7, but military expenditure by 4.2. The major competitors in the Third World's arms market were, in 1978, the USA (47 per cent), the USSR (27 per cent), France (11 per cent), and Italy and the UK with 4 per cent each.[25] But non-aligned Austria and the nation of the Good Soldier Schweik are pushing for their share in the killing.

This is not contingency. It is process. The long waves of the armourers do not move in phase with the waves of diplomatic confrontation. Each international crisis legitimates the process, and strengthens the upswing. But in quiet periods of 'detente' there is an autonomous incremental logic. In the post-war years, the arms race has been like a rocket with three successive stages of thrust: the first Cold War, the Vietnam war, and, then, after a levelling off, the third upward thrust in the mid-1970s, in the midst of 'detente'. The French S3 which came into operation in May 1980 was commenced in 1974. The 'Chevaline' modernization of the Polaris warhead, at a cost of £1,000 millions, was devised in the early 1970s, authorized by Mr Heath in 1973, bequeathed to Sir Harold Wilson, carried forward secretively by Mr Callaghan, and announced triumphantly to a startled parliament in January 1980, by Mr Pym. We have seen that current NATO missile 'modernization' was prepared in the mid-1970s. The upswing in US military expenditure commenced at the same time: US defence procurement increased from $45.8 billion in 1976 to $55.6 billion in 1977 and $69.0 billion in 1979. The US defence budget for 1981–85 is projected at $1 trillion. The increment in Soviet armaments appears to have taken off in the late 1960s and to have been more steady, a product of fewer political variables and of central allocations of plan, although certain surges can be attributed to an action-reaction model. Paradoxically, the SALT I agreement (1972), purporting to establish ceilings for numbers of strategic weapons, provides an example. US strategists assented to these clauses in the foreknowledge that they could make nonsense of them by placing several MIRVs (multiple independently targeted re-entry vehicles) on each missile. In response Soviet armourers successfully developed their own MIRVs by 1975.

It may comfort socialists to see a 'cause' for this primarily in Western imperialism, and only secondarily in Soviet reaction. This is now beside the point. To argue from origins, to nominate goodies or baddies, is to take refuge from reality in moralism. Nations which have been exposed to unremitting destructive attack, famine, and civil war (Cambodia), or which liberate themselves by a prolonged and total sacrificial military self-organization (Vietnam), do not emerge unchanged, to choose between policy options according to theoretical persuasion or moral intention. Superpowers which have been locked, for thirty years, in the postures of military confrontation increasingly adopt militaristic characteristics in their economies, their polity and their culture. What may have originated in reaction becomes direction. What is justified as rational self-interest by one power or the other becomes, in the collision of the two, irrational. We are confronting an accumulating logic of process.

This logic, while reciprocal, is not identical. In the United States a strong contributory thrust to exterminism comes from the normal dynamics of gigantic capitalist enterprise. Moreover, one can observe a collective capitalist General Will for survival or expansion, whether as counter-revolutionary reaction to indigenous anti-imperialist movements in the Third World[26] or whether in pursuit of interests and resources (notably oil) of the most old-fashioned imperialist kind.

Emma Rothschild, in a cogent journalistic essay, has recently re-stated (and up-dated) the argument that in the post-war decades the military industries have functioned in the United States, just as cotton did in the industrial revolution in Britain, as the 'leading sector': not 'as a single or multiple industrial sector . . . but rather as a cluster of industries joined by a common objective and a common customer'. Given an expanding market, and an assured, high, rate of profit, this leading sector has in turn stimulated the boom in electronics, civil aerospace, etc., as well as in secure enclaves of civilian research and development. She suggests that it is this leading sector which has both paced the long wave of growth and determined the national economic structure, in conformity with Schumpeter's criteria of 'breaking up old and creating new positions of power, civilizations, valuations, beliefs and policies'.[27]

Rothschild argues also that this boom is entering upon cyclical decline. It is a sector which carries its own contradictions. It generates both inflationary pressures and unemployment, since the manufacture of advanced weaponry is capital-intensive. It has its own forms of technological obsolescence, as innovation becomes harder to achieve.[28]

But a business boom on the edge of a bust is a snarling, irrational beast. It might even appear that as American hegemony faltered, in the aftermath of Vietnam defeat, and as arms expenditure levelled off, efforts to re-invigorate the leading sector became more deliberate, more highly conscious, and more highly ideological and political in character.[29] What had been 'unconscious' process began to become, when threatened, conscious of itself: impulsive exterminism began to grow an exterminist mind and will. The immense security operations, the organs of political manipulation and information control, revealed by Watergate were not the product of Nixon: they were the natural civilian and ideological support-system for the military-industrial complex. Nixon's blunders exposed them to view, but they have long been resurgent.

Now, in 1980, crisis arrives—Afghanistan, Iran—and is eagerly welcomed. Ageing, overweight arms industries recollect the vigours of their youth. Huge injections of public money are brought to their rejuvenation. 'Defence Stocks Lead Market Up' is the response of the *Wall Street Journal* to Brown's latest budget. Lobbyists (who are often former Pentagon personnel hired by arms contractors) descend on the Pentagon: McDonnell Douglas, Boeing, General Dynamics, Grumman, Lockheed, General Electric, Westinghouse, Chrysler, ATT. Congressmen are approached with promises of investment in their districts. Bribes and excessive commissions oil the procedures. Lobbying extends to regional and local military and air force units, and also to the defence ministries and assemblies of NATO powers. The regular chime of contracts is announced, like the gazetting of top appointments, in the press. A random example—

'Lockheed Missiles & Space Co. unit received an $18.2 million Navy contract for engineering service for ballistic missiles.'

'Grumman Aerospace Corp. was awarded an $8.7 million Air Force contract for horizontal tail stabilizers for F—111 fighter bombers.'

'GK Technologies Inc. said its Automation Industries Inc. subsidiary has received a $9.6 million contract from the Navy for research, development, test and evaluation of weapons systems.'

'Southland Oil Co. got a $4.2 million contract from the Defense Logistics Agency for jet fuel.'[30]

The MX missile system is not yet put to contract. In June 1979 it was costed at $33 billion. By early 1980 it was costed at $56 billion. By mid-April of this year estimates had risen to over $100 billion.[31] The best plum to be landed so far this year has been the $4 billion deal for 3,418 Cruise missiles for the US air force. (Europe's ground-launched missiles have not, at the time of writing, been contracted.) Although Boeing is the winner, some part of the killing will, by quiet pre-agreement, be divided with its rivals.[32]

I cannot, as is well known, understand economics. I leave all this to more competent minds to evaluate. But somewhere within these matters lies one part of the thrust towards extermination.

The Inertial Push of Soviet Policy

We look in vain for comparable thrusts within the placid, plannified features of Soviet bureaucracy. Indeed, if one is not a specialist in Soviet affairs, one looks in vain for anything (NATO propaganda apart), since the press opens up few inspection-covers, and no Watergate scandal affords us a momentary glimpse of the exterminists about their humdrum daily chores of power.

In trying to envisage the nature of Soviet process, I find an analogy with an ill-run, security-conscious university with a huge and overmighty engineering department, so powerful that it can nominate the Vice-Chancellor and the Registrar, dominate the Senate, nobble most of the research funds, attract all the gifted graduates, and pack every committee. The engineering department is of course the military-industrial 'interest'. We are examining, not the self-reproduction and invasive properties of capital, but the self-reproduction and imperative pressures of a bureaucracy.

The Soviet state was born in military struggle: consolidated a ramshackle empire into a Union by military struggle. In the 1930s the priority upon heavy industry had a heavy military accent: militarism was built, not only into the superstructure, but into the base. And militarism inevitably found a huge (and popular) extension in the Great Patriotic War. In a significant sense, the Soviet has always been a 'war economy'.[33]

Arms-related industries have always received the first priority for scarce resources, including skilled manpower; the good conditions of work and pay attract 'the most highly skilled cadres'. In 1970, when arms expenditure had levelled off, in the United States one-quarter of all physicists, one-fifth of all mathematicians and engineers, were engaged in arms-related employment.[34] Today's proportions are probably higher. No comparable figures can be cited for the USSR, but there are strong grounds for supposing that, in a less highly developed economy which has, by a remarkable concentration of resources, developed its weapons-systems close to the point of parity with the United States in force and in sophistication, a significantly higher proportion of the nation's most skilled physicists, engineers, chemists, mathematicians, experts in electronics and cybernetics, are concentrated in this sector.

The arms complex is as clearly the leading sector of Soviet industry as it is in the United States, but this is expressed within bureaucratic modes of operation. There is some spin-off from military technology into civilian industry: civil aircraft, nuclear energy. But Soviet weapons technology, which is paced by its sophisticated American competitor, has opened up a gap between itself and its civilian compatriots: 'recent military technology has become too sophisticated for . . . cooperation to be possible.'[35] The military complex and its successes are upheld as a model of organization and of management techniques, and these are exported to other sectors. Moreover, the needs of the military complex—in particular, the imperatives placed upon centralized planning, priority in access to resources, and direction of scientific skills—affect the structure of the economy as a whole, and colour the decisions of the political managers. It is the threat which might be afforded to the stability and interests of this complex which inhibits any introduction of 'market' mechanisms into the economy as a whole.[36]

At the same time there is a greater direct exposure of the Soviet population to patriotic state propaganda than in most Western democracies: that is, what is (or is attempted to be) accomplished in 'the West' by the 'free' operation of the media is directly inculcated in Russia by such 'voluntary' organizations as DOSAAF: the Voluntary Society for Cooperation with the Army, Aviation and the Navy, with a membership of 80 millions, and with clubs, sports facilities, and military-patriotic or civil defence education organized around factories, farms and schools. Alongside and supporting all this there are the huge, quasi-autonomous operations of the Security Services, inheriting historic traditions of despotism, supporting military-patriotic ideology, and exerting an independent inertia of their own.

In David Holloway's view, such military-patriotic manifestations are now 'a pervasive feature of Soviet life'.[37] 'The Armed Forces and the defence industry occupy an entrenched position in the Party-state apparatus. The high priority which the Party leadership has given to military power has thus become institutionalized.'

But while military officers are awarded high status and privilege, and their influence can be seen at the highest level of political life, that influence (as in 1953, 1955 and 1964) has not been decisive. The interest has been mediated by the Party, and it would be mistaken to view the military—*yet*—as an autonomous interest. Brezhnev, who emerged with close experience of the military-industrial sector and with its backing, has satisfied its aspirations.

In this view, the incremental thrust in the Soviet Union towards extermination is not aggressive and invasive, but is ideological and bureaucratic. Yet it has, in Holloway's view, acquired an autonomous inertia, embedded in the structure of Soviet society, and can no longer be ascribed to reaction in the face of Western exterminism:

'Foreign influences are refracted through the Soviet policy-making process, in which Soviet perceptions, military doctrine, foreign policy objectives and domestic influences and constraints come into play. The effect of foreign actions on Soviet policy is complex and not at all automatic. In many cases the foreign influences combine with domestic factors to speed up the internal dynamic of Soviet arms policies. The very existence of large armed forces, a powerful defence industry and an extensive network of military R & D establishments generates internal pressures for weapons development and production . . . As a system progresses from conception to development, military and design bureau interests become attached to it, building up pressure for production. If it passes into production . . . enterprise managers are likely to favour long production runs.'

It does not look, under this analysis, like an aggressive thrust. Yet it is a dangerous inertial push, with its own hawkish imperatives of ideology and strategy (Czechoslovakia, 1968: Afghanistan, 1980), and which could afford nourishment to a popular culture of chauvinism, xenophobia, and even (when confronting China) racism. It is the more dangerous in that it is unchallenged by democratic exposure: no one may ask, in public, why—after the first ICBMs were in place—the absurd yet decisive decision to match each weapon and to attain to 'parity' was ever taken? Only for a brief period, under the impetuous and contradictory Khruschev, does an erratic challenge appear to have been offered to the process, and this challenge was offered by the first secretary himself: a distinct fall-back in the rate of weapons increment, an explosive speech about 'the metal-eaters', even (as in generous non-military aid to the Third World[38] and as in the long personal exchanges between Russell and Khruschev) a glimpse of an alternative, internationalistic strategy, summoning up a non-aligned movement for peace.

Thereafter inertia assumed the helm: ideological paranoia, fear of dissent, the null orthodoxy of official Soviet intellectual life, terror at Eastern European deviation, hostility at authentic non-alignment or even at Eurocommunist autonomy—all this going along with the games-play of top persons' 'detente',[39] with SALT this and SALT that, with increasingly military injections of 'aid' to the Third World, and with the emplacement of the foul and totally unnecessary SS–20 on Europe's margins: a weapon which beckoned on, like a cue in the common script of exterminism, the entry of NATO's waiting Cruise missle. The Soviet inertial thrust may be as humdrum as the cooked minutes of a captive Senate, but, when in collision with the hectic thrust of capital, it will do for us all.

Annihilation and Security

Let us attempt to assemble these fragments.

I am offering, in full seriousness, the category of 'exterminism'. By 'exterminism' I do not indicate an intention or criminal foresight in the prime actors. And I certainly do not claim to have discovered a new 'exterminist' mode of production. Exterminism designates those characteristics of a society—expressed, in differing degrees, within its economy, its polity and its ideology—which thrust it in a direction whose outcome must be the extermination of multitudes. The outcome will be extermination, but this will not happen accidentally (even if the final trigger is 'accidental') but as the direct consequence of prior acts of policy, of the accumulation and perfection of the means of extermination, and of the structuring of whole societies so that these are directed towards that end. Exterminism requires, of course, at least *two* agents for its consummation, which are brought into collision. But such collision cannot be ascribed to accident if it has long been foreseen, and if both agents have, by deliberate policy, directed themselves upon an accelerating collision-course. As Wright Mills told us long ago, 'the immediate cause of World War III is the preparation of it.'[40]

The clearest analogies are with militarism or imperialism (of whose characteristics exterminism partakes). These may be found to characterize societies with different modes of production: they are something less than social formations, and something a good deal more than cultural or ideological attributes. They designate something of the character of a society: of its drive and the direction of that drive. Militarism and imperialism are founded upon actual institutional bases (the military, the navy, the chartered trading companies and slavers, the arms manufacturers, etc.), from which they extend influence into other areas of life. In mature forms they appear as whole configurations (institutional, political, economic, ideological), and each portion reflects and reinforces the other. Exterminism is a configuration of this order, whose institutional base is the weapons system, and the entire economic, scientific, political and ideological support-system to that weapons system—the social system which researches it, 'chooses' it, produces it, polices it, justifies it, and maintains it in being.

Imperialism helps us both by analogy, and also by revealing the point at which analogy breaks down. Imperialism normally predicates an active agent and a subjected victim: an exploiter and an exploited. Vulgar imperialist theory tended to become enmeshed in an argument from origins: the drive for markets, raw materials, new fields for exploitation—if the originating 'motive' could be identified, this was held to explain all. Yet this failed to explain, not only many episodes—strategic and ideological imperatives, the expectation of rewards, the reciprocal influence of the subjected upon the imperial power—but also the irrationality (in terms of the pursuit of self-interest) of climactic imperial moments: in imperial rivalries, in the First World War, in fiercely irrational ideologies which contributed to fascism. It becomes necessary, then, to see Western imperialism as a force which originated in a rational institutional and economic matrix, but which, at a certain point, assumed an autonomous self-generating thrust in its own right, which can no longer be reduced by analysis to the pursuit of rational interests—which indeed acted so irrationally as to threaten the very empires of its origin and to pull them down.

So far, the analogy is helpful. This gives us the character of exterminism in the 1980s. No doubt we will have one day a comprehensive analysis of the origins of the Cold War, in which the motives of the agents appear as rational. But that Cold War passed, long ago, into a self-generating condition of Cold War-ism (exterminism), in which the originating drives, reactions and intentions are still at play, but within a general inertial condition: which condition (but I am now asking a question which will, I hope, be refuted) is becoming irreversible as a direction.

This is not because of the irrationality of political leaders (although this often helps). It is because the inertial thrust towards war (or collision) arises from bases deeply enstructured within the opposed powers. We tend to evade this conclusion by employing concepts which delimit the problem: we speak (as I have done) of the 'military-industrial complex', or of the military 'sector' or 'interest' or the arms 'lobby'. This suggests that the evil is confined in a known and limited place: it may threaten to push forward, but it can be restrained: contamination does not extend through the whole societal body.

But the more apposite concept, which is employed by some peace researchers,[41] is that of isomorphism: 'the property of crystallizing in the same or closely related forms', or 'identity of form and of operations as between two or more groups'. Viewed in this way, the USA and the USSR do not *have* military-industrial complexes: they *are* such complexes. The 'leading sector' (weapons systems and their supports) does not occupy a vast societal space, and official secrecy encourages low visibility; but it stamps its priorities on the society as a whole. It also inflects the direction of growth. In the US 1981 budget $16.5 billion is allocated to 'research, development, test and evaluation' (RDTE) of weaponry. Of this less than 10 per cent (a mere $1.5 billion) is allocated to MX research. But—'This is more than the combined RD budgets for the Department of Labour, the Department of Education, the Department of Transportation, the Environmental Protection Agency, the Federal Drug Administration, and the Center for Disease Control; over 140 per cent of the RD budget of the National Science Foundation.'[42] Given the technology gap between the two powers, and yet the extraordinary sophistication of Soviet weaponry, the inflection of the direction of Soviet research must be even greater.

Science-intensive weapons systems civilianize the military: but in the same moment more and more civilians are militarized. The diplomacy of 'posture' and bluff, together with the drive to steal some technological advantage, generate covert intelligence operations and the policing of information. The need to impose assent on the public (the US taxpayer, the Soviet consumer whose rising expectations remain unsatisfied) generates new resources to manage opinion. At a certain point, the ruling groups come to *need* perpetual war crisis, to legitimate their rule, their privileges and their priorities; to silence dissent; to exercise social discipline; and to divert attention from the manifest irrationality of the operation. They have become so habituated to this mode that they know no other way to govern.

Isomorphic replication is evident at every level: in cultural, political, but, above all, in ideological life. In a notable letter addressed last year to the California Board of Regents, Gregory Bateson, the social scientist, employed an analogy from biological systems: 'The short-time deterrent effect is achieved at the expense of long-time cumulative change. The actions which today postpone disaster result in an increase in strength on *both* sides of the competitive system to ensure a greater instability and greater destruction if and when the explosion occurs. It is this fact of cumulative change from one act of threat to the next that gives the system the quality of *addiction*.' Frustrated aggression 'backs up' until it permeates whole cultures.

It is within ideology that *addiction* to exterminism is distilled. The confrontation of the superpowers has, from its origin, always had the highest ideological content: ideology, as much as profit-making and bureaucratic growth, has motored the increment of weaponry, indicated the collision course, and even (on occasion) sheltered some victims.[43] In both camps ideology performs a triple function: that of motivating war preparations, of legitimating the privileged status of the armourers, and of policing internal dissent. Over more than thirty years, anti-communism has been the means of ideological control over the American working class and intelligentsia; over the same period communist orthodoxy has imposed ideological controls by a simple 'Stalinist' reversal.

The two camps are united ideologically in only one matter: in mutual hostility to any genuine non-alignment, 'neutralism', or 'third way'. For if such a way were to be possible, it would strike directly at exterminism's legitimacy. Dubcek and Allende must be overthrown, because they have trespassed upon the most sensitive territory of ideology: their success would have challenged the very premises of the mutual ideological field-of-force. The contagion might have spread, not only through Eastern Europe and Latin America, but to the heartlands of exterminism themselves.

The concept of isomorphism provides a clue to developments in the past decade in Britain. In this client state of NATO with its faltering economy, crystallization proceeds with unusual rapidity: Official Secrets trials, burgeoning security and surveillance, the management of Official Information and of 'consensual' ideology, the positive vetting of civil servants, the rising profile of the police, jury vetting, the demotion of parliamentary and other democratic process, the oiling of the machinery of 'national emergency', the contingency planning of the Cabinet Office, the futilities of *Protect and Survive*. While industries wither on the vine, and while 'public expenditure' is hacked at with a Friedmanite axe, new weapons systems are planned and public money is flushed down the exterminist sluice.

Britain, as it enters the 1980s, offers itself as a caricature of an exterminist formation. The imperatives of 'defence' poison the nation's economy; the imperatives of ideology deflect even profitable weapons manufacture into the hands of United States contractors. The subordinate inertial thrust of the national weapons-system complex augments the imposts of NATO: a motive for the £1,000 million 'Chevaline' programme, we learn, was 'finding something for the large scientific establishment at Aldermaston . . . to do'.[44] The politicians who initiated these weapons systems have now left the scene; their successors are now no more than a reflexive part of the support-system for these systems,[45] along with the civil servants, the scientists, the Treasury officials, the television controllers and the defence correspondents who afford these systems logistic supply and protection.

Even here where I write, in the rural West Midlands, I can sense the presence of neighbours: at Cheltenham, the headquarters of GCHQ signals interception; at Hereford, the base of the SAS; at Kidderminster, the manufacture of propellant for 'Sea-Slug' missiles (which came to public notice only after fatalities in an explosion), at Malvern, research into radar, but also into officially secret things.

It is a cumulative process, crystallization in culture accelerating crystallization in the economy, and thence to politics, and thence back again once more. Security operations impinge upon politicians; job security in weapons industries impinges upon trade unions; expansion in military research, usually in the 'public sector', generates bureaucratic pressures in Britain much the same as the bureaucratic thrust of the Soviet managers; the minister of defence and the foreign secretary carry in their portfolios (to China, Oman, Pakistan) the briefs of arms salesmen; and at home, academics are funded to prepare these briefs. Since all these pressures accumulate in the direction of extermination, it is proper to designate them as exterminist.

The Moment of Greatest Danger

The analogy with imperialism takes us a long way, but in the end it breaks down. Imperialism calls into being its own antagonist in the movement for self-determination of the people of the subjected country. Exterminism does not. Exterminism simply confronts itself. It does not exploit a victim: it confronts an equal. With each effort to dominate the other, it calls into being an equivalent counter-force. It is a non-dialectical contradiction, a state of absolute antagonism, in which both powers grow through confrontation, and which can only be resolved by mutual extermination.

Yet exterminism does generate its own internal contradictions. In the West, a science-intensive war economy produces not only weapons systems but inflation, unemployment, and deteriorating services. In the East, a war economy slows down and distorts the direction of growth, and generates shortages of resources and skills. The strains are felt most acutely in the client states of both alliances, where resentment grows against their captive state. As anxiety and dissatisfaction mount, there can be glimpsed, as an intolerable threat to exterminist ideology, the possibility of a truly internationalist movement against the armourers of both blocs.

This brings us closer to the point of crisis. An accelerating thrust has set the superpowers upon collision course, and the collision is to be expected within the next two decades.[46] Yet the economies and ideologies of either side could buckle under this acceleration. The injections of public money, even the MX missile, may not stave off US recession: they might even aggravate its form, in the disjunction between an advancing and a recessive economy.[47] In the Soviet Union and in Eastern Europe it is ideological crisis which is most manifest: how long will those old controls work? The official description of reality induces only tedium; ideology is no longer internalized—it becomes a mask or a patter learned by rote, whose enforcement is a matter for the police.

As we know from history, this conjuncture of crisis and opportunity is the most dangerous moment of all. The ruling groups, habituated to the old modes and controls, sense the ground moving beneath them. The hawks and doves form factions. Actions are precipitate and impulsive. Neutralism, internationalism—democratic impulses in the East, socialist impulses in the West—appear as hideous threats to established power, challenging the very *raison d'être* of exterminist elites. In that situation of impending superpower collision and of ideological instability, it is not likely that 'we'—with our poor resources, our slight political preparation, our wholly inadequate internationalist communications—can succeed. It is probable that exterminism will reach its historical destination.

The Direction of Hell

I have been reading *Arguments within English Marxism*, and, leaving aside local disagreements and assents, have been puzzling over an ulterior difference of stance which neither I nor Perry Anderson have exactly defined. Which difference I will try to identify, in response to Anderson's invitation 'to explore new problems together'—even though this problem is an old one. It is, absurdly, one of generational experience.

My generation were witnesses, and petty actors, in the actual moment of the congealment of the Cold War, and the fracture of power across Europe. That fracture (enlarging the fracture of the 1920s and 1930s) has always seemed to me to be the locus of the field-of-force whose polar antagonisms generate exterminism.

The second generation of the New Left, who have conducted the NLR so long and so tenaciously, arrived on the scene when the Cold War had already congealed, and its ideological imperative had become a habit. At some point around 1960, Khruschev's erratic pursuit of detente together (I would argue)[48] with the growth of CND-type peace movements in the West had offered a check to the exterminist thrust, had forced it to disguise its operations and to modify its aggressive vocabulary. Nuclear war (it was agreed on all sides) was 'unthinkable'.

But at the same time, on the periphery (and South-East Asia was then still on the periphery) a new mobility of national liberation and revolutionary movements was in evidence, which met with a savage Western response. The new generation of the Left was quick to identify this whole opening field of struggle: expert in attention to it, and eloquent in theoretical solidarity with anti-imperialist movements in Africa, Asia and Latin America.

In all this they were right. But in the same moment preoccupation faded with the central emplacements of power: and it came to seem (wrongly) that confrontation between the two blocs *originated* at the periphery, and was carried only thence *to* the centre, so that its thrust and dynamics could be simply explained with the categories of imperialist thrust and anti-imperialist resistance. The role of western socialists became, more and more, to be that of observers and analysts of that external confrontation.

To my generation, which had witnessed the first annunciation of exterminist technology at Hiroshima, its perfection in the hydrogen bomb, and the inconceivably absolute ideological fracture of the first Cold War (the Rajk and Rosenberg trials, the Cominform anathema upon Yugoslavia, McCarthyism and the advocacy of 'preventive war', the Berlin air-lift and the Berlin wall), this never seemed so. We had become, at a deep place in our consciousness, habituated to the expectation that the very continuation of civilization was problematic.

This expectation did not arise instantaneously with the mushroom cloud over Nagasaki. But I can, in my own case, document it fairly exactly. In 1950 I wrote a long poem, 'The Place Called Choice', which turned upon this expectation. The central section of the poem concluded thus:

'. . . Spawn of that fungus settling on every city,
On the walls, the cathedrals, climbing the keening smoke-stacks,
Drifting on every still, waiting there to germinate:
To hollow our house as white as an abstract skull.

Already the windows are shut, the children hailed indoors.
We wait together in the unnatural darkness
While that god forms outside in the shape of a mushroom
With vast blood-wrinkled spoor on the windswept snow.

And now it leans over us, misting the panes with its breath,
Sucking our house back into vacuous matter,
Helmeted and beaked, clashing its great scales,
Claws scratching on the slates, looking in with bleak stone eyes.'

Such an apocalyptic expectation, which has never left me, is no doubt discreditable. Hans Magnus Enzensberger, whom I greatly respect, has recently chided the futurologists of doom, the 'negative utopians'; 'the world has certainly not come to an end . . . and so far no conclusive proof has reached me that an event of this kind is going to take place at any clearly ascertainable point in time.'[49] And, of course, it would be worse, far worse, than an apocalypse for one to make oneself intellectually ridiculous. I would only too gladly read the arguments which show, conclusively, that my analysis of the gathering determinism of exterminist process is wrong.

Yet the arguments have substance, and the technology of the apocalypse exists. Nor have all apocalyptic visions in this century always been wrong. Few of those who prophesied World War I prophesied the devastating sum of the actual event; no one envisaged the full ferocity of World War II. And the apocalyptic prophets of World War III do not match the kind of persons we encounter in our social history: eccentric vicars, zealous artisan sectarians conning *Revelation*, trance-struck serving-maids. Some emerge, with strategic war-plans in their hands, from the weapons-system complex itself: Sakharov, Mountbatten, Admiral la Rocque, Zuckerman. It was not Joanna Southcott who summoned the first Pugwash Conference, but Einstein and Russell. It was not Thomas Tany but Robert Oppenheimer who said, in 1947, 'the world is moving in the direction of hell with a high velocity, a positive acceleration and probably a positive rate of change of acceleration.'

We should, even in the matter of apocalypse, be a little exact. An exterminist climax might be aborted by a 'limited' local nuclear war (China, Africa, the Persian Gulf) whose consequences were so terrible that these frightened even the exterminists, and called up a new global wave of resistance. And even outright exterminist collision, with the full repertory of ICBMs, in the Northern hemisphere would not necessarily extinguish all mammalian life, unless the globe's ozone layer was irreparably punctured.

What this would destroy would be Northern civilization and its economic and societal life-support systems. The survivors (one might suppose) would then be exposed to waves of plague and famine; great cities would be abandoned to rats and to rattish genetic mutants. People would scatter to uncontaminated lands, attempting to re-invent a sparse economy of subsistence, carrying with them a heavy inheritance of genetic damage. There would be banditry: fortified farmsteads, fortified monasteries, fortified communes; and a proliferation of strange cults. Eventually there might be the re-emergence of petty city states, nudging towards new trade and new wars. Or this scenario could be all wrong. Advanced economies might survive, relatively undamaged, in the Southern hemisphere:

Australia, Argentina, South Africa. After an interval for stench and plague to die down, these might come back, with their muskets, to colonize the European tribes: perhaps to fight over the spoils: perhaps to establish one superpower's world dominion.

I do not mean the extermination of all life. I mean only the extermination of our civilization. A balance-sheet of the last two millennia would be drawn, in every field of endeavour and of culture, and a minus sign be placed before each total.

Our Opportunity

If one has come to live with this expectation, then it must modify, in profound and subtle ways, one's whole political stance. Class struggle continues, in many forms, across the globe. But exterminism itself is not a 'class issue': it is a human issue. Certain kinds of 'revolutionary' posturing and rhetoric, which inflame exterminist ideology and which carry divisions into the necessary alliances of human resistance, are luxuries which we can do without.

There are contradictions within this gathering determinism, and countervailing forces in both blocs, as to which I have said, in these notes, very little. It remains to indicate what an anti-extremist configuration of forces might look like, and what its strategy might be, if it were to stand any hope of success.

First, it would have to mobilize itself with great rapidity, since we are already within the shadow of collision. Prophecies are arbitrary: but the successful emplacement of cruise missiles on West European territories in 1983 might signal a point-of-no-return.

Second, the fracture through the heart of Europe remains the central locus of the opposed exterminist thrusts, although the second fracture in Asia (with the unpredictable presence of China) is growing in significance.[50] Hence European Nuclear Disarmament is not a strategy for opting out of global confrontation. It strikes directly at that confrontation, by initiating a counter-thrust, a logic of process leading towards the dissolution of both blocs, the demystification of exterminism's ideological mythology, and thence permitting nations in both Eastern and Western Europe to resume autonomy and political mobility. Neutralism or non-alignment in any part of the globe are not, or are not necessarily, isolationist or 'pacifist' options: they are active interventions against exterminism's determinist pressures.

Third, this configuration must, as a matter of course, forge alliances with existing anti-imperialist and national liberation movements in every part of the world. At the same time, by strengthening the politics of non-alignment, it will develop a counter-force to the increasing militarization, in Africa and Asia, of post-revolutionary states.

Fourth—and this may be the most critical and decisive point—it must engage in delicate and non-provocative work to form alliances between the peace movement in the West and constructive elements in the Communist world (in the Soviet Union and East Europe) which confront the exterminist structures and ideology of their own nations.

This is of necessity; and without such internationalist alliances which reach across the fracture we will not succeed. The exterminist thrust (we have seen) summons up and augments the thrust of its exterminist antagonist. The counter-thrust cannot come from the other, but only from within the resistance of peoples *inside each bloc*. But so long as this resistance is confined within its own bloc, it may inhibit the thrust to war but cannot finally impose alternative directions. So long as each bloc's resistance movement can be categorized as the 'ally' of the other, exterminism (with its powerful bases in the weapons-systems-and-support-complex) will be able to police its own territory, reassert ideological control, and, eventually, resume its thrust.

Hence only the regeneration of internationalism can possibly summon up a force sufficient to the need. This internationalism must be consciously anti-exterminist: it must confront the ideological imperatives of both blocs: it must embody, in its thought, in its exchanges, in its gestures, and in its symbolic expressions, the imperatives of human ecological survival. Such a movement cannot be mediated by official or quasi-official spokespersons of either bloc. (This fact was signalled by those Eurocommunist parties which refused their attendance at the Paris conference in April.) The strategy of Stockholm Peace Appeals and of the World Peace Council is as dead as the strategy (prising open Soviet civil rights by means of US Senate resolutions) of the exile at Gorky.

Internationalism today demands unequivocal rejection of the ideology of both blocs. The rising movement in Western Europe against NATO 'modernization' must exact a real price from the Soviet ideologists and military managers, in the opening of Eastern Europe to genuine exchanges and to participation in the common internationalist discourse. This must not be a hidden tactic but an open and principled strategy. This may be a most critical point in the dissolution of the exterminist field-of-force. It will be contested with equal ferocity by the ideologists of NATO and by the Communist bureaucracy and police. It will require symbolic manifestations and a stubborn internationalist morale. And it will bring friends into danger.

Finally, it should go without saying that exterminism can only be confronted by the broadest possible popular alliance: that is, by every affirmative resource in our culture. Secondary differences must be subordinated to the human ecological imperative. The immobilism sometimes found on the Marxist Left is founded on a great error: that theoretical rigour, or throwing oneself into a 'revolutionary' posture, is the end of politics. The end of politics is to act, and to act *with effect*. Those voices which pipe, in shrill tones of militancy, that 'the Bomb' (which they have not looked behind) is 'a class question'; that we must get back to the dramas of confrontation and spurn the contamination of Christians, neutralists, pacifists and other class enemies—these voices are only a falsetto descant in the choir of exterminism. Only an alliance which takes in churches, Eurocommunists, Labourists, East European dissidents (and not only 'dissidents'), Soviet citizens unmediated by Party structures, trade unionists, ecologists—only this can possibly muster the force and the internationalist elan to throw the cruise missiles and the SS—20s back.

Give us victory in this, and the world begins to move once more. Begin to break down that field-of-force, and the thirty-year-old impediments to European political mobility (East, South and West) begin to give way. Nothing will follow on easily and as a matter of course: but swing those blocs off collision-course, and the blocs themselves will begin to change. The armourers and the police will begin to lose their authority, the ideologists will lose their lines. A new space for politics will open up.

Within the threatening shadow of exterminist crisis, European consciousness is alerted, and a moment of opportunity appears. These notes are rough, and readers will wish to amend them. I ask them also to act.

*Thanks to Ken Coates, Mary Kaldor, Dan Smith, Dorothy Thompson and the editors of *New Left Review*, for comments and criticisms: none are responsible for my conclusions.

¹I am using 'rationality' in these notes to denote the rational pursuit of self-interest, as attributed to a nation, class, political elite, etc. In a different perspective none of these pursuits may appear as rational.

²I take the British adventure at Suez (1956), the Soviet intervention in Czechoslovakia (1968), and the United States helicopter operation in Iran (1980) to be examples of such hot flushes. The Soviet intervention in Afghanistan is a military–political act of a more calculated order: perhaps a cold flush.

³Peter Sedgwick, 'NATO, the Bomb and Socialism', *Universities & Left Review*, 7, Autumn 1959. (My italics).

⁴The literature is now extensive. For a preliminary evaluative bibliography, Ulrich Albrecht, Asbjørn Eide, Mary Kaldor et al., *A Short Research Guide on Arms and Armed Forces*, London 1978. Also the select bibliography appended to Asbjørn Eide and Marek Thee, eds., *Problems of Contemporary Militarism*, London 1980).
Bibliographies are regularly updated in the ADIU *Report* (Science Policy Research Unit, University of Sussex).

⁵And will, I fear, be forgotten through most of these notes. I find Chinese diplomacy inscrutable.

⁶See Régis Debray, 'A Modest Contribution to the Rites and Ceremonies of the Tenth Anniversary', NLR 115, May–June 1979.

⁷At any time before the 1960s, the exactions of OPEC or the truculence of Iranian students would have very certainly elicited a Western military punishment.

⁸Herbert Scoville Jr, 'America's Greatest Construction', *New York Review of Books*, 20 March 1980.

⁹Mary Kaldor, 'The Significance of Military Technology', in *Problems of Contemporary Militarism*, pp. 226–9.

¹⁰See M. Kaldor and A. Eide, eds., *The World Military Order. The Impact of Military Technology on the Third World* London, 1979.

¹¹I take here the conservative estimates of Deborah Shapley. These do not include lesser weapons. In other counts, if all nuclear weapons are included, the world's sum has already passed 50,000.

¹²Deborah Shapley, 'Arms Control as a Regulator of Military Technology', *Daedalus*, 109, Winter 1980

¹³Alva Myrdal, *The Game of Disarmament*, New York 1976, pp. 11–12; Lord Zuckerman, 'The Deterrent Illusion', *The Times*, 21 January 1980 (now reprinted in *Apocalypse Now*, Spokesman Books).

¹⁴For a reliable evaluation of the increment in both blocs, see Dan Smith, *The Defence of the Realm in the 1980s*, London 1980, esp. chapters 3 and 4.

¹⁵Myrdal, p. 8.

¹⁶Lawrence Freedman, Head of Policy Studies, Royal Institute of International Affairs, in *The Times*, 26 March 1980.

¹⁷'The threat of a Soviet nuclear attack on Western Europe could leave NATO the choice only of an early resort to the American arsenal, putting American cities at risk. . . . Missiles in Western Europe would give the American President an intermediate option.' Gregory Treverton, Assistant Director, Institute for Strategic Studies, in *The Observer*, 19 November 1979.

¹⁸Interview in the *New York Sunday Times*, 30 March 1980.

[19]Herbert F. York, 'The Nuclear "Balance of Terror" in Europe', *Ambio*, 4, nos. 5–6, 1975.

[20]*The Game of Disarmament*, Myrdal, chapter two, gives a thorough presentation of the whole 'theatre' strategy, published in 1976.

[21]A chatty account of this bureaucratic delinquency is given by Stephen R. Hanmer, Jr, in *NATO Review*, February 1980.

[22]Stockholm International Peace Research Institute estimates are summarized in Frank Barnaby, 'Global Militarization', *Proceedings of the Medical Association for the Prevention of War*, March 1980.

[23]Myrdal, p. 4. But the Third World is catching up, expending in 1978 (Barnaby, *passim*) 24 per cent of the world's total.

[24]An illuminating account of the present state of chemical warfare preparedness is in the *Scientific American*, April 1980.

[25]See Barnaby, 'Global Militarization'.

[26]The remarkable survey of the 'American Gulag archipelago' by Noam Chomsky and Edward Herman, *The Washington Connection and Third World Fascism*, and *After the Cataclysm* (both Spokesman Books, 1979) has received less discussion in Britain than it merits, perhaps because of differeing interpretations of events in Indo-China. Some of the most terrible episodes (which merit—as do events in Cambodia—the description of exterminist) have been effected by indirection and proxy: see A. Kohen and J. Taylor, *An Act of Genocide: Indonesia's Invasion of East Timor*, obtainable from TAPOL, 8a Treport Street, London SW1.

[27]Emma Rothschild, 'Boom and Bust', *New York Review of Books*, 3 April 1980.

[28]Since writing this article I have read the important report, 'The Role of Military Technology in Industrial Development', presented by Mary Kaldor to the UN Group of Government Experts on the Relationship of Disarmament and Development, May 1980. Kaldor argues a related but more complex case, with greater emphasis upon 'baroque' military technology: increasingly expensive, sophisticated, ineffectual, and leading to technological distortions or dead-ends. Kaldor sees the weapons-systems industries in the USA and Britain less as a 'leading sector' than as a sector constricting and distorting industrial change, and leading to 'technological stagnation, the symptom of a vicious circle in which industrial decline stimulates military spending which then paradoxically accentuates the process of decline'. She finds the export of such technology to the Third World to be wholly negative, implanting decadence within the very pursuit of growth.

[29]See James Petras and Robert Rhodes, 'The Reconsolidation of US Hegemony', NLR 97, and the ensuing discussion in NLR 101–2.

[30]*Wall Street Journal*, 4 April 1980.

[31]See Scoville, *New York Times* (science supplement), 15 April 1980; and *Guardian*, 13 March 1980.

[32]*Time Magazine*, 7 April 1980; *Guardian*, 27 March 1980; and, on the activities of arms lobbyists, *New York Times*, 30 March 1980.

[33]Oskar Lange, *Papers in Economics and Sociology*, Oxford 1970, p. 102.

[34]Rothschild.

[35]Zhores Medvedev, 'Russia under Brezhnev', NLR 117, Sept–Oct 1979, p. 18.

[36]Alec Nove, 'Problems and Prospects of the Soviet Economy', NLR 119, Jan–Feb 1980, pp. 16–17.

[37]David Holloway, 'War, Militarism and the Soviet State', *Alternatives*, June 1980. See also the same author's 'Soviet Military R & D' in J. Thomas and U.

Kruse-Vancienne, eds., *Soviet Science and Technology*, Washington DC 1977. I draw heavily upon David Holloway's paper in this section, and thank him for permission to do so, but he is not to be held responsible for my conclusions.

[38]See Zhores Medvedev, pp. 11–12.

[39]See my 'Detente and Dissent', in Ken Coates ed., *Detente and Socialist Democracy: a Discussion with Roy Medvedev*, Nottingham 1975.

[40]C. Wright Mills, *The Causes of World War III*, New York 1958, p. 47.

[41]See Jan Øberg, 'The New International Military Order', in *Problems of Contemporary Militarism*, esp. pp. 54–64.

[42]Emma Rothschild.

[43]The high ideological visibility of Yugoslavia and of Cuba may have protected them from military operations more than considerations of strategic sensitivity. Contrast the pitiful quasi-official cowboy expedition against Cuba (the Bay of Pigs) with the unprecedented military violence visited upon Vietnam.

[44]*Guardian* defence correspondent, 27 May 1980.

[45]See the ineffable William Rodgers, Labour's defence spokesman, in *Labour Weekly*, 23 May 1980: 'Some three-quarters of a million men and women serve in the forces today or are involved as civilians in support activities and the defence industries. . . . If the Labour Party ceased to care about defence, we should lose their support and never win an election again.'

[46]If China places herself finally in either bloc, throwing her mass into the scales, it is difficult to see how collision will not occur.

[47]See Emma Rothschild, 'Boom and Bust', and Mary Kaldor, 'The Role of Military Technology in Industrial Development'.

[48]I dissent sharply from the analysis offered by Anderson and others which tend to demote CND (pacifist, neutralist, middle-class, 'failed') and to canonise VSC. But, for the moment, this argument can be left aside.

[49]'Two Notes on the End of the World', *New Left Review* 110, July–August 1978.

[50]By 'locus' I do not mean that Europe is the most probable flash-point for detonation. Pakistan or the Gulf States might provide that.

Nuclear Imperialism and Extended Deterrence

Mike Davis

Reading Edward Thompson's 'Notes on Exterminism', every socialist must unconditionally admire the optimism of his will, and respond to the power of its summons to effective action against the dangers of a new world war. But the pessimism of his intellect, expressed no less powerfully, prompts critical reflection. His essay is not only a political call to resistance, but also a theoretical exploration which polemicizes sharply with much of what it takes to be conventional thinking on the Left. Thompson sets out to challenge what he regards as the debilitating 'immobilism' of Marxism towards the imminent danger of nuclear holocaust. In his view this immobilism has several sources. On the one hand he criticizes a misconceived preoccupation of the New Left with the Third World, which has led it to ignore the 'central fracture' of East–West confrontation which more than ever cuts through Europe. On the other hand he rebukes those who reify the Bomb as a mere 'thing' subordinated to the rationality of an abstract international class struggle, when in fact weapons systems in both blocs have acquired a supervening and terrifying autonomy. Thompson insists on the urgent need to reconceptualize the relationship between the arms race and the Cold War in a situation where the former increasingly commands the latter, and where 'imperialism' has become an inadequate category to grasp the deadly symmetry of over-kill on both sides. Instead he proposes the concept of 'exterminism' as the fulcrum of his essay. We should take this not just as a new agitational imagery, but as a real attempt to achieve a theoretical breakthrough capable of explaining, where the old Marxist analysis has failed, the origins of the present nuclear peril, and of indicating the immediate priorities of the peace movement.

In the response which follows, I readily accept the pertinence of Thompson's critique of socialist theory for not generating an original analysis of the specificity of the strategic arms race or the transformation which it has wrought in world politics. The absence is a real one, and it has undoubtedly diminished the political appeal and intellectual authority of historical materialism within the peace movement. At the same time, however, I doubt whether the concept of exterminism provides an adequate analytic framework or, what is more important, a sufficiently realistic assessment of the present war danger. Thompson himself stresses that his Notes are 'rough', and invites readers to offer their own amendments to them. In that spirit I will try to show some of the difficulties of the notion of exterminism. The burden of my argument will be that any concept which collates all the 'inertial', 'irrational', 'symmetrical' and institutionally 'autonomous' aspects of the arms race into a single over-riding process will make it harder to understand the purposeful, strategic function of the current arms build-up within the larger context of the New Cold War. Above all, a focus that is too tightly and exclusively constricted around the arms-complex features of bipolar tension is likely to miss the crucial connection in the present conjuncture (as in past Cold War crises) between the overall nuclear balance and counter-revolutionary initiatives in the Third World. In several steps—beginning first with an immanent critique of the notion of exterminism itself—I will argue that the peace movement in Europe and America must mobilize not only against the general danger of an 'inertial thrust', but specifically also against the open US attempt to create a strategic nuclear 'umbrella' for new military—and possibly tactical nuclear—interventions in the Third World.

I. Deciphering Exterminism

The concept of 'exterminism' is constructed by way of analogy with that of 'imperialism', but also as a replacement for it, in Thompson's essay. It may therefore be appropriate to start by recalling the famous debate over the relationship between capitalism and imperialism in the ranks of the Second International. At the end of the era of liberal capitalism Marxists divided into two camps over their interpretation of the relationship between militarism, imperialism and capital accumulation on a world scale. On the one hand Hilferding, Luxemburg and Lenin argued that militarism and imperialism were the organic and unavoidable expressions of the contradictions inherent in a new stage of capitalism, characterized by simultaneous crises of over-production in the leading industrial nations. On the other hand Bernstein and Kautsky (as well as, of course, radical liberals like Hobson) maintained that war and colonialism were alien excrescences on the body of capitalism which might be removed by the expansion of domestic demand and the restoration of the peaceful norms of free trade. From the 'orthodox' perspective, imperialism was identified with a historically specific stage in the development of capitalism, while for what became the 'revisionist' tendency in the last years before 1914 imperialism and militarism were superstructural phenomena tied to particular contingencies and interest-groups rather than the mode of production itself.

Thompson clearly writes in the grain of the 'revisionist' view of the 'exteriority' of militarism and imperialism to fundamental class antagonisms. Thus exterminism today is a formation common to West and East alike, yet intrinsic to neither. For while it is deeply embedded in the existence of powerful, 'isomorphic' networks of interests (industrial, bureaucratic, military), it is not directly grounded in class structure nor is it coextensive with the reproduction or preservation of any mode of production. Exterminism, in other words, is not the 'highest stage' of anything else, since that would imply organic development and some connection with a 'motor of history'; rather, like a cancer, it is simply a dead end for the whole organism. Acquiring a causal autonomy that is equivalent to a veto-power over the entire social formation, Thompson suggests, the arms race has become its own demiurge. Clearly the relevant theoretical presence here is not Marx, but the ghost of Weber (or his translator *in extremis*, Kafka).

At the same time, while Thompson presents exterminism as the implicit apotheosis of the power of certain interest groups and bureaucratic strata, it is the *unforeseen* convergence of their separate 'thrusts' that threatens to override class or human interests to the point of universal annihilation. I emphasize 'unforeseen' because Thompson also gives a certain Althusserian twist to the concept of an autonomous bureaucratic configuration: that is, he describes exterminism virtually as a 'process without a subject'. It is this which demarcates 'exterminism' from the superficially similar notion of a rampant 'military-industrial complex' that has been a traditional theme of much American sociology. Exterminism, in other words, is not conceived as the domination of any single institutional or political instance, but rather as the vector of different 'thrusts' and 'logics'. It arises, as Thompson puts it, out of a 'collocation of fragmented forces' whose a priori unity or self-recognition is not assumed.

What ultimately confers cohesion on the different components of exterminism is the bipolar confrontation itself. Thompson clearly hints that if the Cold War did not exist, it would have had to be invented—since it provides the indispensible basis for domestic unity. It is the mirror-image demand of internal hegemony, expressed through ideology, in both the United States and the Soviet Union that sanctions, reproduces and 'addicts' the social formation to exterminism. 'Symmetry', in Thompson's usage, thus has two meanings. First it refers to the situation in which state power in each bloc has become the *raison d'être* of its opposite via the permanent brandishing of the Bomb. Secondly it indicates an actual homology between the bureaucratic and military structures of Cold War mobilization in the USSR and the United States. Taken as a whole, this portrait of hyper-militarized establishments imposing domestic order by gearing up for an apocalypse is not unlike Daniel Yergin's explanatory scheme of the dialectic between the American 'national security state' and the Soviet 'total security state'. The difference, of course, is that Thompson takes the possibility of the apocalypse far more seriously than Yergin or the Harvard History Department.

Finally, Thompson expects the actual slippage towards exterminism to come not from politics as we might expect—that is, from field of forces that must be analysed 'in terms of origins, intentions or goals, contradictions or conjunctures' (which he discounts)—but from the 'messy inertia' of the weapons systems themselves. Thus he points to 'pressures from the laboratories', 'impatience amongst the war gamers', 'the implacable upwards creep of weapons technology' or the 'sudden hot flush of ideological passion' as its most likely immediate triggers. The specific scenarios of exterminism that he evokes tend towards either a Dr Strangelove or a latterday Sarajevo. In the first case, an accident—a computer malfunction, a paranoid airforce general, or perhaps only a low-flying formation of seagulls—trips the wire, disconnects the fail-safe mechanism and vapourizes the Northern hemisphere. In the second scenario—where analytic disputation is more possible—elaborate nuclear threats and linkages between conventional warfare and nuclear warfare have been emplaced as safeguards or signals to intimidate the enemy; the 'enemy', however, is not intimidated (perhaps miscalculates) and the mad roulette of deterrence spins to a final halt at mutual assured destruction.

This deeply pessimistic projection, on the other hand, coexists with a diagnosis that also points in a quite opposite direction. For, as we noted above, in Thompson's account exterminism is not only a fatal inertial thrust towards the end of Northern civilization, it is also, more hopefully, a formation in some sense external to and *separable from* the rival social systems which confront each other today, even if at present it prevails within both of them. This side of Thompson's analysis enables him to imagine the possible dismantling of the 'deep structures of the Cold War' without the simultaneous dismantling of the deep structures of capitalist ownership or, for that matter, of bureaucratic domination. This vision finds its fullest and most generous expression in his recent pamphlet *Beyond the Cold War*. Its intellectual foundations are also there most clearly exposed. For in this text, the Cold War today—no longer just the arms race—is seen as a literally purposeless mechanism reproducing itself, whose only function is its own self-perpetuation. 'What is the Cold War now about? It is about itself.'[1] No longer in any sense a rationally intelligible conflict, it is compulsive 'habit' or 'addiction'—if one materially supported by the sectional interests of 'the military-industrial and research establishments of both sides, the security services and intelligence operations, and the political servants of these interests', and psychologically sustained by the need for internal bonding within American and Soviet societies, achieved by the mutual exclusion of a paradigmatic Other. Just because of this, 'a revolt of reason and conscience', in the name of a common 'human ecological imperative', could bring the Cold War to an end. The evidence of this revolt is the growth of the peace movements in Europe. For it was there that the Cold War started, and it is there that it could be overcome. 'The Cold War can be brought to an end in only two ways: by the destruction of European civilization, or by the reunification of European political culture.'[2] Such a reunification would involve a detente of peoples rather than of states, unfreezing the glaciated divide between Western and Eastern Europe. But it would not necessarily abolish the principal economic or social structures of either. 'Immense differences in social system would remain.' But across them would now move 'the flow of political and intellectual discourse, and of human exchange'. As their rigid ideological and military guards came down, 'the blocs would discover that they had forgotten what their adversary posture was about'.[3]

Thompson's arguments and hypotheses have been developing in the past two years amidst every political urgency; they are not a finished case, but an introduction to a common debate that has long been missing on the Left, in which his own views will surely undergo further evolution, or emendation, of emphasis. I want to start my comments by simply pointing out some of the difficulties and inconsistencies of the concept of exterminism itself, and suggesting ways in which the categories excluded in consequence of it by Thompson can, in fact, be reintegrated into a historically materialist explanation of the Cold War. Thompson begins his account of exterminism by suggesting that the present war danger cannot be analysed in terms of 'origins, intentions or goals, contradictions or conjunctures', but rather appears to be 'simply the product of a messy inertia'. The immediate past, likewise, is described as the 'irrational outcome of a collision of wills'. An insistence on these two features—the *inertial* and *irrational* character of arms race (and then by extension of the Cold War itself)—is central to his argument. In part, this deadened unreason is attributed to the sheer mechanical automatism of modern weaponry itself, as 'today's hair-trigger military technology annihilates the very moment of "politics" '. But its sources actually go deeper than this. They reach, in fact, even beyond the kind of anarchic resultant of mutually contending projects conjured up by the phrase 'irrational outcome of a collision of wills'. For the Cold War today no longer embodies—if it ever did—the confrontation of any overall projects at all, representing more or less coherent or unitary historical agents. Its inertia has rather 'drifted down to us as a collocation of fragmented forces', each bound together by no necessary internal logic, and bearing no necessary intention or goal.

What are these forces, whose interplay generates exterminism in each camp? They appear in Thompson's text themselves pell-mell, scattered in different parts of it. In the case of the West, there are the abstracted ambitions of scientists in the laboratories; inter-service rivalry; profitability of weapons companies; most importantly, perhaps 'bureaucratic decisions' (but if these are really *decisions*, aren't we back with some notion of political purpose?) or elsewhere 'inertial thrust'. All of this remains relatively sketchy. Causality in the East, however, is even more tentatively marked in. There are the imperatives of 'ideology', diffusion of military 'patriotism', influence of officers (not yet 'decisive'), technical superiority of arms industries. The enumeration in either case is close to the initial description: it amounts to little more than collection of fragments. Yet the paradox is that Thompson, after insisting on the random and disaggregated character of the forces generating exterminism, then presents their summation as a political culture that is literally all-pervasive, seeping inexorably into every cell of society and addicting it to a fatal toxicant. Having dispersed and miniaturized the *causes* of exterminism, one might say, he magnifies its *effects* out of all scale, to a point where it becomes coextensive with the social order as a whole, as the ubiquitous sickness of a poisoned civilization. 'The USA and the USSR do not *have* military-industrial complexes: they *are* such complexes.' There is a 'cumulative process' in which exterminist 'crystallization in culture accelerates crystallization in the economy and thence to politics and thence back again once more'. The whole vital surplus of East and West alike is symbolically dedicated to the technology of annihilation. Exterminism, the title suggests, may now be built into the very physiological programme of Northern civilization—as the terminal illness of its last stage.

The contradiction within this account is not hard to see. There is a striking disproportion between Thompson's minimization of the sources of exterminism and his maximization of its spread. The discrepancy between the two parts of the argument is covered by the notion of the 'isomorphism' of East and West. Exterminism, from such small beginnings, can be so total and universal because the two sides need it to batten down their own respective social hatches. There is thus a kind of over-arching external causality at work, which can act as a substitute for any more articulated internal explanation. Thompson does not argue that the USSR and USA are identical social formations, or even that their foreign policies are precisely equivalent. Rather it is the reciprocity of their antagonism itself which confers on each their common deadly properties, as ruling groups in Washington and Moscow, the twin citadels of exterminism, come 'to *need* perpetual war crisis, to legitimate their rule'. So long as this reciprocal process holds fast, 'isomorphic replication is evident at every level: in cultural, political, but, above all, in ideological life'.

The effect of the arguments is at variance with its starting-point. For the actual force of the notion of isomorphism is to suggest that despite differences of local derivation, *essentially*—that is, in all that touches on the fundamental issues of war and peace—everything is the same in East and West, and it is a distraction to dwell on secondary differences or past episodes distinguishing the two. This admonition is applied especially to any attempt to explain the Cold War by looking at its genesis in the post-war epoch, or the respective positions and policies of America and Russia at the time. 'To argue from origins is to take refuge from reality in moralism.' Just as Thompson curiously inverts the typical emphases of his history-writing—which honours agency—in a 'structuralist' conception of exterminism virtually without exterminists, so he casts the reproach of moralism on any effort to reconstruct a political history. But in fact it is not moralistic at all to think that the different histories of the USA and USSR are relevant to our understanding of the Cold War today. The fact that the USA has never been invaded in the 20th century, while Russia has been invaded three times, that during the Second World War the USA lost 1 million dead and prospered in the fastest boom in its history, while the USSR lost 20 million dead and a third to a half of its industrial plant destroyed, is pertinent because it helps us to make certain *predictions* about the behaviour of these two great powers, where the notion of 'isomorphism' does not. The flaws in Thompson's stance here find their way into the contradictions of his imagery. In *Beyond the Cold War* he writes: 'I am addressing the question—not what caused the Cold War, but what is about today? And it is no good trying to answer this by standing at its source and stirring it about with a stick. For a river gathers up many tributaries on its way, and turns into unexpected courses'. But on the next page, he unwittingly reverses the metaphor. Here the Cold War, 'an abnormal political condition', is 'the product of particular contingencies at the end of World War II which struck the flowing rivers of political culture into glaciated stasis, and struck intellectual culture with an ideological permafrost'.[4]

Fixed or fluid? The inconsistency condenses the paradoxes of Thompson's general sketch of exterminism: the supreme humanist become arch structuralist, the moralist turned clinician, the historian rejecting history.

These paradoxes are not unintelligible. Behind Thompson's theoretical construct lies a number of very understandable political motivations. To depict the exterminist contamination as omnipresent is to dramatize the dangers of war with the most urgent and mobilizing of tocsins. To represent the sources of exterminism as a medley of involuntary or atomized forces, on the other hand, is to avoid the great divisive breach of class analysis and social identification of political opponents, and with it the risks of ideological hostilities incompatible with an irenic movement. To refuse investigation into the origins of the Cold War is to forestall the possibility of differential judgement of the two sides to it, that would be internationally even less ecumenical. A benign sleight of hand, of a kind familiar—perhaps inherent—in the discourse of all peace movements, is visible here.

Yet the real history of our time still require its answers. These answers have political consequences, for peace and for socialism. In what follows, I shall argue that the Cold War in its wider sense is not an arbitrary or anachronistic feud staged essentially in Europe, but a rationally explicable and deeply rooted conflict of opposing social formations and political forces, whose principal centre of gravity has been for some thirty years now the Third World. That conflict would have existed and developed into a Cold War, even if nuclear weapons had never been invented. The Bomb has shaped and misshaped its evolution, and may yet put an end to it altogether. But it is not its spring. That lies in the dynamic of class struggle on a world scale. The rationality of the conflict derives from the incompatible interests of the major actors in it. Thompson contests this rationality, on the grounds that a drift towards common extermination cannot be in any side's interest. But, of course, this is not the first time in history that a discrepancy has opened up between rational interest and irrational outcome. What typically lies between the two is the recurrent historical phenomenon of class *error*, for which Marxists always need to make theoretical allowance. Class interest, as Hamza Alavi has pointed out, should be conceived not as a source of its own objective, correspondent expression, in an a priori adequacy of means to ends, but rather as the social *basis of calculation* of the agent concerned, that includes in its very definition the possibility of *mis*calculation in a world of antagonistic action and reaction.[5]

In the age of the hydrogen bomb, such miscalculation could indeed lead to mutual annihilation. In that sense, Thompson's warnings of the possibility of accidental triggering or faulty escalation need no further justification; the fear of these must haunt any sober peace movement today. The limitation of 'Notes on Exterminism', however, is that in concentrating so much moral and mental attention on the irrational and inertial dangers of the arms race, it tends to ignore the deliberate and dynamic calculations of nuclear politics. The result is to sidestep consideration of how the Bomb functions as a central instrument of power in an age of revolution. But to pose the question of *nuclear strategy as politics*—and not bureaucratic inertias—it is necessary to retrieve all those categories that Thompson sets to one side as 'irrelevant': conjuncture and crisis, origin and purpose, classes and modes of production. Indeed, to get at the deep structures of the Cold War we may need to dismantle the concept of exterminism.

II. The Dynamic of the Cold War

To pose an alternative we need to offer different interpretations of the fundamental categories of analysis implicitly bound together in the notion of 'exterminism': that is (i) a theory of the *dominant level* of international politics and the proximate impetus towards nuclear war, and (ii) an explanation of the specific role of the strategic arms race in this decisive arena.

Now for Thompson, as we have seen, the strategic arms race *is* the dominant level of world politics and everything else flows from this overarching and terrible fact. Another explanation, reflecting what is undoubtedly the common-sense understanding of the majority of this generation's peace campaigners and anti-nuclear activists, would ascribe the present danger to the domination of world politics by the two 'superpowers' conceived as Orwellian aggregations of uncontrolled power (although individual opinions would, of course, differ as to the relative onus attached to each bloc). In either case—and regardless of whether the two camps are visualized as the antagonistic polities themselves or their specific exterminist complexes—the bipolar contradiction is the constitutive element of the international system, and the only hope for peace (assuming the deadlock of multilateral negotiation) is seen as secession from the dementia of superpower rivalry. Hence the goal of liberating Europe from the Bomb via a 1980s version of the 'positive neutralism' espoused by sections of CND in the 1950s.

Although 'exterminist' and 'superpower' explanations of the Cold War have a certain elegance of simplicity and familiarity, the weakness of both is their inability to elucidate the actual 'why and how' of the Cold War's concrete history. Whether we work from the premiss of a symmetrical need by both superpowers for an external threat to reinforce their internal hegemony, or from simply the abstract notion of geo-political power-craving and war-mongering, it remains difficult to explain why Eisenhower brandished the Bomb over *Korea*, why Kennedy went to the brink—and then almost over it—about *Cuba*, or why Nixon tried nuclear blackmail against *Vietnam*. Why *those* places? A naive question, perhaps, but one which I believe the current commonsense of the peace movement has difficulty answering, and which Thompson's essay does not address.

To begin to answer this question—and thus apprehend the logic of the situations in which the nuclear danger has most often appeared—it is necessary, in my opinion, to reinstate the revolutionary Marxist conception of the modern epoch as an age of violent, protracted transition from capitalism to socialism. From this perspective the Cold War between the USSR and the United States is ultimately the lighting-rod conductor of all the historic tensions between opposing international class forces, but the bipolar confrontation is not itself the dominant level of world politics. The dominant level is the process of *permanent revolution* arising out of uneven and combined development of global capitalism. This is the true motor of the Cold War. In face of the likely reaction of many readers to what may seem jargon, let me be more precise: I am not talking about what Thompson at times self-consciously caricatures as the 'drives of world imperialism' or its 'evil will', but rather the inexorable process by which the international expansion of capital, through its simultaneous destruction of tranditional modes of production and its multiplication of modern forms of exploitation, reproduces new 'weak links' within its own political order and revolutionary explosions against itself. It is not necessary to share an eschatological vision of the World Revolution to recognize that the development of capitalism on a planetary scale has likewise internationalized the forces of revolt against it. True, the emergence of these forces displays no simple, evolutionary tendency, but rather the most baffling pattern of contradiction, retrogression and sudden rupture. Nor does their movement have a single, privileged pivot—either metropolitan or 'peripheral'—since it is the result of the system's continual transformation. As Edward Thompson has in his own way so often pointed out, real history is prodigiously overdetermined by the complexity of the world economy, the innumerable nuances of national class structure, the residues of every traditional social conflict, and the capriciousness of human agency. Yet it seems to me indisputable that the major trend in modern history has been the tectonic action of these elemental class struggles within and upon the international state system.

Before attempting to define the dynamic of the Cold War itself, it may

be helpful to briefly recall some of the antecedent phases in this globalization of class struggles against capital. The era of socialist transition was, of
course, later in arriving than originally predicted by Marx. This was in part
the result of an epic event which neither Marx nor Engels ever theorized
(although they were its contemporaries): the political and ideological
incorporation of the first modern labour movements in Britain and America
by the hegemonic Liberalism of Jackson–Cobden–Lincoln–Gladstone. It
was also in part a by-product of the failure of the Revolutions of 1848
which postponed continental industrialization for twenty to thirty years.
It was only with the formation of the Second International in 1889 (and,
more specifically, with the great international May Day demonstrations of
1890) that it is possible to say that labour became in its own right a
participant in world politics. Significantly the political centre of gravity of
Social Democracy did not coincide with the areas of the greatest development of trade unionism per se (Britain, the United States, Australia), but
rather where extensive recent proletarianization collided with the persistence of absolutism (Central and Eastern Europe). The International
impinged upon the European balance of power as a great, unknown variable. From the standpoint of our exterminist era, it is interesting to recall
how, in their *fin de siècle* divinations, both revolutionaries and reactionaries
were awed by a vision of what was widely believed would be the apocalyptic
weapon of the new century, more mighty than the coming dreadnought or
zeppelin: the General Strike. Yet an internationalism built around militant
resolutions and fine-spirited slogans proved incapable in 1914 of actually
mobilizing that weapon against capitalism and war. Nor did that related
harbinger of the final conflict, international trade-union solidarity
(whether envisaged as the One Big Union or a World Confederation of
Labour) ever become the material force that classical Marxism has assumed
would be the natural concomitant of the internationalization of capitalist
forces of production.

The twentieth century was to take another turn. Class struggles never
acquired a 'pure' international form, but remained compressed inside the
pre-existing state system, with all the charge of nationalism and militarism
it inevitably transmitted to those revolutions that successfully acquired
power within it. Here lay the paradox of October. On the one hand the
Russian Revolution changed world history by creating a territorial base of
support, with increasing industrial and martial resources, for socialist
revolutions abroad, for anti-colonialism, and even, during 1941–44, for
the salvation of bourgeois democracy in Western Europe itself. On the
other hand, the defeat of revolution in the West forced the USSR at home
to resort to a strategy of 'primitive socialist accumulation' (as Preo-

brazhenski called it) on the basis of its own backwardness and underdevelopment, with all the terrible consequences that flowed from this. For a long period the future extension of socialist revolution became dependent upon material aid or political recognition by the Soviet Union (even true in the case of Yugoslavia in 1944–47). Yet the bureaucratic despotism consolidated in the Soviet Union became a virtual dystopia for the Western working class and a huge fetter on the reconstruction of a real internationalism. Thus the vicious circle which commenced with the original isolation of the October Revolution has continued as a reciprocal parochialization of the labour movement in the West and bureaucratic devaluation of socialism in the USSR (and later, Eastern Europe).

The Soviet Union's role in world politics as the material and military cornerstone of further subtractions from the empire of capital has been largely involuntary. Stalin, in particular, made a sustained effort between 1936 and 1947 to disengage the USSR from the dynamic of permanent revolution. Believing that the survival of the Soviet state was strictly dependent upon its manipulation of the violent divisions between the imperialist powers and its own breakneck industrialization, he essentially sought to reclaim Russia's old position as a legitimate great power with its traditional spheres of influence. To this end, he orchestrated the Popular Fronts, traded away (not always successfully) the fates of popular revolutions—Spain, Greece, Vietnam and China—and manoeuvred incessantly for durable ententes with the 'democratic' sections of Western capital. Yalta was the meridian of Soviet efforts to achieve a reestablishment of a traditional international state system based on the recognition of stable balances of power; and Yalta has remained, in the quarter of a century since Stalin's death, the point of reference for continuing initiatives by Soviet diplomacy. No state in modern history has been more consistent and, in a sense, more open in pursuit of its major geopolitical aims than the USSR since 1936 in its quest for some mode of detente with the West.

Two factors, however, have combined to make any lasting stabilization of the relations between the USSR and the capitalist states impossible. First was the post-war restructuring of the world market under American hegemony, which for the first time created a basis for peaceful coexistence between the advanced segments of imperialist capital that allowed them to concentrate their immense economic and military resources against the USSR and international revolutionary movements. Although differences between American and European imperialism were still occasionally to provide space for Soviet diplomatic manoeuvre—notably in the rifts between Eden and Dulles, De Gaulle and Kennedy or Johnson, Brandt and Nixon—there has been no room (at least in the absence of a truly unified and supra-national European capitalist state) for the restoration of a traditional balance of power. Moreover there is a grain of truth in the primarily instrumentalist and 'internalist' theories of the Cold War, to the extent that the Soviet threat was indeed an indispensible condition for the imposition of US hegemony on its allies and the American reorganization of the world economy and Western political system. The Cold War was in this sense 'functionalized' as a forcing-house of inter-capitalist unity and systemic restructuration.

But as I have argued above, it would be a profound mistake to see the origins of the Cold War as primarily an internal or instrumentalist regulation of American (or Soviet) societies. Its driving force, and the second factor mitigating against permanent detente, has been the alloy of socialism and nationalism in the dependent and semi-colonial countries (together with the auxiliary insurgencies of more traditional nationalist movements under often atavistic social leaderships). Between the failure of the German Communist putsch of March 1921 and the liberation of Yugoslavia by Tito's 'proletarian brigades' in 1945 (the second successful socialist revolution in world history), and discounting several ephemeral episodes in Latin America (Chile in 1932 and Cuba in 1933), there were only the historic defeats of the Second Chinese Revolution (1926–28) and the Spanish Civil War. Since 1945, however, there has been, as the American far right never ceases to point out, a socialist revolution on the average of every four years. While none of these postwar revolutions has had the universalistic aspiration or resonance of October ('*patria o muerte*' would have been anathema as a slogan to the Bolsheviks), nor have they been simply national events. In the first place anti-capitalist revolutions, whatever their national epicentre, have always had a seismic impact on distinctive *regional* substructures of the world economy. This is the rational kernel of the 'domino' theory. To extend the geological simile, the most important 'tectonic plates' of postwar revolution have been, respectively, the Balkans (1944–48), East Asia (1946–today) and Latin America (1959–today). These are the regions where (unlike the Arab world) socialist vanguards of workers and intellectuals were able to win the leadership of mass upheavals of peasants and semi-proletarian rural poor. Secondly, these revolutionary waves have had two, successively different geopolitical orientations. The 1944–54 revolutions in the Balkans and Far East were centred in the historically contested borderlands (especially the Lower Danube Valley and Manchuria) where Russia since the Tsars had confronted and battled German and Japanese expansion—indeed, all these revolutions germinated as national resistance movements against German and Japanese fascist occupation. In contrast the post-1959 revolutions have been centred in the strategic areas of the traditional European colonial empires or in the very backyard of American imperialism. This distinction between the *'Eurasian'* and *'Third World'* phases of postwar revolution, along with a recognition of the *regional* dynamic of each national revolution, is indispensible for an understanding of the development of the Cold War.

Within this pattern, however, there was one special area. In the more developed regions of Central and North-Eastern Europe, the post-war upheavals would not have led to the overthrow of capitalism without the decisive presence of the Red Army. The communization of this zone, which included the more important nations of Eastern Europe—Poland, Czechoslovakia, Hungary, Rumania—was a process apart, dictated essentially by Stalin's determination to create a protective *glacis* round the USSR. The creation of these buffer states was totally unwelcome to the USA, which had looked forward to profitable opportunities for trade and investment in them after 1945. But in the last resort it could and did accept them, for two reasons which hold good to this day. Firstly, it knew that the USSR was likely on the most traditional of strategic grounds to want a security belt on its Western frontiers, and would claim a 'moral' right to one after the Nazi attack and its consequences: it was well aware that this aim did not involve any principle of messianic revolutionary expansionism. Secondly, Eastern Europe was far the poorer half, and its forcible sovietization by an even poorer USSR logically implied a corresponding US sphere of interest in the far richer Western half of the continent; more, it actually consolidated capitalism in the latter by the spectre of authoritarian austerity it henceforward presented. Thus although there were seismic waves in the *Balkans*, which threatened capitalism in Greece, once the socialist revolutions of the Lower Danube were integrated into the Soviet bloc as such (or expelled from it, precisely because of their autonomy, as in the case of Yugoslavia), there was thereafter never any 'spread-effect' to be feared from the People's Democracies. On the contrary, their very existence contained its own dual—ideological and strategic—self-limitation, the two assisting Washington to clinch the lion's share of the Old World. For just as 'artificial' socialism was introduced into Budapest, Prague or Warsaw, so capitalism was the 'natural' tendency of growth in Paris, Hamburg or Turin, given the balance of political forces in the West. The USA was working with the spontaneous socio-historical grain there, as much as the USSR was working against it beyond the Elbe. The result, of course, was the triumphant consolidation of bourgeois democracy in Western Europe, with the aid of the Marshall Plan, and the repression of any vestige of proletarian democracy in Eastern Europe, with the inquisitions against Titoism.

Ever since, the official history and ideology of the West has always magnified Europe as the central *Kampfplatz* of the Cold War, because it was there that political and economic contrasts worked in its favour, that capitalism enjoyed a moral and cultural superiority, and that the USSR could be portrayed as a national oppressor. The Europeanism of Thompson's own vision of the Cold War is itself partially a victim of this orthodox Western construal of the conflict to its own advantage. In reality, however, the first act of the Cold War was to provide a completely misleading image of the structure of the drama as a whole, as it has unfolded to date. For the European theatre had been stabilized by 1950. Capitalism had nothing to fear from an impoverished and 'satellite' socialism in the East, once it had contained the labour movement in the West. Thus it is striking that though the USSR has had to intervene militarily three times to keep control in Eastern Europe, the deployments of Soviet troops in the DDR, Hungary and Czechoslovakia have never seriously disturbed the international peace. The West has each time exploited the occasion to the full ideologically, while remaining essentially passive diplomatically and militarily. There has never been a major war crisis in Europe since the Berlin airlift. This pattern would be inexplicable if the Cold War really pivoted on Europe. By contrast, first 'Asia' and then the 'Third World' have been active arenas of Cold War conflict in the past thirty years, because there the USA and its allies have faced spontaneously generated, uncontrollable outbreaks of revolution, which—from China to Nicaragua—*have* had an ideological and political spread-effect rather than counter-effect, and which could not be fitted into any division of spheres of interest of the European type. In other words, the greater vulnerability of capitalism in the 'periphery' (so far) has dictated the greater importance of this zone for the permanence of the Cold War.

Even at the outset, however, Asia intervened directly in the emergence of the Cold War in Europe. For it is not difficult to identify the two events which totally undermined the Soviet effort to establish a durable accommodation with the United States: these were the Chinese Revolution and the integration of West Germany into the American alliance (an act prior to the establishment of the DDR, at a time when Stalin sought the neutralization of Germany). The two arenas were inextricably interlinked, and it was precisely the crisis over Germany that forced Stalin reluctantly to provide arms and support to the revolution in East Asia which he had tried to barter away in 1945–46. A fundamental pattern was thus established in the development of the Cold War: first the principle of linkage between the European and Asian spheres of Soviet security (recently demonstrated by the compensatory intervention in Afghanistan following NATO's nuclear escalation in Europe); and secondly, the implacable strategic constraint on the USSR, in the face of American pressure, to support and arm at least *certain* revolutions. In other words, the Soviet Union has attempted to blunt the ceaseless attempts of the USA to enforce its geopolitical and military paramountcy by strategically 'annexing' appropriate socio-economic upheavals in the dependent capitalist countries. Thus in the case of the first great Cold War crisis the USSR, faced with an American nuclear monopoly and a new ring of hostile encirclement, tried to safeguard Soviet cities and Russian interests in Central Europe by transforming the mass peasant armies of Red Asia into instruments of its own conservative national diplomacy (a design made dramatically clear by the Geneva conferences of 1954). In contrast to the American imperium, the 'Soviet Bloc' emerged, not out of a grand design for a world order, but as the accretion of battered and besieged 'socialisms in one country' huddled together for sheer survival round the preponderance of the first-comer.

The alternative to the Soviet bloc model of bureaucratic and nationalistic socialism—in the absence of a revolutionary wave in post war Western Europe—would have been the crystallization of a new pole of socialist internationalism around a regional federation of revolutionary states. 'Regional', because only such a supra-national entity in the Third World could command the economic and military resources to defend its dependence from imperialism and to negotiate a fully autonomous alliance with the USSR. During the sixties and early seventies both Cuba and Indochina temporarily appeared as the potential nuclei of regional revolutions with strong internationalist outlooks independent of the Sino—Soviet conflict. For this very reason, together with the important geopolitical shift which they represented in the axis of world revolution, they threatened to transform the Cold War qualitatively by challenging any bi-polar management of revolutionary crises. In the event, however, the Cold War was 'triangulated', but not by the emergence of the new Tricontinental International, but by the formation of Mao's unholy alliance with Nixon and the Chinese lead in containing the shock waves of the historic triumph of the Indochinese Revolution in 1975. Simultaneously the renewed pressures of United States—with the overthrow of Allende in Chile and the continuing blockade of Vietnam by 'other means'—as well as severe internal economic problems, forced both Cuba and the Indochinese states into closer dependence upon the USSR.

It would be illusory to imagine that the Indian Summer of detente in 1972–75 was forced upon the United States by its defeat in Indochina, as some sections of the left have maintained. The conjuncture was more complex. On the one hand, the USSR was for the first time approaching parity with the United States in the strategic balance of nuclear power; on the other hand, the China Card represented a major shift in the global balance of power against the USSR. Simultaneously the USSR had managed to bring both Cuba and Vietnam within its bloc, while the Nixon administration was confident that global 'Vietnamization'—the strategy of substituting sub-imperialist police powers for conventional US forces—would guarantee stability in the main sectors of the American Empire. As the Soviet academician Trofimenko has explained in an exceedingly frank and revealing essay in a recent issue of *Foreign Affairs*, the essence of the Nixon and Ford administration's approach to the USSR at the summit meetings of the seventies was a trade-off between nuclear parity and the containment of Third World revolution.[6] 'Linkage' in the jargon of Kissinger meant the US codification of the strategic arms status quo in exchange for Soviet ratification of the socio-political status quo in the Third World. The contradiction, of course, in Kissinger's grand design for a neo-Bismarckian settlement of the Cold War was that the Soviet Union, even with Cuba and Vietnam now under tow, could no more prevent the outbreak of new revolutions in the 1970s than it could in the late 1940s (when international communist discipline was incomparably stronger).

I have no disagreement with Edward Thompson's assessment of the importance of the armourers' lobby in Washington in promoting its vested interests in MX missiles, Trident submarines, and B-1 bombers. But again I do not think that a primarily 'internalist' analysis enables us to understand why, at the mid-point of the Carter administration's brief career, the Brzezinskis and Browns suddenly carried the day against the proponents of detente like Vance and Young. An analysis of the shift in the international conjuncture becomes absolutely necessary. I think the origins of the new Cold War in that sense are not hard to seek. In a sentence, *the new Cold War is principally the product of a gigantic and relatively synchronized destabilization of peripheral and semi-industrial capitalism in the wake of the world economic crisis.* I will argue the particulars of the Third World crisis in a moment; suffice it to say that growing real immiseration and super-exploitation combined with militarization, industrialization-by-debt and extensive proletarianization have created explosive situations on three continents. Without any new initiative by the USSR, the walls of containment began to crumble simultaneously in Africa, Central America, the Middle East, with temporary tremors in the Iberian Peninsula and new cracks in East Asia. Some of the weak links which have recently broken—the Portuguese colonies, Afghanistan, Ethiopia, Nicaragua—were amongst the poorest and least well-fortified bastions of the world market; Iran, in contrast, was a crucial imperial relay with the most advanced military machine in the Third World apart from Israel. From Washington's point of view, these ruptures had a distinctly 'wild' and unpredictable character; particularly because the ability of the USSR to modulate or take 'responsibility' for the level of revolutionary activity in the Third World has decreased with the weakening of the traditional communist movement and the disappearance of most of the USSR's old 'non-capitalist' allies. Another distressing development has, of course, been the emergence of an atavistic religious populism in the Middle East and Sahel which confounds regular Cold War categories.

If these revolutions and popular anti-imperialist upheavals have been unprecedently autonomous in their origins from the orthodox Communist movement—or its febrile opponents in Peking—the very success of the United States in playing the China Card and in exploiting its renewed technological-military lead (since 1974) over the USSR, has forced the latter to assume a more militant stance in arming and providing a logistical backstop to the new revolutionary regimes. While prudently cultivating Ostpolitik in Western Europe, the Soviet Union in concert with Cuba undertook in the second half of the last decade bold new military interventions in Africa. It is important to note, however, that this does not so much indicate a Brezhnevite return to neo-Cominternism as it expresses a defensive geo-political response by Moscow to the growth of the Washington–Peking axis. Meanwhile on the American side, the collapse of the Nixon Doctrine and its strategy of sub-imperialism has brought US strategy (via the so-called Carter Doctrine) almost full circle back to the impossible project of maintaining a universal American military presence. This time, however, there is a new and more ominous nuclear twist.

III. The Quest for 'Extended Deterrence'

It is at those moments when the institutional mechanisms stabilizing the Cold War give way under the full assault of the logic of permanent revolution that the time of the Bomb arrives. As Daniel Ellsberg has chronicled, this moment has recurred repeatedly in the course of the Cold War: during the retreat from Chosin Reservoir in 1950, in the last days of Dien Bien Phu in 1953, during the Formosa Straits crisis of 1959, during the 1962 Cuban Missile crisis, at the siege of Khe Sanh in 1968, and, most recently, during Nixon's 'nuclear alert' after the encirclement of the Egyptian Third Army in the Yom Kippur War of 1973.[7] On each occasion it was the United States that moved to the brink—usually without consulting its European allies—and in virtually every case the arena of crisis was in the Third World.

To understand why the present danger of nuclear brinkmanship is again so grave, we need to analyse the specific role of the nuclear arms race in the dynamic of the new Cold War. Such an analysis, however, begs an answer to Edward Thompson's original question: what—first of all—is the Bomb? This apparently naive question is really the Sphinx's riddle which has long barred the way to adequate Marxist explanations of contemporary world politics. For understandable reasons most left-wing commentary on the arms race has traditionally concentrated on demystifying the arcane fallacies and pure disinformation of official military spokesmen and their think-tank shadows, rather than specifically theorizing the role of nuclear build-up as a political plane in its own right.

As a first approximation let me propose that the strategic arms race must be conceived as a complex, regulative instance of the global class struggle. As I have tried to argue, every modern revolution has taken place within an organized system of international constraints and counter-revolutionary violence. With the pacification of inter-imperialist military rivalries, permanent mobilization for 'total war' acts as a force-field which defines the terms of contestation between capitalist and post-capitalist social systems. Within the Cold War's aggregate balance of economic, geo-political, ideological and military power, the nuclear build-up plays the double role of preserving the structural cohesion of each bloc and of regulating the conflict between them.

Illustrative of the first function has been the 'alliance-building' role of nuclear weapons deployment in Western Europe. As Thompson's essay makes clear, 'exterminism' has always been an implicit cornerstone of Atlantic unity, and devotion to the Bomb and NATO has been a fundamental precondition for a party's admission to governmental power in the major Western parliamentary states. Thompson exaggerates, however, in imputing a neo-colonial or captive-nation status to Britain or other NATO countries. The 'American yoke' has been worn willingly by European capitalism precisely because it has served its needs so well. American *hegemony* is exactly that—not mere usurpation or dictation: and the NATO states have derived major benefits from its maintenance. The availability of the American strategic deterrent, together with the stationing of a large American garrison to act as 'tripwire', has allowed the European allies to devote a minimum of their budgets to support of conventional armies; although, with a population equal to that of the USSR and GNP more than twice as large, they are clearly capable of 'balancing' Soviet conventional forces if they so wished. This has greatly redounded to the competitive advantage of European capital. It has also allowed significantly higher levels of welfare expenditure to contain its more combative working class. At the same time, European and Japanese capital have been able to participate as virtual 'free riders' in the hi-tech spinoffs of the mammoth American military research programme—the primary engine for the generation of applied science in the postwar world. All in all, Atlanticism—as a kind of contemporary Concert of the Powers—has made possible an unprecedented concentration of military might against both international revolution and any potential surge by a domestic far left, while at the same time allowing a more flexible and rational international division of labour amongst the advanced countries, based on the relatively unhindered diffusion of advanced technologies. It has, thus, been the precondition, not just for the survival of European capitalism, but specifically for the reconstruction of European *imperialism*, with its major interests in the Mediterranean, Africa, and the Middle East.

The situation on the other side of the Cold War divide is far from symmetrical. The Soviet Union, unlike the United States, has stubbornly refused to permit any proliferation of its nuclear capability amongst other members of the 'Socialist Commonwealth'—a position which played no small part in precipitating the original Sino–Soviet split of 1959–60. At the same time, however, the survival of every revolutionary regime since October has depended at some critical stage upon the countervailing military and economic support of the USSR and its industrial allies. The *primary*, although by no means exclusive, function of the Bomb, therefore, has been to regulate the parameters of Soviet intervention in and support for global class struggles, anti-colonial revolts and nationalist movements. Since 1945 the United States has attempted to exert this *extended deterrence* against the USSR in at least four different ways:

First, by maintaining the strategic arms race as a form of economic siege warfare against the social system of the USSR and the Comecon bloc. Although this aspect of the bipolar conflict has all too often been ignored or underestimated, it has increasingly become the focus of long-range American hopes for 'rolling back' or internally disrupting Soviet and allied regimes. Arms competition, grain exports and strict control of Western technological patents all form components of a grand strategy. The projected one-and-a-half-*trillion* dollar Carter/Reagan defence budget for 1981–85 is ominously the first military build-up in American history to have economic warfare as an overt objective. In a sarcastic but serious play upon the words of Khrushchev's famous 'We Will Bury You' speech, Reagan has recently warned the Russians: 'We Will Bust You'.

Secondly, by forestalling any possibility of Soviet actions in Western Europe comparable to those in the Third World through NATO's strategy of responding to a Soviet conventional campaign with a nuclear blitz. It should be remembered that first use of nuclear weapons has been the pillar of NATO's strategy since the formation of the Alliance in 1949, and that the European allies have been its most zealous guardians. (Thus the French and Germans, believing that the Kennedy Administration's commitment to nuclear first use might be weakening, forced it to deploy an extravagant number of new, 'tactical' nukes in Europe as additional collateral.) Furthermore, the current US campaign to make Europeans 'think the unthinkable' in accepting the strategy of 'limited' nuclear war is not so much a sudden descent into the 'theatre of the apocalypse' as a return to the status quo ante. From 1949 (when the USSR first acquired the atomic bomb) until 1965–68 (when it first acquired a credible capability to strike the continental United States with solid-fuel ICBMs), the United States enjoyed sanctuary while Western Europe was mortgaged against the USSR's medium-range bombers and missiles.

Thirdly, by threatening nuclear retaliation against all Soviet attempts to achieve 'forward basing'—either as an attempt to redress the American strategic advantage or to extend a regional shield to new revolutionary regimes. (Soviet motives in installing missiles in Cuba in 1962 undoubtedly involved both goals.) In the endless debate about the nuclear numbers game, the Russians have always insisted that it is essential to take into account the unequal geo-military positions of the USSR and the United States. What underlies the claim is the fundamentally assymmetrical character of the overall balance of military power. The United States has immense forward-based nuclear striking capacity, the Soviet Union has none. The USSR is surrounded by thousands of miles of hostile border-lands, from Turkey to Japan, while the United States enjoys the security of three oceans and the largest of all satellite blocs, the Western hemisphere. Finally the United States has twice attempted to bomb 'established' social-ist states—Korea and Vietnam—'back into the stone age', while virtually every important American ally is defended against Soviet intervention not only by forward-based US nuclear weapons, but also by the tripwire of American soldiery directly connected to the so-called 'ladder of escalation' and the strategic arsenal.

Fourthly, by constantly buttressing its qualitative strategic-nuclear superiority to limit conventional Soviet military and economic aid to Third World struggles, and to prevent a Soviet response to the potential usage of tactical American nuclear weapons against a Third World foe. Ideally, as Arms Control and Disarmament Agency head Eugene Rostow (a leading war criminal of early Vietnam days) recently testified, American strategic nuclear superiority should 'permit us to use military force in defence of our interests with comparative freedom if it should become necessary'.[8] The concept of extended deter-rence that can be seen at work here is something of a rosetta stone for understanding the underlying logic of the complex of weapons systems and their deployment in a range of modes. For example, the ceaseless accumulation of nuclear overkill has entirely different implications if we conceive 'deterrence' in a defensive or offensive sense. In the first case—understanding deterrence as simply the most effective disincentive to an enemy first-strike—the growth of the nuclear arsenal beyond the 'counter-society' threshold appears absurdly redundant, and Thompson seems more than justified in seeking irrationalist forces and autonomous drives within the weapons systems themselves. In the second case, however—when the strategic systems (ICBM, submarine, bomber) are conceived as the basis of extended deterrence in support of conventional or tactical-nuclear engagement in a subsidiary theatre—the acquisition of 'counter-force' and first-strike capacities assumes quite a different meaning: for what are now projected are disincentives against interference in the 'dominant' side's offensive actions. 'Limited Nuclear War', 'Flexible Response' or 'Ladder of Escalation' can then become functional deterrents in their very obscurity or absurdity. As a leading New Right strategist has emphasized, 'Much of the deterrent effect of our nuclear force is, in the final analysis, the result of forcing the Soviet Union to live with uncertainty. . . . Ultimately the Soviet Union will see the wisdom of accepting serious constraints in their military efforts, both in force deployments (nuclear and conventional) and in geopolitical expansion'.[9]

The problem, of course, is that all this is easier (and more safely) theorized than done. The actual implementation of 'extended deterrence'—that is, the translation of US strategic superiority into effective, 'on-the-ground' supremacy—has been the elusive will-o-the-wisp of every post-war administration and the hub of every major debate on nuclear strategy. For nearly forty years the American deterrent has chased the World Revolution largely in vain, as Pentagon policy has alternated back and forth between nuclear brinkmanship and on balance unsuccessful attempts at direct counter-revolutionary intervention. Thus Truman's bid for global containment did win the Civil War in Greece, but it was totally stalemated by a million Chinese volunteers in Korea. In face of the huge human reserves of the revolution in East Asia, the Eisenhower Administration, dominated by budget-conscious Midwestern Republicans, attempted to retreat from conventional warfare behind the shelter of 'massive retaliation.' Although this strategic 'New Look', with its reliance on the H-Bomb and the Strategic Air Command, managed to forestall the liberation of Taiwan and extorted the division of Vietnam at Geneva, it failed to prevent a handful of guerrillas from growing into a revolutionary army a mere ninety miles from Florida. The Kennedy doctrine of 'flexible response' was the answer to the prayers of the strategic revisionists of the 1950s (including General Maxwell Taylor, Nelson Rockefeller and all the hungry young PhDs of the Rand Institute) who had been demanding a more aggressive global posture. The fiscal conservatism of the Republican years was replaced by the military-Keynesianism of the 'New Frontier'; with unlimited largesse, MacNamara's Defence Department systematically staked out its targets—special warfare, a fifty per cent increase in ICBM 'throw-weight', a new generation of tactical nuclear weapons, and the enunciation of the 'counterforce' doctrine (yes, Virginia, in 1962, not 1978). While this escalation in strategic arms held the Soviets at bay, the Green Berets and B-25s were supposed to be able to finish off the Viet Cong in an efficient climax of technocratic genocide. Instead the Vietnamese finished off Lyndon Johnson, the doctrine of 'flexible response' and the myth that the American economy could finance both welfare at home and a major counter-revolutionary war abroad. It is possible that the Soviet Union's approach towards strategic nuclear parity in 1970–73 (the first Russian ICBMs were MIRVed in 1972) stayed Nixon's hand from the final, nuclear escalation as much, or more, than the fears of domestic explosions at home. At all events, the *deus ex machina* of entente with China temporarily created the illusion of a costless US withdrawal from Indochina, as like Eisenhower before him, Nixon attempted to find way out of the Democratic morass of an Asian war. The solution was the Nixon–Kissinger doctrine of using the rapidly industrializing dictatorships of the periphery as regional military surrogates for the United States, while securing the neutralization of the Soviet Union in the Third World in exchange for the SALT treaties and the recognition of the Eastern European status quo. But at the same time as Nixon and Brezhnev were discussing quantitative ceilings on strategic arms, Washington was making every effort to widen the qualitative US superiority in missile accuracy and undersea warfare.

Then came Luanda, Managua and Teheran. As mentioned earlier, the collapse of the Shah and the new wave of Southern revolutions brought the Ford and Carter Administrations back to the same problem of combining nuclear and conventional weapons in an effective system of 'extended deterrence' that Kennedy had faced in 1960. The Carter Administration agonized, hesitated and then plunged into the New Cold War without ever quite being aware of the massive domestic retrenchment that would be necessary to sustain it. Then the New Right came to town and liberated the US war budgets from the incubus of residual New Deal claims for welfare or human rights.

Americal global strategy, as we have seen, passed through four distinct stages on the road from Potsdam to Vladivostock: the Truman Doctrine or

'Containment' (1947–52); 'Massive Retaliation' (1953–1960); 'Flexible Response' (1961–70); the Nixon Doctrine (1970–75). All were different solutions to the common quest for extended deterrance. What is the emergent doctrine of the *fifth* strategic epoch that has now opened? In particular, what is the relationship between the strategic nuclear build-up and renewed US military intervention in the Third World? To some analysts the Carter–Reagan New Cold War has looked like a hasty and impromptu resurrection of the Kennedy Administration's pretence of a 'two-and-half war' capability, dovetailing strategic, theatre and special-war forces. In contrast, other observers have doubted whether any coherent plan underlies the current arms mania beyond the appetites of the military-industrial complex for the Congressional pork barrel, covered by Pentagon propaganda diverting the public with a re-fabricated red menace. A closer reading of New Right defense theorists, however, suggests that there are indeed deeply reasoned and very alarming elements of a strategic new departure in the Administration's actions. The distinctive features of the Reagan strategy seem to be these:

First, the Administration is intransigently opposed to any new 'multilaterization' of international politics. It has opposed the so-called 'North-South dialogue', not only because of a frozen heart, but also because it fears the emergence of any new axes of diplomacy or political-economic cooperation that might increase the autonomy of the EEC vis-à-vis the United States. With the failure of a voluntarist Trilateralism, and as inter-imperialist economic competition reaches a post-war height, the New Cold War provides an invaluable framework for reimposing Western 'unity' and American hegemony.

Secondly, the New Right and its hawkish allies in the Democratic Party (including most of the AFL–CIO executive) have made the restoration of American strategic superiority their central and overriding objective. 'Superiority' for them, however, has little to do with any quest for a fail-safe protective deterrent around the United States itself. Rather it consists of acquiring the means of projecting US nuclear strength as a global umbrella, especially over the Third World. The New Right has been adamant in its opposition to proposals to put the US deterrent out to sea (the idea of a so-called 'strategic dyad') because it would lack—at least at this point in technological development—the precision accuracy to be a credible 'counter-force' deterrent. The virtues of the $30 billion dollar MX system, in tandem with MARVed Trident-2s, Cruise missiles, Stealth Bombers, is that it would supposedly provide the Pentagon with a selective ability to knock out any or all levels of Soviet conventional and 'theatre' forces. The dangerous implication here is not so much the likelihood of an all-out American first-strike, as a US ability to impose on the USSR a de facto recognition of 'limited nuclear war'. The deployment of strategic superiority to attain what Haig calls 'escalation dominance'—i.e. the ability to confront the other side with the choice between acceptance of a limited nuclear *fait accompli* or total escalation to societal suicide—is what links counter-force to counter-insurgency.

Thirdly, the Rapid Deployment Force is radically different from the Kennedy-era special warfare forces in one outstanding regard: its deployment openly integrates a tactical nuclear backstop. As Daniel Ellsberg has pointed out, the RDF is in many respects a kind of 'portable Dien Bien Phu' waiting to enmired and besieged. The difference, of course, is that the Pentagon is now expressly prepared to rescue the RDF with tactical nuclear weapons.

Fourthly, in face of the potential vulnerability of key semi-developed relay states like Saudi Arabia, Egypt, Nigeria, and perhaps even Brazil, the US is moving towards a more intimate embrace with the bunker regimes in Israel and South Africa. One of the gambits of the new Administration has been its exploration of a possible 'South Atlantic Alliance' between the Southern Cone dictatorships and South Africa which would be closely linked to NATO–Atlantic and US–Indian Ocean war plans. Such an alliance would be an implicitly *nuclear* one and clearly emphasizes the growing danger that Israel and South Africa (as well potentially of Brazil, Argentina and Pakistan) might in the future become nuclear surrogates for the United States in regional Third World arenas.

The Reagan strategy, in other words, appears to be based on an extremely dangerous widening of 'flexibile response' to include limited nuclear war in Third World theatres, under the umbrella of a buttressed counter-force superiority, in a general context of increased bipolar tension and a tightened American command structure over NATO. In one sense the goal of this strategy is actually deterrent—i.e. to constrain the Soviet Union in 'force deployments' and in 'geopolitical expansion'. On the other hand, actual scenarios of nuclear warfare are all too grimly imaginable. As I have said earlier, one of my chief criticisms of any unilateral emphasis on the 'irrational' dimensions of the exterminist thrust, is precisely its elision of the *purposeful* escalations and strategically contrived confrontations of the Cold War. Perhaps the maximum exterminist danger in the present period would concentrate in one or both of the following Third World centred scenarios: (I) The employment of tactical nuclear weapons by American Rapid Deployment Forces or one of the US's rogue allies against a Third World revolutionary or nationalist regime that itself possesses relatively sophisticated conventional armaments: e.g. Libya, Iran or North Korea.

(II) The Reagan Administration's persistent threats to take military action against Cuba (in violation of the 1962 agreement that was the cornerstone of detente), or its support for military infiltration (via a Savimbi or Pol Pot) against African and Indochinese allies of the USSR, might prompt the Soviet leadership to again consider the forward basing of nuclear weapons, leading to a rerun—or much worse—of October 1962.

The possibility or otherwise of nuclear crises breaking out in the next year in the Third World, however, will be inextricably bound up with the tempo of the class struggle and the emergence or absence of new pre-revolutionary situations in the South. Thus today the danger to Cuba is acute because of the growth of people's war throughout Central America, while the extension of Libyan influence in Africa has been based on the disintegration of the traditional economy in the Sudanic belt. It is necessary, therefore, to make some brief, final remarks on the general causes of the deepening crisis of capitalism in Africa, Asia and Latin America.

IV. The 'Collapse' of Dependent Capitalism?

It has become conventional wisdom that the last decade has witnessed a major transfer of economic power from the OECD nations to the new petro-chemical and industrial boom economies of the Third World. The press has been awash with glowing—or glowering—accounts of the economic miracles of Korea, Taiwan, Singapore, Brazil, Venezuela, Mexico and even the Ivory Coast and Sri Lanka (only yesterday, of course, it was singing the praises of the Shah and his accomplishments). More alarmingly, the conviction appears to be growing in the ranks of the metropolitan labour movements that much of the current high unemployment in the West has been caused by a process of 'de-industrialization' which has literally scooped up capital, jobs and even machinery from the West Midlands, Youngstown or the Ruhr, and transferred them en masse to the sweated factories of São Paulo or Seoul. This perception, combined with the widespread belief that OPEC has caused the last two recessions, has created a congenial climate for the thunderings of the Anglo–American New Right against the 'menace' from the Third World. *Business Week* openly came out for the seizure of Middle East oilfields, while bumper-stickers on thousands of American cars urged Carter to 'Nuke Iran'. Meanwhile even relatively progressive currents of opinion, including trade unions and social democratic politicians, have rushed to combat the foreign threat in more 'responsible ways' by urging the revival of protectionism or selective import controls.

The theory of the Third World as culprit of the current crisis is of course factually absurd. On the one hand it ignores the central fact that most of the job loss in the OECD bloc has been the direct result of *internal* restructuring: i.e. the massive shift of capital from secondary to tertiary sectors, job flight from older to newer 'sunbelt' regions of the United States and Europe (e.g. Spain), and deliberate under-consumptionism (via monetarist belt-tightening). On the other hand, it obscures the real phenomenon of a dramatic expansion of a restricted number of industries in a restricted number of non-OECD countries, amidst a generalized and entirely illusory impression that major resources have been transferred from North to South. In fact the opposite has been happening.

First of all, absolute immiseration is expanding at an unprecedented rate in the history of the world economy, and the economic infrastructures of some societies are literally collapsing. It is necessary to insist on the horrifying specificity of this process. There has never been a 'subsistence crisis' of the ferocity or global dimension of the current, unfolding catastrophe. The Great Depression, by contrast, had a relatively benign impact upon large parts of the colonial world: a paradox explained by the fact that the collapse of cereal prices allowed millions of Asian and African peasants to consume their own crops or buy cheap wheat. The present crisis is entirely different because of the well-nigh universal impingements of the market on former subsistence farming, the marginalization of domestic foodstuff cultivation by export agriculture, the gigantic displacement of peasant tillers from the land, and expansion of socially parasitic layers (soldiers, bureaucrats). The worst-hit countries are the so-called Fourth World of non-oil producing, primary-product economies which have been afflicted by the triple curse of stagnant or falling prices for their exports, huge oil (and weapons) bills, and astronomical interest rates. In the words of one recent survey, these 'countries are forced to bear a major part of the adjustment required by instabilities in the world economy over which they have no control'. Declining real income, combined with the greater share extracted by American bankers and Arabian oil feudatories, has squeezed the reproduction fund of local oligarchies and military elites precisely at a moment when their appetites for luxury goods, retainers and, above all, weapons are exponentially increasing. The result has often been a terroristic strategy of super-exploitation that has, in turn, evoked desperate resistance. The logic of what is happening to societies like El Salvador, Guatemala, Haiti, Bolivia, Upper Volta, Niger, Chad, Zaire or the Sudan is in some ways reminiscent of the disasters that overtook European society in the fourteenth century, compounded of exploitation, famine and revolt (but this time with a nuclear plague?). Absolute pauperization is what is fuelling the flames of Islamic revivalism across the Sahel (where nomadic society has collapsed after 2,500 years) and providing the will-power for the incredible revolutionary ordeal in Central America.

A different set of structural conditions threatens crisis in the so-called 'newly industrialized countries' of Latin America and East Asia. While it remains true that the semi-industrialized countries of Latin America contain their own 'fourth worlds' in the form of vast and severely underdeveloped rural regions (Southern Mexico, North-East Brazil), the real focal point of social revolution in these societies is more likely to be their gigantic, hypertrophic cities. Despite an irresistible rise in popular expectations amongst the enlarged working classes of these countries, none has yet made a real transition to the 'Fordist' unification of mass production and mass consumption that characterizes the economies of the OECD bloc. Moreover there is little sign that any of the political conditions could be mobilized which would allow a restructuring of production away from export markets or middle-class consumer durables towards truly mass domestic goods. The increasing addiction of these countries to 'debt-led' growth reinforces their need to preserve or expand their international competitive capacity, while it simultaneously increases the invigilation of OECD banks over their domestic policies. The resulting pressures to force wages down and reduce social expenditure—radically more severe than under even the most right-wing of the current OECD regimes—are likely to close the space for reform or partial democratization. In the short-run the enormous indebtedness of these countries could bring the international financial system itself into jeopardy, and provoke new forms of US intervention. But in the longer-run the greatest danger to Western capitalism is the emergence of autonomous, self-organized labour movements in these countries. If the centre of gravity of the international class struggle were to shift to them in the 1980s, it would have immense repercussions for the entire system of world politics. The United States would not resign itself lightly to the loss of any of the major semi-industrial countries; here might lie the seeds of another *casus belli* for World War Three, if a powerful movement for peace and solidarity with the people of the South is not built within American society today.

The two-fold crisis of dependent capitalism in the Fourth World and the semi-industrialized world, while creating broad new opportunities for socialist advance, also creates new dilemmas. The Soviet bloc now offers diminishing resources to accommodate or sustain anti-capitalist revolution in the poorer countries, or to inspire emulation in the more advanced. Together with the Sino—Soviet split, the failure of Comecon to organize any real international division of labour or integrated trading system amongst the post-capitalist states reduces the relief available to new revolutionary regimes of the Third World. Furthermore any inclination by the USSR to counter-balance American (or American–Chinese) initiatives with its own manoeuvres in the Third World is certain to be tempered by wariness of the United States and by fear of too much instability in the South. While new social explosions are inevitable, the further consolidation and extension of socialism may have to rely on alternative bases of international aid as well as upon greater regional self-help.

Meanwhile for the United States, the political-economic resources for keeping a velvet glove over the iron fist are dwindling. Brandtian schemes for reflating North European capitalism by pump-priming Third World demand look utopian beside the enormous exposure of American banks in the Southern hemisphere. The Carter Doctrine, with its wild brandishing of six-shooters over the Persian Gulf, has for the moment played taps over neo-Wilsonian pretensions to a 'reformist' American foreign policy. Whether the New Right stays in Washington or not, the consequences of the reaction and recession of the turn of the decade will be with us for years to come.

V. Actually Existing Exterminism

As future megadeaths multiply to incomprehensibility in their underground crypts, present slaughters are dulled in our conscience and made matter-of-fact by repetition and sheer enormity. Twenty years of 'revolution in the counter-revolution'—to borrow Debray's still apt phrase—have produced a penultimate apparatus of 'conventional' terror. The old-fashioned technicians of human extermination that yesterday organized 'Operation Phoenix' in Vietnam or ran a clandestine mission or two over the border in Cambodia, are now rendering their crew-cut (but slightly grey) service in the barracks of San Salvador or Guatemala City. No bastion of the free world is too poor or humble not to possess the ultimate status symbol of America's trust, the airborne weaponry for rural fusillades. Meanwhile in the cities—*many* cities—torture is not only routinized, it is now computerized. Counter-revolution no longer simply hunts down revolutionaries, it pre-emptively destroys families, villages, whole social strata. The costs of making revolution in these lands would be unbearable if the costs of not making it were not higher. This is the actually existing exterminism.

I wish not to be misunderstod. Edward Thompson's passionate call to protest and survive should not be deflected by radical platitudes or appeals to Marxist orthodoxy. But it can be sharpened by a more acute attention to

64

the interlinkages of the actual struggles unfolding across five continents. Whatever the errors of its immaturity, the 'New Left' should not be disparaged for having emphasized the dependence of the hopes of socialism in the Northern hemisphere upon the desperate and courageous battles being waged on the other side of the world. It will not weaken the resolve of peace campaigners in Western Europe and North America to understand more accurately and realistically why the struggle against the Pershing and Cruise missiles, the MX and B-1, will lessen the dangers of a holocaust in the Third World, as well as the First. The new movements for peace must mobilize the deepest levels of human solidarity, rather than pine nostalgically for the restoration of a lost European or Northern civilization. And within these new movements, the Marxist left must continue to honour the injunction of the Communist Manifesto to 'point out and bring to the front the common interests of the entire proletariat, independently of all nationality.'

[1] *Beyond the Cold War*, Merlin Press, London 1982, p. 17.

[2] *Beyond the Cold War*, p. 30.

[3] *Beyond the Cold War*, p. 34.

[4] *Beyond the Cold War*, pp. 9–10.

[5] Hamza Alavi, 'State and Class Under Peripheral Capitalism', Alavi and Teodor Shanin, eds., *Introduction to the Sociology of the Developing Countries*, London 1982.

[6] Henry Trofimenko 'The Third World and US–Soviet Competition: A Soviet View', *Foreign Affairs*, summer 1981.

[7] Daniel Ellsberg 'A Call to Mutiny', in E. P. Thompson and Dan Smith, *Protest and Survive* (US edition), New York 1981.

[8] Senate Confirmation Hearings, 1981.

[9] Jan M. Lodal, 'Deterrence and Nuclear Strategy', *Daedalus*, Fall 1980. See also Kenneth Adelman, 'Beyond MAD-ness', *Policy Review*, No 17, Summer 1981.

The Politics of Nuclear Disarmament

Raymond Williams

Since autumn 1979 there has been a vigorous renewal of campaigning against the nuclear arms race. Its immediate occasion was the NATO decision to deploy Cruise missiles in Western Europe, with further effects from the failure of the United States to ratify the Salt II agreement. But it was then rapidly intensified by the development of a complex international crisis, involving the Iranian Muslim revolution, the Soviet military action in Afghanistan, and heightened tensions in the Middle East and in the Gulf oil states. Yet while these conjunctural reasons are evident, it now seems that the specific campaigns against nuclear weapons have emerged with renewed authority, independence and strength. Residual and new campaigning formations have attracted many new members; successful meetings and demonstrations are again being held; and there has been a significant body of new writing and new analysis. The issues are so fateful that there can be nothing but welcome for this vigorous renewal of attention. Yet it is at just this moment that we have to look very closely again at the politics of nuclear disarmament. It is not simply that we have been here before; that in the late 50s and early 60s we had a powerful Campaign for Nuclear Disarmament which, for whatever reasons, was contained and dissipated. Indeed the most salutary effect of the renewed campaigning is that the more complacent conclusions about the decline of CND have been decisively challenged by the more substantial dimension of actual strategic and weapons developments, which the merely political conclusion—'we've had CND'—sealed off in thousands of minds. Anyone who has read the details of these new developments must be shocked by the extent to which 'the Bomb', as fact or slogan, has operated in the culture as a static if terrible entity, provoking resignation, cynicism or despair, while the reality has been the unceasing development of new and ever more dangerous systems. Moreover, in left politics especially, 'the Bomb' has for the most part been pushed into the margin of more tractable arguments about political strategy and tactics. When we now read, with full attention, the most sober descriptions of the appalling new military systems and strategies, it can seem like a waking after sleep, though it is not really that; it is yet another and perhaps now absolute demand, when we have already given available time and energy to other necessary work.

This is now the central political question. As the nuclear arms race again dominates attention, where is the rest of our politics, or is there indeed any other important kind of politics? Many comrades and friends are now arguing, eloquently, for an absolute priority of specific, autonomous and collaborative campaigning against the nuclear arms race.[1] The shock waves of recent events are pushing many thousands in that direction. But then it is here, at whatever risk of misunderstanding, that we must, as comrades and friends, ask and indeed insist on certain fundamental questions, and begin to suggest some answers.

Which Anti-Nuclear Campaign?

There is a first and relatively simple set of questions. They can be summarized as: give absolute priority to *which* campaign against the arms race? In Britain, for example, there are at least three campaigns, all gaining support. There is the revived Campaign for Nuclear Disarmament (CND), campaigning broadly but centred on a demand for unilateral British nuclear disarmament, in very much its original terms. Coherently but not exclusively associated with this is the urgent campaign against the siting of Cruise missiles in Britain. Then, second, there is the new and important campaign for European Nuclear Disarmament (END), still needing to resolve its relations with an older unilateralism, but centred on proposals 'to free the entire territory of Europe, from Poland to Portugal, from nuclear weapons, air and submarine bases'.[2] Third, there is the World Disarmament Campaign, centred on the comprehensive proposals of the United Nations Special Session on Disarmament, convened in 1978 and to be renewed in 1982. In the urgency of actual campaigning against powerful opposing forces, the differences of emphasis, some radical, between these campaigns can and at times must be set aside. Yet it is not only that the differences are already being exploited by the political and military establishments. It is that arguments drawn from these differences of emphasis become confused, even in single minds, and that genuine differences of policy and affiliation are overridden by the too simple conclusion that since all are against the arms race, all know how they will work to end it.

This state of mind was memorably and damagingly indicated at the

1980 Labour Party conference, when motions deriving from all three positions were passed, allowing endless opportunities for subsequent confusion and double-talk. Moreover it is significant, as was again evident at the Labour Conference, that at just the points where these differences of emphasis need to be discussed there is a regular reversion—of course in its own terms impressive—to simple restatement of the horrors of nuclear war, which are indeed the beginning but cannot function as the conclusion of any of the arguments. Nobody is quicker to agree about these horrors than the defenders and actual executants of the arms race, who then derive their own models of deterrence and swing much public opinion behind them. If a version of absolute priority to the anti-nuclear-weapons campaigns is then practically dependent on simple restatement of the terrible consequences of nuclear war, it is plainly insufficient.

There seem to me to be three broad questions. First, whether the development of nuclear weapons, and of the political and military systems associated with them, has so changed the character of otherwise determined social orders, that what we now confront, as Edward Thompson has powerfully argued, is in effect a new social condition of 'exterminism'. Second, within a different context, there is the question of the current real meanings of the leading terms of the general argument, notably 'deterrence', 'multilateralism' and 'unilateralism'. Third, and now of critical importance (though it depends on our answers to the preceding questions), what is or should be the specifically socialist contribution to activity against the nuclear arms race, whether autonomous or as an element in broader collaborative campaigns?

I. Nuclear Weapons and the Social Order

'The Bomb' and Technological Determinism

'If "the hand-mill gives you society with the feudal lord; the steam-mill, society with the industrial capitalist", what are we given by those Satanic mills which are now at work, grinding out the means of human extermination?'[3] The question is urgent and relevant, but behind it, of course, is another question: who 'gave us' the hand-mill, the steam-mill, the missile factories? The intricate relations between a technology and a mode of production, and indeed between a mode of production and a social order, are only rarely of a kind to permit simple analysis of cause and effect. Technological determinism, as indicated in that combined sentence from Marx and Edward Thompson, is, when taken seriously, a form of intellectual closure of the complexities of social process. In its exclusion of human actions, interests and intentions, in favour of a selected and reified image of their causes and results, it systematically post-dates history and excludes all other versions of cause. This is serious everywhere, but in the case of nuclear weapons it is especially disabling. Even when, more plausibly, it is in effect a form of shorthand, it steers us away from originating and continuing causes, and promotes (ironically, in the same mode as the ideologies which the weapons systems now support) a sense of helplessness beneath a cast, impersonal and uncontrollable force. For there is then nothing left but the subordinated responses of passivity or protest, cynical resignation or prophecy.[4] That the latter response in each pairing is infinitely better, morally and politically, should go without saying. But that the tone of a campaign can be radically affected by the initial assumption of so absolute and overpowering a system is already evident, mixed incongruously as it also is with the vigorous organization and reaching out to others which follow from different initial bearings.

In the case of nuclear weapons, nothing is more evident than that they were consciously sought and developed, and have continued to be consciously sought and developed. It is true that, as so often in modern technological innovations, much of the basic research had been done for quite other reasons, without foreseeing this particular result. But again as in many other comparable cases, the crucial moment of passage from scientific knowledge to technical invention, and then from technical invention to a systematic technology, depended on conscious selection and investment by an existing social order, for known and foreseen purposes. Thus the atomic bomb was developed within a situation of total war, under the familiar threat that the enemy might also be developing it, by states which were *already* practising the saturation-bombing and fire-bombing of cities and civilian populations. The atomic bomb gave them very much greater destructive power to do the same things more absolutely, more terribly, and (with the new genetic effects of radiation) more lastingly. Yet while it is true that massacre is not a twentieth-century invention it has made a radical difference that massacre was first industrialized, in the nineteenth-century development of high explosives and the twentieth-century development of the bombing plane, and then, in the late-twentieth-century development of guided missile systems, in effect automated. It is not only, though it is most immediately, a matter of nuclear weapons. Contemporary developments in chemical and bacteriological weapons, also capable of combination with missile technology, belong to the same escalation in the extent and practicality of massacre.

Military technology has often, perhaps always, been a significant factor in the constitution of a social order. It also directly affects the struggles of classes. If the characteristic effective weapon is within the reach or use of peasants and workers there is a different ultimate balance of class forces from those periods in which effective weapons depend on control of major industrial plants or advanced scientific research. What we have really to ask, about the full range of nuclear and related weapons, is what specific *variations* they have introduced into the shifting but always crucial relations between a military technology and a social order. Two types of variation are evident: international and internal.

Nuclear Weapons and the International Order

It was commonly said, when the atomic bomb had just been invented, that there were now only two or three states capable of waging major war. Indeed this perspective, learned with much else from James Burnham, was the basis for Orwell's projection of *1984*, in which three super-states, in shifting alliance and counter-alliance, with absolute repressive and propagandist control of their internal populations, were in a state of effectively permanent war. It is essentially this Orwellian nightmare ('1984' as 'exterminism') which is now being revived. The mere fact of revival does not affect its truth, either way. But it is worth comparing the prophecy with the history. The emergence of superpowers was correctly foreseen. As it happens this was not primarily a function of the atomic bomb or even of the hydrogen bomb, even though these had conferred immediate and in certain situations decisive military advantages. For there were definite stages within the new technology, and the crucial stage, we can now see, was the combination of nuclear weapons with advanced missile technology, from the mid-1950s: a combination, at its continually rising level, which still keeps the United States and the Soviet Union as superpowers in a period in which other states have acquired nuclear weapons but less effective or more vulnerable means of delivery. All the other projections are more arguable. There has been a very powerful and dangerous grouping of secondary states in direct alliances with the superpowers. In the dimension of nuclear weapons and related military strategy these alliances have indeed taken on something of the character of super-states, though at other levels this development is much less complete and is subject to other, often major, political interests and processes.

At the same time, the rest of the world, which had been conveniently incorporated and in effect neglected in the Orwellian perspective, has been both object and subject in this dominating and dangerous history. It is ironic that one of the principal (mainly Chinese) arguments against agreement on the non-proliferation of nuclear weapons has been the evident danger of superpower hegemonism: an impulse to political independence which, combined with certain regional rivalries, has in fact multiplied the nuclear arsenals. In direct military ways, in the search for bases in the global strategy which accompanied missile-nuclear and related technology, there has been constant pressure to reduce independent or ex-dependent states to objects in the superpower military competition. But then while much of this has followed from the imperatives of military technology, and has even been continued, in blind thrusts, when changes in the technology made it no longer so necessary in military terms, it is also true and crucial that the central thrust of this deadly competition has been not primarily military-technological but, in the broadest sense, political. But this fundamentally political character of the competition in its turn modifies the directly military competition. It is necessary for the superpowers not only, as often, to pretend, but in many cases actually to be concerned with those broader interests which originate in the rest of the world. Thus political and economic struggles which a simple military hegemonism would have a priori excluded have in fact continuously and powerfully occurred, and have included the substantial if still incomplete liberation of many peoples who are nowhere near having nuclear-weapons capability. At the same time not only the superpowers but many secondary states have exported other forms of armament with a recklessness, often distinct from the terms of the primary competition, which has led to twenty-five million (and rising) war deaths in a period in which nuclear weapons had been supposed to be determining and in which none had been actually used. Nothing in this argument reduces the central danger of direct nuclear war between the superpowers and their locked-in nuclear alliances. But, as we shall see again in analysing the ideology of deterrence, the apparent technologically determined process has been at most imperfectly realized, and in many significant cases has been inoperative, within the complexities of a necessarily broader world history.

Nuclear Weapons and Internal Controls

The other half of the Orwellian projection has also to be taken seriously. First, in the Cold War competition for the development of nuclear weapons, then in their continuing technical development, there have been dramatic increases in the levels of surveillance and control, and of espionage and counter-espionage, in capitalist societies like our own. Whether there has been a similar increase in Soviet-controlled societies, and especially in the Soviet Union which before nuclear weapons already had an immense apparatus of this kind, is more arguable. But there can be no denying that, taken as a whole, as not only direct repression and control but as an increasingly powerful propaganda for war preparations, secrecy, xenophobia and distrust, these internal developments have been contemporary with nuclear weapons. Yet there is again a major qualification. Precisely because the central competition is not only military-technological but is also, in the broadest sense, political, it is an underestimation of the dangers to suppose that they relate to nuclear weapons alone. On the contrary, what is now most dangerous in capitalist societies is the powerful attempt, already too widely successful, to achieve a symmetry between the external (military) threat—directly identified as the Soviet Union—and the internal threat to the capitalist social order which is primarily constituted by an indigenous working class and its organizations and claims. We should be in a much better situation than we now are if surveillance and secrecy were directed only against actual and possible Soviet agents, or for national military security. In fact, significantly, there is at least as much use of these controls, now aided by major technological developments of their own, against indigenous working-class and related political organizations. If this threatening symmetry of an external and an internal enemy is ever fully politically achieved, we shall indeed be in extreme danger.

At the same time, while the centralized secrecy-and-security state cannot be reduced, causatively, to nuclear weapons and their systems, there is one particular and vital respect in which the threat to democracy is indeed, in effect, technologically determined. This is not the possession of nuclear weapons as such, but their combination with missile technology. There has been a dramatic shortening of time for effective military decisions. The greatly increased accuracy of recent guidance systems, in the period of microprocessors, and the related shift from counter-city to counter-force strategy, have again reduced this margin.[5] It is then not only that secondary states have ceded their powers of ultimate political decision while they remain in nuclear alliances, but that within such a technology this ceding and centralization of powers is, in its own terms, rational. While much might be done in the more normal political areas of approaches to such a crisis, the fact remains that to assent to missile-nuclear technology is to assent to the loss of independence in ultimate decisions and, spreading back from that, to a steady loss of independence and openness in a much wider political area. It is this dangerous reality which now confronts the peoples of Europe, East and West. Combined, as it now is, with the siting of medium-range missiles, controlled from the same foreign centres, in the developing strategy of a 'theatre' (European) or 'limited' nuclear war, it compels, while we still have time, the most far-reaching political struggles.

II. Deterrence, Multilateralism or Unilateralism?

Deterrence as Strategy and Ideology

Deterrence is both a strategy and an ideology. We should be wrong if we failed to acknowledge some limited validity of deterrence as a strategy. Just because there is no effective general defence against nuclear weapons, or more strictly against nuclear missiles, there is some initial rationality in the argument that if an enemy possesses them, the only policy, short of pacifism, is to acquire and maintain a deterrent capability of the same kind. We have only to look at the international politics of the mid-late 1940s, when the United States but not the Soviet Union possessed atomic weapons, and when proposals for use of this monopoly to destroy the world centre of communism while there was still time acquired significant support, over a surprising range, to realize that in this as in so much else a monopoly of such terrible power, in any hands, is profoundly dangerous. It was then argued (as by Burnham in *The Struggle for the World*, 1947) that as soon as two hostile nations possessed atomic weapons nuclear war would follow almost immediately, and predictions of this kind—that possession implied inevitable use—have been made ever since, with a recurring confidence (in fact a recurring despair) unshaken by the passage of several predicted crucial stages. It has not been only military deterrence which has so far falsified these predictions. The whole complex of political struggles, the widespread public revulsion from any *first* use of nuclear weapons, and further those characteristics of nuclear weapons themselves, which in the unpredictable effects of fallout introduced a new qualitative, and, in some respects, qualifying element in calculations of aggression have been powerful and at times even leading factors. Yet also, in its limited direct context, deterrence has not been ineffective. Indeed it is significant that when we place this fact of 'mutually assured destruction'—in itself so insane a basis for any lasting polity—within actual world-political relations since 1945, we find that it was just because deterrence was operative in direct relations between the United States and the Soviet Union that steadily, and very dangerously, it had to be masked as a real strategic concept and replaced, confusingly under the same name, by deterrence as an ideology.

The crucial dividing line, now so vital in the struggle for public acquiescence or support, is, to put it bluntly, between deterrence from direct military attack, which is still widely and understandably supported, and on the other hand the deterrence of communism *per se*. Of course in practice the strategy and the ideology are intricately connected, but at the level of public argument they are intolerably and often deliberately confused. If it is evidence of Soviet aggression that an Asian or African country makes a socialist or communist revolution, then the simplicities of deterrence against a direct military attack are left far behind. The natural and wholly reasonable desire of all peoples to be secure against direct attack, which ought never for a moment to be denied or even questioned by those of us who are against nuclear weapons and the arms race, is systematically exploited for these other and only ever partly disclosed objectives. It is then a necessary element of any effective campaign to so clarify the differences between the strategy and the ideology that it will be possible to isolate all those who can, without hyberbole, be called warmongers. Thus it is only on the powerfully organized right of West European and North American politics that the ideology becomes again a strategy: to destroy communism everywhere. Yet it has in practice been far too easy for this grouping to enrol natural desires for security and independence into their quite different objectives. Moreover we make it easier for them if we do not ourselves start, genuinely, from these desires, and go on to show their ultimate (if not always immediate) incompatibility with nuclear weapons and the arms race.

We can best do this if we can show that it is indeed from the limited success of deterrence against direct nuclear attack that the most dangerous recent strategies have been developed. It is clear that it has been in periods of significant political and economic change beyond the terms of direct US–USSR relations that intensification of what is still called deterrent nuclear weapons development has occurred. This has been so especially in periods of intensified national liberation struggles, with peaks around Cuba in the early sixties and after Angola in the seventies. At these points the distinction between strategy and ideology is particularly evident, and it has been evident again, though in confused ways, in the complex of changes in Iran and Afghanistan. Moreover it is clear that *direct* deterrence had been achieved by the mid-late 1950s. We have then to allow something—perhaps much—for the internal improvement and modernization of these systems, at this level and within this strategy. It then becomes clear that the vast development of overkill capacity, now continuing at a rising rate, belongs strictly to the ideology, and has to be firmly referred not to matters of national security but to a both overt and covert world political struggle. Moreover it is within the limited success of direct US–USSR deterrence that the particular and now exceptional danger for Europe has developed. It is from the facts of that standoff that Europe has been nominated as a 'theatre' for another 'scenario', in which it is (on the military evidence, quite irrationally) believed that a limited nuclear war could be fought, as a controlled part of the global struggle. Here, decisively, for the peoples of Western Europe—and especially in these years in which the nuclear weapons for just such a war are being actively deployed—the strategy and the ideology can be seen as distinct. From deterrent subjects, which we could still, however unreasonably, imagine ourselves to be, we have become objects in an ideology of deterrence determined by interests wholly beyond us as nations or as peoples, though significantly not beyond our frontiers as the interests of existing ruling classes. Whatever the scenario might be for others, for us as peoples it is from the opening scene the final tragedy. Global deterrence would have achieved a Europe in which there was nobody left to deter or be deterred.

Multilateralism: Codeword for Rearmament?

'Multilateralism', as a concept, is often paired with 'deterrence'. This is the consistent orthodox argument which has so far commanded majority support. We can begin to break the pairing when we have distinguished between deterrence as strategy and as ideology. It is not impossible that from deterrence as military strategy, at a certain phase of its development, staged mutual disarmament might have been negotiated. But within the *ideology* of deterrence, in which vast political forces of an absolute kind are at once and necessarily engaged, there can and will be no disarmament. The long-sustained promise, that from this necessary strength disarmament can be negotiated, has been thoroughly falsified, and it is extraordinary that it can still be so brazenly asserted, as cover for yet one more stage of military escalation. At the same time, however, multilateral disarmament is indeed the only way to security. The World Disarmament Campaign is on very strong ground when it argues not only for this, but for the urgent inclusion of other than nuclear weapons. Nuclear war is indeed the worst possibility, but chemical and bacteriological war are only minimally less appalling. Even what is called conventional war, with the combined use of advanced high explosives and the present capacities of missile technology, could now destroy urban civilization. Thus only multilateral disarmament can be accepted as an adequate objective. At the same time we have to distinguish between multilateralism as a political strategy and multilateralism as an ideology.

To a very large extent, in current debates, 'multilateralism' is in fact a codeword for continued acquiescence in the policy of military alliances and the arms race. In deceptive or self-deceptive ways, the longing for disarmament is ideologically captured as the cover for yet another stage of rearmament. It becomes an essential objective of any campaign to break this false pairing, but again this can only be done if the reasonableness of genuine multilateralism is fully acknowledged. One important way of doing this is to break the multilateralist 'code' at its weakest point which while speaking of 'multilateralism' really entails an exclusive *bilateralism*. It is not, for example, the governments of Europe who will attempt negotiation on the deployment and possible reduction of nuclear missiles within their territories. Within the logic of the alliances, this primary and indeed multilateral responsibility is virtually without protest surrendered and displaced to bilateral negotiations between the United States and the Soviet Union. 'Multilateralism' is then only a code for those processes of polarization and submission to the loss of national independence. It is against this dangerous and habitual obscuration that an impulse to genuine multilateralism has much to contribute. This is the crucial significance of the campaign for European Nuclear Disarmament, both in its own terms, of resuming direct responsibility, and in its genuine compatibility with the World Disarmament Campaign.

Unilateralism Today and Yesterday

This may and in my view should be the way in which the campaign for European nuclear disarmament develops. But it is already evident that the campaign overlaps with both a residual and a revived 'unilateralism', and the current meanings of this concept have now again to be carefully examined. 'Unilateralism' must first be distinguished, historically, from pacifism, which has always, and coherently, proposed the unilateral pacific act, including the renunciation of all weapons, as the first move to break the dangerous deadlock of armed confrontation. But 'unilateralism' acquired more specific and more limited meanings in a particular period—the late 1950s—in which certain circumstances were operative. Britain was at that time the only nuclear-weapons state other than the superpowers, so that on the one hand unilateral British renunciation could be argued as the first necessary practical step to prevent the proliferation of nuclear-weapons states and on the other hand as a moral example to all states including the superpowers. Furthermore, there was the desire to get out from under this dangerous superpower rivalry, whether positively as a non-aligned state, or negatively as 'leaving them to get on with it'; in either case on the assumption that Britain could be independent and autonomous. What matters now, within a resurgence which is also in some respects a continuity, is to re-examine circumstances before we simply resume old responses. Thus the argument against proliferation is significantly different in the 1980s as compared with the 1950s, and in any case has now to include attention to the problems of superpower monopoly ('hegemonism') which, quite apart from being insufficiently analysed in that earlier phase, are now major political realities. Deprived of this immediate practical bearing, the argument of moral example has, in my view, no reasonable resting place short of pacifism, which remains, in the multiplying dangers of international violence, one of the most profound and accessible responses to evil in our world and culture.

Thus unilateralism of a non-pacifist kind, in the 1980s, has either to be coherently political, with all its consequences followed through, or to resign itself to rhetorical evasiveness. It is clear that the loose assembly of diverse political forces around unilateralism, which for a time held but then failed to hold in the late 1950s and early 1960s, cannot now for long be reconstituted on the old terms. What has always been insufficient in its arguments, but now much less forgiveably, is any realistic facing of the full significance of such an act by a state like Britain. It is significantly often at this point, when in any political campaign aiming for majority support the most stringent realism is an absolute requirement, that there is a rhetorical loop back to the undoubted evils and dangers of nuclear war and to the abstraction of 'the Bomb'. What then must we really face? The central fact is that Britain at every level—military, political, economic and cultural—has been locked into 'the alliance', which is at once a life-or-death military system and a powerful organization of the most developed capitalist states and economies. To take Britain out of that alliance would be a major shift in the balance of forces, and therefore at once a confrontation of the most serious kind. Every kind of counterforce, certainly economic and political, would be at once deployed against it, and there could be no restriction of the resulting struggle to the theoretically separable issue of nuclear weapons. Thus a theoretically restricted campaign, based on an eventual popular refusal of the dangers of nuclear war, would arrive, in reality, at a stage of general struggle for which it would be quite unprepared.

At the same time the general notion of the unilateral act, now commonly construed as 'renunciation', has in practice to be divided into separable political acts and stages. What most immediately enters the political argument is, first, on a European scale, the decision about medium-range missiles specifically designed for a 'limited' nuclear war on our own territories; and second, in Britain, the decision about the renewal, into a third generation, of the so-called independent nuclear capability, by the purchase of Trident missiles from the United States. Political campaigns around each of these decisions can, but need not, be conducted in terms of old-style unilateralism. It is significant that there already seems to be more political support for the refusal of these stages of escalation than for a general and indiscriminate 'unilateralism'. It is understandable that many who have taken the full measure of the existing dangers of nuclear weapons and nuclear-alliance strategy should advocate absolute positions, which can alone express our full moral sense, and reject or even despise more limited positions as mere political calculation. But since the dangers are indeed so great, there is also a case for saying that we must advance wherever we can, and that campaigns against Cruise and Trident need not, in these critical years, involve, and often be politically limited by, the full unilateralist case. For to refuse the siting of Cruise missiles on our territories, as part of a process of demanding multilateral European negotiations for the removal of all such missiles and the related bomber and submarine bases from the territories of 'Europe from Poland to Portugal', is not, in any ordinary sense, 'unilateralism'. It is the exercise of independence and sovereignty as a stage in a negotiating process for which there is still (just) time. Similarly in the case of the Trident purchase; it can be also a conscious entry into the negotiating process of strategic arms limitation, by refusing the (in fact unilateral) escalation of British-based missile-nuclear systems. Positive campaigns for these specific initiatives can then in practice be very different from the relatively unfocused demand for 'unilateral renunciation', and should be kept rationally distinct.

Of course, what remains to be faced, although at a different level from old-style unilateralism, is the full consequence of such positive refusals and initiatives. For these more specific moves would not only challenge existing strategic dispositions and calculations but would also, just as radically, challenge the logic of superpower hegemonism. The consequent political struggles would be on an even wider stage than that of the consequences of old-style British unilateralism. But that the stage would be wider is an opportunity as well as a problem, and it is in this context that we must examine one of the deeper structures of British unilateralism.

The Problem of 'British' Nationalism

It is very noticeable now that there is a congruence, within that spectrum of opinion which we can describe, broadly, as the Labour Left, between economic, political and peace campaigns which are all, in a general sense, unilateralist. Proposals for a siege or near-siege economy, protected by the strongest version of import controls; proposals for the recovery of political sovereignty or actual withdrawal from the EEC; proposals for the unnegotiated unilateral renunciation of nuclear weapons and bases: all have this common style. There are strong arguments within each of the positions, but the decisive common factors seem to be a radical overestimation of Britain's capacity and effect in independent action, and a radical underestimate of the degree of actual penetration of British economy and society by both international capitalism and the military–political alliance which exists to defend it. There can be no question that we have to find ways to contain this penetration and to roll it back, but it is then a matter of very intricate and realistic economic and political argument to find the most effective ways. The Labour Left position, at its simplest public level, seems to be not only an abstract short-cut through all these actual difficulties, but based in a very deep political structure which characteristically idealizes desirable conditions and forces, while, as a protection against more radical perspectives, reducing real opposing forces to abstract and alien entities. For the question is never what we could legally do, or find some temporary majority for doing. The question is one of broad struggle. And if the question is one of struggle, the political campaign must be a matter of mobilizing real forces on the most favourable possible ground. It would be unfair to say that the passing of resolutions, even within relatively etiolated structures, is a deliberate evasion of this much harder political reality. Properly understood, it can be part of the process of actual mobilization. But what does seem to be an evasion is the simple rhetoric of 'go it alone'. A characteristic, but a crucial example, can be given in this context. If we are seriously proposing a collaborative campaign for European Nuclear Disarmament, is it sensible at the same time to propose simple withdrawal from the EEC? What is necessary and possible, in both cases, is a radical negotiation, and this can only really be undertaken on a European rather than simply a British scale. None of the actual negotiating steps is easy, but I have found in discussion that the dominant mood thus far, on the EEC as on nuclear weapons, is an impatient insistence on the 'swift, decisive unilateral act', after which all the radical consequences, and the radical struggles, for which a maximum of carefully prepared collaboration and alliance would undoubtedly be necessary, would be faced *ad hoc*.[6] Yet in any of these struggles, and especially in the struggle against the polarized hegemonism of the nuclear alliances, only combined action, on a European scale (of course based on what are also nationally conducted and to some extent uneven and differently inflected campaigns) has any realistic chance of success. Thus we must consistently advance *European* rather than British-unilateralist arguments and objectives.

III. Socialism and the Nuclear-Weapons Systems

It is understandable that some comrades should argue that the danger of nuclear war is now so great that we should set aside all other considerations and unite to achieve disarmament and peace. Anyone who does not at times feel like this is indeed underestimating the appalling immediate dangers. Yet some of us at least must go on to say, first, that specifically socialist analyses of the production and reproduction of these dangers are, while undoubtedly incomplete, still centrally relevant; and, second, that we have still to look to specifically socialist analysis and mobilization to generate the linked forces that will in fact be capable of significantly reducing and finally ending these dangers.

This should never be said arrogantly, or within some exclusivist rhetoric. There is an urgent duty on all socialists to join in collaborative campaigns in at least seven general areas: (a) heightening public consciousness of the specific as well as the general dangers of modern missile-nuclear and other weapons systems; (b) exposing the deceptive official campaigns about the possibilities of 'civil defence' against nuclear attacks; (c) organizing public pressure for all possible measures of arms limitation and negotiated disarmament; (d) publishing and explaining the details of current weapons development and rearmament, and, in close relation to these, the complex of actual offers, counter-offers and stages of negotiation in limitation and disarmament negotiations; (e) organizing campaigns to widen the negotiating process, not only between states but within societies, thus including opposition to arbitrary secrecy and security controls; (f) demonstrating the real links between nuclear-energy and nuclear-weapons programmes, including the realities of some consequent proliferation of nuclear weapons (as in the newly formed Anti-Nuclear Campaign); (g) opposing the naturalization of arms production and export as part of the economic strategy of the advanced industrial world.

This is already a heavy list, yet on each of these issues there is already significant public campaigning and active socialist involvement. What has then still to be asked, however, is whether there are further specific socialist contributions to be made both within collaborative campaigns and independently. Some answers can be suggested in three areas: (i) relations between the concepts of a 'ruling class' and a 'military-industrial complex', with evident effects on the question of substituting 'exterminism' for existing or possible categories of socialist analysis; (ii) the very difficult question of what is called, in some circles, the 'socialist bomb' or 'the missiles of the international working class'; (iii) the problem of linkages between military and economic crisis.

The Ruling Class and the 'Military-Industrial Complex'

It is obviously correct to identify and to stress the specific complex of arms-production, military, research and state-security interests within contemporary advanced capitalist societies. It is also necessary to identify an analogous but far from identical complex within such socialist states as the Soviet Union and China. Yet it is almost certainly wrong, first, to fuse these different formations as a single entity, and, second, to override more general concepts of a ruling class by the priority of these specific complexes. The problem would have to be analytically separated to recognize its specificity within the two contrasting systems, but there are still some preliminary general points. It is of the essence of a ruling class that it possesses a monopoly or a predominance of overt or threatening violence. This is not a consequence of nuclear-weapons systems, and indeed it has been mainly in non-nuclear societies that the specific military-state-security formation has acquired absolute or determining power. The realities of more general productive development have created, in more advanced and complex economies, other effective major formations within the ruling class; and the true political process, at this level, is much more a matter of the shifting relations between these formations than of any inevitable dominance. The military-security formation has major advantages, and these are increased in conditions of international conflict. But just because what it produces is at once so deadly and so negative, it can only temporarily achieve that command of resources and policies which would ensure its stable dominance. It is then true that the present nuclear arms race is producing conditions in which the possibilities of dominance form a rising tendency. Yet the ruling class as a whole still has other interests, both in its own immediate terms and in relation to assuring its continued dominance over the whole life of the society, which must include satisfying increasing non-military economic needs and demands of its people. It has also political interests in its need to present its central objectives in those broader terms which can command a necessary consent or acquiescence. Therefore, no ruling class, and *a fortiori* no whole social formation, can be reduced to the military-security element. If it is true that the military-security complex, just because of its negativity, moves on its own towards certain ultimate irrationalities, in which the whole social order exists to serve and supply it, it is also true that other ruling-class formations, to say nothing of other classes, exert constant and powerful practical pressures of a different kind, which are then the materials of real politics. The observable fluctuations of military spending programmes and of broad political strategies are the indices of these continuing internal and externally affected struggles.

In lieu of more precise analysis of these dangerous internal formations, within the different social orders of the two major systems, we can note certain contradictions. Within capitalist societies, the military and related industries may not, for all their command of research, be a genuine leading sector. Their crude counter-cyclical role, and their privileged rate of profit, can distort the programmes and the interests of the capitalist class as a whole, while their massive levies of public revenue can disrupt investment programmes and produce unintended crisis and socio-economic discontent. The present crisis of ordinary manufacturing industry, with its consequences in major unemployment, is perhaps just such a case, and it is significant that it is often from within the ruling class that campaigns against the 'military-industrial complex' have been mounted. Meanwhile in the centralized socialist systems it is evident that the scale of military expenditure is economically crippling and has virtually no advantages for any productive sector. There the linkage is different, between the bureaucratic formation of the ruling class itself and the necessary support of military and state-security formations. The contradiction between an unproductive high-military economy and the dependence of a political leadership on exceptional monopoly of power and force is indeed very dangerous, but is itself reciprocally affected by external developments within the contradictions of its opponent system. Thus we need not conclude that there is any genuine inevitability in the formation and tendency to dominate of these powerful internal sectors. A full analysis must include a recognition of the 'dysfunctional' aspects of the arms race for both social systems.

'The Socialist Bomb' (sic)

The simplest version of the argument that Soviet nuclear-weapons systems are in effect the 'socialist bomb', demanding the support of the international working class, scarcely merits attention. It is an inescapable fact of nuclear weapons, with their indiscriminate destruction of whole populations, that they cannot be class-selective. The real consequence of that kind of argument is an impotent alienation and, ultimately, treason against every particular working class. Yet there are more serious arguments, as for example the position taken by Ernest Mandel in 1970.[7] In place of the essentially abstract propositions of 'international tension' and the 'dangers of war', such arguments begin from the facts of the imperialist world-system, including its ineradicable hostility not only to existing socialist states but to all national liberation struggles which threaten imperialist economic and strategic interests. All socialists who share this analysis of the present world crisis are faced with exceptionally difficult questions when they also, as they must, recognize the extraordinary and quite unprecedented dangers of nuclear war. It is one thing to hold to a strategy of victory against imperialism, but it is quite another to suppose that there can be any victory worth having through the ultimate devastation of a nuclear war.

There are then two possible positions. The first, which is more often drifted into than consciously adopted, involves using the legitimate fear of nuclear war, which after all can in the West be very freely expressed and campaigned on, as a way of objectively weakening the imperialist defence systems, thus tilting the strategic balance. The fact that this is constantly alleged, by the right, against *every* campaign for nuclear disarmament (and then often with ludicrous mis-identifications), ought not to blind us to the fact that it can be, in some cases, objectively and even subjectively true. It would make for intellectual honesty if those who have really adopted this position would say so; elaborating the radical case for a non-pacifist unilateralism. What is wrong with this position (and with any of the tactics and emphases which consciously or unconsciously follow from it) is, however, its uncritical identification of the interests of socialism and of anti-imperialism with the Soviet *state*. It is necessary, of course, to oppose absolutely all those who wish to destroy or threaten the Soviet state and its allies, or socialist China, or the new revolutionary states. This involves radical opposition to nuclear rearmament, to strategies of global containment, and to the whole complex of imperialist military alliances and arms-export client regimes. Yet this duty of all socialists must be distinguished from naive or false-naive positions in the matter of the central nuclear-weapons confrontation. There are duties of defence of the international working class, but these necessarily include the whole working class, in each of the systems and beyond them, and cannot be discharged by deliberate or as it were accidental projection to the interests of a single state military order.

The second available position is more complex, but more adequate. It begins from the fact that it has been primarily the long pressures of imperialism against the new socialist and national-liberation states that have distorted, often disastrously, the realization of revolutionary socialism and democracy. From such a position it is possible both to recognize and struggle to end the crimes of imperialism and at the same time look full in the face the consequences, within the revolutionary states, new and old, of prolonged militarization and a state of political siege. Nor is this some neutralist position. It is centrally in the interests of socialism itself that these dangerous and objectively anti-socialist conditions should be diminished and finally abolished. Thus initiatives for disarmament must be primarily directed to the *inseparable* processes of weakening the imperialist offensive and strengthening the forces of socialism against those formations which now distort it. This requires, in the matter of proposals, the most scrupulous attention to real popular interests, rather than to any existing state interests. There is then an overwhelming socialist interest in nuclear disarmament, since the missile-nuclear systems objectively strengthen bloc politics, hegemonism and centralized military-security state apparatuses.

This emphasis can be the particular merit of the emerging campaign for European nuclear disarmament. Committed, as it must be, to East–West reciprocity, to the steady enlargement of demilitarized zones through the various layers of weapons systems, and then to the necessary gaining of some real *political* space in Europe, it is the only campaign which is entirely congruent with the long-term interests of all European socialists. It will remain very difficult to keep the emphases right, not only against misrepresentation and opposition, but between ourselves. Real responses will be required from within the Soviet alliance, and these are more likely to come if we make it clear that our disarmament proposals are integral with renewed efforts to advance socialism within our own countries; that they involve significant and difficult breaks with the strategy and ideology of the imperialist and anti-communist alliance; and, crucially, that the condition of success of any of these struggles is a serious reciprocity, allowing the development of movements of national-popular support, rather than any simple taking of advantage of peace campaigns. It would be a very serious misreading of our campaign by anyone in the East to conclude that it is manipulable in the interests of bloc-politics and military advantage. But then it would be also a serious misdirection of our campaign if it became, at any point, in fact or by default, manipulable.

Necessary Linkages

To support the Campaign for European Nuclear Disarmament does not necessarily mean believing that the central fracture and confrontation is in Europe. The most dangerous nuclear arena is here, but the crucial political struggles and dangers are very much more widespread. Thus the socialist contribution to the politics of nuclear disarmament must be more than simply collaborative, and must include solidarity with Third World struggles gainst an imperialist economic system which globally reproduces hunger and exploitation. This is no matter of riding the peace campaigns for some partisan objectives. There is now a profound linkage between the most actual and recurrent dangers of war and the specific crises of the imperialist world system. The use of military force and intimidation to maintain systems of power and exploitation—over and above the systems of military-strategic deployment—is still the central threat to peace. If we are to understand and explain this fully, we have to move on from the known and still crucial facts of the international economic order, to the now rapidly emerging facts of the crisis of resources. It has become an absolute duty for Western socialists to prepare, in good time, the positions from which we can oppose and defeat attempts to secure scarce resources—the case of oil is the most urgent current example—by military interventions, whether direct or indirect. Such interventions will of course attempt to recruit popular opinion by appeals for the protection of our (privileged) 'way of life'. Given the effects of the simultaneous crisis of imposed unemployment and deprivation on the working peoples of the West, no socialist can suppose that these attempts will be easy to defeat. But there is no contradiction between such work and campaigns for nuclear disarmament. Indeed unless such campaigns are developed, in practical and predictive ways, the more isolated peace campaigns could be simply overwhelmed. Such considerations are also relevant to what is now the major problem of the traditional linkage between opposition to rearmament and opposition to unemployment and social deprivation. There are still real links between essentially wasteful military spending and poverty and deprivation in the rest of the social order. But here, as elsewhere, there is not going to be any simple return to the status quo ante. We may have to face the old problem of a reactionary connection between rearmament and the revival of employment. But beyond this there are new and quite major problems of change, if both peace and decent living standards are to be maintained in the old capitalist world. It is not just a matter of cancelling useless or obscene military expenditure, nor even of redirecting investment to alternative civilian manufacture. The changes will have to involve radical transformations, internally and externally, rather than simple cancellations or reversions. Despite the difficulties of such transformations, they must be central priorities within any agenda of working for peace.

This can appear only to add to our burdens, for which our present strength is still insufficient. But this must be the final point of the present argument. It is, fortunately, still possible to generate movements for peace and for disarmament on the most general human grounds. That these are again growing is a significant gain against the culture and politics of violence. Yet alike for their intellectual adequacy and for extension of their support it is necessary to reach beyond the moving and honourable refusals on which many of them still characteristically depend. To build peace, now more than ever, it is necessary to build more than peace. To refuse nuclear weapons, we have to refuse much more than nuclear weapons. Unless the refusals can be connected with such building, unless protest can be connected with and surpassed by significant practical construction, our strength will remain insufficient. It is then in making hope practical, rather than despair convincing, that we must resume and change and extend our campaigns.

---

[1] The most eloquent example of this position is Edward Thompson's 'Notes on Exterminism, the Last Stage of Civilization'.

[2] END statement of which the present author was a signatory; reprinted in E. P. Thompson and Dan Smith, eds., *Protest and Survive*, London 1980, p. 224.

[3] Ibid., p. 7.

[4] The common use of the term 'apocalypse' (cf. *Apocalypse Now?*, Spokesman Pamphlet, London 1980, and Thompson), with a curious shift from the sense of 'revelation' to a sense of ultimate destruction, marks this development. For a nuclear war would not be an 'apocalypse'; it would be at once more terrible and more sordid, with no revelation.

[5] See Michael Pentz's excellent pamphlet *Towards the Final Abyss?*, Bernal Peace Library, London 1980.

[6] An idealized projection of a Labour government, under 'Left' leadership, which would resolve and execute such policies, may be as misleading now as it was in the early 1960s, when the cause of nuclear disarmament was widely entrusted to just such a projection.

[7] 'Peaceful Coexistence and World Revolution', in Robin Blackburn, ed., *Revolution and Class Struggle*, London 1978, pp. 284–293.

A New Approach for the Peace Movement in Germany

Rudolf Bahro

The New Sounding-Board

Edward Thompson argues that the dominant tendency of the present epoch is exterminism—an impulse towards mass destruction, annihilation and extinction that is generated by our industrial civilization and radiates outwards from it to threaten the whole world.[1] This is a view that I share. Thompson's thesis, in fact, has implications that go far beyond his rejection of the very different definition of our epoch given by Lenin: imperialism as the highest stage of capitalism. For his case radically puts into question that traditional historical optimism for which the very essence of the human species points towards socialism, and not to barbarism, let alone a premature self-destruction.

The basic issue here is whether the course of human evolution has not taken a wrong turn; and it must be conceded that the perspective which has governed the Left up till now does not allow this question to be posed unflinchingly enough. If history is a process with certain immanent laws, and we believe it is, it cannot be accidental that our civilization should generate a tendency towards the self-destruction of its subject as a defining trait of its most recent stage. Rather, such an impulse must have long been inscribed in human nature (conceived as the 'ensemble of social relations').

The first precondition for the arms race is, of course, modern industry as such. Exterminism is rooted in the very foundations of this system and its innermost driving forces. Exterminism does not just find expression in nuclear weapons and power stations; it is the quintessence of the whole complex of tools and machines operative on humanity and the planet. Those particular elements within it that bear a different stamp—elements which Illich calls 'convivial'—have so far been subordinate to the exterminist principle. Our collective practices break up and destroy natural conditions, degrade energy potentials, suffocate the Earth's surface and isolate human beings from spontaneous energy cycles. The result is inevitably a distortion of both body and mind, whose consequences range from cancer to crime.

It is plain that this impulse to self-destruction is rooted in European industrial capitalism, at least as far as its current acute form is concerned. From 1750 onwards, all the familiar curves of 'growth' and pressure on resources start to show the ever more precipitous ascent that heralds a collapse. But the phenomenon has its origins further back than capitalism, and it persists on the other side of capitalism as well. European society had long been preadapted for its capitalist constitution: all its antecedent historical trends, from antiquity onwards, contributed to this outcome. There is a good deal of evidence that the 'Fall' took place already with the transition from female-centred societies of gatherers and hunters to patriarchal societies of agriculture and cities (paralleled by nomadism). This transition occurred at so many more or less independent points in time and space that it must necessarily be seen as a historical law—that is, as unavoidably inscribed in the endowment of our species.

In this sense, therefore, our starting-point should not be a *superficial* critique of (contemporary) political economy, but a more *fundamental* critique of human nature itself. This does not mean we should cease to concern ourselves with economics, simply seeking the source of evil in ourselves, in defiance of the whole legacy of the Enlightenment. The impending catastrophe is evidently linked to that social dynamic which has made all written history a history of class struggle[2] and caused the process of human development so far to hurtle forward in limitless material expansion and acceleration.

If this is so, then so long as we continue to see class struggle as the key to the contemporary crisis, we will only remain trapped in the very circle out of which it is imperative to break. Even the goal of socialism shares the same limitation in a decisive respect: it sets our sights on a classless *industrial* society,[3] without stopping to criticize the origins and consequences of industrialism. Traditional socialist analysis has fixed its focal point 'too high', in a 'base' which is not yet the base—in other words, in 'relations of production' instead of 'forces of production'. Marxism was precisely conceived from the standpoint of the proletariat as the second *industrial* class. In the common field of struggle of *both* contemporary classes, therefore, it seeks only to abolish the deforming processes of exploitation and domination. Almost invariably, we have attacked only the *capitalist* form of our societies, scarcely ever the *industrial* system of capitalism. Since we were unable to do away with capitalism, this neglect has now caught up with us. The 'gathering determinism of the exterminist process'[4] is evident enough. With or without a complete explanation of it, we must now orient ourselves to a practical critique of the industrial system and its military spearhead.

Unexpectedly, as it were, red flags are now a minority in demonstrations against nuclear power stations that challenge the very basis on which the traditional labour movement emerged. Wage-labour stands accused not just because it is 'abstract' and 'alienated', but because its results are in large measure simply deadly. The abolition of at least half the work now performed in the industrialized countries must take unquestioned precedence over the demand for full employment within the industrial system. The same applies to education as to work: education for the industrial system is quite rightly rejected by more and more young people.

No contemporary movement that seeks anything less than a transformation of the entire system, right down to its material and cultural foundations, that attacks only the military programmes, and weapons technologies which exterminism relentlessly and inexorably produces, can achieve anything more than minor modifications or variations of this perverted production. The whole question of human emancipation has taken a new form. The insight that the impulse to obliteration, to the self-extinction of humanity, lies in the very foundations of our industrial civilization and pervades every structure of its economy, science and technology, its political apparatus and its sociology and psychology, is today of such immediate importance that the socialist perspective takes second place, and in any case must be redefined.

Our whole social organism is riddled by the disease of militarism; and just as it seems that cancer can only be cured at the level of the organism as a whole, so we cannot hope to root out militarism, which now consumes resources in the region of £200,000 million per year and transforms these into murderous waste products, without a similarly holistic therapy. 'The ultimate dysfunction of humanity: self-destruct'[5] can only be prevented by a movement that goes beyond reactive defence—a movement that actively seeks to live a different life, and to release hitherto obstructed and untapped potentialities of the human species. The concept of exterminism tells us why the peace movement has found an unprecedented new sounding-board in the ecology movement. The connection between the two was not immediately apparent from the start to all of those involved. Those political ecologists who early advocated an integration of the two currents can themselves testify how difficult it often is to link specific campaigns to more far-reaching horizons. Now, however, their labours are bearing fruit, above all because the facts themselves are being forced on people's awareness. Whenever I have spoken on the ecological crisis in recent months, it has been a matter of course that the discussion has moved on to the problems of foreign policy and peace.

The new peace movement is based right from the start on the premiss that exterminism is simply the rank outgrowth of a parasite attacking and consuming the tree from root to crown. I too did not at first understand why the ecology movement started by attacking not nuclear weapons, but nuclear power stations and even establishments less harmful than these. I have since come to see the essential condition for its breadth and strength, and above all its potential for victory, in its growth from the bottom upwards. Peace can only thrive in a mental soil quite different from the culture of domination. The humus first needs to form. The abolition of both nuclear weapons and nuclear power is a far stronger demand than the 'ban the bomb' slogan of the late 1950s and 1960s, not just because of the addition, but because the new slogan aims deeper. It strikes right at the fundamental exterminist axiom of our misdirected civilization, which is aggressive in its innermost being, based on the principles of expansion and explosion. This response will be all the more effective, the more clearly nuclear power itself is seen as only the most prominent outgrowth of the tumour, which could go on poisoning our social life even if the button is never pressed to unleash the missiles, as in our (I hope) most pessimistic fears.

Even where the ecological movement has not yet found a comprehensive expression, it provides the explanation for the increased strength of the peace movement. In Denmark and Holland the fusion of the two is unmistakeable. It is surreptitiously present even in Britain, although there the close linkage of nuclear disarmament with the more traditional social policies of the Labour Left, a strength in the short run, still impedes its wider extension. I am personally convinced that the potential for a politics of peace on the part of the entire social-democratic, socialist and Eurocommunist left in Western Europe depends on a fundamental modernization of its general strategy.

If these socialist forces do not abandon their traditional union with capitalist industrialism and achieve a radical change in the concept of well-being inherent in it, they will be unable to put up an effective resistance either to the ecological crisis or to the arms race. Such a break with the industrial system is, moreover, a precondition for a settlement with the peoples of the Third and Fourth Worlds. Without 'industrial disarmament'—that is, an absolute reduction in global demand for raw materials and energy, and a corresponding technological transformation—it will be possible neither to attain a genuine military disarmament nor to restore the ability of the South to provide itself with adequate means of subsistence. The voracity of our giant machinery cannot do without rapid deployment forces and neocolonial production branches. That is why it reproduces a majority consensus for these as a matter of course. There is no way of avoiding this fatality. We have to embark on a psychological revolution that starts with ourselves, and liberates our politics from the aggressive model of reactive class antagonism that only reinforces and accelerates exterminism.

It goes without saying that an understanding of this connection is not an 'entrance condition' for joining the new peace movement, but rather an argument for its prospects. Those opponents of war and armaments who are not yet convinced ecologists can conclude from their own experience that a single-issue peace movement will very probably remain stuck in its tracks. But borne forward by the ecology movement, which is something quite other than a single-issue campaign—it includes, among other things, the women's movement—but represents rather the beginning of a general awakening to that new phase of our evolution which alone can promise us any future, it has a far greater chance of success, as an alliance of all life-preserving and emancipatory forces. There is, of course, no guarantee of success, but so far the attempt is still afloat.

The protection of life is a fundamental principle of infinite scope. Thus the struggle against war and the arms race is a natural consequence of an ecological orientation, an organic development of its basic stance. Here should be the general soil and sounding-board of the peace movement. The rescue of the planet and our species requires the systemic dismantlement of all structures that threaten life. This principle includes within it the core of the traditional goals of socialism, even if the form of these is certainly changed.

Survival, in any case, will mean a very different way of life. If everything goes on as it does today, there will indeed be a Third World War, as the most extreme consequence of the everyday war against Earth and humanity that is inseparable from the capitalist industrial system. We have to generate the mental preparation for a change in the totality of this system. That will involve agreement on means and aims, in a common project capable of subordinating the opposing special interests of all those engaged in it to their own fundamental and long-run interests.

Away With the Blocs!

The basic premise of Thompson's approach in his warning of the most immediate danger, is the notion that 'the fracture of power across Europe . . . [is] the locus of the field-of-force whose polar antagonisms

generate exterminism'.[6] This does not mean Thompson sees the collision as
necessarily starting here. Like others who have considered this question, he
thinks it quite possible that the catastrophe might be triggered off in the
Middle East, for example. In my view, it is perfectly valid for Thompson to
shift attention from the war-breeding internal structures of the two rival
systems to the process of their confrontation itself, and from the underlying
motive forces on either side of the arms race, which are beyond reliable or
secure assessment, to the tendency for these to generate only too similar
results.

It goes without saying that the causes internal to each system and their
political and psychological dimensions remain important questions. These
are explained in an essay published in *Tageszeitung* of 26 June 1980 which
argues that the present *increase* in East–West tension has arisen not
primarily from the competition between the two blocs, but rather from
contradictions within the two systems. Hostile depictions of the other side
are nurtured in order to suppress resistance at home. The arms race is in
this sense also a strategy for the maintenance of power on either side.
Anyone who rejects the consensus of 'security through strength' thus
disturbs the basic legitimation of the system of domination. It is very
instructive, again, that Thompson's description of the complex of interests
that underlie the nuclear arms race in the West coincides entirely with the
findings of Klaus Traube's study of the West German nuclear energy
lobby.[7] The mechanisms involved here are thus quite 'normal' ones. Similar
conclusions are likely for the Eastern bloc and the Soviet Union.
Thompson's argument sits perfectly well with my own analysis of the
'anatomy of actually existing socialism' in *The Alternative in Eastern Europe*.
The capitalist profit motive is only one specific form in which interests of
domination come to prevail. Certain apologists for the Soviet Union argue
as if no other ruling class but the bourgeoisie had ever been marked by
militarism.

But whatever the internal forces that profit from the bipolar
confrontation between the two blocs, and have an interest in its
reproduction, the confrontation itself is the precondition for any profit
made out of it and any career that is built on it. In a society without an
external enemy it is impossible for anyone to make a living out of weapons
production or to seek personal affirmation in the fame of war. This is in
itself a trivial observation, but what it suggests is that confrontation and
competition must themselves be abolished if the arms race is to come to an
end.

Since the arms race has now reached a technological level which
threatens the mutual extermination of those states and peoples caught up in

it, there is no other solution but to do away with bloc confrontation. In previous history, all such complexes of power as those presently facing each other in Europe and across the Atlantic have led to war. This time, another way must be found. But we cannot hope to find it if we are not prepared to tailor all our actions to this necessity.

We socialists must understand, above all else, that the fracture dividing the world, Europe and Germany into two systems no longer represents any kind of positive perspective, that it no longer shows any trace of a boundary between revolution and counter-revolution, socialism and anti-socialism, world proletariat and world bourgeoisie—in so far as this ever was the case, at least in a favourable interpretation. This fracture is rather the immediate obstacle to the most radical revolution that humanity has ever needed: its rapid transition to a different basic pattern of civilization, at a time when the present pattern has put the further advance of the human species into question, over the last 200 years.

Further scrutiny only confirms that the confrontation of blocs in the Northern hemisphere, which has generated the arms race, is indeed the number-one world problem—the *general* barrier that prevents a solution of all remaining problems, by both absorbing and perverting the energies and forces needed to resolve them. Unless it is overcome, it will be possible neither to solve the basic social question facing humanity, the tendency towards absolute impoverishment of more than half of its members, nor to restore the balance between civilization and nature.

Of course, each of the two blocs has its own conception as to how their confrontation can be overcome. Somewhat simplified, the Western version is to make the East 'capitalist' once again, the Eastern version to make the West 'socialist'. Both of these concepts are preeminently designed to lead people astray. Neither, in fact, means anything more than an attempt to redeem the evil system on the other side by reshaping it in the image of one's own good system.[8] On occasion it will be conceded that one's own system is not without its faults, and that the other system cannot be compared with it in every particular, but the effect of such provisos is actually to reinforce the principle behind these projections, rather than to dispense with them. In Germany, for instance, we have a whole industry of 'system comparison', in which many social scientists are stubbornly engaged.

The first commandment, in coming to grips with the actual reality of the two systems, is to abandon the idea that the other system can be cured or even improved by applying the standards of one's own idealized system. For some socialists in the West, unfortunately, this commandment must be for the time being reversed: to abandon the idea that one's own system can be cured or even improved by applying the standards of the other idealized system. There is *nothing* we can learn or adopt from the *system* over there. The same applies to those on the other side too.

Those who claim a dialectical heritage, in particular, should stop resorting to the idea of a distinction between good and bad elements, as if some kind of organ transplant were possible, for example of an educational or medical system. (In general, the supposed superiorities of the other side are mythological.) Those too weak emotionally to do without a strong homeland far away should at least understand rationally that the trap it represents undermines their entire socialist commitment. The peace movement can only be made up of those ready to break with the justificatory ideologies of *both* blocs.

The network of peace organizations in West Germany still bears the marks of its Cold War origins. There cannot but be problems in integrating the ecology movement and the peace movement, so long as the latter even indirectly sees the Soviet Union as the head of the forces of peace. These problems only increase when this allegiance is concealed, as it would have no influence if it were openly admitted. A new approach for the peace movement based on independence from both blocs requires that we bypass its traditional structures, whatever new forms of organization may be adopted.

I deliberately use the word 'structures' here, to refer to traditional organizational connections. We must certainly offer access to individuals, even if they have been involved in these structures and identified with them for a long time. But there is a necessary process of education. Is it not an indisputable experience that if any peace initiative—indeed any initiative in general—favours the interests and intentions of one superpower, no matter how indirectly or even unconsciously for the individuals concerned, it ends up integrated into the logic of exterminism? This applies equally, of course, to any 'loyalty to the Atlantic Alliance'. Fixation on the 'peace-loving Soviet Union' can only damage the mobilization of our people against the arms race, and thus in the last instance even injures the false purpose that underlies it.

Conversely, a negative fixation on only one side also leads into an impasse, as in the case of protest against American aggression in Vietnam, or Soviet aggression in Afghanistan. In particular, we would only follow the logic of deterrence and contribute to the spread of conflict were we to oppose the image of the Soviet Union as the enemy—which the West deploys in its preparations for war—with a similar image of the United States as the enemy. There is no point even in depicting particular representatives of exterminist policies as the enemy; to do so only mystifies the real dangers.

Neither anti-Sovietism nor anti-Americanism! Freedom from both blocs! Thompson notes, as we experience for ourselves every day, that *refusal* of the blocs and their logic is either vehemently attacked as neutralism and pacifism, or scoffed at as an illusion. Neutralism and conscientious objection, however, for all the risks they involve, still remain arrested in a stance of negation, so long as we do not manage to transform such attitudes into a growing political movement that can overthrow the present political and psychological balance of forces. Freedom from blocs, on the other hand, is a positive idea. It clears a space for exploring the possibilities that escape from the logic of blocs might offer.

If the competition for power between the two industrial systems is to be overcome without war, then we must seek a different way for their integration, their convergence, the construction of an order embracing both. The demand for Europe 'from Portugal to Poland' to be free from military blocs is thus only an anticipation in foreign policy of a movement for a Third Road that still awaits closer definition. If both systems are simply two sides of the same coin, and their pernicious interaction is no more than the most acute expression of the general crisis of civilization, it follows that any future we may hope for depends on continuing processes of *internal* transformation in both East and West. There is no better home for these than the ecology movement, in the broadest sense, which by its very nature is not fixated on images or relations of friend and foe.

A different way of life means the restoration of inward and outward balance with nature, the protection of life in every respect, the securing of human rights from the most elementary provision of food, clothing, housing, education, work and leisure, through to guarantees of personal freedom and political participation as indispensable needs of human dignity. This is a programme rising above the conflict of the superpowers and the blocs crystallized around them. Just for that reason it can cross their frontiers without using means of subversion and psychological warfare. It would be the bearer of that new internationalism for which Thompson calls, an attitude and a practice which can be termed alike truly human, planetary, or ecumenical: the sense of each of these terms is becoming increasingly identical.

If the weaker Eastern side in the ideological battle can find no other response than to attribute a practice of this kind to the opposite bloc, it will risk losing its last remaining scrap of credibility vis-à-vis its own population. The suppression of political liberties in the Eastern bloc even damages the inadequate level of official efforts for disarmament and detente. From the standpoint of the interests of humanity it is an ancillary function of exterminism, whatever the external and internal causes that originally generated it. It stifles those energies the peoples of Eastern

Europe need for the necessary transformation of their own conditions, which they cannot undertake so long as they do not even enjoy political democracy. The stubborn defamation in the East of projects for reform as 'anti-socialist' is the mirror image of the slanderous use that reactionary forces in the West make of the word 'communist'.

The psychological war between two systems that mutually condition, reinforce and stabilize each another, a war with its rituals of boast and threat, intimidation and adventure, embellishment and vilification, not least of self-deception even when the facts are known—this is the conspiracy that the new peace movement must defeat. However familiar it may be, the peace movement today has a quite new prospect of success, arising from the ground of the ecology movement and aiming not simply at an equal distance from the two superpowers but at an unconditional independence from them.

The Collapse of Deterrence

Partial victories here, such as West European rejection of Cruise and Pershing II missiles, would be very significant. But these will be a function of the speed at which a comprehensive new orientation of the peace movement develops. This is all the more true in that new missile developments—especially of the Cruise type, in which the Americans have a lead of several years, as they have always had since 1945—and military planning based on these now have an inherent tendency to widen the difference of strategic interests between the USA and Western Europe, and to increase not the security but rather the insecurity of the latter vis-à-vis a possible nuclear attack from the other side.

The deployment of these new weapons evidently provides a space (if only a mathematical one) for the USA to wage a 'limited' nuclear war in the European theatre. The possibility of a nuclear exchange that would destroy Europe from the Atlantic to the Volga, yet leave the USA unscathed, is admitted by the transatlantic big brother to be precisely the ultimate rationale for its current 'modernization' and 'renovation' of NATO—a rationale long since prepared but now suddenly brought to light, for it lies in the logic of the new weapons systems themselves and so defies concealment. Just like the more than 7000 nuclear warheads that are already stored in West Germany, supposedly to 'defend' our domestic battlefield, the new Euro-strategic systems are also to be in the sole charge of Reagan and his ministers. Moreover, the drastic reduction in flying time gained by European deployment, the tremendous precision and flexibility of these missiles (especially Cruise) virtually impose a resort to a preemptive first strike by the other side as soon as there is a threat of military conflict. In an emergency, the Soviet Union would have no other way of trying to protect its western half than by eliminating what would inevitably be the most immediate threat to it.

Under the Carter Presidency, Brzezinski provoked a storm of indignation by declaring that he could not hold his post as security adviser if he were not ready to press the nuclear button without flinching. The indignation was naive, in as much as his statement only expressed the permanent logic on which 'security' through mutual deterrence has rested for the last thirty years. It is a necessary condition of the latter that responsible politicians and soldiers on both sides, and the entire chain of command beneath them, are 'credibly determined' to press the buttons as soon as their instruments indicate that the other side has unleashed its monsters. In this insane logic, Brzezinski would no doubt have been deemed a war criminal if he had ceased to advertise his readiness to behave in this way.

Yet the technical development of weapons systems, escaping the control of both contestants, has now itself brought the 'balance of terror' to an absurd conclusion, since the rules prescribed for the superpower duet have long been thrown into question by the incessant spread of nuclear weapons. For the peoples of Europe, at any rate, the risk to our security has become incalculable even within the framework of military planning. 'Missiles are magnets!' No one need look to the stars to predict for the 1980s the decline of the West, indeed—since the United States will find it difficult to escape the same fate—our whole Northern civilization.

What is new in the present situation is that it is necessarily provoking profound contradictions *within* NATO (i.e. between the dominant interests either side of the Atlantic) and *within* the official political establishments of Western Europe. This time, the ruling classes and other 'elites' cannot avoid sharing in every respect the fate of their peoples, and they know this very well. In any case, such information as we have indicates that there is more to fear from surviving a nuclear explosion than from instantly dying in it. No one knows better than the initiated the growing probability of a breakdown of both systems when zero hour comes, and the impotence of political leaders in the face of the megaton machine.

This puts the formal discipline of *all* established political formations to a severe test, as well as that of the military and civilian specialists. There *must* be an interest in these circles in seeing a pressure from below, from outside the established power, outside the institutions, which alone could permit a fracture within the official apparatus, and after a certain point would make it inevitable.

I am assuming, therefore, that the new conditions of the arms race and international contention, once these find their way into people's consciousness, will arouse greater concern than they ever have in the past, and will enlarge the space for practical political changes. Of course, even people who are completely informed do not necessarily act in a rational way; if they did, we could immediately do away with the whole doctrine of defence that has prevailed up till now. Enlightenment must also find a psychological point of entry. Even in a public opinion that is poorly or wrongly informed, the customary stereotype of threat and security-through-deterrence is not just the result of direct manipulation, but is supported by what were originally less patently misguided attitudes—which is why the latter must always be challenged at every point.

This can more readily be achieved the more people *feel* that their former responses have themselves helped to conjure up the terror against which they seek protection. Our task is not to do away with fear, but to enlighten people so that their fear leads to a rational solution. We do not have to stop depicting the present danger in its full and frightful extent. We shall only escape the apocalypse if we take its possibility seriously and are prepared to use the appropriate models of prophetic adjuration against it. In the last analysis, these have been a necessary part of human development, and have served it well from time to time. We urgently need appeals that are direct and palpable, not so much addressed to intellectuals, vividly depicting the present danger and the way of avoiding it.

The Russians Aren't Coming

The crisis of Western military strategy happens to coincide in time with an increasing crisis of general political stability in the Eastern bloc, ultimately tending to affect the Soviet Union itself. Given a total product that is less than half that of the USA, a productivity that is still further behind, and the very much less favourable integration of the military sector into the economy as a whole, the Soviet Union with its poorer population has to spend at least twice as high a proportion of its national income to keep up in the arms race.

It is common knowledge that, with the exception of a leap forward in missile propulsion from the mid 1950s to the early 1960s, the Soviet Union has always lagged behind in military technology. Nothing of this has changed. It has no equivalent to the Cruise missiles that adapt to the contours of the terrain and can fly beneath the enemy's radar defences. Comparisons of troop numbers, which are so fondly bandied about and purport to show the superiority of Warsaw Pact forces, in actual fact prove just the opposite.

The Eastern bloc finds itself obliged to make up by quantity what it lacks in technological quality. In the key field of nuclear warheads, NATO has numerical superiority, as a result of its typical lead in MIRV technology, even though the Soviet Union has a greater number of missiles as such. The gigantic Soviet tank armies are designed above all for intervention in allied and less developed countries, and are of little use against NATO's armoury of anti-tank weapons.

The dynamism and efficiency of the Soviet economy, moreover, are in notable decline. Even if it would not be easy to stifle Soviet economic growth as a whole purely through the pressure of the arms burden, the logic of mutual deterrence contains a real danger of technological defeat for the Soviet Union in advanced electronics and computerization. The Western arms industry is already playing on this possibility, one which will surely surface in the current decade. The only indubitable strength that the Soviet Union possesses, today more than ever, is its gigantic territory. The peoples of the Warsaw Pact countries, with only a twelfth of Earth's population, occupy more than a sixth of its surface, with a more or less complete spectrum of natural resources, even if access to these is sometimes difficult. The Soviet Union's geo-strategic situation, within the present bloc confrontation, thus in the long run dictates a clear imperative of stability. The USSR seeks to gain time; expansion into more industrialized regions, rich in population but poor in raw materials, would be a senseless goal for it.

There is no doubt that the SS-20 missiles permit a Soviet missile attack on Western Europe, though the Soviet Union has no motive for a preemptive strike so long as the space between Poland and the Urals is not threatened from Western Europe, or the Warsaw Pact attacked in any way. I hope that the Soviet Union will be ready to withdraw these weapons in exchange for the Americans abandoning Pershing II and Cruise.

One thing, however, is obvious in the light of the Polish situation (and quite apart from the fate of the Soviet intervention in Afghanistan, which it is to be hoped will be a salutary failure): to introduce the greater number of soldiers in the Warsaw Pact forces into the strategic debate today is merely a gesture to impress the uninitiated. The situation in Eastern Europe is clearly such that, except in the event of blatant Western aggression, an emergency would in practice subtract not only the troops of almost all the East European countries from Warsaw Pact strength, but also considerable Soviet contingents. Adelbert Weinstein has made the following noteworthy assessment in the *Frankfurter Allgemeine Zeitung* of 12 February

1981: 'The Warsaw Pact, too, has its weaknesses, for example the strategic situation in Poland. For months now, 26 Russian divisions have been positioned along the Polish borders. How monstrous this situation is can be seen from a comparison. What would it mean for NATO if the Americans had to invade West Germany on this scale in order to hold the strategic zone of central Europe for the West as a field of operations? For on top of the ideological danger, the unrest in Poland is a warning to Russian strategy. The 20 Soviet divisions in the East German glacis can be used neither for attack nor for defence unless their supply lines through Poland are firmly under Moscow's control. Then there are the psychological burdens afflicting the Warsaw Pact. Already, both Polish and Russian troops have been put to a severe psychological test in the present atmosphere of crisis . . . A violent solution . . . would release forces which in normal times remain concealed, though they are not politically inactive: those historically conditioned elements of tension that have contributed for centuries to shape the lives of the East European peoples. These emotional forces would also have their effect on the fighting power of the satellite armies, if it came to a military showdown with the West. The Poles could only be mobilized to fight against NATO if they believed that the Bundeswehr was threatening their country. In that case, their dislike of the Germans would be greater than their antipathy towards the Russians. But Polish soldiers have scarcely any hostile feelings towards the Americans, French or British. The Czechs, for their part, see the East German forces as their enemy rather than the West German; it was the former, after all, who invaded Prague. The other Western allies, especially France, the Czechs view as potential friends. No Hungarian or Romanian can be convincingly motivated for war against the West. The Warsaw Pact armies are mostly made up of conscripts, and conscripts are not readily influenced by ideology.'

Its internal constitution makes the Soviet Union quite incapable of effectively securing the political system it has dictated even in its immediate sphere of influence in Eastern Europe. The positive significance of the Polish example for Western Europe lies first and foremost in the fact that it has once and for all removed from the realm of what is rationally conceivable the prevalent fear of the post-war epoch that the Soviet leaders have it in mind to incorporate the population of Western Europe into their empire.

The Soviet system has totally exhausted its original revolutionary impulse. As far back as 1945, its *counter-attack* to the Elbe (and it is only in the form of counter-attack that the Russians have ever advanced massively to the West, drawn in by the armies of Bonaparte, Wilhelm II and Hitler) was in no way inspired by the socialist ideals of the October Revolution, themselves borrowed from the West, but rather by the impetus of the Great Patriotic War. The 'Bolshevik danger', whatever positions were adopted on it when the Russian revolution still exerted an influence beyond its geographical limits, simply no longer exists. The domestic proof of this is the political decline of Third International communism in most of Western Europe, and its hopeless political isolation in those countries where it still retains a certain numerical strength, for reasons only indirectly connected with the Soviet Union. Compare the situation today with the importance of the Comintern in the West European labour movement in the 1920s!

Just as it was in the 19th century, so Russia today is once again under pressure from the West to adapt its political system to the exigencies of self-preservation as a continental empire—now however in conditions where its shadow falls not only over Europe, as before, but over the whole world, in its role as the second superpower. In this sense, the Soviet Union is fundamentally on the defensive, additionally troubled at its rear by a newly industrializing China. The Soviet Union is overburdened by its great-power status, regardless of whether the Russian General Staff does or does not think in terms of preventive attack rather than a more indirect strategy, depending on the conjuncture of the arms race and international military balance.

This situation has already led to a visible relaxation in West European political debate. Even in West Germany, the neurotic fear of Bolshevism is losing its virulence. There is an increasing space for rational discussion of the Soviet Union and East Germany, aided by the growing generational distance from 1945. This might gradually open the way for a 'new Ostpolitik' quite different in kind from that of twelve years ago.

Naturally, if we were to continue identifying the prospects for peace with the balance of terror, the decline in Russian power would be a matter for concern not just to those who still identify with Soviet interests. On the left, residues of traditional illusions in the supposedly socialist character of the Soviet Union and the Eastern bloc combine with reverence for the ideology of deterrence in a tendency to tolerate the efforts of the materially weaker of the two superpowers to achieve military parity. The result is an untenable and indeed unrealistic position. We should be well aware that such parity has never existed, and that given the internal situation of the Soviet Union and the Eastern bloc it is less attainable today than ever before.

Some, like Cornelius Castoriadis,[9] now claim that the USSR is the leading military power in the world today, possessing conventional superiority and nuclear parity—on the basis of 'facts and particulars' we supposedly can find 'in any newspaper'. I would not rely on these. From everything I know or have read, the United States has been explaining to the world at large that 'balance' has been upset because the USSR is *preparing* to achieve parity. But even if we leave this aside, and accept the thesis that the Soviet Union has a numerical superiority in conventional arms, kitchen arithmetic is equally ludicrous in this domain, according to the very logic that Castoriadis otherwise favours. It is mere illogical bias to conjure up a 'Russian scenario' for taking advantage of the 'socio-politico-ethno-military' complexity of Iran, without mentioning a word about the unfavourable complexities of East Europe, not to speak of its own Baltic or Ukrainian territories, for Moscow. Castoriadis makes it appear as if the Kremlin merely had put its divisions in motion for them to be 'in a few days in Biarritz'. His text reads in parts like a briefing for Reagan, Haig and Weinberger, or rather—since it was written before the US presidential elections—like a call to elect this trio. No doubt this was not his deliberate aim, but he did not take the trouble to prevent the misunderstanding.

Moreover, when Castoriadis talks of Soviet or Cuban activities in Africa, he never makes it clear whether Africa should be left to the Africans, or reclaimed by the West—which has far more effective means of intervention there than soldiers dressed in civilian clothes, and furnishes fraternal aid to Mobutu when 'need arises'. He who speaks of Angola and Ethiopia but keeps silent about the whole history of Zaïre since the eviction and assassination of Lumumba has no independent standpoint, but simply voices the interests of NATO and the 'defence of the free world'. The established 'logic of blocs' inevitably drives the high contracting parties, naturally including the Soviet Union since it started to act as the second superpower, towards global strategies. But without ignoring the strategy of the Eastern bloc, the first concern of whoever lives *here* should be to shield the peoples of Africa from the far more powerful structural violence of the Western model.

If the Soviet model is gaining ground in Africa today, it is because it represents a version of development that promises a path of industrialization that will be semi-independent from the capitalist world market. In this sense Russian hegemony there is more power-political than economic: the peoples it 'protects' have less to fear for their natural resources. So long as Soviet protection affords the only chance of avoiding dependent integration into the reproduction mechanisms of the metropolitan West, it will again and again be taken up, directly or indirectly. He who condemns the imperial intrusion of the USSR in Africa or anywhere else in the name of Western interests and pretensions to control and influence, seeks the victory of one bloc over the other, not the overcoming of both.

Even left social-democrats—in my brief experience of them in West Germany—constantly make the mistake of confusing their specific 'export ware', an unbacked cheque on democratic socialism, with the genuine 'exports' of the metropolitan economies. Similarly, at home they make the alterations and modulations which reformism has won from or imposed on the system into an alibi for the system itself. The precarious democratism of the Western metropoles, their one point of positive identity vis-à-vis the politbureaucratic dictatorships of the East, is thus the epiphenomenon of a process that in the whole of the rest of the world calls forth conditions that render even a democratic minimum impossible.

Repression of the historical and material connections between the crimes of both blocs is of course essential, once one is determined to remain in line with regime or alliance orthodoxy in basic questions of foreign and military policy. Castoriadis practises this silent repression throughout. Since the beginning of the colonial epoch, and the onset of the dominance of the European capitalist societies on a world scale, it is an invariable rule that he who sits on a chair in the metropolitan countries, analysing any phenomenon in any other part of the world, without first asking whether its final origin is not be found *here*, can arrive at no correct conclusion. Criticism, no matter how pertinent in itself, then inevitably falls into the twilight of indirect apology. When a tone of self-righteousness is added, the end-result is fatally phariseeism.

Thus anyone who knows something of the history of the Russian Revolution, while giving all due weight to internal factors in its destiny, cannot possibly fail to point out the monstrous deforming pressure of the imperialist West that lay on it from the hour of its birth. Indeed its very prehistory is inexplicable without the constant West European challenge to the Tsarist Empire, which received its own despotic structure from its role as a absorptive barrier against Mongol invasion into Europe (the 'Christian West' has the East Slavs to thank for the fact that the battle of Liegnitz was merely a passing episode). Ivan the Terrible, Peter the Great, Catherine the Great 'modernized' and perfected this despotism in response to the pressure of advanced Europe. Without Napoleon's invasion of Russia, there would have been no Decembrist rebellion. Without English and French military—because industrial—superiority in the Crimean War, serfdom would not have been abolished in 1861, as the prelude to capitalist underdevelopment. The sinking of the obsolete Russian fleet at Tsushima was the prologue to the Revolution of 1905. October itself is unthinkable without the rivalry between the 'late-comer' German and older-established Anglo-French imperialisms which triggered the First World War, that Tsarist Russia lost on the side of the victors because its whole economic and social structure was not ready for the test.

Has the continuity of this line of determination really stopped since 1917? Did Leon Trotsky by chance become Commissar for War, before he could even shut up shop as Foreign Minister, because he and the Bolsheviks were enamoured of militarism? Even Castoriadis must once have heard of those 14 foreign powers that forced the USSR to create its first mass armies. His indices lack any indication that the oldest cadres of the present party and government leadership in Moscow once served as officers. What kind of a time was it when Marshal Stalin kept all other comrade marshals under party control? How did power relationships so change shortly thereafter that Marshal Zhukov came to be considered dangerous as a military man?

If one simply emphasizes the conclusion that the Soviet Union has undergone such a structural change, one makes it appear as if militarization were a diabolical specificity of the system over there. Yet Soviet militarism—despite Marx's *Secret Diplomatic History of the Eighteenth Century*—is the most significant proof, the most substantial victory of the strategy of expansion and encirclement that brought the first anti-imperialist, anti-colonial revolution to a standstill and drove it towards involution. Today the result of the Russian Revolution presents itself as the second superpower, incontestably dangerous to more than its original opponents.

In this respect, Castoriadis is not wrong to point to the structural overweight of the military sector in Soviet society as a whole. Because the politbureaucratic system has no possibility of achieving equality with the United States at the level of the national product as a whole, the only way it can approach military parity is by operating the armaments industry as a state within a state. The great disparity between civilian and military production naturally means that the military power of the USSR, as the aspirations of its population for a higher standard of living increase, is a colossus with a feet of clay, and that the ground under its feet is going to become steadily hotter. This is why the NATO idea of 'forcing the Kremlin to arm itself to death' is no idle fancy. The Soviet leadership on its side, even if it were not otherwise inclined in this direction, would be interested in demonstrating external strength and successes, to legitimate its authority at home. In my view, however, it is not to be excluded that in the post-Brezhnev epoch it will be the Soviet generals themselves who will press for economic and even societal reforms, since most of them know that the USSR will in the medium-run lose the arms race if the economy continues to walk on two legs of unequal length. This is naturally only a speculation. What is not a speculation but a certainty is that any concession whatsoever to the current hysteria about the Soviet menace directly serves exterminism.

The inability of the Soviet Union to control 'its' East European perimeter is in no way the result of any intervention by the Western Left in favour of the forces of reform there. The most optimistic prospect, from the standpoint of peace too, would be that of a profound renovation of the entire social system in these countries. The growth of the ecological and peace movement in the West would help to secure the room for manoeuvre that the East European countries need for such a development, and to prevent reactionary forces in the West from taking advantage of the transformation of institutional structures in the East.

Since the East has irrevocably crossed the threshold of advanced industrialization, and military conflict can yield no thinkable outcome between industrialized soceites, there is only one reasonable perspective in the long run. That is the integration of Eastern Europe and the Soviet Union into a European community of nations of a new kind. In the last analysis, the underlying cultural basis of Russia is no more distant from the West than is that of Turkey. I note here in passing that the contrast in economic organization between *so-called* market economies and *so-called* centrally planned economies is customarily exaggerated; both in fact combine elements of market and of planning, if with different emphasis.

To resume: the fracture of Europe along the frontier between the blocs is no longer historically productive. On the contrary, the two systems—both in their different ways non-socialist—mutually obstruct each other's chances of internal development. Because they have the same industrial foundations, and ultimately face the same ecological challenge, they should both seek to evolve towards a common goal, whose governing coordinates would be ecological humanism and democratic socialism.

For a Nationwide Debate on Security

To summarize the arguments of the last two sections:

1) The idea that the civilization of the industrialized North can be preserved through a balance of terror between the superpowers or military blocs—an idea which underlay detente policies in the 1960s and 1970s—has completely broken down.

2) The logic of contemporary weapons development has led to the perspective of a 'limited nuclear war' on our continent.

3) The Eastern bloc countries now exhibit a visibly advanced stage of

internal destabilization. The nerves of the bankrupt politbureaucracy in this region are wearing thin, and this can lead them to a risky resort to their cudgels. The state of its empire, however, makes any massive invasion of Western Europe impossible, whatever view is taken of Soviet appetite for one. Russian missiles may come, especially if attracted by American ones, but the Russians themselves will not.

Given these three conditions, the entire security policy of Western Europe falls to the ground. All decisions taken since the 1950s must be rethought anew. What is needed now is a comprehensive debate to produce a new definition of our security interests.

The conclusion that directly forces itself upon us is that Europe, including our German homeland, *must not* be armed with nuclear missiles designed to reach the territory of the other superpower, as this only attracts the evil of total destruction. The stationing of these missiles must be prevented at all costs.

Europe, including our German homeland, *cannot* be defended by so-called tactical or battlefield nuclear weapons, as this would mean the certain annihilation of the civilian life to be defended, rather than its protection.

Europe *does not need* nuclear weapons, since there is no real threat of a conventional war of conquest.

What nuclear armaments mean for tomorrow, moreover, is that we are preparing not just for mutual mass murder with the Eastern bloc, but with the entire non-Western world as well. The new security debate must widen out to explore alternative directions for our economy and society in general, if we are not to be set on a collision course with the vital interests of other peoples, as well as with the Earth and its biosphere.

Life depends far more on decisions in this field than it does on such pressing short-run problems as prices, rents and jobs—issues that often crowd in to such an extent that they absorb all public attention and energy. There can scarcely be a single person in this country who would not be *fundamentally* interested in his own and our security, once a civilly conducted debate got under way and the institutions that are supposed to represent society and its subdivisions politically were compelled to do their duty.

Psychological motivation is the key to a new security policy. The promotion of a debate over it falls within the terms not only of the formal constitution of West Germany, but also of its actual constitution—for all the criticism that may be made of it. Neither the mass media nor the political parties, neither parliament nor courts, neither private and public sectors of the economy, nor federal and local government at all levels, are immune to popular influence. The proof can be found in the effect of protests against nuclear power stations, against new international airports, against the consequences of property speculation in the cities. If a popular movement against a new airport can cut right across party divisions, why cannot a similar movement against the military establishment, in favour of conscientious objection of all kinds? It is just that resistance has not yet reached the necessary level of intensity, and above all the necessary ubiquity.

The effect of such a campaign will be all the greater, the more the sweet force of reason prevails in our methods. Peace with nature, peace among nations and individuals, are values and goals unattainable through violence. (I do not of course question the right of both individuals and whole peoples to defend themselves against murderous terror, as recently in Nicaragua, and now in El Salvador.) Happily, it seems to have become accepted on almost all sides that actions should not be directed against the life of political or administrative opponents. It should also be similarly accepted that violence against material objects generally fails in its purpose, unless this purpose is precisely to vent aggression. There will always be someone who has to break a window, or a few people who cannot keep from overturning a car. The problem begins when a strategy is made out of this, and intellectual justifications are produced, instead of addressing those involved as in the recitative from Beethoven's 9th Symphony: 'Oh friends, not these tones, but more joyful ones'. It is still open to debate whether it might not help things now and again to give a signal by an act of destruction. But this can always be done in a demonstrably non-aggressive and communicative fashion. In that case, symbols will serve equally well. A calculated and fundamental opposition to the status quo can always convey its message to women and men in such a way that not only are the indifferent neutralized or converted, but even the adversary is troubled. As for the mega-machine, anyone who understands what it is made of knows that it cannot be seriously challenged by blowing up a pylon carrying electricity from a nuclear power station, and that it is only exercised and strengthened if people put on helmets and throw Molotov cocktails against it.

I do not rule out—unfortunately no one can rule out—that the great machine might prove so immune to popular influence that the only way to avert general disaster would be outright civil war. But then this would be no act of liberation, simply the penultimate catastrophe. We have not even attempted a fraction of the possibilities that lie between our present concern and that extreme situation. Much depends on the intellectual and moral quality of the pressure we bring to bear on the established institutions. Such pressure will appear pointless only so long as we forget that for all their alienated character these are still staffed by human beings. If we fetishize the apparatuses by lumping together the whole administration and all who perform its functions as the 'enemy', then matters will pursue their present destructive course.

It is still too easily forgotten, or at least not sufficiently heeded, that the proper 'target' of our attack is the consciousness of those on the other side. If we make this our explicit aim, then we maximize our chance of influencing those who are undecided, those who waver between listening to us and listening to the enemy. Goliath must be hit on his forehead, the place which his armour doesn't cover. That is the proper way to practise the necessary 'love of the enemy'. We should even avoid needlessly antagonizing someone like Franz Josef Strauss, but rather work towards a position where we can invite him, listen to him and debate with him without personal abuse. We need to do this in every town and every village in the country.

Exterminism does not divide society into social classes of the traditional kind. Certainly, classes still retain their influence, but exterminism rather divides society into servants (active and passive) and opponents (or victims) of the mega-machine. The decisive demarcation is which of these roles predominates in each particular individual. We shall not be saved, therefore, by a small and sham-radical protest movement which is sometimes itself destructive, often still echoes the great machine and drives the majority over to the other side by the anxiety it inspires, but rather by a politics which aims at the divide between the two souls that exist in each person's breast, and seeks to release their energies by widening it.

There is no possibility of defeating exterminism except in the minds of the exterminists. Please don't laugh: there are far more people in the governing cliques than the handful of self-proclaimed 'hawks'. Not the least of these, moreover, are those ambitious physicists given charge of various murderous projects. Certain 'fighters for peace', on the other hand, themselves belong among the exterminists—those not prepared to see the beam in their own eye, the crimes of those good, brave battalions with which they identify. We should never forget how much we are ourselves still trapped in the worship of idols, both with and without realizing it.

At the risk of labouring the point: we shall only defeat exterminism if we can make inroads into its own elites, far beyond the periodic 'treason' of a few individuals. Is there really only ever one General Bastian? Without a scission in the elites, we shall fail to stay the spontaneous march of the mega-machine. What other way is there, given that we shall find it hard to get near the death-dealing buttons ourselves and switch them off?

To preempt misunderstanding: what I have in mind is totally different from the tactic of paper petitions to governments and parliaments, which feed the fatal illusion that we can do our duty by delegating our responsibilities to institutions which are by their very nature incapable of bearing them. The former British diplomat Ronald Higgins, in his excellent popular book *The Seventh Enemy*, has shown very accurately that nothing can be expected of those in government, where all kinds of special interests, no matter how sinister, exert greater real pressure than the long-run vital interests of the great majority that are now jeopardized by the impending catastrophe.

Campaigns such as those around the Berlin housing squats, the Frankfurt and Munich II airports, as well as the Brokdorf nuclear power plant, show *in nuce* the only way in which the great machine can be forced to something like an adequate response—that is, by actions of such scale that the interest in question is brought to the head of the agenda for the sake of the system's own stability. It is only thus that the more alert and conscientious elements within the apparatuses will find any opportunity of expressing their sensibility, normally blocked by everyday political routines and the pressures of special interest groups.

In short, transactions are possible with the state and its institutions without absorption or recuperation, if there exists a genuinely autonomous movement in the country, which is not a reflection of its governing structures. The problem is how to promote such a non-violent popular uprising directed at the minds of its opponents. The spread of information and understanding, forms of communication that transcend existing barriers and fears of contact, are the most important services we can provide our society and ourselves.

The Prospects for Germany

Bonn has of course already been disturbed by the first signs of the new security debate. The Chancellor, as leader of the SPD, fought the last election campaign with a strong emphasis on peace and security, rightly aware of growing popular fears about the international situation. For all the limitations of his policy, which remains within the logic of the blocs, he won a majority for moderation against the calls for greater confrontation from the CDU candidate. It is clear enough that the CDU's attempt to regain power on this platform failed to persuade even its own ranks.

What the election also confirmed is the declining force of conviction of those attitudes on which the CDU candidate based his appeal, even in a

West Germany where fear of the Russians is congenital. We can assume that the CDU is itself less than completely agreed on this issue. As a former Latin teacher, Dr Strauss should possess some feeling for historical connections and processes. Can those 'symptoms of decay' against which he blusters really strike a nation by accident, let alone a continent or a bloc of states? We could ask what Roman history teaches us of the prospects of defending an imperial metropolis based on tribute from the whole world, with the method of *limes et legiones*. Is not the fundamental reason why the Roman Empire came to grief that militarism increasingly became the major force holding it together—a rise of militarism accompanied by a progressive decline not only of morals, but above all of agriculture, marginalizing ever broader sections of the population and driving them into discontent?

Today, a conservative outlook might well give rise to quite different preoccupations than those towards which the CDU has been pulled by its right wing: a genuine concern for long-run consolidation and security, as against military risks and resource shortages. It may be that the line of division on this fundamental question no longer runs between the governing coalition and the opposition, but right through the whole establishment. It was Herr Genscher who found it necessary to issue a warning against neutralism and pacifism among the population, to the full agreement of Herr Apel, as if the Social Democrats had never had an anti-militarist tradition.

The only hopeful sign here is that warnings of this kind are deemed necessary. We can assume that these gentlemen are well informed as to where attitudes are undergoing a shift. It is certainly not a question of first converting leading politicians and beginning with the most stubborn among them. The task is rather to understand and respond to the readiness in the population to rethink the whole nature of security, so that we can contribute best to the crystallization and clarification of this change.

What we need are two things: most essentially, the development of a practical political campaign that can affect decision-making processes in our country, but also an idea that summarizes it and carries the force of conviction. A short while ago, Robert Havemann concluded an article published in Britain with the remark that the key to a solution of the European problem might be found here in Germany, more so than people generally suspect. How can we relate this to Edward Thompson's central notion, and turn the fracture that divides Europe into the object of a practical criticism, a critical practice?

The first factor to take into account is the particular significance of the two German states in their respective blocs. The movement for European

Nuclear Disarmament, which is already growing in some other West European countries as well, may restrain the arms race in certain particular national contexts, but it cannot have any major or conclusive success as long as the Federal Republic of Germany remains the model pupil of the traditional 'Atlantic' defence policy. Something must happen here, and from below, if we do not want our country to become the bottleneck of the whole campaign. A breakthrough in the Federal Republic, moreover, on such sensitive subjects as nuclear disarmament and disengagement from the blocs, would have major consequences in East Germany, even if in the immediate future it could only be supported there by the churches. Through television, it would reach the entire politically interested section of the population, including SED members and functionaries. The effect would combine with dissatisfaction over the Soviet big brother's adventure in Afghanistan, and with unease over the stability of the alliance in the wake of the events in Poland. There should still, moreover, be interest in the Rapacki plan for a nuclear-free zone composed of West and East Germany, Poland and Czechoslovakia, which at the time was completely serious in its intent.

If the new peace movement gains some palpable success, then the precarious position of Germany, divided by the bloc frontier, could perhaps be turned to good use, as it was in 1968–69. It has since become only too clear that reunification by a policy of strength—in the last instance the incorporation of one half of the country in the existing social system of the other—is not only unrealistic, but would be playing with the fire of a new world war, by proposing a shift in the demarcation between the two zones of the continent. The old-style rhetoric of German reunification has thus become so hollow that even the CDU no longer believes in it. NATO and German reunification were incompatible right from the start; this is something every citizen of West Germany now understands. Thus not only the theme of Europe, which has resurfaced against Atlanticism as at no time since 1945, but also the theme of reunification are escaping the grip of strategies of confrontation. In its proper place, the German question belongs to us.

At the Second Socialist Conference in Marburg, I was somewhat surprised at the unreflecting vehemence with which large sections of the left proposed to hand over this issue once and for all to the right. This is an expression of the unduly negative and defeatist outlook which German reaction has imposed on us for generations—the feeling that if we want to change something, we must not encroach on areas that are the traditional prerogative of the right. Yet today it is imperative that we leave no field unoccupied. On the contrary, we must develop a discourse that among other things is capable of putting the favourite issues of the opposite side in a different light.

I find it hard to understand why so many of us seem to reject the opportunity we now have of reorienting national sentiments in a direction to which they have never greatly tended in Germany: that of 'peace without weapons', of popular sovereignty and democracy from below, of regional and local connections, of protection of home, landscape and customs from terroristic levelling by the central state apparatus and cosmopolitan capital, of an ecumenical solidarity with the resistance of all peoples against the ubiquitous aggression of the military–industrial mega-machine.

In Germany, and in the Federal Republic in particular, the theme of nationality—precisely because it is thwarted by the overwhelming reality of the frontier between the two blocs and perhaps even because it has been so massively repressed—may well have not a lesser importance than elsewhere, but an even greater one. Yet its complexity, too, is far greater. Eruptions are possible here which we must anticipate by a rational canalization of the energies in question. Just like every other level of supra-individual interest in which we are involved—from our various primary groups, through work associations, to local and ultimately planetary communities—the nation too has its own reality, both in particular institutions and organizations, and in the minds of individuals affected by them. It matters to every German whether the two German states are drawn more closely together or each falls more in thrall to its respective protector and superpower. In the same way, there are interests that concern our whole continent. If the Brussels bureaucracy is an alienated Europe, a movement for European Nuclear Disarmament could provide the kernel of a regained continental identity, the starting-point for an initiative capable of checking the rivalry of the superpowers.

We must of course guard against treating the German question in the perspective of a reduced Great-German unitary state, and strictly avoid pandering to nationalist emotions. The problem of Germany, for us, is how the two German states can gradually be prised loose from the blocs, from the tutelage of the superpowers that endangers the very existence of both sections of the German people. In truth—in what direction could the two partial German states move, if not towards each other? A nuclear-free zone in Central Europe, a nuclear-free Europe from Portugal to Poland, an atmosphere favourable to neutralization and disengagement in West Germany—all these things would be made easier by a new rapprochement. A peace movement in West Germany that arose from the ecological ground and was oriented to a Third Road would also have a greater opportunity of fostering an East German equivalent. It would be something genuinely new, if instead of consumerism, which whips the needs of the East German people into line with the Western model of growth, it was an alternative to the exterminist industrial system that crossed the frontier.

In East Germany, an eco-socialist reform movement could also be *the* long-run perspective, though its point of departure and its progress would be quite different from the 1968 reform movement in Czechoslovakia or that of today in Poland. Much would then depend on what we have managed to change on our side. The true challenge to the East German political system would occur if it were freed from military pressure and from any kind of project for reunification proceeding from the Federal Republic. If West Germany could change its military policy, accepting for example 'nuclear pacifism' and replacing NATO with an unambiguously defensive defence of frontier and territory, then the entire East German military posture would forfeit its ideological legitimation, right through to the presence of Soviet troops in the GDR. The SED would never have been able to govern without the cement of a plausible military threat from the other German state.

Some Points on Steps and Methods

Finally, how could we proceed, how must we proceed—assuming that we are more or less in agreement over both our goal and the political and psychological preconditions for achieving it? The latter, as we have seen, must include: readiness for action 'at the face', a break with the logic of blocs, rejection of foe imagery, an attempt to communicate even with the adversary, a search for allies in the apparatus, including its central instances, and commitment to change in the framework of legality, including change in the orientation of the institutions themselves.

First and foremost, we must realize how far our possibilities depend on ourselves, on changing ourselves for the task in hand, on a new adaptation to it as our goal and means, on our positive action. For it *is* possible to prevent the deployment of Euro-strategic nuclear missiles in our country. It *is* possible to achieve the withdrawal of those 'tactical' nuclear weapons that are already in place. It *is* possible to establish an independent Western Europe, with a particular type of freedom from the blocs. It *is* possible, in this European context, to alter the whole position of this partial German state in world politics, and thus put the national question in a new perspective. It *is* possible to influence the development of the other German state in a constructive, unarrogant and unchauvinistic way, without the intention of remodelling things there according to the fashion here.

Second, we must acquaint ourselves in an all-round way with the fundamental structures of military and industrial exterminism. This great subject, which includes also the hunger and poverty of the South, should have a particular claim on our time. Each one of us must be in a position to provide concrete refutations of those who manipulate public opinion, to expose their tricks and enlighten those whom they seek to manipulate.

Third, what we learn in this way must be propagated in every conceivable way: that is, it must be transformed into well-drafted addresses to people. The mass media are the crucial nerve centre here, for us as for others. In this respect, especially, we have to break out of the ghetto of the left. No local paper is too small or too reactionary for our intervention. Nor can we afford to ignore the Springer press itself, unless we want to cripple our own capacity for communication; we may often need to expose and rebut it, but we can also make selective use of it—even this branch of the media is not impervious! The current international danger and the failure of official security policy is all too apparent. There is no journalist, of whatever stripe, who cannot and must not be morally forced to rethink his opinions on the subjects that concern us. Many of them indeed want to be forced to 'get something in'. Articles or readers' letters can still have an effect even if they are not published. The need is to find a way of expressing ourselves that cannot be side-stepped.

Fourth, we must organize debates, preferably in manageable groups rather than large halls, where representatives of the other side are actually present. In such debates, the mechanisms of anxiety and projection described by Horst Eberhard Richter should not just be repressed, but actually worked through. Given the new situation, it is possible to bring the argument to a head and redirect people's anxiety. When it comes to the crunch, it is not just the launching-ramps that are targets for incoming missiles; so are all other military establishments, as well as every significant factory and traffic intersection, and our own nuclear defences would carve empty holes for the other side's tanks to advance through. So long as the majority of the population still believe in security through armaments, there can be no political breakthrough.

Fifth, we have to tear away the curtain of talk about balanced disarmament, troop reduction, arms limitation and arms control. Berta von Suttner once wrote that the delegates of the great powers at the Hague disarmament conference of 1899 seemed to her like a meeting of shoemakers convened to decide on the abolition of shoes. We must ceaselessly repeat what everyone already knows: these people just talk past one another, and cooperate in driving one another on. Treaties simply channel the arms race. The only way forward is for the people of each country to force through major steps of unilateral disarmament, of a kind that the peoples on the other side cannot fail to see and to appreciate.

Sixth, we should be quite serious, and quite expert too, in spreading the idea of an alternative defence policy, which has already been developed in its basic elements (for example by Afheldt, Ebert, Mechtersheimer, Vilmar) and is the only viable strategy:

—*non-nuclear*: without long-range nuclear missiles, which only attract destruction, and without self-destructive tactical nuclear weapons for the domestic 'battlefield';

—*unambiguously defensive*: without any capabilities aimed at the territory of the opponent; but a massive frontier defence with the most modern non-nuclear armour, aircraft and possibly also non-nuclear missiles;

—*decentralized territorial defence*: scattered across the whole country, not concentrated into large units presenting large targets; specialized forces with light armour and anti-aircraft weapons;

—*social defence*: that is, in combination with territorial defence, non-military forms of popular resistance deployed at the right time, as well as technical sabotage designed to make any occupation problematic in advance;

—*civil defence*: important also as a psychological compensation for the renunciation of retaliation in kind against an enemy attack.

The essential difference between such a policy and the existing strategy of deterrence (through retaliation from an already destroyed territory) can be summed up in the concept of 'restraining' the adversary. Just as is the case with energy supply, the two options—nuclear and non-nuclear—are not both possible simultaneously. The population must decide on which they want to spend the immense tax resources involved.

Seventh (last but not least): even this alternative defence concept, still governed by the 'reality principle', does not escape the exterminist framework. For a definitive break out of this vicious circle we need a more radical model of behaviour, which I would like to call *eco-pacifism*. Not only must we maintain the demand for general and complete disarmament; this must be supplemented by a programme for the industrial dismantling of our Northern civilization, or rather a constructive re-mantling of it. This should be both our own choice, and the basis of a widening effort to bring about a change of thinking among the majority of the population.

Politically, this means standing for an alternative defence policy; morally, however, it means rising to that higher reason and trust visible in the declaration distributed by certain Protestant circles: 'I am prepared to live without the protection of armaments. I intend to support a policy for our state that seeks peace politically and not by weapons.'

We should take on the task of distributing the declaration in millions of copies, engaging in personal discussion with every single child, woman and man without exception. The questions and answers that are important in

116

this connection should be composed in the style of a catechism. Everyone who helps distribute the declaration must have at their disposal arguments that take into account the mental barriers, prejudices, hostilities that the division of Europe and the manipulation of both blocs has created. It is impossible to think of any better starting-point for a debate on the entire complex of problems discussed in this essay than by challenging people in this way to make a thought-out existential decision by individually signing their name on a sheet of paper.

It may be that we find ourselves here at a point of unconditional agreement with the message of Christ. It is in this precise sense that I adhere to this declaration, convinced that there was never a moment in history when the words of the Sermon on the Mount were more pertinent or pressing: 'Blessed are the gentle in spirit; for they shall inherit the Earth.'

---

[1] Edward Thompson, 'Notes on Exterminism, the Last Stage of Civilization'. The present essay is written as a 'supplement' to Thompson's article, in the sense that I endorse Thompson's arguments and aim to extend them, though not necessarily in a way with which he would agree. But I can literally say that I agree with every one of Thompson's points. If he says that he 'do[es] not claim to have discovered a new "exterminist" mode of production', I would only add that he has provided the concept for the prevailing tendency in which the 'two imperial formations' converge. The question then arises: what is the ultimate basis of this tendency, if not the prevailing presence of the one and only industrialism which has so far existed? It is scarcely very meaningful to say that industry is deformed by certain well-known class interests, given that these are evidently dependent subfunctions of an apparently spontaneous 'progress', and the stimuli on which this 'progress' seems to thrive. We must accordingly consider, far more radically than in the past, not how these 'historical laws' can be as it were obediently fulfilled, but rather how they can be broken.

[2] 'Manifesto of the Communist Party', *The Revolutions of 1848*, Penguin/NLR, Harmondsworth 1973, p. 67 and note.

[3] Wolfgang Sternstein, for example, draws attention to this in *Marx, Lenin, Mao. Darstellung und Kritik der marxistischen Industriegesellschaft*, Frankfurt 1980.

[4] Thompson, see above, p. 27.

[5] Ibid., p. 14.

[6] Ibid., p. 25.

[7] Klaus Traube, *Frankfurter Rundschau*, 4–5 December 1980.

[8] Horst Eberhard Richter, 'Und ist es Wahnsinn, hat es doch Methode', *Kritik* 26, 1980.

[9] Bahro is referring here to C. Castoriadis' book *Devant la Guerre*, Paris 1981—a manual of the new cold war in France (NLR).

The Peace Movement and Europe

Lucio Magri

A movement for peace and disarmament has exploded in Europe in these last months that has stupefied even those—like ourselves—who believed from the start in the possibility of building one, and worked to bring it about. There are many reasons for that stupor.

First of all, there is the range and variety of the forces that have mobilized. Bonn and London, Brussels and Rome, have witnessed the largest demonstrations ever seen, on any issue, in the whole post-war period. Quantity has also been quality: there is no way of gathering together hundreds of thousands of people in the streets and squares of our cities without finding side by side different generations, different political forces, different cultural traditions. This diversity alone has put the demonstrations above any suspicion of tactical or partisan calculation, and has multiplied the impact of each on society as a whole.

Secondly, there is the geographical spread of the new movement. This is probably the first time that a mass movement has emerged simultaneously, with essentially analogous demands and similar protagonists, in virtually all the countries of Western Europe. Not even the great wave of 1968 had this European scale and this spontaneous kinship of language.

Thirdly, there is the new and unusual relationship in the peace movement between mass spontaneity and political organization. In the past we can recall either broad movements—in the fifties—that were highly structured and led by parties or trade-unions; or broad movements—in the sixties and seventies—that emerged outside and often against political institutions, and never succeeded in inter-acting with them. By contrast, the growth and impact of the new peace movement (similar in this perhaps only to the working-class revolt of 1968 in Italy) holds the promise of a fruitful dialectical convergence between the spontaneity—hence autonomy—of the masses and established political forces. It effectively selects those political organizations that are closest to it, which themselves become participants and promoters of a movement that by the same stroke

117

tends to condition and transform them, and thereby to impinge directly on parliaments and governments.

Nevertheless all this, if it constitutes the initial novelty and strength of the peace movement, could also subsequently become a source of weakness. The tremendous variety of social and cultural forces that make up the movement, its rejection of political schemas that have long since become impoverished and sclerosed, are the grounds of its richness and of its first practical results. It can already be said that the superpowers themselves cannot ignore, in either their propaganda or behaviour, the existence of these struggles for continental disarmament, and their ability to influence the governments of Europe. But these advantages also contain the danger that the movement could remain arrested at a stage of relatively generic or amorphous protest. Such a danger would increase if and when these governments react by diversionary or obfuscating manoeuvres, casting blame on each other and postponing options for peace and disarmament behind a screen of solemn declarations of principle and good will; or if the major political forces closest to the movement, imbued as they are with a traditional 'realism', try to reduce it to a mere pressure of opinion to which they are not accountable and whose objectives are not to be taken literally. These are no mere contingencies: just such processes are already more than evident in Germany and Italy. Conversely, it is also possible that the more radical sectors of the movement—as happened in the seventies—react mistakenly, counterposing and isolating themselves from broader currents of opinion, by an exclusive and one-sided insistence on their own objectives and forms of struggle.

It is thus neither premature nor sterile, but rather urgent and necessary, to start common discussion on the ways in which the movement can both keep its unitary and pluralist character and yet acquire a more permanent and organized basis, and above all a more definite political physiognomy. For this is the condition of its stamina and real autonomy. A mass political movement that does not have an organizational discipline holding it together, or consolidated ideological traditions giving it identity, precisely for that reason needs a set of concrete objectives and strategic priorities all the more.

So I would like to give our view of what—not 'the movement should do'—but what the movement already potentially is (which therefore it is our duty to sustain with our analyses, to render explicit with our programmes); and also to say something of those problems which still remain absent from the consciousness of the movement but which the real world will not allow to be evaded in the long run. I will begin with the short and medium term platform of the struggle for peace, with the problem of those objectives which can or cannot be achieved.

To any attentive observer, above all to anyone in the streets of Bonn or Rome, it was obvious that overwhelming majority of the movement is agreed on a set of demands that are neither vague nor utopian. People are not demonstrating merely to oblige the great powers to negotiate, towards an ultimate goal of universal disarmament. On the contrary, they plainly and rightly have no confidence in the will of the great powers to bring serious negotiations to any conclusion, or not to void even those agreements that are reached by further and graver measures of rearmament outside their framework, as has always happened in the past. In other words, the peace movement believes neither in the subjects of the negotiations (USA and USSR), nor in the premisses of these negotiations, which still remain the balance of terror. For that reason it maintains that a unilateral initiative must be taken to break the spiral that is leading to war, by the subject that has a direct and particular interest in denuclearization—Western Europe. There may be different opinions about the scale of such an unilateral initiative, or different motivations given for it. The specific goals appropriate to each country may be diverse: for Italy, rejection of the Cruise installations at Comiso, of the doubling of military expenditure, of the dispatch of troops to Sinai; for England and France, renunciation of the independent deterrent; for Spain, refusal of entry into NATO. But there is a broad collective awareness that only actions of this type can reverse the basic thrust of the Reagan Administration in America and induce the Soviet government to opt for political rather than military solutions to its difficulties.

The peace movement in Europe is thus neither pro-Soviet nor pro-American—it includes countries and parties that have never been connected in any way to the USSR. It seeks to dismantle not only the Cruise and Pershing but SS-20 bases, indeed all old and new 'theatre' nuclear weapons. It argues that Western Europe should 'give an example', by reducing wholly or in part its own nuclear arsenal: not only because we must live and struggle here, on the terrain of our own direct commitment, but also because this is the only way to impose genuine negotiations between the great powers, by a political act with some hope of effect.

Now there is no doubt that this position is a disconcertingly new and radical one for much orthodox opinion. There is still a tendency among governments and parties of the left in Europe to regard it as a generous utopia—a useful provocation to arouse public opinion, but not a political line that could actually be adopted. We believe on the contrary that in the strictest sense this is the only realistic policy, that is, one which is both necessary and possible. We of the PDUP do not represent, either by tradition or culture, a pacifist force in the Gandhian sense. History has taught us—above all in the arena of international relations—the hazards of any literal translation of the doctrine of 'non-violence' and unilateral disarmament. Dubcek and Allende are there to remind us how difficult it is for a good political cause to prevail over an enemy with a bad cause but good weapons. Still less do we have any illusions as to the peaceful nature of the Soviet Union. Our rupture with the PCI as a group derived from our judgement of the nature and tendency of Russian policies after Prague—just as more recently we were among the few on the Italian left to warn of the adventurist turn of Soviet foreign policy before Afghanistan, in the Horn of Africa and South-East Asia.

Why then do we hold acts of unilateral disarmament by Western Europe to be a just and realistic prospect? Would they not expose European security to unacceptably high risks, and even end by encouraging the leading group in the Soviet Union in its worst illusions of power? Our choice is based on a number of factual considerations, and a number of political arguments free from ideological predisposition, which I will try to set out schematically here—although they warrant much more extended development and discussion. *Firstly*, I will look at the claims that the Soviet Union has in recent years gained a general strategic superiority over the United States, or a particular advantage in Europe, that necessitates acceptance of the NATO 'modernization' demanded by Washington. *Secondly*, I will review the new pattern of the arms race that emerged in the seventies, and which threatens world peace more acutely than at any time in the past thirty-five years—above and beyond the question of so-called 'theatre' balance in Europe itself. *Thirdly*, I will consider the structural processes at work in each of the superpowers which have created the dual political crisis that now jeopardises detente. *Fourthly*, I will emphasize the long-term problems of global development—the inter-related drama of the Third World and impasse of the First World—which pose in the last analysis the deepest and most intractable menace of all to a peaceful conclusion to the twentieth century.

1. The Strategic Balance: USA, USSR and Europe

It is not true that the military balance of forces has shifted in favour of the USSR—indeed shifted so decisively that to counter an immediate Soviet menace we must accept the new American missiles without regard for the loss of European autonomy they involve, or the peril of a new spurt in the arms race they represent. An incessant propaganda campaign by the American Administration and its friends in Europe has hammered on this theme. This campaign should itself have created suspicion of its claims, since if a real military imbalance did exist it would be all the more dangerous to broadcast it to the enemy, who should logically then be tempted to exploit his position of force before equilibrium was restored again. Nevertheless, this ideological operation has achieved its objective of creating a diffuse 'common sense' on the subject of the Soviet peril.

Now I have no wish to attempt armchair strategy, or start to enumerate missiles, delivery-systems, and radar-networks on the basis of official data which everyone knows are infinitely manipulable. But there are certain incontestable facts that suffice to disprove the current US propaganda. When the Carter Administration—which was certainly not pacifist or eager for disarmament—signed SALT-II, the SS-20s were already being installed: yet the Administration publicly acknowledged an effective balance of forces on each side. Since then, if the deployment of these Soviet missiles has continued, a completely new phase of American strategic rearmament has been launched. There are thus no grounds for supposing that Carter's judgement could be radically reversed.

But there is another consideration that is even more important, yet more often forgotten. The military balance of forces itself is not commensurable simply with the stockpile of arms on each side. It is determined at least as much by the economic and technological hinterland that each camp can mobilize rapidly for a war effort, and by the geopolitical diplomacy of the world at large. Now there is no doubt that the economic and technical lead of the West over the Soviet Union has become more pronounced, less easily eroded, in recent years. It is equally evident that the net changes in international diplomacy of the past decade have not been to the disadvantage of the West. If the USSR has made some gains, often with aggressive initiatives, in Africa, Indochina, Central America or Afghanistan, far weightier shifts have occurred in the opposite direction. Whatever our interpretation of the origin or meaning of the policies pursued by the regimes in Egypt or China, it is plain to all that these two major regional states—each decisive for vital zones of the world—have radically altered their external postures towards alignment with the United States.

Many object that a local military imbalance still exists in Europe in favour of the USSR, and since it is this imbalance that is threatening it must if necessary be countered by rearmament. In fact, any argument that subdivides the military balance between the blocs by 'theatre' is a perilous one. What would happen, for example—what did happen in the past?—if the USSR were to install missiles close to the American coast-line in order to guarantee Cuban independence in the Caribbean 'theatre'? Such arguments are even more erroneous and arbitrary when applied to Europe, at least so long as the continent is not an autonomous political subject free from any military alliances. For a limited nuclear war in Europe—the new aberration envisaged by the latest strategic doctrines—would in practice inevitably lead to a generalized atomic holocaust. This is so because the European theatre is not internally symmetrical: it comprises on the one side no more than the periphery of the American strategic military complex, but on the other side it represents the metropolitan heart of the Soviet strategic military complex. Thus even if a perfectly equal number of 'theatre' missiles could be defined and controlled in each zone of Europe, the fact would still remain that those on one side could strike in the space of a few minutes at the entire strategic defences of the other. Precisely because of this 'asymmetry', the only way forward for Europe is the total dismantling of the two theatre nuclear systems—SS-20, SS-4 and 5, Cruise and Pershing, but also NATO's air and sea 'forward bases', and the English and French *forces de frappe*.

2. The Military Mutation: Precision of Weapons, Proliferation of Users

The idea that a balance of terror, if it is not enough to ensure a real peace, at least guarantees us against a new world war, has dominated the culture and politics of the last decades. But it is false, and becoming ever falser.

Experience has shown that the very pursuit of a balance of terror, instead of convincing the great powers of the futility of the arms race, has acted as an alibi and an incentive for a continual acceleration of military spending in both camps, as each seeks to neutralize in advance the possible gains sought by the other. Every agreement on arms control, even when signed and respected, has meant no more than a pause in a race rapidly resumed in other sectors. Experience has likewise demonstrated that military arms and equipment very rarely remain a purely defensive reserve, but fatally tend to become instruments of aggression for the extension of imperial power, or its forcible preservation when jeopardised. This is all the more true in our own epoch, when the sheer scale of military expenditure, its interconnexion with the most powerful and vital sectors of the economy, and the enormous political and organizational apparatuses that administer it, tend to create a state within a state whose logic and interests become relatively autonomous from the very societies that they are supposed to serve. But to repeat these truths today is not enough. For there is much more to be said, and worse to be considered, as we enter the eighties.

In the past decade the pursuit of the balance of terror has produced a veritable qualitative leap forward in the acceleration of the arms race. Two factors in succession, and then multiplication, have been responsible for this. In the first instance we have witnessed from the early seventies onwards a change in the 'general philosophy' informing the military strategy of the great powers. Hitherto the guiding notion, at least so far as nuclear weapons were concerned, was that of deterrence: each side sought security in its own capacity to respond to any attack by physically destroying its adversary. Whoever contemplated unleashing an atomic war could be certain of signing his own death-warrant too. This strategy, however terrifying, contained within itself a principle of objective limitation: once the ability to destroy enemy cities and territories several times over was reached, there was no sense in further multiplying nuclear weapons. Military expenditure could be concentrated on other and more conventional means of armed intervention—even if, as the war in Vietnam was to show, these were no insurance against heavy defeats in local wars.

Recently, however, the novel opportunities opened up by the sophisticated technologies of the electronic revolution and space research have seen the emergence of a new 'philosophy' of nuclear arms. The objective of this doctrine is the capacity to destroy the military forces of the adversary and so 'render him harmless'. Two consequences follow from it. It commits its adherents to the logic of the 'preemptive strike'; and it plunges them into an unlimited race to acquire new weapons-systems before the adversary can do so, and to achieve a capacity to neutralize the latter's defence systems. 'Deterrence', instead of constituting an objective limit to rearmament, becomes an uncontrollable stimulus to the constant renewal of armaments consigned to obsolescence.

Meanwhile a second, and no less important, mutation has occurred in the seventies. There has been a sudden multiplication of the subjects of military spending and arms utilization. In the fifties and sixties major military establishments were an affair of the great powers, who bore the burden and retained the control of them. Since then two new factors have intervened. After its defeat in Vietnam, the United States, unable and unwilling to undertake further direct interventions of a similar sort, promoted the growth of local systems of political control in the Third World through the establishment of sub-imperialisms: Brazil or South Africa, Israel, Iran and then Egypt. These sub-imperialisms emerged out of the internal dynamic of each region, but the USA sustained them with military aid and encouraged their nationalism as an instrument of its own global penetration. Meanwhile, the USSR showed signs of moving in a similar direction, if with much more limited means: using different states in the same kind of role in the Horn of Africa and Indochina. The result has been a proliferation of military powers, but one that has not reflected a genuine multipolarity so much as a more complex and mediated system of bipolar domination. Yet in this system a multiplicity of national interests and logics now intervene in ever less controllable ways, so proliferating the risks of local conflicts setting off a global war.

Moreover, this military tendency has found a new social and material basis since the oil crisis. For within the underdeveloped world as a whole, those countries which command valuable natural resources have finally become able, in the new international context, to profit substantially from them. But since in general, both because of internal reasons and external pressures, this unexpected wealth has not been directed to productive investment or real development, it has found a natural outlet in demented military expenditures in the Third World, which in their turn have unleashed new local conflicts there.

This great leap forward in the arms race is pregnant with very grave consequences. In the underdeveloped world it constitutes an ever more central determinant of the genocide and oppression which we see daily there, even prior to the eruption of outright armed conflicts. Two thirds of humanity lives on the edge of physical starvation and social brutalization, in the first instance because gigantic planetary resources are absorbed by military spending and the largest part of scientific research is devoted to means of death rather than life. At the same time the militarization of states and societies in the Third World poses in itself an insurmountable obstacle to genuine policies of economic and civil development. How can we imagine that a general war could be avoided in the long-run, if an absolute contradiction between development and underdevelopment persists and worsens in the 20th century? What kind of peace is it, for the rest, that condemns millions of people to death by hunger every year?

In the second place, the effects of the last decade of rearmament have been equally new, and disquieting, within the metropolitan societies themselves, West and East. For a whole historical epoch, that of so-called Keynesian capitalism, military spending—like public expenditure in general—was a flywheel of growth and employment, and as such often won the consensus of the trade unions. Today, however, as the crisis of the Keynesian state explodes amidst chronic inflation and fiscal disequilibrium, the objective necessities of the economic system and the subjective pressures of the dominant classes are combining to impose drastic reductions in public spending. At the same time productive investments are more often generating technological unemployment than new positions on the labour market. In these conditions, military outlays become stark alternatives to social spending and increased employment. To maintain their level, it will be necessary increasingly to dismantle the welfare state. To achieve this end, it will be necessary to conjugate political repression of marginal groups who must now be deprived of social security safeguards, and nationalist mobilization of those intermediary groups which must also suffer diminution of their relative standard of living.

In the Soviet Union, too, the contradiction between rearmament and socio-economic development is deepening. This contradiction has always weighed on the system in the East, and has been one of the basic causes of the authoritarian degeneration of its political order: a society like the USSR whose per capita income is a third of that of the USA has traditionally had to sustain a military burden comparable to that of its adversary. This discrepancy was in the past tempered by the fact that national income was itself registering constant and steady growth. But from the moment that growth rates start to decline in the USSR as well, and ideological enthusiasm among the masses slackens, how can such a disproportionate military effort be continued—if not by recourse to a new nationalism and to harsher repression? For all these reasons a balance of terror, even were it perfect, henceforward leads only in the direction of war. For all these same reasons, only a rapid and radical reversal of direction towards genuine disarmament can save us from the prospect of disaster.

3. The Political Crisis of the Superpowers: from California to Poland

The danger of war between the superpowers today does not derive from the expansion of rival empires so much as from the mutual crisis of each of the two great antagonists—or rather, from the growing discrepancy between their inability to solve the economic, cultural and political problems facing them within and without their borders, and their perdurable material—above all military—might.

Let us look at the United States first. The past year has seen a historic turning-point in American politics. Already under the Carter Administration the first symptoms were visible of a change of outlook, as the effects of 'after Vietnam' wore off and the USA started to resume more aggressive postures once again. But the victory of Reagan has represented much more than a mere accentuation of this tendency. It is reminiscent rather of the advent of Roosevelt at the start of the thirties, if with a very different connotation. For the first time in forty years a man of the right, advocating a programme expressly and organically of the right, won a massive electoral victory, pulling in behind him social strata and regional interests hitherto unfailingly loyal to the Democratic bloc. The ground of this shift has the general internal crisis of American society, and the processes of restructuration it has started to engender. This crisis is on the one hand ideal and cultural: the collapse of traditional values and disintegration of the texture of everyday life has been not less but more marked in America than in any other major capitalist country, in the course of the past twenty years. It has generated a cry for 'law and order' that has now engulfed broad layers of the Democratic electorate. On the other hand, the crisis is also economic and social: manifested above all in the popular discredit into which the 'welfare state' has fallen. What was once seen as a humane system of provision born of the experience of millions of unemployed in the thirties is now widely perceived as a mere administration of parasitism and decay, parking an increasing slice of the population in marginality, presiding over inefficient services, generating inflation and bureaucratism—all in contrast with the dynamism of decentralized high technology and new zones of industrialization. The mass revulsion against it has fused with sectors of the business establishment chafing at the pressure of Japanese and European competition, and with a financial community determined to restore the prestige and stability of the dollar. The result has been a repetition of the Thatcher operation in the United States, with the difference that there it disposes of far larger economic and military resources and encounters far less organized resistance from the labour movement.

A new social and political bloc has thus crystallized in the United States, amidst the crisis of the 'social state' and in reaction to imperial decline. Its economic programme is neo-liberalism (which does not contradict but presupposes direct support for capitalist redeployment and military industry) and cuts in social spending. Its ideology seeks to refurbish the traditional moral codes of bourgeois society and to exalt national identity anew. Its financial policies include truculent revaluation of the dollar and liquidation of even notional aid programmes to the Third World. Its social objectives involve confrontation with the trade unions and women's rights, and negation of assistance to racial minorities. All these trends underlie and condition a new and coherent international policy. What defines this policy is not a desire to restore a situation of balance with the Soviet Union, which the United States has never ceased to enjoy, but a will to impose its own clear-cut supremacy. For the crisis of American imperialism today is not one of the force it can command, but of the hegemony it has lost. America today knows that it is still the largest economic and above all military power in the world; but it also feels that its global paramountcy is ebbing away. The decline of its hegemony is due as much or more to the slow and uneven emancipation of the oppressed peoples, and to the 'disloyal' competition of a European and Japanese capitalism that seems to be shifting military burdens onto the US while ousting it from its markets in the periphery, as it is to Soviet initiatives. Reagan's Administration consequently seeks to reassert the coercive force of US power, to check and reverse the process of hegemonic decline. It is this purpose that is behind the monetary moves to upgrade the dollar, the collision course with democratic and national liberation movements in Central America, the support for South African aggressions, the resolve to militarize American allies in the Middle East, the provocations in the Gulf of Syrte. The current arms programme of the USA is thus no empty exhibition of bravado, but the necessary foundation of a vast international design.

This military programme itself is something new. Simply in quantitative terms, it is the most gigantic project of investment for war ever recorded. But it is its qualitative novelty that is even more disturbing. If we look at the theatre missiles planned for Europe, the construction of the neutron bomb, and the new insistence on the need for 'civil defence' as an inter-related set of measures, it becomes plain that what they amount to is not a mere programme to enhance existing military potentials, but one intended to render the contingency of a limited and controlled nuclear war technically and materially feasible. It thereby marks the passage from a philosophy of nuclear deterrence to another philosophy, which deems atomic weapons normal instruments of thinkable war, and thinks of total war in terms of preemptive attack.

Is it possible, would it be reasonable for Europe to confirm the decisions taken at the NATO council in 1979 to install the new American missiles, already questionable enough at the time, without taking into account a context that has changed so radically since then? Even in the US itself, it is not difficult to foresee that Reagan's policies are soon going to run into major difficulties—whose initial symptoms are already visible. His promises of economic revival will probably prove as hollow as those of Thatcher. Social tensions and conflicts are likely to intensify. Imperial bullying will provoke local conflicts and no doubt desertions. These very setbacks might then propel the United States even more tragically along the path of bellicose adventure. But they could also engender a broad and effective front of domestic opposition. The war in Vietnam has already shown how difficult it is in practice to mobilize a contemporary capitalist society, divided by corporative interests and pervaded by a crisis of traditional values, for nationalistic goals that involve real costs for the population.

Thus if resistance to Reagan's strategic design could develop early and strongly enough in Europe and elsewhere in the world, it would be possible to bring it into crisis politically rather than through an eventual military conflict as happened in Vietnam. The 'New Right' in the West can and must be confronted now, before it becomes powerful enough to drag us all into its adventures.

Meanwhile, the past year has also seen decisive new developments in the other camp. The Soviet system is currently being shaken by a crisis no less grave than that of the West. The Polish upheaval is no mere repetition of the Prague events of ten years or so ago. Its causes are much deeper, its consequences vastly more far-reaching. For what they reveal, and accelerate, is the cracking of the architrave on which 'actually existing socialism' has always rested: the relationship, or at any rate compromise, between party and working class. This cracking is not simply a product of the national particularity of Poland, or the specific conjuncture of the food crisis there, even if these are the factors which have obviously allowed it to widen. It is also and above all the result of structural processes. For the material basis that ensured modest security of employment, tolerable work rhythms and steady social progress is now failing in Poland, and elsewhere, because the Eastern system of centralized planning has not succeeded in making the transition from a model of simple and extensive to one of complex and intensive growth. At the same time, the ideological mechanisms which once allowed the working class to identify with a power structure that in fact escaped its control, have dissolved—partly for objective historical reasons, but partly also because of subjective options by the ruling groups in these countries. Finally, the system of economic and political privilege which always existed in the East, but in the past remained precarious and subject to perpetual rotation, has now been consolidated into a dominant stratum, perceived as such by the masses, and vitiated more gravely than ever before by incompetence and bureaucratism. The established order has tried for years to postpone the maturation of these contradictions by opening itself in one direction to foreign trade with the West, and in the other by multiplying consumer expectations. But since its opening to the West abroad has not corresponded to any capacity to organize new economic or social mechanisms at home, it has ended by becoming a factor of destabilization—bringing with it foreign debt, financial difficulties and growing distance between authorities and masses. In the Polish case, social rebellion in the working class and national aspirations have become the new and formidable vectors of a revolt that threatens to become contagious.

It is this that explains the fact that for the first time conservative forces within Poland, and their powerful Soviet ally, have hitherto been unable to repress the movement, or deemed it unwise to try to do so. If the Polish experience survives and develops, it can open up a new and unpredictable road for this whole area of the world. But it is also true that one of the peculiar characteristics of the crisis in the East is that the forces of opposition, even when they are so deeply rooted in society as in Poland, typically lack a historical background or a political project capable of providing a coherent immediate alternative. The economic and political crisis thus persists and deepens, teetering at every moment on the verge of an abyss. This should make us realize the real space, and responsibilities, for a European politics aimed at overcoming the blocs. The East of the continent is no less concerned by one than the West; and explosive potential is building up there. If Western Europe responds to the internal crisis of Soviet monolithism (which is now gripping other countries like Romania as well) by simply aligning itself with Reagan's aggressive postures, it is all too probable that everything will end tragically in Eastern Europe. No one can doubt that an invasion of Poland today would have far larger and worse consequences—political and military—than that of Czechslovakia in 1968.

4. The Economy of Hunger and Oil

These then are the very concrete facts and political considerations that make the emergent demands of the new peace movement no vague pacifist utopia born of an understandable fear of war, but a realistic programme derived from a lucid analysis of world politics and of its principal tendencies: in a word, an adequate response to the question—what is it immediately necessary and possible to do to build peace? The task of parties and trade-unions on the European Left is then not to interpret and mediate away this platform, but to transfer it into the seats of public decision-making by doing everything to impose the essential objectives of the movement on national governments and supranational organisms alike.

Yet we cannot rest with these immediate objectives, nor stop at a discourse which still tends to isolate the question of disarmament, and in particular the denuclearization of Europe, one-sidedly from the political, social and economic background which is the real soil of the drive to rearmament, and on whose resolution the fate of peace in the long run must depend. I am thinking above all of that problem which we of the West are continually tempted to evade (or to rediscover sporadically only when some great drama like Vietnam makes it inescapable): the primordial and quintessential structure of exploitation, the vast clot of suffering and violence, that is constituted by underdevelopment and domination of some peoples over others. That domination remains today, in the new forms of economic and technological subordination, as grave as it ever was in the colonial epoch. It is no surprise that most explosive zone in the world today, where immediate occasions for war are most numerous and most probable, is that of the underdeveloped countries. It is there that the majority of the human race struggles for a precarious physical survival, there that tumultuous demographic growth has created new megalopoles of despair, there that the aggressivity of the superpowers is most concentrated and exercised, there that international financial crises loom, there that local wars now multiply.

After the end of the war in Vietnam, it seemed for a time that a new and positive phase might be beginning at last for these regions. A more polycentric metropolitan world appeared to hold out the possibility of more stable national independence in the ex-colonial world. The decentralization of manufactures with which Western capitalism reacted to the growing costs of domestic production, seemed to be creating a new international division of labour that favoured industrial take-off in at least some parts of the periphery: Iran and Brazil, Korea, Mexico and North Africa. The increase in oil and raw material prices for the first time broke the traditional schemas of unequal exchange, and promised new funds for development.

In the event, however, the very rise in oil prices proved to be the trigger of a dynamic of a quite different—indeed opposite—sort. Formally, it looked as if it could lead to a compression of wasteful consumption in the advanced societies, a transfer of resources towards investment in the least privileged regions of the capitalist world, and a progressive reconversion of the patterns of international output and trade. The fact that oil wealth was concentrated in a few countries was no insurmountable obstacle in itself—since in theory nothing prevented a triangular recyling of petrodollar balances from those states which could not fully use them through the advanced economies to countries poorer in industry but richer in labour-power. But for that to occur social and cultural conditions favourable for development had to exist in the Third World, and political and entrepreneurial subjects able or willing to direct such a reconversion in the First World. Above all, moreover, the Western model of development itself had to be extendable on a world scale. None of these conditions obtained.

So the opposite occurred. High oil prices generated fearful balance of payments deficits in the majority of underdeveloped countries, absorbing up to 80% of their export earnings and crushing them with debt interest charges. The type of dependent industrial development towards which they had oriented was now blocked for financial as well as technological reasons. Meanwhile, this model of development—based on starvation wages, organized as a decentralized unit of the metropolis, supported by an avid and deracinated bourgeoisie, administered by a corrupt bureaucracy—proved to be very short-winded in Brazil or North Africa; unleashed a socio-political explosion in Iran; and nearly everywhere aggravated the terrible scourge of food shortages. The result has been that the vast mass of oil capital—finding no reliable outlets for investment and no subjects capable of promoting it—was funnelled back into the international financial markets, unleashing a tidal wave of generalized inflation and speculation. The advanced countries in their turn, gripped by their own crisis, have intensified their mutual competition and fallen back towards protectionism. The final economic outcome of the decade has been disastrous for the Third World: 800 million victims of malnutrition, thwarted projects of industrialization, escalating prices, declining agricultural production.

But the social and political mechanisms set in motion by these processes are no less explosive. The conditions for a new anti-imperialist upsurge are undoubtedly building up. But their forms appear perilously confused and often sterile. In some areas authoritarianism, nationalism and renewed dependence on the United States have been a direct response to the crisis: the Arab conservative regimes, the Latin-American dictatorships, South African racism. In other cases, authentic national liberation movements—Cuba, Angola, Mozambique—have been driven to accept the discipline of the Soviet camp by the military threat from the United States and its local allies, and to reproduce many of the vices of the Soviet model under the pressure of economic hardship and lack of viable alternatives. In still other cases new revolutionary forces, emerging on the broken social and ideological deserts neo-colonialism has left behind, have evolved towards exasperated forms of populism, incapable of furnishing any answer to real problems and therefore seeking imaginary solutions in integralist religion or regressive nationalism. The case of Iran is not a unique one: similar tendencies were already evident in Libya or in the Moroccan opposition well before the fall of the Shah; the return of Indira Gandhi is preparing another version of them in India. The common element in all these different trends, however, is a propensity towards military fortification just as economic and political development encounters increasing difficulties. What perspective, then, can the counterposition of this Third World to a metropolitan world divided into aggressive and antagonistic blocs, proposing an economic model already familiar and already failed, offer—other than new incitement to wars, further cultural and political involution?

Any prospect of a lasting peace needs the emergence of another pole, outside this field of force. Western Europe today possesses—as it did not thirty years ago—the economic, technological and cultural resources to assert its own political autonomy and to help sustain another path of development for the Third World. Non-alignment could then become an effective international reality, the active subject of a different kind of political economy. But for this to occur, of course, two fundamental conditions would be necessary. Firstly, European unification would itself have to advance, as a collective project of the left. The present Europe of bureaucratic 'coordination', of continual stagnation, of furtive competition, of petty corporative interests, has no international future. A constructive world role for the continent presupposes a rediscovery of its real unity, and a creation of common institutions and policies capable of giving effect to a will independent of the two blocs.

More important than its forms, however, would be the content of that unity. For a pervasive crisis is now gripping the metropolitan societies themselves, in the common disarray of our industrialism, our welfare state, our parliamentary institutions, our primary social groups, our forms of conviviality. The problems of the Third and First World are in this sense inseparable from one another. For it is not possible to confront the problem of underdevelopment seriously without putting into question our own ways of producing and consuming, our whole system of values. Any new relationship with the Third World presupposes a qualitative change in our own type of development. Such a change would have to involve a reorientation of the European economies away from the quantitative multiplication of goods for consumption and export, and the wasteage of natural resources that goes with it, towards another style of development: one that was sober in its consumption, exported technology and knowledge rather than commodities, sought a reduction in labour-time performed, gave priority to improvements in the quality of living. Such a model of development would no longer find its centre of gravity in heavy technology and industrial concentration, but in decentralized production and communication systems. It would be based not on the expropriation of nature, but on its reconstruction and valorization. The fact that only this kind of development could be extended to all humanity without breaking against physical barriers of the relative scarcity of resources is its strength. But it is also true that its realization would demand the radical overthrow of the economic tendencies that rule us today, and which the recession accentuates. It could only be the product of an alternative social and political bloc, consciously struggling for the transition to a new kind of socialism.

It is on this terrain that the new peace movement, more than that of 1968, remains uncertain and retarded. Some of its sectors—ecologists, squatters, feminists—are aware of the radical dimensions of the problem, but in a very elementary, confused and nearly always (in this case, genuinely) utopian fashion. The movement as a whole, however, and yet more so the trade-union left within it, has virtually no consciousness of this dimension. It still acts as if peace could be defended without tackling the most difficult nodes of our society and politics, without changing the structures of power in Europe and the world. It would seem as if the disappointments which followed 1968, the painful discovery of the inadequacy of old ideological frameworks, and of the misuse of the most accredited concepts (class, imperialism, socialism), have produced in this new movement a kind of reaction, a reluctance to undertake any global analysis, to define any long-term perspectives. But this state cannot last long. Indeed it is already a brake on common action because certain basic connections impose themselves as of now—for example, between disarmament and reconversion of military industries, between refusal of military blocs and progress towards European unity, between the release of resources by disarmament and their effective use for the development of the Third World, between detente in Europe and resolution of the explosive problems of the Middle East and Central America or Afghanistan.

It is these themes that will separate a passive neutralism, solely and delusively concerned with its own salvation, from an active neutralism looking outwards to new shapes of world development. Let it be clear that in raising them, I in no way wish to cast a suspicion of ambiguity on the movement that is now in gestation. I have already said that the objectives for which it is so effectively fighting are not only absolutely just in themselves, but represent the indispensable premiss of any longer-term policy for peace. I only wish to say that if it is to endure, and develop, this movement has a long road ahead of it, among other things in the growth of its political culture.

In this respect, the political and intellectual forces of the left active within the movement can make a specific contribution that is not just one of support. But it is equally important that the movement itself generate its own means of qualitative growth, in permanent organizational structures and bodies capable of fulfilling its goals and developing its culture. Finally, it is no less vital that it move outwards and make links with other sectors of struggle, actual or potential—workers' struggles for jobs, the struggles of young people and of women for another kind of life, the struggles of all over energy and environment; and with other protagonists of the cause of non-alignment—Yugoslavs, Palestinians, Salvadoreans among many examples. Here too if we are serious about putting the traditional policies of the status quo in question, we cannot avoid the risks of practising politics ourselves.

The Long March for Peace

Etienne Balibar

It is not an easy task for a communist militant in France to intervene in the present international debate on the nuclear arms race; yet it is an urgent one. In most other European countries, both North and South, the mass demonstrations of the last few months have expressed a clear awareness of the danger of escalation and a determination to drive it away. This campaign has put no reliance on the 'good will' of states, and still less on their calculations of 'strategic balance', but has sought instead to mobilize the energies of the men and women marked down as the victims of nuclear 'exterminism' themselves. In France, however, the picture is very different. With the exception of a few courageous initiatives taken by activists—mostly intellectuals—associated with the movement for European Nuclear Disarmament, the country as a whole seems remarkably insensitive to the urgency of the problem. In the fifties the French labour movement, especially the PCF and CGT, was vigorously committed to the peace movement, as it was also (despite certain contradictions) to the struggle against the Vietnam War and Nixon's policies in the sixties and the early seventies. Even today the ideals of the new European peace movement would seem close to those which inspire that sector of the Left which identifies with 'self-management' in France. Yet what we see now is apparently paralysis.

I fear that in these conditions many of our comrades abroad will find the French Left guilty of 'betraying' or abandoning its historical tasks. All the more so, no doubt, in that the causes of this paralysis do indeed lie in certain patterns of political behaviour that are very characteristic of France (but perhaps also of other countries as well), and which may suggest that we are incapable of developing *any alternative* to the practice of the traditionally dominant classes and their political personnel.

Last summer, it is true, the French Communist Party launched a protest campaign against the neutron bomb and the installation of Pershing missiles in Western Europe. But this short-lived initiative inevitably aroused all manner of questions about its political background. The PCF denounced the Pershing missles, but did not breathe a word about the French *force de frappe* which it had unexpectedly endorsed in a spectacular policy-change in 1977. Only at the last minute did the slogans for the 25 October 1981 demonstration formally correct a blatant ideological imbalance, by calling for 'No Pershings, no SS-20s!'. Above all, the ephemeral nature of the campaign may indicate that its main function was to test out the Party's room for manoeuvre, a few months after its election defeat had reduced it to a back-up force for a socialist government. In all likelihood, it was thereupon rapidly reminded that this matter belonged to the President's 'exclusive prerogative', not to 'emulation' among the parties of the new majority. In any event, since the PCF leadership would not run the risk of 'losing control' of the protest, its bureaucratic methods of mobilizing public opinion did not leave much chance of a real popular movement.

At least, however, the Communists—whatever their intentions—have had the merit of raising the issue in France. The Socialist Ministers and the top PS leadership immediately made clear, in both word and deed, their determination to follow the military policy of the previous governments of the Right: not only to continue building nuclear submarines, but also to resist the democratic demands of national servicemen's committees of which Defence Minister Charles Hernu is a resolute opponent. Even more disturbing has been the change of tone in the French press. Breaking with their previous indifferences to the issue, all but a few papers have waged an intensive campaign against the 'Soviet military threat' and the danger of 'Finlandization' of Europe, relentlessly arguing in support of the American policy of military superiority. Francois Mitterand, meanwhile. has conjured up the 'risk' that the strategic balance will shift against the United States in coming years. Naturally enough, the press campaign has exploited the military coup in Poland to the fullest extent. It has also turned its fire on the German peace movement, which one left-wing daily went so far as to label *Nazionalneutralismus*. The traditional right-wing press has been joined in a common front by far-left, 'libertarian' papers, some of the same signatures appearing in both. Yet the fact that this *militarist* tendency stretches right across the traditional political spectrum does not, unfortunately, prove that a broad *anti-militarist* movement could also hope to find support among all classes and parties!

The weakness and division of the resistance in France to the renewed dangers of war today calls for collective reflexion and public discussion, without preconceptions or exclusions. In my view, the problem stems from something deeper than the mere mistakes, shortcomings or even scleroses of the political and trade-union apparatuses of the Left. If the Socialist Party is paralysed by its position as 'the party of government'; if the Communist Party, now 'in the government' and drawing the CGT in with it, wavers between the temptation to take up the question to regain an audience of its own and the weight of its allegiance to the USSR; if the CFDT is immobilized by its attempt to combine anti-nuclear positions with a certain return to Atlanticism—all this is so, because of objective contradictions which run deep in French society and within the labour movement, heavily affecting the present situation itself.

For this very reason, however, French 'backwardness' could have a beneficial side-effect. For it may help to focus our attention—and when I say 'our', I am also thinking of comrades in neighbouring countries—on *the reality of the contradictions and obstacles* which the movement for peace and disarmament will have to overcome before it acquires the scope and level of support to have an effective impact on events. Some of these contradictions are, no doubt, particularly strong or salient in France. To say this is *in no way to set prior conditions* for a commitment to militant anti-war activity, it is rather to consider how the developing movement can dispel certain ambiguities which break, block or weaken it. For the problems of war, imperialism and international relations do not lend themselves to simple or spontaneous solutions—even, or above all, if they find their common point of concentration in a race towards an 'apocalypse' in which the alternative is All or Nothing (mutual survival or extermination); and even if the stark simplicity of this alternative drives hundreds of thousands, potentially millions, of people to search for a way out of it.

There is no simple solution, because although nuclear blackmail seeks here and now to force the masses to 'choose' between submission and death, and threatens to issue in death ultimately anyway, the victims of this blackmail have at the same time to fight *a plurality of struggles*, for the survival of civilization, but also for independence and against exploitation. They cannot be asked to sacrifice one of these struggles to any other. Nor is it the submergence of the specificity of these struggles beneath a single resounding concept, whether imperialism or exterminism, that will make them converge in a common front against the inhuman 'system' which called them all into being. If the peace movement is to arouse the broadest masses of people durably, it must have great ideals that are clear to everyone, and *therefore* must also possess deep roots in their material conditions of life and struggle. Bombs may rain down from the sky, but the collective 'act of self-determination' for which Edward Thompson calls cannot fall from heaven. Indeed that is why he, and others like him, are sparing no effort to create the concrete conditions for the exercise of such an act. These conditions will no more result from the sheer 'logic' of capitalism and the class struggle, than they will from pure 'will' or the 'conversion' of everyone to hopes of peace. The fight against exterminism will be fought with men and women as they are, or it will not be fought at all. It is the struggle itself that can gradually transform them into 'new' people, possessed of greater liberty and solidarity with one another. Hence the crucial importance of the movement that has *already begun* in Europe and elsewhere; without it the major problems could not even be posed.

These problems undeniably exist, however. The boundary-line between hypocritical or unwitting compromise with the system and genuine capacity to engage with real contradictions is not one traced out in advance. Thus in my view, no concessions should be made in insisting that the French *force de frappe* belongs to the global arsenal of nuclear escalation, or that, in Africa and elsewhere, the French socialist government is willy-nilly imbricated in the same imperialist relations as were its predecessors. On the other hand, can we oppose—in the name of pure principles'—French (or Cuban, or Soviet) arms supplies to Nicaragua, Angola or Mozambique, whose poverty-stricken peoples have to defend themselves day in and day out against the most powerful colonial and neo-colonial armies on earth? But then is it possible to reject *a priori* the argument, doubtless present in the mind of many Socialist Party members, according to which Mitterand's partial (provisional?) support for Reagan's claims of 'strategic imbalance' is a clever way of keeping his hands free to counter US imperialism on other terrains, for example with aid to certain liberation movements in the Third World? We have to demonstrate *concretely* that any such calculation—if it exists—is doomed to failure, and that there is a real alternative. But we are still a long way from that.

Similarly, it is not enough to assert that 'in the last analysis', the peace movement in the West has the same goal as the popular struggles in the East against 'socialist' oppression and exploitation. It must be concretely shown that they can assist and reinforce each other, at a time when sizeable forces tend to paralyse both by *counterposing them* in the real world. The contradiction is only sharpened by the fact that, after a year and a half of intense class struggles, the revolutionary process in Poland has for the moment concluded in a military coup. Of course, this is just one result among others of the 'logic of Yalta', which divided the world between opposed 'empires' and instituted a 'balance of terror'. But we now have to prove that a movement against that logic *can* give effective support to the Polish revolution which it will certainly not receive from the sanctions brandished by Reagan and Thatcher, whose function is simply to re-establish a Cold War consensus in empires and countries gangrenous with a crisis of their own.

These are very real contradictions, then. They result neither from illusions generated by the system, nor from propaganda orchestrated by its defenders. Only if they are directly faced, from several sides at once, without preordained theoretical 'solutions', will it eventually be possible to build a new internationalism. My own conviction is that not insignificant forces already exist for this.

Our 'Socialism' and the International Context

The rebirth—to general amazement—of a great peace movement in Europe, starting from Britain, the Netherlands, Germany and the Scandinavian countries, is a major historical event. It also affords an opportunity we in France must absolutely seize. For even if it should encounter all manner of obstacles in the immediate future, this movement both helps us and compels us to try to discern the convergence of different forces which alone can challenge the imperialist tendencies in the world around us. If the vital task is to discover new political practices, and the new forms of internationalism necessary to that end, then it offers us *one* element of a solution.

Whatever the press would have us believe in France, the peace movement is neither a chance development without a past or future, nor the simple result of a psychosis of fear. The young Germans, for example, who stand in the front line against the installation of Cruise and Pershing missiles, no doubt preparing themselves for harsh repression, are in no way a pack of overfed cowards fearful for their own tranquillity. They represent a responsible and conscious popular force, in a country already riddled with atomic weapons. Indeed, it is this that has allowed them to reject the blackmail of Western governments that is an essential part of the system of escalating terror. Together with hundreds of thousands of British, Dutch and Italian demonstrators, they have made their priority the struggle against *our* Western militarism, demanding *unilateral* measures of disarmament if necessary. Thereby they have already upset 'the rules of the game' and begun to endow 'pacifism' with a new meaning. It is, of course, no accident that the movement has sprung up at a time when unemployment is reaching new heights in every European country, including West Germany. Yet behind it lie years of revolt and reflection in West Germany on the ideology of 'security', on the real meaning of 'the strong state', and on the military-industrial model of capitalist society which is no longer even a Welfare State for all. Most crucially, there seems to be a determination and capacity to go beyond the web of terrorism and counter-terrorism which threatened to ensnare every initiative critical of the established social order in the Federal Republic.

But should we not also reckon the electoral victory of the French Left another factor helping to upset the 'strategic balances' of domination? Everyone knows that the new socialist government aroused great hopes throughout the world: above all, in national liberation movements fighting with their back to the wall, and in countries making the most serious effort at independent development. Their hopes may be exaggerated and premature, but for their sake as well as ours it is vitally important to give them body and reality. To do that presupposes the political autonomy of Europe, which a socialist experiment in France would already help to make more credible.

It is sometimes said that the victories at the polls of May–June 1981 were just a mechanical effect of an 'erosion of power' which, in the present crisis of advanced capitalism, produces 'swings to the left' here and 'swings to the right' elsewhere. However, this does not seem to me a serious explanation, for it overlooks the fact that the new French government arose out of a long process rooted in mass social struggles. No doubt, coming after the decline of the elan of 1968 and the deplorable break-up of the Union of the Left in 1978, it was a 'last chance'. But the workers of this country knew how to seize this last (and therefore first) chance. What we must now understand is that no projects of social transformation will take any concrete shape in the absence of an active popular movement, and that such a movement will never be born from a hermetic cultivation of 'socialism in freedom' or 'a national solution to the crisis'.

For any consistent attempt to base the socialist experiments in France on 'a new international order' will inevitably involve a clash with the logic of imperialism, and especially with American interests. A whole section of the French Left accepts, at least in words, that the axis of mutal aid between North and South must as far as possible prevail over confrontation between East and West. This is crucial, too, if the French workers' movement is to overcome those false paths and historical lags which stem both from its relative weakness vis-à-vis 'our' national imperialism and from its own divisions. Nor is this all. Government 'decisions' are not here the critical element—or, rather, they will only assume a clear character and take the necessary risks of confronting external constraints and threatened interests if there gradually develops a movement of sufficient strength and cohesion, in which social demands are fused with anti-imperialist goals and the struggle for peace and disarmament. Instead of abstractly wondering whether the French 'socialist project' (which has hardly begun even on paper) corresponds to such and such a progressive theoretical requirement, we would do better to ask ourselves how the conditions could arise for it to develop or be compelled in that direction. The dramatic openness of European youth to mass movements and world-wide liberation struggles is obviously one favourable condition.

At this point, I would like to dwell for a moment on the international context of the French socialist experiment. This context has a crucial European dimension. The experience of the last few years is sufficient proof that the 'supra-national' perspective offered by the most diverse ideologies is nothing but a myth. National social formations are, and will remain, the principal framework within which the political orientations of various classes and social forces actually crystallize. Nevertheless, a distinctively European *political space* has now existed for a number of years, structured by state institutions, an economic balance of forces, and class strategies which cannot merely be reduced to the traditional political space. So far, the initiative in this respect has always belonged to capitalist governments and companies interested in extending their activity across frontiers, and as such it has continually divided and weakened the workers' movement. In fact, the 'building of Europe' has always served as a gigantic outflanking manoeuvre designed to shift, at least in appearance, the site of political decisions beyond the reach of class struggles. For their part, the unions have never been able to co-ordinate activity at the same level, even when mass struggles have broken out simultaneously against similar plans for unemployment and industrial restructuring (as for example, in 1978 in Lorraine and the Ruhr). Eurocommunism, in its ascendant phase, could not or did not know how to transcend the ossified divisions of the European workers' movement; still less can it do this in its present state of decomposition.

At a time when world economic crisis and sharper rivalry among capitalist powers are opening up deep contradictions between the interests and policies of European states, *the labour movement has still not overcome this historical lag.* Quite the contrary. This is a formidable source of weakness for any process of social transformation in France or elsewhere. We should therefore unhesitatingly welcome and support any progressive movement whose mass, Europe-wide character helps to correct this imbalance. For then the European political space is no longer just the arena of NATO, the Brussels Commission, the banks and the 'currency snake'—it also includes popular initiatives, such as meetings between major labour-movement organizations (or significant parts of them), as well as deep aspirations of young people, intellectuals, women. Or, at least, it could include these.

However, the international context has another, inseparable side to it.

The present capitalist crisis is inherently also a structural crisis of the imperialist 'division of the world'. Jean-Pierre Vigier has shown in a recent article[1] the menace represented in these conditions by the arrival in power of an American government determined to practise a form of 'unbridled liberalism' in external policy, to repress by force any organized opposition to US domination (or the dictatorships it protects), and to ground its political offensive on an unprecedented development of the arms race.

Of course, this imperialist drive stems from growing difficulties in the fight against popular resistance in the superexploited and martyrized Third World—difficulties which, even before the Iranian revolution, rapidly dispelled the flights of concern with 'human rights', or rather brought out their true content. At the same time, American and US-based multi-national capital has lost ground in the face of Japanese and European (mainly West German) competition. Before it is too late—that is to say, before the United States loses its massive economic superiority—an attempt is therefore being made to reverse the process if necessary, by bringing the whole world to the brink of the precipice. 'We should not underestimate Reagan', Vigier has rightly argued, 'he is no more a B-movie cowboy than Hitler was a failed painter. The success of such men merely testifies to the profound mutation in the social forces which carry them to power. The fires of nationalism and great-power chauvinism will mark the new America of the 1980s'.

The current crisis is thus plainly leading both to sharper East–West confrontation, and to heightened antagonism *among* the imperialist powers. Far from being braked as a result, the 'logic' of military escalation which characterizes the world supranational system is being hugely strengthened. A third world war is still one possible outcome, unfortunately a prospect more dire and devastating than ever before. For during the Cold War of the fifties and sixties, there was an overall balance between two blocs, very unequal and profoundly dissimilar in social character, yet both dominated by a 'superpower' that held an absolute monopoly of political and military initiative.

If the present relationship of forces between capitalist powers is simply extrapolated into the future, apocalyptic visions cannot fail to suggest themselves. We know from the last few decades, however, that history does not follow such a linear course. The logic of imperialism, of which the 'irrational' arms race is an integral part, meets resistance *at the very heart* of the system, as well as of course from liberation struggles against it. Whatever was the role played by nuclear 'deterrence'—about which we could speculate at length—the Vietnam War would not have ended in a defeat for imperialism if the patriotic struggle of the Vietnamese people had not combined with the movement of the American people against the aggression of the US State in Indochina. Movements like this may break out anew; and insofar as the internal development and external policy of the Soviet bloc have become increasingly moulded by the same imperialist logic, the new historical stage of democratic and national struggles within the socialist countries must also be counted among the inner forces of resistance to it. Even if at the same time the development of this *other crisis*, in its origins relatively independent of the world economic crisis, serves in its own way to render the international situation even more perilous.

A Super-Imperialism?

It is these contradictions, together with the realities of popular resistance, which should be our starting-point for an analysis of the contemporary imperialist system that may, if need be, fundamentally correct our inherited images of it. The 'exterminist' process is incontestably revealing of the character of the system: its effects extend into every field of social life, from production to culture. Yet if we are to gain any purchase on these effects, we must do more than simply record their infernal logic. Exterminism, as Thompson rightly observes, is a *social relation*, like machine-production or the conquest of the world by European and North American armies. It does not, therefore, reproduce itself automatically. We must examine all the aspects of its reproduction if we are to discover not only its *origin* but also—above all—its future *direction*. Let us begin with some hard facts.

It is impossible to overemphasize the major danger posed by the present policy of US imperialism. From the standpoint of the Third World, the United States is of course still the main enemy of liberation struggles, constantly intervening to maintain or re-establish the conditions for capitalist pillage and to widen the scope of its exploitation within 'a new international division of labour'. This new division of labour, based on present-day technology, in no way involves full use of the human resources furnished by the earth's soaring demography, but rather creates zones of exploitation of interest to multinationals chiefly concerned to corner scarce raw materials; it may indeed be accompanied by a repression so systematic as to involve physical annihilation of anything that moves—not the least important form of exterminism. I do not know whether the present stockpiles of strategic weaponry are in mathematical 'equilibrium': anyway, that is only a crucial issue if we situate the debate within the framework of a terror which fuels escalation and objectively paves the way for war. The fact remains that the global configuration of the conflict between 'blocs' stems from the strategy of expansion and encirclement which American imperialism, despite all its temporary or local setbacks, has methodically pursued for many decades.

This principal aspect of the danger of war no longer, however, operates in isolation. Over the last twenty years, the position of the socialist camp on the world arena has undergone a complete transformation. Encircled from the start, and then wracked by internal crises, it has tried to combat this American strategy with one of the same kind. The socialist countries are themselves now caught up in the logic of inter-imperialist relationships, even, indeed above all, at the military level. This has critically affected the evolution of the state and the relations of production within them, as well as generating an ideology ever more clearly marked by nationalism. Thus, when the PCF leadership, among others, persists in talking of 'the improvement in the world balance of forces', not only does its posture seem absurd in relation to the mounting crisis of 'actually existing socialism', but it also keeps alive the worst kind of mystification. From Czechoslovakia to Afghanistan, from the Sino-Vietnamese to the Vietnamese—Cambodian conflict (which led in turn to the Vietnamese occupation of Cambodia), a tendency towards imperialist international relationships has increasingly prevailed over the struggle against exploitation and underdevelopment. Indeed, this logic becomes dominant even as it expresses a worsening relationship of forces for the 'socialist camp'.

As Brecht already feared at the time of the German—Soviet Pact and the invasion of Poland,[2] the socialist states as such have long been incapable of representing *by themselves* a revolutionary, anti-imperialist force in the world. It is not their existence or example which arouses revolutionary movements in other countries. Yet at the same time they confront national liberation struggles with a dramatic dilemma. The power of Western neo-colonialism makes 'self-reliance' an absolutely necessary, yet not a sufficient option. *To whom can they turn, then, if not the USSR and some of its allies?* Yet, how can they do this without becoming hostages of Soviet foreign policy, and thus of the 'strategic' calculations imposed by the arms race between two superpowers? How can they avoid entering into a new economic and political dependence that severely curbs the possibility of an original socialism, at once viable and liveable? The Angolans, Mozambiquans and Vietnamese experience this contradiction every day of the week. Nor is it a secret that Cuba's efforts to strengthen the unity and autonomy of the Non-Aligned Movement were torpedoed by the Soviet intervention in Afghanistan. This action placed a socialist country for the first time in a situation of direct colonial war, at the very moment when US policy-makers were dropping the mask of 'human rights' and openly reviving the principles that led to Vietnam and Chile.

I do not see how we can separate this development from *the progressive reintegration of the socialist countries into the world capitalist market*. Usually operating through the mechanism of state-guaranteed long-term credits, this reintegration offers the multinationals huge openings into the Eastern-bloc markets, tending to subordinate them to the imperialist process of accumulation with its characteristic division of labour. It thus makes it possible to play off the socialist countries against one another, and to insert them in the process of inter-imperialist competition (for example, through the delivery of fully equipped factories and advanced technologies against future supplies of food, raw materials and manufactured goods below West European prices). Although only part of their economy is integrated in this way, the phenomenon has gravely affected the 'division of labour' among the socialist countries themselves. It did not, of course, *create* the social contradictions which led to the current political crisis in the East. But it has manifestly accelerated and aggravated their evolution. (One has only to think of Poland's 27 billion dollar external debt, which resulted from the 'flight forward' of the Gierek government from rising workers' demands.) It has thereby directly contributed to the present instability in these countries. We must recognize that the process is irreversible: the clock cannot be turned back to an autarkic, centralized 'socialist camp'; the only way out is a sweeping transformation, whether violent or peaceful, of 'actually existing socialism'.

If these points are correct, then the 'balance of forces' on a world scale simultaneously involves three aspects: a heightening of the antagonism between blocs; 'isomorphism' of their military strategies; and, contradictory though it may seem, a progressive reintegration of the socialist economies into a single world market, dominated by rivalry among the big capitalist powers and the exigencies of intensive accumulation. These heterogeneous tendencies do, however, point to a single interpretative hypothesis that I shall now try to formulate as a contribution to the debate initiated by Thompson.

It is doubtless true that we are no longer in the period of classical 'imperialism', whose definition in any case needs to be re-examined. But nor are we in that period of 'ultra-imperialism' which certain Second International Marxists understood as the transcendence of national antagonisms within a single multinational 'trust'. Rather, things seem to have developed in the *opposite* direction, including a revival of militarism. Since the reality of 'superpowers' is an unmistakable one today, I shall refer to the present phenomenon as *super-imperialism*: not, that is to say, the 'fusion' of imperialisms and growing uniformity of their social relations, but the rise of *new* political and economic structures which allow imperialism as a world system *to control, encompass and reverse the course of socialism itself* by exploiting its internal contradictions. This is a 'post-revolutionary' imperialism, then, although not in the sense that there are no longer any revolutions. Rather, these have constantly to face *both* preventive counter-revolution *and* the uninterrupted reconstitution of relationships of domination and exploitation on the ground of 'actually existing socialism' with its étatism and its planning. A two-way *circulation of state forms*—including in the first instance military technology—between countries 'with different social systems' is one characteristic feature of super-imperialism. Like its predecessor, the latter is no flawless mechanism. But the great task facing the men and women of our time is to analyse its contradictions and to develop new forms of struggle (and organization) which will help popular movements to loosen its hold on us.

At this very moment, events in Poland are casting a brutal yet illuminating light on all these questions. It is a simple and obvious fact that the revolutionary movement of Polish workers incarnated in Solidarity, which drew in behind it peasants and intellectuals, expressed particularly clear forms of class struggle that were inseparably bound up with democratic and national demands. For its part, the Polish ruling caste not only represented the interests of the 'Soviet bloc' and defended its own politico-economic privileges (what is euphemistically known as 'corruption'); it also managed the unequal exchange between the surplus-labour of Polish workers and Western finance capital. This *twofold dependence* partially explains why even in certain western circles the Polish coup could quite untruthfully be described as an 'internal affair'.

While the European situation is now only remotely connected with the agreements reached thirty-five years ago, François Mitterand touched on a critical issue when he said that the Polish events proved the need to challenge the division of the continent at Yalta—although, of course, such a challenge must attack the reservation of the Western half of it to capitalism as well. It is a far cry, however, from this very general thesis to a concrete programme of action against the structures of the two blocs. In the meantime, their very antagonism allows the social status quo to be everywhere preserved, while at the same time it in no way guarantees—quite the contrary—that the international 'equilibria' of domination will remain forever stable.

Dispelling Some Ambiguities

Nevertheless, we should not imagine that, by virtue of some fortunate angelism, the manual and intellectual workers of France (or other countries) have a *clearly perceived* material interest in a thoroughgoing campaign for nuclear disarmament. Although such a course does, indeed, correspond to their long-term interests, tens of thousands now live on the arms industries or their technological 'spin-offs'. As is well known, France not only has its *force de frappe*, but is one of the main arms-suppliers to the Third World. The 'conversion' of these industries is, in fact, one of the greatest difficulties facing any attempt to transform present industrial structures and to redistribute the labour-time of society among the various sectors and products. The problems become more acute, and potentially explosive, in times of high unemployment and unstable foreign markets.

This kind of problem can only be really tackled within a socialist perspective. In a recent work,[3] Christian Baudelot, Roger Establet and Jacques Toiser have shown with remarkable clarity the extent to which 'two centuries of bourgeois domination have moulded the structure of the active population, organized the productive apparatus, and shaped landscapes and regions according to the needs and designs of the class in power'. 'The capitalist production apparatus,' they continue, 'consists of rigid compartments—whole networks of production and transmission adapted to the existing class structure. As such, it cannot be placed overnight in the service of the popular classes'. Especially since, in a manner of speaking, they live off that apparatus. The direct or indirect militarization of a growing segment of production is not a 'foreign body' within the productive apparatus, but a part of the 'needs and designs' which materially regulate productivity and the utilization of the surplus. Conversely, a root-and-branch reorganization of social production could release huge monetary, material and human resources for collective consumption, rationalizing and easing work-loads, expanding development aid, and rendering foreign trade more secure. This evident contradiction threatens to divide the workers against themselves. It is therefore necessary to pose the problem very clearly, not only at the level of intellectuals, parties, government and public pressure groups, but above all *at the level of the trade unions*, which are alone capable of launching a mass debate on the question.

When they chose to elect a government which proposed to fight the crisis through *a reduction in work-time* rather than the methods of 'neo-liberalism', the French workers probably did not make a very sophisticated economic analysis. But they did show that they were ready to discuss the relationship between fundamental changes in the system of production and their most immediate material demands. Any given pattern of production involves a specific social structure of consumption. So far as present-day society is concerned, the 'consumption' of weapons is one of the most ponderous forms of 'mass consumption'.

Perhaps we can assist debate here by dispelling some ambiguities. At the risk of shocking the reader or committing a gross error, I would include among these the notion that nuclear weapons and nuclear energy are essentially one single force of actual or potential destruction which call for identical forms of mobilization against them. Of course, there is no watertight separation between these two questions: the same industrial plant can have civilian and military uses; while the same military-industrial complex pushes with all its might for the construction of both nuclear power-stations *and* nuclear submarines or intercontinental missiles. A new qualitative and quantitative level has been reached since the time when Krupp or Schneider manufactured tanks and artillery alongside locomotives and hydroelectric turbines, or when Boeing and Tupolev produced both strategic bombers and civil aircraft. It is not by accident, nor by some artificial linkage, that the peace movement in Northern Europe has rooted itself in the solid tradition of ecological struggles for 'a different kind of growth'. Those struggles have been directed against a militarized police society of universal electronic surveillance, induced by an 'all-nuclear option' in energy.

There can be no question, then, of dissolving anxieties about 'civilian' nuclear industry with a simple return to traditional pacifism or bare anti-militarism. For these reflect genuine concern for the safety of workers and local communities, while the development of 'high-risk' technologies, even more centralized and statified than anything before them, poses a threat to personal and political freedoms. Nevertheless, the word 'nuclear' must not become a new fetish—a 'Thing' as Thompson would say—a bogey to bemuse the masses or ourselves. Politics, including mass politics, is the art of drawing distinctions and winning acceptance of them. I would therefore suggest that the debate has everything to gain from exploring the conditions of the distinction between nuclear weapons and nuclear energy, or rather the transformation of these conditions. It may be that nuclear energy corresponds, for the moment, to a requirement of current production. But even if there are different views on the constraints, benefits and dangers of nuclear power, all the forces resolutely determined to break the infernal logic of the arms race can come together in a fruitful unity. Perhaps we may also assume that the struggle against nuclear weapons will create better conditions for a struggle to ensure democratic control over 'civilian' use of this source of energy. Certainly the links

between the two, and between the interests threatened by such a
movement, make this a worthwhile wager.

Active Neutralism

Voluntarist methods, resorting to propaganda to 'force' the barriers to
popular mobilization, will not be capable of solving any of the problems
raised so far. I have tried to situate the problems of nuclear weaponry in
what seems to be a more concrete framework, and not at all to minimize
their gravity. Yes: the fact that nuclear arms have existed for nearly forty
years, with ever greater destructive capacity, has had a determining
influence on our history. It has qualitatively altered the risks to humanity,
while it has at the same time increased, if that were possible, the power of
ruling classes and castes over their subject populations. Yet a certain lack of
awareness—not to say a certain 'European' hypocrisy—is involved in any
isolation of this question from *the endemic state of war* in which most of the
world has been living, or rather dying, ever since the existence of the
'nuclear umbrella' gave out that the Apocalypse was suspended over our
head by the slender thread of the 'Hot Line'. Pershing and Cruise, the
SS-20s, the French nuclear submarines and silos on the Plateau of Albion,
do not belong to another world from the bombers in Vietnam, the paras in
Kabul, Belfast or Bangui, the tanks in Warsaw and Santiago, and the
anti-guerrilla helicopters in El Salvador. They form part of the same system.
In the present period, as atomic weapons proliferate to China, Israel, India,
South Africa, soon to Argentina, Iraq, Pakistan and others, and as 'tactical'
nuclear weapons are brought into service and the development of chemical
and biological weapons is speeded up, the gap between 'conventional' and
'nuclear' is constantly closing. The whole apparatus of destruction is passing
to a higher level and already functioning in various 'theatres'; while the
'irrational' character of the scenarios of deterrence and pre-emptive attack
may cause *any* armed conflict to set off a chain reaction.

At the same time, precisely at the moment when a mass peace movement
is growing in the West, the countries of Eastern Europe have been shaken
by the mightiest revolutionary wave since the last war, in the struggle of
the Polish people. Now that the possibility of compromise between state
power and popular forces has collapsed in Poland, it is still more crucial to
ask ourselves how these two movements, with a common aspiration to
freedom, can avoid being instrumentalized against each other. I see no
other solution than tireless work to build a large, diverse and independent
European movement, rooted in its own variant forms in East and West,

which will campaign for *progressive disarmament* and *the dissolution of military blocs*. The struggle of French and British workers and the revolt of German youth against their 'authoritarian constitutional state' can assist the growth of such a movement, just as the Polish people has already objectively contributed to it. Marxist and non-Marxist labour organizations, Christians, libertarian currents, social-democrats—all can unambiguously participate. We may even see the involvement of some East European communists: not only dissidents, but even those ruling communists who, as in Hungary, seem to be searching for a 'third path'.

It must be said that a number of French historical traditions here require serious critical examination—especially the double-edged legacy of Gaullism, which includes not only the Phnom-Penh speech but also the *force de frappe*, to which first the Socialist Party and then the Communist Party have officially rallied. The existence of this nuclear force became associated in people's minds with a policy of 'independence' which was never more than a fiction, or increasingly turned into one, except insofar as it coincided with a clash of inter-imperialist interests. Today, France—pregnant with a 'transition' for which a number of fragile yet precious conditions have already been present for a year or so—still inherits its own imperialist position within the international system of dependence and exploitation (most clearly in the case of Africa) and the system of world militarism, just as it inherits all the other structures of French capitalism.

The present world upheaval requires the French Left to think clearly about the real content of national independence, and to set as its conscious goal not a nominal 'withdrawal' from but *the effective dissolution of* NATO. But how can this be persuasively argued, in such a way as to mobilize support, if the question of the Warsaw Pact is not posed in the same breath? For it has to be shown that such demilitarization will not proceed at the expense of the workers and peoples of Eastern Europe. Our objectives, then, will be at once difficult and necessary: to overcome the division between the two Germanies, to reactivate the Rapacki Plan, and to create a nuclear-free zone 'from Portugal to Poland'.

In this perspective, we may gradually be able to dispel the ambiguities which still afflict the notions of *pacifism* and *neutralism*. Since Munich and the last World War, since 'non-intervention' in the Spanish Civil War, the term 'pacifism' has had a deservedly negative connotation in France, particularly for the workers' movement. It puts many people off today. Matters are very different in Germany, for good reason! There, despite thirty years of official Atlanticism, its currency is one of the great moral victories of the present movement. The ideas of peace, then, do not have a self-contained meaning fixed for all time. When circumstances permit and demand it, they lend themselves not to resignation, but—becoming profoundly revolutionary forces—to *active* historical intervention. Around them it is possible for workers and young intellectuals to link up with very broad popular aspirations.

Marx, himself, at the height of US-British tension during the American Civil War, already pointed out that the working class was capable of 'appearing on the historical stage no longer as a docile executant, but as an independent force . . . capable of dictating peace where its self-styled masters are calling for war'.[4] Later, in the early years of the twentieth century, social-democracy fatally underestimated the difficulties which militate, even in its own ranks, against the adoption of such a historical course. Yet the Zimmerwald and Kienthal conferences of the socialist left, held in the midst of the carnage of 1914–18, pointed in the direction indicated by Marx, this time with more clearly revolutionary perspectives that were partially translated into reality. As we know, they were also one moment in the eventual formation of communist parties. Although the conditions and potential bases of struggle today are very different, it does not seem utopian—although, I agree, it will not be easy—to fight for an *active neutralism* that will go beyond the traditional meaning of the word. Already the slogan 'No Pershings, no SS-20s!' takes us some of the way.

Through his essay on 'the logic of exterminism', Edward Thompson has greatly helped the peace movement to unite and organize against the projects of NATO 'modernization' and a 'new balance' of terror. Arguing that this logic tends to replace politics with automatic technological and strategic mechanisms, he writes: 'The very notion of "political" options becomes increasingly incredible'. This certainly poses a very real threat. The menace does not stem merely from the new techniques of war, however, but also from a social structure in which the problems of peace and war, 'security', armaments and international politics are part of *a special domain* closed to simple individuals like you and me. For, by definition, 'the masses' are supposed to understand nothing of such matters. The entire practice of states, and of political parties insofar as they base their decisions solely on state interests, tends to confirm that things happen in this way. The PCF is a good case in point: after consulting 'its' experts and updating 'its' analysis of the international relationship of forces, it suddenly made a complete about-turn and sprung its support for the *force de frappe* on a dumbfounded membership.

The monopoly of 'experts' can be broken by public debate that is at once patient and persistent. It is not utopian to think in terms of a mass political culture that will legitimately include a balance-sheet of 'the world relationship of forces', the present contours of imperialism in all its forms, and various 'military' questions. Such a culture would increase the field of possibilities for a transformation of our own society. Only when it is in possession of it will the French Left cease to be, on one crucial issue, the *petrified hostage of its own government*. Instead of passively awaiting a decision from above or holding forth against the government's 'mistakes' and 'betrayals', it could then actively pave the way for a progressive change in its policies.

Only in this way, too, will we begin to see a democratic impetus *from below* towards an independent Europe of the workers and revolutionary youth, standing in solidarity with the oppressed peoples of the whole world. Without this last, French 'socialism' will eventually face a mere choice between its own defeat, and repression of the disappointed hopes of those who have sought and prepared it for fifteen years or more.

[1]"L'Offensive Reagan", *Franc-Tireur*, No. 1, November–December 1981.
[2]Bertolt Brecht, *Arbeitsjournal*, Frankfurt 1973; see particularly the entries for 18 September 1939 and 1 January 1940.
[3]*Qui Travaille Pour Qui?*, Paris 1980.
[4]Marx Address of the International Workingmen's Association to the National Labour Union of the United States of America (May 1869) Marx and Engels, *Werke*, vol. 16, p. 355.

The USSR and the Arms Race

Roy Medvedev
Zhores Medvedev

In face of what Edward Thompson has called the 'present war crisis', we welcome the invitation from our comrades in the peace movements and anti-nuclear campaigns of Western Europe to join in a cooperative project of dialogue and action. We want to reassure them that despite the barriers thrown up by the official media—West and East—there are Soviet citizens who hear their voices and share their deep concern about the peace of Europe and the world. Precisely because of the urgency of the situation, however, we must be patient in trying to understand the sometimes different premises and experiences that lie behind our respective perceptions of the present crisis. In particular we would like to respond—critically yet with positive solidarity—to the very powerful arguments on behalf of a movement for European Nuclear Disarmament that Edward Thompson has recently advanced for discussion by the left. It is important for peace forces in the West to understand why much of the argument that Thompson makes so eloquently would not be received with the same agreement or unanimity by the peace forces within the Soviet Union.

By 'peace forces' we do not mean the official Soviet bureaucracy or Party apparatus, but the ordinary Soviet public whose fierce aversion to war has been conditioned by the historical tragedy—still vivid and haunting to all generations—of twenty million dead and twenty million more wounded and disabled in the fight against the German invasion. In particular, we think that the rank and file of Soviet society, including many of those who contest bureaucratic authority within it, would be unlikely to accept Thompson's argument—so central to his analysis of the dynamic of 'exterminism'—that responsibility for the current crisis can be divided equally between the USA and the USSR. Moreover, as partisans of socialist democracy in the Soviet Union ourselves (and thus, 'Soviet dissidents'), we are also unable to agree with what seems to us to be the too fatalistic assessment made by Thompson. In representing a symmetry between the

aggressive impulses of the American war machine and the equally
'dangerous inertial push' of the Soviet military-industrial complex, we
think that Thompson overlooks important contrasts between the nature of
American and Soviet society. In the interests of a realistic understanding of
the current crisis and the tasks facing the peace movement, we cannot
accept the notion of a functional equivalence between the 'deep structures
of the Cold War' within both blocs.

Such ideas obscure, in our opinion, major differences in the bipolar
confrontation—whether we consider the institutional role of military
spending, official attitudes toward the usage of nuclear weapons, the
history of previous attempts at arms limitation, popular perceptions of
nuclear policy, the problem of proliferation or the ultimate logics of
strategic rivalry. In the notes that follow, we try to indicate some of the
asymmetries which we feel are most relevant to understanding the origin of
the present arms race. It is of course true that Western societies are more
open to analysis than the USSR, where state decisions are shrouded in
much greater secrecy, and information about military strategy or
technology is especially rigorously kept from the citizenry. Readers should
bear this limitation in mind as we try to set Soviet actions and responses
since 1945 in context: in some cases, moves by the USSR can only be
subject to speculation. Nevertheless, despite the more open character of
American society, we will argue that the role of successive US
administrations has been, and continues to be, more provocative and less
predictable in the global inter-relationship between East and West.

A Soviet Military-Industrial Complex?

Military-industrial complexes exist in all modern industrial societies, but
these are under much less responsible control in the United States than in
the USSR. Undoubtedly military-industrial-research interests in the Soviet
Union exercise important influence over the selection of particular weapons
programmes and the manner of their production, but it would be wrong to
suggest that they have ever acquired any control over the long-term
strategic policies of the Soviet government—whether under Stalin,
Khrushchev or Brezhnev. They do not constitute a 'state within a state' as
they do in the United States, but remain a subordinate part of the state.
Thus we believe Edward Thompson is mistaken to believe a situation could
ever reach the point in the Soviet Union when 'hair-trigger military
technology annihilated the very moment of "politics" '.[2] The Soviet system
is too conservative and densely bureaucratized for this to happen. If the
government and Party apparatus do not allow any freedom of action even

for editors of small and obscure provincial publications; if they refuse to allow any film or play to be presented without a special session at the Ministry of Culture; if they ban the formation of any professional association without state and Party authorization; and if not a single person can go abroad without approval of several different Party 'travel commissions' (not to speak of local and regional police authorities)—then how can one imagine that those military experts who manage the Soviet Union's ICBMs could possibly launch them in an emergency without collective decisions at the highest levels of the Party and state? Although we do not know the exact command structure within the Soviet nuclear forces, it is a safe assumption that strict and comprehensive safeguards exist against any possibility of either a mistaken or deliberate initiative by any level of the military hierarchy alone.

There are further reasons why the intersection of military and industrial interests in the USSR comprises a much weaker and less autonomous complex than in the United States. Neither munitions workers nor factory directors fear loss of employment in the event of reconversion to civilian production; in fact most defence workers would probably welcome it, since they would no longer be exposed to some of the dangers inherent in arms manufacture. The scientists and researchers in the defence establishment would likewise welcome transfer to civilian projects, since at present their work is so tightly classified that they receive no public honour or acknowledgement for their achievements—a source of intense frustration to them. A case in point is the late Sergei Korolev, architect of Soviet rocket technology, whose prizes were classified and who remained quite unknown in Russia until after his death in 1966. For its part, the Soviet officer corps is a secondary component of the political establishment; generally speaking it is not in a strong position to control the flow of procurements. Moreover, unlike the United States where competition between the Army, Navy and Air Force has traditionally propelled a persistent tendency toward the 'overproduction' of arms systems, inter-service rivalry is insignificant within the more unified and subordinated Russian military establishment. Finally, Politbureau members are typically more generalist in their careers than most US politicians or government bureaucrats—they are less tied to special interest groups on whom they depend for the maintenance of their career positions.

Cold War Perceptions

Let us now turn to the question of the perceptions each of the parties have of each other in the Cold War. There are at least three possible scenarios in which a full-scale nuclear exchange might occur: as an act of deliberate aggression, as a pre-emptive strike in anticipation of aggression by the other side, and as a retaliatory strike. If we confine the arena of possible nuclear war to Europe, then the likelihood of a sudden blitzkrieg by either NATO or the Warsaw Pact seems zero. In our opinion there are no longer any border disputes, 'Danzig Corridors' or revanchist tendencies capable of producing the kind of crises that paved the way to the past two world wars. Even if one tried to adopt the mentality of the American cold-war right, and attempted to imagine (as has Frederick Forsyth in his bestseller, *The Devil's Alternative*) that the Soviet Union was ultimately forced to invade Western Europe for economic reasons, it would, of course, be absurd to think that the USSR would destroy it first with nuclear weapons and contaminate it with radioactive debris for centuries. Equally, Western aggression against the USSR or the Eastern bloc that might provoke a Soviet nuclear retaliation seems also highly improbable. This leaves the possibility of a pre-emptive first strike as the remaining scenario. Now a pre-emptive strike is conceivable only if one side sincerely believes *or* has clear knowledge that the other side is preparing deliberate aggression.

The problem—and potential fatal danger—is that there is a huge difference between 'sincere belief' and 'clear knowledge'. 'Sincere belief' is an entirely subjective notion implying a range of different levels of interpretation and imputed probability. In our opinion, the evolution of the strategic arms race since Hiroshima has been in part based on this problem of the subjective perceptions of the intentions and world-view of the other side. For example, if we consider the public explanations advanced by the Western leaderships for the 'modernization' (in fact, a qualitatively new build-up and escalation) of NATO's nuclear arsenal, they purport to be based on the 'sincere belief' that the Soviet Union really does have aggressive intentions toward Western Europe. Even where the Western media take a liberal view of Soviet attitudes, they almost always assume that these can be regarded as essentially similar to those on the American side. Thus in CBS's recent major documentary about the dangers of nuclear war ('The Defence of the United States'), which greatly irritated Weinberger and the Pentagon, Walter Cronkite was sent to Moscow 'to see what general impressions the "enemy" may have of us. Not surprisingly, they tend to think of America as the aggressor and are quick to refer to a long list of alleged grievances. . . . Mr Cronkite reaches the conclusion: "Who are these Russians? No one can say with certainty. But if their perception of America is as flawed as we believe it is, then our perceptions of the Soviet Union just could be flawed, too. In the absence of any real dialogue, the same old fears and doubts continue to dominate our relationship." '[3]

The assumption of a basic symmetry of outlook is unfounded, however. This is particularly true in regard to Soviet perceptions about the intentions of the West European powers. If a television commentator from Norway, Sweden, Greece, France, Italy, Holland or Spain arrived in Moscow, what evidence would they find amongst the Soviet public of the fear of aggression from *Europe?* Almost none. There would be no 'long list of alleged grievances' against any of these countries. It could be argued that West Germany is a special case, and, indeed, until 1958–62 there was still anxiety amongst ordinary people and sections of Soviet officialdom over possible revanchist tendencies on the German right. The memories of Nazi aggression were still too fresh to allay all suspicions about Bonn's ultimate intentions, whatever common sense might suggest. But the perception of a 'German threat' has slowly receded with time, especially since the emergence of Ostpolitik; and although not completely extinct, these fears no longer play an important role in forming the general Soviet view of Western Europe. Everyone in Russia would feel it as a personal tragedy if any war or accident led to the destruction of Paris, London, Rome, Amsterdam, or Madrid. (Do people in Britain or Italy feel the same about Moscow or Leningrad?) If Warsaw Pact missiles and tank divisions face westward today, it is not because anyone in the Soviet Union actually thinks that Western Europe by itself is a real threat to the security of the Soviet Union. Rather it is because Europe has for a generation been the primary 'operational military theatre' for the United States. The difference is all important.

If a fundamental antagonism between the USSR and Western Europe does not exist either in terms of the foreign policy objectives of the USSR or its citizenry's perception of the world, it still remains to explain why there is a pervasive fear of the USA in the USSR. We, therefore, will try to explain the general strategic situation which has made *defence* the permanent obsession of the Soviet leadership. East-West tensions have passed through successive cycles of confrontation and detente, crisis and relaxation. There were two hopeful periods—both initiated on the Soviet side—when it appeared that a basis might be laid for co-operation in mutually reducing the arms race. The first was Khrushchev's policy of 'peaceful coexistence' (1955–63), and the second was Brezhnev's strategy of 'detente' (1971–79). The most important agreements achieved during these interludes of comparative sanity were the ban on atmospheric nuclear testing and, later, SALT I. SALT II—frequently depicted in the Western press as the victim of events in Afghanistan—had in fact been fatally undermined by the resistance of right-wing forces in the US Senate and Carter administration, months before the Soviet intervention in Afghanistan.

Here we must emphasize a crucial difference between Western European and American attitudes toward the Soviet Union, and thus in perceptions of the current crisis in superpower relations. For the countries of Western Europe, the Soviet Union is a state with which Europe has lived for centuries: Russia—pre-revolutionary or post-revolutionary—is widely perceived in terms of the evolution of the traditional European state system. The political order in the USSR is seen as the long-term outcome of historical trends in European development, for which Russia herself did not always have the main responsibility. Thus West Europeans are aware that the First World War rendered the collapse of Imperial Russia inevitable, while the Second World War made the USSR a military superpower, whose tendency to take every possible measure to guarantee its survival and avoid any repetition of the catastrophe of 22 June 1941 they can understand. In 1944–45 there was a unanimous feeling in Russia that the strategic frontiers of the USSR must be pushed a long way back: Romania, Hungary, Bulgaria and the Eastern half of Germany were occupied as ex-enemy states, and Western opinion initially accepted this.

The creation of the peoples' democracies in this zone was, on the other hand, widely seen as the formation of a 'satellite' region, lacking popular support—even if Soviet strategic interests in Eastern Europe were acknowledged. There is here a certain distinction between West European attitudes towards East Europe and towards the Soviet Union itself, though never an absolute one. At the same time, however, the Communist character of the USSR does not as such unduly frighten West European societies, in which Marxist ideology and Communist parties have long played an important part in public life.

American attitudes towards the Soviet Union have historically been very different. It is important to recall the relative isolation of the United States from the politics of Europe in the nineteenth century, and the (related) fact that Russia only emerged as an important consideration in American foreign policy in the immediate aftermath of October. Whereas West Europeans tend to accept the USSR as a legitimate state, the last survivor of the great European empires after the collapse of the British and French imperial systems, Americans still often see Russia as the fount of world revolution and left-wing 'subversion'. European political leaders have always had to deal with important local socialist movements—many of them much older than Soviet communism. By contrast, the United States has lacked any experience of an influential national party of the left. Thus the absence of American socialism and the long isolation of American politics from the affairs of the European state system have contributed to the underdevelopment of a rational understanding of international politics in the United States. This óne-sided American perception of the Soviet Union, together with the strength of the left in France and Italy at the end of the Second World War, in large measure determined the initial American course which gave rise to what was later labelled the 'Cold War'—a course then confirmed by the consolidation of Soviet control of Eastern Europe.

The Strategic Balance of Power

To what extent was the Cold War also a response to a real military threat to American capitalism from the Red Army? Indisputably the Soviet forces which greeted the American and British troops on the Elbe and Danube constituted the strongest land army in world history. Despite the Soviet Union's immense wartime losses, it possessed in 1945 an army of three hundred divisions, well-equipped with modern weapons and highly mobile tank corps. Soviet analysts—corroborated by not a few eminent Western historians—have generally viewed the American decision to destroy Hiroshima and Nagasaki with atomic bombs in August 1945, at a moment when the surrender of Japan was already imminent, as a demonstration of force primarily designed to intimidate the USSR at this juncture. Most discussions of the formidable military power of the Soviet state at the end of the Second World War neglect, however, an extremely salient fact: despite extensive modernization of its armed forces in the course of the war, the one kind of conventional weapon which never received priority was long-range bombers. The Soviet air force was certainly well equipped with many types of new fighters and special short-range bombers to support ground combat, but it lacked strategic bombers and, indeed, never attempted to carry out massive raids on German cities and industrial centres. The capability to conduct long-range strategic bombing was a wartime monopoly of the United States and Britain. When this advantage was combined with the exclusive possession of atomic weapons (and the proven will to use them) which the Truman administration enjoyed from 1945 to 1949, the unequal military position of the USSR at the beginning of the Cold War should be obvious. US superiority was further enhanced when the USSR, faced with the enormous task of reconstruction, demobilized the bulk of the Red Army and significantly reduced its military presence in Europe during the same period.

It was during this phase of American nuclear monopoly that Soviet perceptions of the aggressive intentions of the United States began to take shape. Despite the military reductions undertaken—no doubt reluctantly—by Stalin, the United States made no effort to construct a durable peace. Despite the absence of a single other nuclear power in the world, the United States accelerated the development of its atomic arsenal and the fleet of special bombers which allowed it to strike anywhere in the USSR. Nobody tried to conceal the American threat: Pentagon generals spoke freely of their country's nuclear supremacy and the coming of the 'American Century'. Meanwhile the war-devastated countries of Western Europe and the Mediterranean basin, who desperately needed American economic aid, opened the door to the creation of US airbases encircling the Soviet Union. Eventually this ring of bases extended from Iceland, Britain, France, Italy, Greece and Turkey to Japan and Alaska. Before the USSR was able to produce even one, primitive thermonuclear device, the United States possessed hundreds. And—what is so often forgotten—even after the first Soviet bomb, the Americans continued to retain their monopoly of delivery systems. There was, in fact, no Soviet nuclear threat to the United States in the early fifties, since the USSR did not have a single bomber which could cross the ocean. The strategic dominance of the United States was complete, and during this time (and only during this time), there was a crash programme of building special atomic shelters near the government buildings and big apartment blocks of Moscow and other cities—a clear index of Soviet apprehension. Even after the testing of the first Soviet intercontinental missiles in 1957 (Korolev's *semerka*), the fundamental strategic equation remained basically unchanged. Despite the impression given by the launching of the first Sputnik, the early Soviet ICBMs were highly unreliable, a handful in number, and no serious match for the American B-52s.

The Legacy of the U-2 Affair

It was in the context of this continuing strategic imbalance (in the American favour) that Khrushchev launched his policy of 'peaceful coexistence' and the search for atomic test bans. The failure of this policy is often attributed to the Cuban missile crisis, but in fact Khrushchev's creditable disarmament initiative was undermined much earlier by the US reluctance to stop the periodic surveillance of Soviet territory by American spy planes. Many in the West, and even more people in the USSR, remember the dramatic shooting-down of the U-2 piloted by Francis Gary Powers in 1960, as well as Khrushchev's subsequent and skilful exposure of Eisenhower as a liar. But neither Khrushchev nor the US sources ever described the U-2 affair as it really was. For the Soviet leadership it would have been an embarrassment to acknowledge that it had been completely helpless for years to prevent overflights at 70,000 feet of its largest industrial centres by American planes; while the United States government obviously wanted to minimize the political damage done by the revelation of its previous falsehoods, and their disgraceful ending. In fact the American decision to overfly Soviet territory had been made during Stalin's lifetime, and not just for the purposes of military espionage, but for political intimidation. The Soviet government did not publicly denounce these flights at the time but made confidential protests which were dismissed by Washington. As Khrushchev later remarked in his autobiography: 'The Americans knew perfectly well that they were in the wrong. They knew they were causing us terrible headaches whenever one of these planes took off on a mission. . . . We were sick and tired of being subjected to these indignities. They were making these flights to show up our impotence. Well, we weren't impotent any longer.'[4] Moreover, for special effect the dates of these overflights were often selected to coincide with Soviet national celebrations and parades. The U-2 which was finally shot down—with the first proper Soviet anti-aircraft missiles—was engaged in an overflight of the May Day parade in Red Square. It took off from Peshawar in Pakistan, crossed Afghanistan and flew over the Urals, en route for Leningrad and a landing again at a US base in Norway. It was brought down near the industrial centre of Sverdlovsk.

Khrushchev seems to have expected some sort of apology from Eisenhower for the Powers flight. He had himself just visited the United States, and had gone to great lengths to demonstrate his commitment to 'peaceful coexistence'—including a sacrifice of previously close Soviet ties to China.[5] The Soviet leadership expected some response in return to preserve the momentum towards the Paris summit. When Eisenhower instead foolishly justified the spy missions, the Paris talks collapsed. The significance of the episode was in this sense symbolic. The overflights were a contemptuous expression of United States technological superiority over the USSR which had existed since 1945. The American refusal to disown these violations of international law during the 1960 'thaw',[6] signified Washington's rejection of any equality in the negotiation process, a posture that rendered disarmament talks in a new situation futile. Khrushchev wrote later in his memoirs: 'As far as we were concerned, this sort of espionage was war—war waged by other means. . . . Americans were using military means. And they couldn't hide behind their technology forever.'[6]

The U-2 episode happened almost a generation ago, but the essential American approach to the problem remains the same. Successive administrations have made the preservation of a clear US military-technological lead over the USSR the precondition to any serious negotiation. Looking at this from another angle, *every* significant new technology of nuclear warfare—nuclear missile submarines, MIRVs, cruise missiles, the neutron bomb, and so on—has been introduced into the arms race by the United States. Rather than viewing the negotiation process as one of preventing the development of further systems of annihilation, the United States has traditionally seen new strategic weapons as bargaining counters to force the Soviet Union to ratify the permanence of the post-war imbalance of military and political power. In fact, until 1965–66 the Soviet Union did not have any real ability to reach American territory, while the United States could reach any part of the Soviet Union. In this respect it is incorrect to speak of a 'new' nuclear danger facing Europe; the logic of the arms race from 1949 onwards always meant that Western Europe would be the only real hostage of an atomic war. The United States was comparatively safe, and this is why the Kennedy brothers could so confidently threaten military actions during the dark days of the Cuban missile crisis.

Following the failure of the summit, the USSR made several unsuccessful attempts to revive the disarmament process. If these initiatives had succeeded, the world could have been spared the great arms race of the next decades, and the superpowers might have achieved some reasonable stabilization of their mutual defence systems. But as Khrushchev had been forced to learn twice through the bitter experiences of the U-2 and Cuban crises, the only chance of getting serious negotiations under way was to show the United States that 'they couldn't hide behind their technology forever'. Thus the new Soviet leadership, in the aftermath of the Cuban ultimatum and the breakdown of diplomatic overtures, decided to pursue the massive national effort required to attain a credible deterrent capability. It was only in the late 1960s and early 1970s, while the United States was mired in Vietnam, that the USSR finally acquired the means for massive nuclear retaliation against the continental United States. This change in the military-technological balance of power, combined with the effects of the US defeat in Indochina and the Watergate scandal, induced a major alteration in the American attitude toward disarmament talks. Suddenly it became possible to have mutual dialogue with godless communists and even to sign and ratify SALT I.

Finally it is important to appreciate how the legacy of the U-2 epoch is likely to have a very different weight for the Soviet and American leaderships. In the twenty years since Powers was shot down, the US administration has changed completely several times. In all probability, neither Ford nor Carter—still less Reagan today—have any recollection of the history of the U-2s and the decade of deliberate American intimidation of the Soviet defence system. The current Soviet leadership, on the other hand, remembers these events only too clearly. In 1960 Andrei Gromyko was minister of foreign affairs, as he is today; Leonid Brezhnev was chairman of the presidium of the Supreme Soviet; Dmitri Ustinov, now minister of defence, was at that time deputy prime minister; Yuri Andropov, current head of the KGB, was secretary of the Central Committee section responsible for foreign relations; Mikhail Suslov, now the chief ideologist, was another secretary of the Central Committee; Alexei Yepishev, head of the Political Department of the Red Army, held the same post twenty years ago. While these men's perception of American policy may well not be entirely correct, it is incontestably grounded on a much longer and more solid personal experience than the opposite perception of Soviet policy by the current administration in Washington.

The Shift in Strategic Axes

The origins of confrontation between 'East' and 'West' date back to the emergence of Russia as a great power in the eighteenth century. Many of the decisive conflicts of modern world history were, in fact, fought out on Russian soil: Napoleon's invasion of Russia in 1812, the Crimean War of 1854–55, the Eastern Front of the First World War in 1914–17, the Entente intervention in the Civil War of 1918–21, and the Nazi aggression of 1941–45. At the end of the Second World War, the principal American strategic aim became the defence of Western Europe on the basis of an overwhelming US nuclear and air superiority. For twenty years, bases in Europe, Turkey and Japan gave the United States the capacity to strike with relative impunity against the Soviet heartland, while the USSR possessed only the limited ability to retaliate against Western Europe and Japan. The American continent remained secure as long as the Soviet Union lacked either strategic aviation, fleets of nuclear submarines or reliable intercontinental missiles; the Atlantic and Pacific Oceans still remained the best protection of the United States. This confidence in nuclear superiority and de facto immunity to nuclear retaliation allowed American administrations until the late 1960s to pursue fairly active confrontationist policies. At the same time, however, relations between the USSR and Western Europe developed more favourably—in part because both sides had everything to lose in a general war. 'East-West' confrontation shifted from its historic Western Europe-versus-Russia axis to the United States-versus-the USSR. With the great European empires in decline, the absolute and relative importance of Western Europe in world politics was gradually decreasing while the countries of the 'Third World' that had once been European colonies assumed more and more significant roles in the global balance of power.

By the advent of the 1973–74 oil crisis, the American leadership had begun to sense a major shift in the geo-economic and military balances of power. The Soviet Union's success in modernizing its navy and developing an ICBM system made the traditional deterrence of oceanic distance a dwindling factor in American defence. Moreover, with the increase in Western dependence upon oil imports, the former geographical advantage of the United States—its distance from the Eurasian land-mass—was slowly being transformed into a practical disadvantage, as the Soviet Union's greater proximity to the Middle East and, more importantly, its independence of Third World resources strengthened the USSR's strategic position against it. Finally, as potential conflicts developed in Third World arenas where relative superiority in nuclear weapons was no longer a decisive factor, the Soviet Union's assets in conventional warfare tended to acquire a new weight. The overall effect of this narrowing of the strategic imbalance between the superpowers was to pave the way for a revival of the 'peaceful coexistence' approach—now relabelled 'detente'. With the beginning of the SALT negotiations it seemed at last that an era of relative sanity had arrived, with the promise of gradually phased stabilization, and even perhaps reduction, of the massively redundant 'overkill' capacities of the Soviet and American nuclear arsenals.

Why, then, did detente suddenly collapse in the last year of the Carter administration? The Soviet intervention in Afghanistan was not the main determinant—if anything, it was more a result than a cause of the demise of detente. SALT II was dead long before, in fact within a few weeks of its signature by Brezhnev and Carter, when it became clear that the US Senate would refuse to ratify it. This refusal was the starting-point for the degradation in the international situation, which was then sharply intensified by the Brussels decision to re-equip NATO in December 1979—again before Russian troops entered Afghanistan. What were the real reasons for this change in US policy? We think the principal cause of the return to confrontation was the fact that SALT II did nothing to redress the disadvantages of the United States in the Third World—where America had just suffered another setback with the Iranian Revolution after its failures in Indochina and Angola, with the result that both the Carter and Reagan administrations became determined to restore the strategic importance of Europe, and thus of the US nuclear arsenal in it. Washington has repeatedly claimed that America is now in a position of strategic 'inferiority', but in reality it is rejection of the prospect of *parity* with the USSR that motivates US policies in the present period, as Stephen Cohen has recently shown in the *New York Times*.[7]

The United States refuses to accept that wide areas of the Third World are now escaping its grasp or that the USSR has won a new capacity for presence or freedom of movement in them. American leaders tend to see only strategic points on a military map when they look at the Third World—as in the recent case of Namibia and Angola—while their Soviet counterparts are more inclined to assess developments there in terms of underlying social and economic processes. Moreover it is generally easier for Third World countries to adopt elements of the Soviet path to industrialization than to emulate the American way of life, so creating further fears in Washington. So far as the USSR is concerned, revolutions in far-away regions like Central America or Southern Africa—events which occur independently of Russian policies—tend to pose costly and inconvenient problems of assistance or support; but generally speaking the Soviet leadership under Brezhnev has felt that it could not refuse aid when asked: Nicaragua is a recent example. The Reagan administration presents this to the American public as evidence of Soviet aggression and responsibility for 'terrorism'.

The New Danger in Europe

At the same time the United States seems to have become increasingly concerned at the possibility that detente might open the door for a further growth of West European-Soviet relations and perhaps an eventual delinking of Western European defence from the global American military posture. The tendency towards parity of the Soviet ICBM and submarine systems with their US counterparts could potentially emancipate Western Europe from its hostage role in any general nuclear exchange. By the mid 1970s it had become conceivable that a nuclear war could break out between the United States and the Soviet Union which might leave Western Europe more or less intact. Such a contingency might, in particular, occur if the conflict originated somewhere else in the world where Western European interests were not involved. This possible reversal of previous cold-war scenarios—in which Europe was most vulnerable—opened a new space in European politics for disengagement from the arms race. This possibility of European reluctance to join in a nuclear war has been of great anxiety to American military planners, and explains the urgency of a new arrangement for US forces in Europe. Thus under the euphemistic label of 'modernization', the United States is trying to induce the NATO countries to accept a deployment of nuclear missiles that would be free from the old 'double key system' (i.e. nominal joint control) and, for the first time, give America overriding authority to unleash the latest generation of rockets against the Warsaw Pact. Naturally the United States has sought to disguise this with promises of consultation, but in fact only the American Army will possess authority to fire the new nuclear weapons from NATO territory. If in an earlier period the United States attempted to protect Western Europe with an American nuclear umbrella, now, under the new plan, Western Europe would be protecting the United States.

We do not find it surprising, therefore, that Moscow views the so-called 'modernization' of NATO with an alarm reminiscent of Washington's twenty years ago when Khrushchev installed medium-range missiles in Cuba. We have no means of knowing exactly what the calculations of the Soviet leadership have been in the latest period. This is a field, as we have said, where Soviet citizens are kept in virtually total ignorance by their government.[8] But it is a safe surmise that there are two major reasons for the acute concern the USSR has shown at the plan to install Cruise and Pershing II missiles in Western Europe. The first must be seen in the context of US-Soviet military relations as a whole since the Second World War. Historically, the USSR has never been able to pioneer a single new weapons technology since 1945 (its brief satellite advance of 1957–58 remained non-military, and was rapidly overtaken by the United States—today the USSR no longer even tries to compete in planetary exploration). At every stage, America has always been ahead, taking the technological lead and obliging the USSR to try to catch up from a position of inferiority. This permanent dynamic has structured Russian responses deeply, creating a pervasive inferiority complex that probably prevailed over rational calculations in the 70s. SALT I was signed at a time when the United States had approximately 6,500 warheads, the USSR some 2,200. Soviet weapons were thus more than enough to destroy the United States by the early 1970s. Why then, it may be asked, was production continued, till today the Soviet Union has some 6,000 warheads? A number of factors were probably at work here. One was no doubt the sheer discrepancy in absolute numbers itself—the United States did not volunteer to reduce its stockpile to Soviet levels, so that there was a temptation to follow upwards to American levels. These could be rationalized by the contingency of a war extending beyond the United States itself to other continents. Much more important, however, was the constant Russian fear of the American lead in weapons technology. Just at this time, Washington was introducing multiple-re-entry vehicles (MIRVs) into its strategic delivery systems, giving it a wide new advantage in the arms race. The SS-20s which the Soviet Union is now deploying represent part of the belated Russian response to US MIRV-ing of its warheads a decade ago—a decision in Moscow whose results only started to come off the production line in the late 1970s, but which dates back to the time of SALT I. The SS-20s are presented to the Russian public simply as new models of the old rockets, with no more strategic significance than a new fighter or tank replacing old ones. In reality, the Soviet propensity for very long production runs of weapons they have mastered (tanks, old-fashioned ICBMs, the new IRBMs), to a point of quantitative redundancy, is a kind of compensation for the failure to keep up with new weapons, in a defence economy that has been persistently unsuccessful in generating real innovations. By contrast, the Cruise missile represents for the Soviet leadership a *qualitative* jump in the arms race, because it embodies a totally new technology that is far in advance of anything the USSR could hope to emulate in the short run. Termed the 'winged rocket' in Russian, its accuracy and radar-evadability are seen as a deeply menacing initiative by the United States. The Cruise missile reawakens all the fears and feelings of technological inferiority of the past: hence the pitch of Soviet reaction to it.

There is, however, a second reason for the gathering diplomatic crisis that NATO 'modernization' has created. This is the fact that the new generation of missiles will be an integral part of the American military machine and could be used without the consent of the European allies. If France, Italy or Britain had developed their own new missiles and retained full control over their usage, the USSR would not be nearly so nervous. Nobody in the Soviet Union can imagine that either France or Britain would have reason to start a nuclear war. But a preemptive strike by the United States is a much more imaginable and frightening scenario to the Soviet leadership; hence it sees the new 'single key' command structure implicit in the deployment of Pershing II and Cruise missiles as a very dangerous lowering of the nuclear threshold. From the Russian point of view, the installation of the new generation of Soviet medium-range missiles—the SS-20s which are the formal pretext for NATO's own projected modernization—cannot be compared with the escalation of the arms race that Cruise and Pershing II, targeted on the USSR, represent. For the SS-20 cannot reach the United States and does not, therefore, constitute an upset of the balance of strategic power equivalent to the new NATO system.

The Threat of 'Limited' Nuclear War

In official Western discussions about the new generation of nuclear weapons and their delivery systems one can discern a profoundly troubling change of attitude. If in the past nuclear weapons were considered almost entirely as deterrents, now there are suggestions about the practicality of so-called 'theatre nuclear weapons' and certain *rules* of nuclear warfare. This discussion of 'limited' or 'flexible' nuclear war has only occurred within NATO. The Soviet official attitude remains the old-fashioned belief that nuclear war is unthinkable, criminal and unwinnable. At the same time it is noticeable that American discussions about limited nuclear war have been mostly focused on Europe. American military experts apparently believe that it might be possible to confine a nuclear exchange to the mutual destruction of Western and Eastern Europe. While hundreds of new missiles will be installed near major European metropolitan centres where military and civilian targets are indistinguishable, the United States has decentralized its own domestic missile systems to sparsely inhabited desert areas. As popular insecurity and apprehension grows in Western Europe, the Reagan administration assures the American electorate of the prospect of renewed US supremacy.

In the Soviet Union, by contrast, there are no illusions about the rationality of nuclear war. Despite periodic claims by NATO spokesmen, there is no planning in the USSR for mass survival in a nuclear conflict: shelters are non-existent in the new Moscow housing districts, while civil defence training in the provinces is confined to perfunctory bus trips into the forests. Likewise, no serious official statement has ever envisaged the USSR winning such a war. In fact the Soviet population is told that global nuclear war is lunacy and that no one would survive it. As far as 'theatre' war goes, it is not discussed and its possibility is officially denied. The USSR in this sense does not entertain contingency plans for a limited nuclear war in Europe as does the United States. On the other hand, should any country launch or permit an isolated nuclear strike against the Soviet Union, then in all probability the USSR would make a comparably limited retaliation against the territory of the aggressor. But the Soviet leadership has gone to great lengths to warn the Americans repeatedly that such hypothetically contained exchanges would not only be impossible to guarantee, but are just the kind of delusion that could speed the way to a global holocaust.

The Western media frequently dwell on the political and economic advantages of the 'free world' and the necessity to defend the democracy it represents. Democracy, however, scarcely exists as far as modern military machines are concerned. In both camps all really major decisions are secret, and neither parliaments nor publics have any serious influence over the formation of military strategy. It is true, and important, that in the Western-style democracies of the capitalist world, the population is freer to express itself, to organize peace movements or anti-nuclear campaigns. Periodic elections and parliamentary debates are a reality in the United States or Britain. Nevertheless, even with a 'free press' and 'free elections', the public had no say in such decisions as the escalation of the Vietnam War, the invasion of Cambodia, the British purchase of the Trident missile or the production of the neutron bomb. Life-and-death decisions for humanity, involving billions or even trillions of dollars, entirely elude the supervision of general democratic processes. The new cold war and the accelerated arms race will only amplify these tendencies. Military systems exist as virtual states within states in the West; no one can really vouchsafe where nuclear weapons are under 'responsible' control. Thus the argument that the Soviet Union is more likely to employ nuclear weapons because it is not a democratic power is absolutely false. In both systems, capitalist and communist, the general population is excluded from the relevant decision-making processes.

The Deadly Side-Effects

Furthermore, once we consider the spectre of nuclear proliferation in Third World countries, the behaviour of the West must induce far more alarm than Soviet or Chinese policies. The dangerous and irresponsible spread of the technology of nuclear war in the 'hot spots' of the world is, in face, the most frightening development of the last decade. This has happened entirely because of the availability of *Western* nuclear technology and raw materials. Neither Israel nor South Africa could have developed their present nuclear capability without external assistance, primarily from the United States and France. The test of a nuclear device by India in 1974 was possible only because of Canadian-supplied uranium and nuclear engineering skills. The controversy about a possible nuclear-military programme in Iraq has to do with technology sold by the French and the Italians, while the so-called 'Muslim Bomb' suspected of being under construction in Pakistan will also be based on mainly French technology. Brazilian nuclear plant, meanwhile, has been supplied by West Germany. Thus potential or actual producers of atomic bombs in the Third World now indifferently include democracies like Israel and India, dictatorships like Pakistan, Iraq or

Brazil, and racialist or even 'outlaw' states like South Africa or Taiwan. The Soviet Union, in stark contrast, has always refused to share its nuclear secrets even with its closest allies; it is a well known fact that Khrushchev's denial of bomb-making technology to China was a major precipitant of the Sino-Soviet conflict.

The problem of proliferation is also obviously connected to the role of private profits and the international arms trade in the Western 'military-industrial complexes'. In the West issues of national security are highly commercialized and linked to the overall contradictions of capital accumulation. In many respects the production of new types of strategic weapons—including nuclear bombs and missiles—is based on the same economic determinants that regulate the production of new cars, television sets or washing machines. The incentives of the market-place, combined with inherited technological superiorities, give the 'free world' one important if dubious advantage over the Soviet bloc: its permanent priority in the design and output of new forms of nuclear weapons and armaments systems generally. On the other hand, the side-effects of the arms race are probably more damaging in the long run for the capitalist economies. There was a time when it was typical for some Soviet dissidents to think that the Western economic system was much more rational and efficient because it was regulated by 'competition' rather than by ideological principles. If they had looked at the role of military spending in the West, however, they would have seen how the false this view was. The 1.5 trillion dollars which the Reagan Administration plans to devote for military purposes over the next decade will create new inflationary pressures within the US economy and, far from the promised balancing of the budget, will lead to enormous deficits. The diversion of astronomical quantities of social resources to build MX and other new nuclear systems will slow down investment in other sectors and weaken the United States still further in the face of the competitive pressure of the Japanese in high-technology consumer-goods industries. As not only money, but also the talents of its best engineers and scientists are concentrated in efforts to create more sophisticated means of mass murder, it will be harder for the United States to maintain its economic leadership in the West or its celebrated standard of living. Needless to say, these negative consequences of military spending apply with redoubled force to a much weaker economy like that of Britain, as it prepares to take on the burden of paying for US-made Trident missiles. The only Western economies to escape damage will be those which continue to stave off American pressure to expand military expenditure (the current economic power of both Japan and West Germany is clearly related to their low levels of arms spending). In the long run the side-effects of the arms race might destroy the capitalist system without war, as mass unemployment, inflation, reduction of foreign aid to poor countries, give socialist ideology greater influence abroad than thousands of new nuclear missiles or neutron bombs can do.

What is the situation in this respect in the USSR? Soviet defence spending, contrary to widespread belief, is not generally perceived as a major cause of their economic difficulties by the Russian people. The ordinary Soviet citizen blames the omnipresent bureaucracy for shortages, inefficiency and poor quality products, not the army. Partly this is because of the low visibility of the military establishment, much of which is camouflaged in ostensibly 'civilian' ministries and budgetary programmes. Partly it is because the Russian masses are aware of major improvements in the standard of living over the past decades, even without any reduction in arms expenditure. The 85% of the Soviet GNP spent on non-military purposes looms far larger in the public eye than the 15% allocated to arms; and the 7.5% excess of this over US military spending would not even be registered as such. Above all, Soviet arms production is maintained at a planned, regular pace over long periods, whereas US military spending is cyclical—with sharp intervals of downturn and mass unemployment. Thus the military sector of the Soviet economy is not associated with dislocation of employment or investment; it creates neither regional joblessness in downswings nor inflationary pressures in upswings. In this sense defence spending—although it is actually a heavier burden on a poorer economy—is also more compatible with price and planning stability. The result is to allow the Soviet government to maintain and legitimate a proportionately higher level of military investment than the West without the same range of disruptive side-effects.

The Responsibility of the Peace Movement

The origins of the new cold-war atmosphere in world affairs are complex, and we have not tried to discuss all of them here. It is clear, for example, that all the new nuclear weapons systems now being prepared for the modernization of the Western armoury—the neutron bomb, Cruise and Pershing II missiles, the Trident programme, the ATB 'Stealth' bomber—started to be designed some 10–12 years ago, long before the coming of the new Cold War. Whatever the diplomatic conjuncture, implementation of these programmes was bound to create an acute political confrontation. Similarly, the deep economic recession of the capitalist world was likely to generate strains in the United States' global posture, regardless of other circumstances. In the event, however, it has coincided with a series of popular revolutions in the Third World, hostile to Western interests—in Ethiopia, Angola, Nicaragua, Zimbabwe, Iran and elsewhere. Long-standing regional conflicts in the Middle East and Southern Africa have worsened, and the Western powers have proved impotent to resolve them. Meanwhile, Soviet interference in Afghanistan and the increase of Soviet influence in Vietnam, Laos and Cambodia have exacerbated tensions in Asia. The surprising ineptitude of the Carter and Reagan administrations in Washington, and of the Thatcher government in London, in attempting to increase pressure on the USSR by playing the 'China card', has further accelerated the deterioration in the international situation. All of these factors have contributed to the condensation of the new cold-war climate.

Fortunately, however, America does not have the same following in the new Cold War that it possessed in the old. It seems unlikely that the United States will be able to recreate the same kind of anti-communist consensus that it enjoyed in the NATO bloc during the Korean War period. Western Europe and Japan have come to share very different perceptions of the problems of the Third World from those of the United States. The West European viewpoint has generally become more objective, paying less heed to the notions of 'Soviet conspiracy' that still haunt paranoid visions in America. The existence of broad differences between Western Europe and the United States will, in fact, probably become of central importance to world politics in the near future. Already many West European countries like Holland, Belgium, Norway, Greece and Federal Germany are trying to avoid participation in an East-West confrontation, and are fighting to preserve the rudiments of detente by playing the role of moderators. Popular opinion in the Scandinavian countries is leaning to the creation of a regional nuclear-free zone, while centre-left coalitions in Belgium and the Netherlands will probably refuse to accept the American gift of the new nuclear missiles.

The new cold war and the future spiral of the arms race cannot survive very long without active West European participation, and we are optimistic that this participation will not be forthcoming. It is pertinent to compare the present logic of events with the previous build-ups to world war. Both world wars developed out of internal contradictions and aggressive rivalries within European society, and both involved major military miscalculations (in 1914, the German expectation of a lightning success of the Schlieffen Plan; in 1941, the German misestimation of Soviet industrial power and tenacity). The new Cold War is based on equally dangerous military miscalculations and geo-political delusions, but this time Western Europe has no fundamental stake in the logic of the confrontation. If, therefore, the United States continues its drift towards the reactionary right and super-militarization, it seems probable that Western Europe will move correspondingly to the left and towards disengagement from confrontation. Should the USA refuse to take part in constructive arms negotiations with the Soviet Union, the movement for unilateral nuclear disarmament in Europe will surely grow. There is no longer a single genuinely European problem which cannot be solved by non-military means, and the call for mobilization has never sounded more irrational and atavistic. Millions of citizens of Western Europe are coming to realize that they have little to gain from entrusting their fate to the military establishment of a superpower which does not have either a competent government or a consistent and balanced international policy. The peace movements in Europe are already a powerful pressure for moderation: it is they who can halt the prospect of a dangerous new round in the arms race, threatening to all mankind.

[1] Edward Thompson, 'Notes on Exterminism, the Last Stage of Civilization', see above.

[2] Ibid, p. 10.

[3] *New York Times*, 14 June 1981.

[4] *Khrushchev Remembers—The Last Testament*, New York 1974, pp. 443–453.

[5] In September 1959 the bombardment of Quemoy and Matsu began, and Eisenhower promised full support to the Kuomintang to repel a Chinese attack—including the use of nuclear weapons. Khrushchev, despite the urging of the Chinese leadership, nevertheless refused to cancel his trip to the United States, and when he later visited Peking for the tenth anniversary of the Chinese Revolution, he was given a bad reception and cut his visit short.

[6] After the Powers flight the United States ceased U-2 flights over the Soviet Union because it was clear that Soviet missiles could now destroy them. But it did not repudiate the practice of overt surveillance, and in fact continued U-2 flights over Cuba, Korea, Vietnam and China. To this day, the United States remains the only country in the world which—despite its possession of space satellites—still maintains a programme of such flights over the territory of other countries.

[7] 'For the United States, the parity principle involves one essential question: can Americans acknowledge to themselves that the Soviet Union, whether they like the Soviet political system or not, has become a legitimate great power with comparable global interests—that the Soviet Union has attained political parity with the United States in world affairs? Plainly, the United States, unlike most nations, has not yet learned to live with that geopolitical, historical fact. Enthralled by 64 years of anti-Sovietism and by a long history of being the only superpower, many US leaders and substantial segments of public opinion persist in seeing the Soviet Union mainly as "godless", "terroristic" and an "evil force" without any legitimate political status or entitlement in the world. Americans do not even discuss the parity principle openly. It remains, like sex in Victorian England, a forbidden, repugnant subject. But it is this unwillingness to concede political parity that repeatedly causes US diplomacy to succumb to militaristic policies, as acceptance of the necessity of military parity succumbs to the chimera of superiority, and episodes of detente succumb to cold war.' (Stephen F. Cohen, *International Herald Tribune*, 4/5 July 1981.)

[8] It is symptomatic that the technical provisions of the SALT treaties were never published in the general press in the Soviet Union. There are some signs, however, that this policy may be changing, as official anxiety over the present crisis rises. In August, a General Staff officer, Major-General Starobudov, explained Soviet military technology and dispositions in Europe in greater than usual detail in an address on Russian television.

A 'Limited' Nuclear War

John Cox

There has been much talk recently about whether a nuclear war could be confined to Europe. Personally I feel sure that any outbreak of nuclear hostilities will end up as an all-out nuclear war. If anyone is mad enough to start a holocaust they are hardly likely to become cool and rational once it is under way.

However it is a fact of life that thousands of nuclear weapons are in place and are targeted on European locations. Table I summarizes the world totals: a large proportion of the 20,000 plus warheads and the 3,000 plus megatonnage under the heading 'Other Systems' are destined for Europe as well as perhaps half the US strategic nuclear forces. So the threat to Europe is measured in *thousands of megatons* and *tens of thousands of warheads*.

These weapons could be used either in a limited European war or, more probably, as part of a world-wide nuclear war. My intention here is to discuss the consequences of a 400 megaton attack on Europe with a minimum of assumptions about the possible wider context. It must be emphasized at the outset however that 400 megatons is not an exceptionally high presumption. A much derided British civil defence exercise in 1980 (code-named 'Square Leg') assumed a 200 megaton attack on Britain alone (less than 5% of the megatonnage available from Soviet medium and long range warhead systems). In postulating a 200 megaton attack on NATO Europe as a whole, and an equivalent 200 megaton attack on WTO Europe, we are dealing with quite a 'small' limited nuclear war.

Nevertheless, 400 megatons could do a great deal of damage. Way back in 1968 the US Secretary of Defence (Robert McNamara) said that no more than 400 thermonuclear bombs (of average yield one megaton) 'delivered on the Soviet Union would be sufficient to destroy over one third of her population and one half of her industry.' Europe as a whole is about three times (and Central Europe ten times) more densely populated than the European sector of the Soviet Union. So 400 megatons would do a great deal of damage to Europe, however it were to be distributed.

Table I

Current nuclear arsenals

	Strategic	Other Systems	Total
(a) Number of Warheads			
USA	9,000–11,000	16,000–22,000	25,000–33,000
USSR	6,000–7,500	5,000–8,000	11,000–15,500
Others	—	—	<1,000
Totals	15,000–18,500	21,000–30,000	37,000–50,000
(b) Explosive Yield (Megatons)			
USA	3,000–4,000	1,000–4,000	4,000–8,000
USSR	5,000–8,000	2,000–3,000	7,000–11,000
Others	—	—	500–1,400
Totals	8,000–12,000	3,000–7,000	11,000–20,000

Sources: UN and SIPRI data, 1980

The Weapons

European-based missiles could deliver far more than 400 megatons—indeed, the now obsolete SS-4s and SS-5s (currently being replaced
by SS-20s) could deliver this much destruction on their own. Alternatively,
the total megatonnage of the NATO tactical nuclear weapons also exceeds
400. So they also need be the only weapons used. Moreover, in terms of
megatonnage the European-based aircraft carry even more destructive
potential than the missiles and can deliver this from at least 2000 nuclear
warheads. With no warning at all of an impending nuclear war, Europe
could inflict many times 400 megatons-worth of destruction upon itself.

Yet, important as the European-based nuclear weapons are, they do not
complete the threat to Europe. As many as a half of America's strategic
nuclear forces may be targeted on WTO Europe—equivalent to perhaps
4,000–5,000 extra nuclear warheads. Moreover, as shown by Table II, the
USA could treble its 'nuclear-capable tactical aircraft' in Europe within 30
days of a decision to mobilize. By the same token, the WTO threat to
Europe is greater than suggested merely by an examination of its
European-based weaponry.

Table II

US nuclear-capable tactical aircraft available for European contingencies

Aircraft	Year first deployed	Strike radius (km)	Speed (Mach)	Inventory Normal	Inventory After 30 days
USAF F-4	1962	1300	2.4	528	888
F-111	1967	2700	2.2	72	288
F-105D/B	1960	1800	2.2	0	158
F-100C/D	1955	1100	0.9	0	352
USN A-6	1956	1600	0.9	24	48
A-7A/B/E	1966	1600	0.9	60	120
			Totals	684	1854

Source: *Tactical Nuclear Weapons; European Perspectives* SIPRI, 1978

The Targets

In a 'controlled' nuclear war the targets are unlikely to be the same as for a fast-moving no-holds-barred full-scale nuclear war. In an all-out nuclear war the priorities are missile silos, airfields, military communications—to reduce the enemy's retaliatory capacity—and, later (during the retaliatory phase), population centres and economic-industrial targets. The 'ideal' limited war would end with all military targets destroyed and before the retaliation phase began. . . . 'An important objective of the assured retaliation mission should be to retard significantly the ability of the USSR to recover from a nuclear exchange and regain the status of a 20th-century military and industrial power more rapidly than the United States' (from the 1977 Annual Report of the US Department of Defence).[1]

Unfortunately, the 'logic' of a controlled nuclear war suggests that it is more likely to *begin* with the step-by-step destruction of economic-industrial targets. A strike against military targets would run the risk of being interpreted by the other side as the first phase of an all-out war. On the other hand, the destruction of population centres would not provide a suitable psychological climate for an early end to hostilities (what could?). On balance, the *least unlikely* scenario for a very limited nuclear war (i.e. only 400 megatons) is one in which both sides, with deliberation and plenty of prior warning, systematically 'take out' key economic-industrial targets, (using the forward-based systems in preference to the land-based ICBMs in order to reduce any incentive to widen the area of conflict).

This may be why almost one-half of the 40,000 listed targets of America's SIOP-5 (the Single Integrated Operation Plan first introduced in 1976) are economic-industrial. These targets include power-stations, ports, road/rail junctions and oil refineries. Of the several thousand or so nuclear warheads that could be used in a limited (400 megatons) European war, many can be assumed to be intended for economic-industrial targets. Most of these targets could be destroyed quite effectively by nuclear warheads in the 20 kiloton range.

The Success Rate

According to authoritative military sources, many bombs and missiles will not hit their intended targets. Not many people realize how many warheads may explode off-target. Missile reliability is only about 80% and other weapons are even less reliable. Penetration capability varies from 40% for the oldest aircraft to 100% for ballistic missiles. Survivability (against enemy attacks) is estimated at 90% for the mobile SLBMs and SS-20s but below 50% for the most vulnerable bomber aircraft. Combining all these factors gives an overall 'success rate' estimated at below 30%.

Although this may be a limitation for a military strategist contemplating a pre-emptive strike against missile silos and airfields, it is one which offers little comfort to the peoples of Europe. Most of the 'failures' will explode somewhere or other in Europe, probably as ground-bursts. The long-term radiation hazard and fallout is not significantly reduced by off-target explosions—indeed, the total amount of radiation could be greater and its distribution wider.

The Initial Death Toll

Descriptions of nuclear war usually begin with a step-by-step account of a single nuclear explosion in the megaton range (see, for example, Chapter Three of *Overkill*[2]). This approach has the merit of explaining the physical phenomena logically and chronologically (fireball, flash, blast, firestorm, radiation); but it is far from satisfactory as an introduction to the social, economic and psychological effects of nuclear war. The detailed and necessarily gruesome descriptions of these initial phenomena tend to overshadow

Table III

Environmental damage from nuclear explosions (excludes long-term radiation/fallout effects)

	Areas (kms²) for specified type of damage		
Explosive yield damage	*1 × Mt*	*1 × 20Kt*	*50 × 20Kt*
Dry vegetation ignited	213 (f)	7.5 (f)	374 (f)
Vertebrates killed	364 (r)	10 (f)	500 (f)
Trees destroyed	128 (r)	3.6 (b)	181 (r)

Notes: The references are to the major causes of damage in each instance: (b) – blast, (f) – fire and thermal radiation, (r) – nuclear radiation.
Source: *Weapons of Mass Destruction and the Environment*, SIPRI 1977.

the descriptions of the aftermath—a period which is likely to witness at least as many deaths as in the war period itself.

For our purposes it is not necessary to make detailed assumptions about the events of the war (or how it might end). Nor is it necessary to be specific about the distribution and size of the nuclear explosions. Table III shows that the environmental damage from a single one megaton explosion is only marginally less than for the same yield expressed as fifty 20 kiloton explosions. The death toll from a 400 megaton onslaught would be about the same whether inflicted by four hundred one megaton bombs or twenty thousand 20 kiloton bombs, or any combination of yields and numbers that total 400 megatons. In any event the death toll is likely to *exceed 150 million* (this being about the same proportion of Europe's population as McNamara's estimate of one-third dead from a 400 megaton attack on the much less densely populated Soviet Union).

Initial Damage

The distribution and size of the nuclear warheads is relevant however to the economic-industrial destruction. Assuming that about a quarter of about 4,000 nuclear warheads (of average yield 100 kilotons) destroy their intended targets, at least a thousand key economic-industrial centres will have been irreparably damaged and several thousand more put out of commission. In all probability the irreparable damage would include over 70% of Europe's oil-refining and electricity-generating capacity (including a hundred or so nuclear power facilities whose destruction, as shown by Table IV, would increase the long-term radiation hazard dramatically).

Table IV

Areas (in km^2) affected by radiation after a 1Mt explosion alone and on nuclear power facilities

Dose accumulated from one month to one year after the explosion	On its own	On a 1GW(e) reactor	On a spent fuel storage tank
1.0Gy	2,000	34,000	61,000
0.5Gy	4,000	46,000	87,000
0.1Gy	25,000	122,000	164,000

(Note: Scientists differ in their assessment of the risks from radiation exposure. Whereas most would accept that a 1Gy dose could result in a 10% mortality rate, some scientists believe that mortality rates are negligible for 0.1Gy)

Other damaged facilities would include ports, airfields and road and rail networks, virtually all of which would be in need of major repairs. It is very unlikely that electricity, petrol, diesel oil and gas and other basic services will be available to more than a handful of industrial enterprises in the immediate aftermath of the war.

Water supplies would be another major casualty. Although direct attacks on reservoirs are unlikely, distribution networks will be severely damaged. The prudent action for water engineers will be to cut off supplies to areas suffering major water losses, in order to conserve the service for less affected areas. In practice piped water supplies would cease for most people and, even without allowing for radioactive contamination of the remaining water supplies and the problems of untreated sewage, the incidence of water-borne disease is likely to rise.

Food will be another major problem. Whatever the loss amongst humans, the death toll will be incomparably greater amongst the unprotected livestock. Moreover, as food supplies are interrupted (initially due merely to distribution difficulties), the surviving sheep, cows and poultry will be prime candidates for slaughter. Within a short period it is realistic to assume the effective disappearance of farm livestock and most animals and resident birds throughout Europe.

Plants are much more resistant to radiation but, in the case of crops, increasingly dependent upon human control over the cultivation cycle. If a nuclear war interrupted any of the critical steps of ploughing, sowing, reaping, gathering, etc., an entire year's harvest could be lost and subsequent harvests threatened. Moreover, the disappearance of birds and animals will upset the ecological balance on which the plants depend. For example, the absence of birds may result in a massive increase in the insect population which, in turn, would cause major damage to crops. Furthermore, in the aftermath of a nuclear war, farmers will be deprived of electricity and fuel to drive machines and tractors, fertilizers to feed the crops, let alone pesticides to control the expected plague of insects.

The Aftermath

Modern industrial society may be likened to an extremely complex machine. Its operations depend upon the smooth working of many small yet essential components, often involving a small handful of key workers. When any one of these components fails, as occurs fairly often nowadays with industrial disputes involving petrol tank drivers, power station supervisors, coal miners and dockhands, the economy quickly reaches the verge of collapse (prior to the statutory last-minute settlement of the dispute), with numerous industrial undertakings, large and small, unable to continue to operate.

These industrial disputes rarely involve more than a minute proportion of the total workforce (2% at the most, usually far less). Moreover, they usually are independent disputes taking place in an otherwise normal industrial environment. By contrast, in the aftermath of a limited nuclear war, up to 30% or more of the workforce may be dead and many more again incapacitated. Whether by direct destruction or by the loss of workers and supplies, many key industrial enterprises will stop work simultaneously. Meanwhile, the environment will be abnormal in a whole variety of ways (social, physical, industrial). It is valid to query whether a modern industrial society could be rebuilt at all after such a catastrophe.

In many respects Europe would be more likely to recover if it were more primitive, based like many Third World countries upon numerous self-sufficient village communities. Our vulnerability is our highly developed interdependence upon widely dispersed skills and capital assets. The power station worker needs coal from coal miners and fuel oil from refineries. The coal miner needs electricity from power stations and food from the farms. The road transport driver needs petrol from refineries and food from the farms. The refinery worker needs electricity, crude oil supplies, customers for refined products—and food from the farms. The farmers produce a surplus to their personal needs because they have an assured *sale* for their produce and are able to do so because of the basic services provided by the rest of the community (electricity, fuels, fertilisers, etc.). If only one sector were to fail completely, the entire structure of the economy would collapse.

There are, in practice, two distinct elements to the problem of recovery. (a) Is it *physically possible to rebuild the economy?* In other words, can sufficient equipment be put in working order to re-establish the basic components of a modern industrial economy. (b) Is it *psychologically feasible* for people to work cooperatively together in the aftermath of a nuclear war *to rebuild the society?*

Whatever the answer to (a), it is (b) that should cause the most concern. Experience with natural disasters (earthquakes, droughts, etc.) suggest that the psychological factor is crucial to survival. Many of the more active survivors succeed by safeguarding their own personal interests (or those of their immediate family) rather than concerning themselves with the community (looting is prevalent in all communities after earthquakes, major fires, etc.). There is no basis whatsoever for the myths purveyed by certain war historians to the effect that suffering in a catastrophe brings out the best in people, to share burdens and cooperate in the face of adversity.

These considerations have led governments to plan *military-style administrations* for the post-war period. They have accepted implicitly that voluntary cooperation is unlikely to be forthcoming from a shocked, wounded and bereaved population. In the aftermath, people will be *directed* to work in key areas (power and fuel supplies, agriculture, etc.). Only those that cooperate with society's perceived needs will enjoy the benefits of such food and warmth that the economy still has to offer. This aspect of official plans seems realistic since the coercion inherent in our money-exchange, wealth-owning economy will have little force in the post-war period. But, to be accepted, even a military government has to offer hope of an end to privations—will this be feasible?

Help From Outside?

The casualty figures quoted earlier are for Europe as a whole but, naturally, will be greater in territories of the main belligerents. Sweden and Switzerland, for example, may be spared the direct effect of nuclear explosions and their extensive networks of shelters should reduce their fatalities from the subsequent fall-out. It has been suggested that these countries could provide the base from which European society could be rebuilt.

There are a number of problems with this theory. In the first place, the countries outside NATO and WTO Europe constitute less than 20% of its population and produce only a roughly equivalent share of its wealth.

Secondly, to the extent that these countries do escape the worst of the destruction, they could be overwhelmed by refugees from the less fortunate areas. Thirdly, and most important, they also will be covered by radioactive fall-out (see map), disruption of fuel supplies, deaths to livestock, diseases and many more of the numerous problems affecting the worst-hit countries. Although the non-belligerents may be better off than the NATO/WTO countries, they are unlikely to be strong enough to take responsibility for the recovery of Germany, Poland, France, Britain. . . .

Alternatively, since we have stretched our imagination to accept the concept of a nuclear war confined to Europe, perhaps it requires no greater effort to imagine the people of Europe welcoming the generosity of their unscathed destroyers if the USA and USSR offered to help rebuild Europe (for another nuclear battle?). Although such a contingency would be physically possible, one doubts whether the USSR and USA, having first destroyed Europe as a by-product of their mutual hostility, would then promptly collaborate in a joint venture to reconstruct it.

In Short

Even a very limited nuclear war would devastate Europe physically. In the aftermath the risks of psychological and political breakdown could prove fatal to the prospects of any form of social recovery at all.

---

[1] Discussed further in Rogers, Dando, van den Dungen, *As Lambs to the Slaughter*, London 1981.

[2] See John Cox, *Overkill*, Harmondsworth 1981.

[3] The best recent scientific study is Rotblat/SIPRI, *Nuclear Radiation in Warfare*, London 1981.

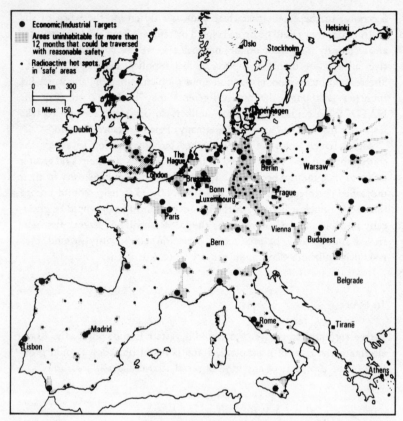

Effects of a Nuclear Exchange in Europe

The Nuclear Umbrella in East Asia

Saburo Kugai

for Peggy Duff

Edward Thompson's excellent essay on the new dangers of nuclear war has a universal message. At the same time, it is primarily concerned with the European theatre of the reemergent Cold War. Thompson argues that Europe was the original focus of the confrontation between the two blocs, and continues to be the main arena of their conflict today. Yet Japan was no less important an objective for the United States to hold for capitalism in 1945; China represented a greater loss to it than Eastern Europe; while all the occasions on which the Cold War actually became hot occurred in the Far East—above all, in Korea and Vietnam. As a Japanese, then, I will naturally concentrate on the Asian and Pacific dimension of the present perilous international situation—which one can argue has historically been as significant as the European and Atlantic dimension. Moreover, East Asia has not only been the region where the most destructive conventional wars between capitalism and communism have been fought. It is also the only region in the world where nuclear weapons have actually been used—in my own country. The Japanese experience thus probably has some lessons for the peace movement in Europe and the United States. In my response, I will discuss a number of themes. Firstly, I will say something about the moral and scientific background to nuclear weapons development in the West, and then about the human effects of their use on Japanese cities at the end of the Second World War. Next, I will discuss the grave deterioration in the nuclear arms race in the last decade. Finally, I will look at the whole concept of the 'nuclear umbrella' that the USA at its own initiative 'extends' to Japan, and now to China as well—a concept that is highly relevant to the situation in Europe, of course: a form of protection that in fact threatens only destruction of those whom it purports to cover. In conclusion, I will suggest common positions that peace forces in the Atlantic and Pacific zones should struggle for together.

The Genesis of Nuclear Fission

In 1938 Bertolt Brecht, then in exile in Denmark, was working on *Galileo* when he approached a group of young scientists under Niels Bohr (who later took part in the Manhattan Project) for advice on the role played by Galileo in the history of science. Through his encounter with these contemporary scientists, Brecht learned, to his great astonishment, of their involvement in the study of nuclear fission. The experience prompted him to revise his text at this early date. Later, in his notes on the staging of this play, starring Charles Laughton in Los Angeles in 1945, Brecht wrote: 'Just as we were working on a revised version, the "atomic age" made its debut in Hiroshima. The biography of Galilei, the founder of the new physics, came to be interpreted differently overnight. The infernal effects of the huge atomic bomb shed a new, more penetrating light on the conflict between Galilei and those in power in his time. . . . As the first press reports of the atomic bombing reached Los Angeles, the metropolis made a show of mourning to a surprising extent. The author of this script heard bus drivers and hawking women at the vegetable market talking only of how terrible it was. It was no doubt a victory, but one with a disgrace that is usually brought by defeat.'[1]

In his notebooks, Brecht left numerous illuminating remarks on the philosophy that was supposed to inspire the very foundation of science but has in reality all but eluded modern science. Galilei's crime, he commented, can be considered the original sin of modern science itself. The Catholic hierarchy which summoned Galilei before the Inquisition should be represented on stage not as an ecclesiastical but as a political power. Brecht called modern science a rightful bride of the church, saying it developed in continuity from medieval theology and was originally intended to alleviate the burdens of human life.

I start my discussion with these reflections on Brecht not because I subscribe in any way to the theories of counter-science which have lately become fashionable in some quarters, but because his penetrating intuition as an artist seemed to presage the unfolding horrors of the nuclear age. It is a striking fact that in November 1945, about the time that Brecht was writing these notes, Robert Oppenheimer—who played a leading role in the Manhattan Project—was speaking bitterly to researchers in the Los Alamos Laboratory of the predicament of his contemporaries who had created the atomic bomb. He said in part: 'The real impact of the creation of the atomic bomb and atomic weapons. . . to understand that one has to look further back, look, I think, to the times when physical science was growing in the days of the Renaissance, and when the threat that science offered was felt so deeply throughout the Christian world. The analogy is, of course, not perfect. You may even wish to think of the days in the last century when the theories of evolution seemed a threat to the values by which men lived. The analogy is not perfect because there is nothing new in atomic weapons . . . there is certainly nothing that we have done here, or in the physics or chemistry that immediately preceded our work here, in which any revolutionary ideas were involved. I don't think that the conceptions of nuclear fission have strained any man's attempts to understand them, and I don't feel that any of us have really learned in a deep sense very much from following this up. It is in a quite different way. It is not an idea . . . it is a development and a reality . . . but it has in common with the early days of physical science the fact that the very existence of science is threatened, and its value is threatened.'[2]

Another scientist who collaborated in the Manhattan Project, Victor Weisskopf, was to express a very different view of the relation between modern physics and the creation of nuclear weapons, in the light of later knowledge of the damage and after-effects of nuclear weapons, the vicious cycle of the post-war arms race, and the accelerating development of nuclear power in the 35 years since the creation of the first atomic bomb.

'There is indeed something different in the latest developments of physics which I would call "the leap into the cosmos." Previously we were dealing mostly with processes similar to those occurring in our terrestrial environment. In the past few decades, however, we have made a decisive step: we now deal with extraterrestial phenomena. Nuclear physics and subnuclear physics deal with the excitation of quantum states that are beyond the reach of ordinary terrestrial energy exchanges. In general, nuclear reactions do not take place on Earth. Nuclear dynamics are dormant in our environment. . . . Today nuclear physicists are dealing with cosmic processes in which many millions of electron volts per atom are exchanged rather than the few electron volts that are customary here on Earth. The fission reaction was one of the first of these cosmic processes which led to major technological applications. . . . It is not surprising, therefore, that people are fearful and bewildered. . . . *In 1940 we took no time to speculate about these questions.* The discovery of fission came at a dark time in the history of mankind. . . . The whole world was threatened by the expanding cancer of Nazism. The Germans discovered fission and they might have used it if it had been usable at that time. . . . From then on, political developments, and not scientific ones determined the course of events.'[3]

An embryo of what is now called the doctrine of nuclear deterrence may be found in Weisskopf's recollection that 'in 1940 we took no time to speculate about these questions'. In fact, there was an exception here. At least one colleague, Joseph Rotblat, gave much deeper thought to these issues at the time. In August 1980 he visited Tokyo and told his story.[4] Being a Polish-born Jew and an exiled scientist, Rotblat said he was well aware of what the Nazis had done and were intending to do in occupied Europe. He also knew that the Germans had the necessary scientific know-how to produce the atomic bomb and had gained access to the uranium mines in Czechoslovakia. Under the circumstances, he willingly took part in the Manhattan Project, via the British Tube Alloy Project, in the firm belief that the Allied powers had to acquire the bomb before the Nazis in order to deter them from using the weapon. So saying, Rotblat commented wryly that people at the time, including himself, were already seized of the notion of what is now called nuclear deterrence, even before the atomic bomb was created. He also recalled his astonishment at hearing Major-General Leslie Groves, military director of the Manhattan Project, declare to Rotblat and his fellow-scientists towards October 1943 that the projected bomb was directed not so much against the Germans or the Japanese as ultimately against the Russians.

One of the remarkable things about Joseph Rotblat was that of all the European scientists who took part in the Manhattan Project, including those who were exiles, he was the only one to resign from the programme immediately after the defeat of the Germans in May 1945, on the ground that the project had now lost its purpose and that the bomb should not be used on Japan or any other country. Furthermore, he abandoned the study of nuclear physics after returning to London and has since specialized in the medical application of radiation and radiological protection. The significance of his course of action acquires its full relief when we remember that organized peace initiative by scientists, such as the Russell—Einstein Manifesto and the Pugwash Conference, began to appear only in the 1950s when the nuclear arms race had already begun.

The Significance of Hiroshima and Nagasaki

The 36 years since the dropping of atomic bombs on Japan have been a period of ever-intensifying nuclear arms race. Authoritative studies of recent years, such as the *Comprehensive Study on Nuclear Weapons* compiled by United Nations Secretary-General Kurt Waldheim in September 1980, or the Yearbook of the Stockholm International Peace Research Institute, *Armaments or Disarmament 1981*, estimate that the current level of nuclear weapons stockpiled in the world amounts to some 1.0 to 1.3 million

Hiroshima-type bombs, or three tons of TNT for every person in the world. But since Hiroshima and Nagasaki are the only precedents so far for the actual use of atomic bombs in war, nuclear weapons remain an abstraction to a vast majority of the world's people—including even those informed few who have some knowledge of the latest series of weapons such as MIRVs, neutron bombs, SS-20s, and Pershing II missiles. Accordingly, descriptions of the destructive power of contemporary nuclear weapons in terms of their kilotonnage or scale relative to that of the Hiroshima bomb, however precise their estimates, tend to create a most misleading image of the disastrous consequences of a possible nuclear war, by reducing them to a set of abstract figures.

Let us consider, for example, the bombing and shelling of the three countries of Indochina, notably the southern half of Vietnam, by the United States and its puppet regimes in the eleven-year period from 1965 to 1975, which amounted to 18 million tons. (For comparison, the total amount of bombs dropped by the USA during World War II on all fronts—European, North African, and Asian-Pacific—was 2.3 million tons.) Approximately, this figure would translate into more than 900 Hiroshima bombs. Having visited Vietnam at war on three occasions, including May–June 1972 during the carpet bombing by B-52s immediately after Richard Nixon's decision to mine the harbours of North Vietnam, I am well acquainted with the inhuman war crimes committed by the United States and the lingering after-effects of the war—including thousands of casualties caused even after the total liberation of the country by unexploded shells, frequent incidence of liver cancer and microcephaly as a result of chemical warfare using defoliants such as 2,4,5T, and the wholesale destruction of the ecological system which has seen the sprouting of bamboo forests in South Vietnam in place of the more vulnerable mangroves which died out in the war. Yet massive as this damage may seem, it bears no comparison with what would have occurred if 900 Hiroshima bombs had been dropped over Indochina. Such an attack would have caused irreparable damage to human life and the natural environment not only of Indochina but also of surrounding regions, as radioactive fall-out was carried to them by monsoon winds. Recent evidence of the extent of these dangers has been provided by the revelation of the consequences of nuclear tests on the Pacific and in the Nevada deserts, which emerged as a major epidemiological issue in the latter half of the 1970s, some 20 years after the tests were conducted. In view of the fact that these were, after all, the result of controlled experiments which did take into account, at least to some degree, the probable effects of the detonation on human lives and environment, the experiences of Hiroshima and Nagasaki acquire a decisively important significance today as the only precedents of actual nuclear attack on urban population centres and as a minuscule prototype of the annihilation that a future nuclear war would bring.

A considerable amount of documentation is already available on the damage and after-effects of the nuclear attack on the two cities, including the report of the 1977 International Symposium on the Damage and After-effects of the Atomic Bombing sponsored by a group of international NGOs. Much remains unknown, however, of the long-term effects of neutron and gamma ray doses; new findings appear almost every year, presenting an ever more horrifying picture of the injuries they cause. For our purposes here, let us simply make a brief review of the damage inflicted on the two cities which served as prototypes of the effects of a future nuclear war. In so doing, we hope to convey a more concrete sense of what nuclear weapons really involve.

While the first atomic device detonated in the desert near Alamogordo on 16 July 1945 was a plutonium bomb, the weapon dropped on Hiroshima, dubbed 'Little Boy', was the first uranium bomb. The critical mass of uranium-235 was known at the time to be six to eight kilograms: the Hiroshima bomb was composed of some 60 kilograms of 95% uranium-235. But in the event only 700 grams of this material was consumed in the chain reaction after the apparatus was set off just above the city. The rest was blown away in the original state of uranium-235 without going through a chain reaction, although the inside of the bomb was presumably made of tungsten to render the chain reaction by neutron irradiation more effective. The 700 grams of uranium-235 that did undergo nuclear fission would have been the size of a ping-pong ball. Yet it created a ball of fire around the centre of the explosion with a temperature of nearly 4000 degrees centigrade—lava flow, a terrestrial phenomenon, has a temperature of about 1000 degrees centigrade—incinerating all things in its path—both living and non-living—in an instant, hitting a 500-metre radius area with a 280-metre-per-second blast, which is more than five times the speed of the strongest typhoon, and showering a far more extensive area with radiation—mainly neutrons and gamma rays—far above lethal doses.

The plutonium bomb dropped on Nagasaki three days later, on 9 August, unleashed some 22 trillion calories of energy and an explosive yield of 20 kilotons, which was 1.7 times that of Hiroshima's uranium bomb, though the amount of plutonium to undergo nuclear fission was a meagre one kilogram or three tablespoonfuls. The two cities were annihilated in an instant by these non-terrestrial weapons, and while the exact death toll remains unknown to date, at least 200,000 are estimated to have died from the strikes by the end of 1945, followed by more than 100,000 in the ensuing years. Hibakusha, or surviving victims of the nuclear onslaught, number upwards of 370,000 today, many of them still suffering from the after-effects of the bombing.

The plight of the Hibakusha is not confined to the fact that they are generally sickly, susceptible to illnesses of all kinds, haunted by constant fear of being suddenly struck by leukemia or other cancers. What needs to be noted is that they have been compelled by their predicament to conceal their identity as Hibakusha out of fear of discrimination in marriage and employment, and that many of them have tended to be wary of having children due to fears of genetic effects. The sufferings of the Hibakusha cast a most suggestive, if indirect, light on the range and depth of human damage that would ensue from a possible nuclear war. A considerable amount of knowledge is now available on the physical, psychological, and social sequels of the atomic bombing of Japan, including the problem of *in utero* victims, through various studies such as those of the International Symposium of 1977. It should be remembered, however, that the question of genetic effects has generally been skirted as a virtually taboo topic and has yet to become an object of scientific study because of the enormity of the social and psychological consequences that might ensue from it.

In both Hiroshima and Nagasaki, residual radiation contained in the radioactive fall-out and irradiated material affected those who had not been in the city at the time of the attacks but subsequently entered the area for relief operations or in search of families and friends. In this regard, the case of Nagasaki warrants particular attention. Incidence of leukemia and other cancers has been reported since the beginning of the 1970s among former US servicemen stationed in Nagasaki after September 1945. They were apparently affected by the residual radiation of plutonium through their drinking of river water while the city's normal water system remained out of commission. The U.S. government has now been obliged to conduct a thorough investigation into their case as well as that of some 300,000 atomic veterans who took part in more than a hundred nuclear tests in Nevada in the 1950s. The case of the Nagasaki veterans is significant because, as noted earlier, only one out of the eight kilograms of plutonium in the Nagasaki bomb underwent fission, while the rest descended on the area or was driven into the ground by the blast in the form of tiny particles of plutonium-239. (The half-life of plutonium-239, incidentally, is 24,400 years.) With investigation still continuing into the question of residual radiation in Nagasaki, epidemiological follow-up research on the US veterans has revealed noticeable variations in the effect of plutonium depending on which river was used as the source of drinking-water. This suggests the existence of considerable differences in the distribution of plutonium contamination over the hilly terrain of Nagasaki, but publication of such data is thought certain to provoke unpredictable social, economic, and psychological repercussions.

The effects of the Nagasaki bombing take on a particular significance today, in face of the trend towards production of cheaper, smaller, and lighter nuclear weapons such as the neutron bomb, nuclear artillery shells, Cruise missiles, and other types of theatre nuclear weapons. Since the critical mass of plutonium-239 is far smaller and can be obtained far more cheaply than that of enriched uranium-235, it seems virtually certain that plutonium-239 (instead of the more expensive americium) will be used for the mass production of 'triggers' for these weapons, including the neutron bombs ordered by Reagan. Despite all 'progress' in nuclear weapons technology in the 36 years since Nagasaki, it is difficult to imagine that such nuclear weapons have become so 'humane', as is claimed in the case of the neutron bomb, as to kill only those inside targeted tanks, trenches, and buildings—while all their plutonium supposedly undergoes fission, leaving no residual plutonium that could be the source of secondary radiation, and expediently avoiding the deadly heat rays, blast, mushroom cloud, and nuclear fall-out of the Hiroshima and Nagasaki bombs.

The Vicious Circle of the Seventies

Since the mid-1970s there is a growing awareness that the threat of nuclear war has been intensified by the US preparation of a nuclear first-strike or counterforce strategy aimed against Soviet arsenals. Public knowledge of this first-strike strategy has widened in the United States itself and in the Asian Pacific region, including Japan, above all since former Lockheed engineer Robert Aldridge resigned from his post as a designer of the Trident missile in protest against it, and embarked upon a non-violent campaign to galvanize public opinion into a sense of crisis, prompting the spread of similar movements elsewhere. But in reality the first-strike strategy was conceived as long ago as 1962 by the Pentagon under Robert McNamara, when it was believed that the United States was behind the Soviet Union in the number of delivery vehicles.[5] Our peace movements thus have never been able to get ahead of our opponents, always allowing them to keep the initiative.

In 1978 Bernard Feld, a physics professor at MIT, who was then chairman of the Pugwash Conference, remarked that engineers and other experts involved in the research and development of nuclear weapons have always asked for 'four or five more years' to complete a perfect weapon for certain specified purposes, and then succeeded in obtaining the necessary budget and other resources for it. But in the meantime, the other side would also build weapons just as formidable, or set up defences against the projected new weapon by the time it was complete and ready for use. So when at last the new hardware is ready, it regularly proves ineffective against the reinforced armaments and defence systems of the enemy, and so only prompts further attempts to develop even more sophisticated and deadly weaponry. This is the way the unending vicious cycle of the nuclear arms race constantly escalates. Feld argued that it would never be possible for the United States to build a strategic weapons system capable of delivering a disarming first strike on the Soviet Union by destroying all of its ICBM silos, SLBMs, and other means of retaliation, so enabling the USA to emerge from the fray unscathed. The first-strike scenario, he said, was nothing but a pretext for continuing the nuclear arms race. I could not agree more.

The nuclear arms race was, in fact, bound to generate a vicious circle. For while the USA and USSR have always claimed that their goal was the attainment of a military balance, no such thing has ever been possible in the nuclear age. Neither side can hope to achieve security or military balance by deploying two or three times more nuclear weapons than its opponent, not to speak of gaining a first-strike capability, since even countries with such an immense expanse of territory as the United States and the Soviet Union could not survive as a nation if they were hit by a first strike. The attacking nation might be behind in the arms race, and some of the opponent's SLBMs and other means of retaliation might escape such a pre-emptive strike, but no nation as such will survive a nuclear war.

It must be noted that the United States has always taken the lead in the arms race with the Soviet Union. Although the Russians pioneered certain technological breakthroughs such as the development of portable hydrogen bombs made of lithium deuteride, and intercontinental ballistic missiles, it was always the United States that actually deployed these and other nuclear weapons systems first. The rationale of the constant US preponderance in the arms race has lain equally in American designs of imperial domination over the world, in the profit motive of the capitalist 'military—industrial complex', and in a coldly calculated bid to exert pressure on the socialist economies and ultimately ruin them, by provoking the USSR into an arms race on an unprecedented scale.

But this is where the problem begins, not ends. During the administration of Nikita Khrushchev, now an unpopular figure in the socialist world, the Soviet Union proposed measures in the United Nations for general and complete disarmament, phased peace initiatives, and openly spoke of its ambition to catch up and overtake the USA not in an arms race but in an economic race. But since the start of bilateral arms control negotiations following the 1962 Cuban Missile Crisis, the nuclear arms race has, ironically, actually intensified. As the two powers sat down at the negotiating table and became familiar with each other's hand, they began to play a game based on a common set of rules, trying to outplay or overtake the other while following these rules. It seems unavoidable that, in the interim, there have emerged in the Soviet Union various social groups with a vested interest in a military build-up, even if a different type of interest from that of their counterparts in the capitalist countries. The stockpile of nuclear weapons possessed by the socialist countries today cannot possibly be justified as necessary for the defence of socialism. This is precisely the proof that the present nuclear arms race has become a vicious circle. The nuclear arsenal of the Soviet Union, like that of the United States, is built upon a strategy of maximum, instead of minimum, deterrence.

Furthermore, since the signature of the US–Soviet Nuclear War Prevention Treaty at the time of Brezhnev's visit to Washington in 1973, suspicion has been growing that the two powers have reached a tacit agreement to regard each other's territory as a sanctuary, opting for the development of 'usable' nuclear weapons in 'theatre' warfare elsewhere. This suspicion has given a major impetus to the recent rapid growth of anti-nuclear movements in Europe, as people in the Anglo-Saxon countries will be well aware. On this score, a recent statement by Erhard Eppler, a leading member of the West German Social Democratic Party and a former Cabinet member under Chancellor Brandt, is symptomatic: 'But there is an attempt to make nuclear war limitable, manageable and even "winnable". Every step forward in nuclear technology—in which the United States is ahead of the Soviets—encourages this attempt. Thus, there is an increased danger of limited nuclear war in Europe.'[6]

USA, China and Japan Today

The strategic situation in the Asian-Western-Pacific region has undergone a major change in recent years. In this part of the world, the US nuclear 'umbrella' was long thought to cover Japan, South Korea, Taiwan, the Philippines, and other ASEAN countries along with the Pacific islands. But in the late 1970s, two critical developments altered the whole military map of the region. The first has been the extension of the US umbrella to China. The second has been a modification of the role of Japan within the umbrella.

Let us start with the position of China. After a few years of ephemeral China fever among American businessmen in the aftermath of Nixon's visit to Peking, US firms have shown little interest in the Chinese market or Chinese resources, except for the cash sale of a few goods including passenger jets and their parts. In this attitude, they have followed a time-tested, unwritten law of American private capital—not to invest in or trade with countries lacking a domestic infrastructure capable of guaranteeing such capital political security, a policy not shared by their Japanese or European counterparts. Consequently, American banks and corporations as well as the US state had no need to scurry frantically for cover, as Japanese and West European firms did, when official Chinese policy shifted in 1979 from the ill-fated 'Four Modernizations' to the present 'period of adjustment'. Instead, ruling circles in the US had from the mid-1970s onwards started to view China as a weak link in the world military balance, breaking with their past visions of China as an immense and enigmatic menace that needed to be contained by American might. What finally clinched this American assessment was the debacle of China's supposedly 'punitive' invasion of Vietnam in 1979 and its aftermath.

Washington now learned for the first time that the Chinese People's Liberation Army, in contrast to the Vietnamese forces with which US troops had fought so long, lacked the ability to fight a modern war.[7] The US thus seems to have reached the conclusion that it had to extend its nuclear umbrella far west of the line connecting Japan, South Korea, Taiwan, and the Philippines, to cover the entire length of the Sino-Soviet border. Failure to do so would, according to the Pentagon's concept of nuclear deterrence, create a vast military 'vacuum' extending from North-Eastern continental Asia all the way to Turkestan. There is little doubt that this is the explanation of the recent series of overtures to Peking, starting with the lifting of the ceiling on an Export–Import Bank loan and the granting of most-favoured-nation status to China by the Reagan administration, in a reversal of the earlier pro-Taiwanese Republican platform of 'Two Chinas'. These overtures have continued with the lifting of a COCOM ban on the export of militarily applicable computers, aircraft, electronic equipment and parts prior to the first visit to China by Secretary of State Alexander Haig on 14 June 1981. The State Department has now taken care to redefine China as a 'friendly developing country' instead of continuing to refer to it as a constituent of international communism. The Chinese government, for its part, has effectively conceded its acceptance of the US nuclear umbrella—as can be seen from the welcome it has extended to Reagan's decision to produce and deploy neutron warheads, and the permission it has given for the deployment of US monitoring equipment for detecting Soviet missile and nuclear tests in its strategic border province of Sinkiang. Within the Reagan administration's massive arms build-up, meanwhile, proposals are emerging for deploying theatre nuclear weapons in Asia and the Western Pacific—notably the positioning of Cruise missiles on land and seaborne vessels in the region by 1984. Similar plans will doubtless involve the redesigned B-1 bombers.

At the same time, a series of recent nuclear-related incidents provides disturbing evidence that the Reagan administration is constructing a new role for Japan within the framework of its expansion of the US nuclear umbrella to China. In early April 1981 a 2,300-ton Japanese freighter was sunk in a hit-and-run collision by a US Polaris submarine, George Washington, close to Japanese waters off the southern coast of Kyushu. The US Navy later announced that the incident had occurred while the submarine was on its way to a South Korean port during an exercise with P-3C anti-submarine patrol aircraft. The hit-and-run collision fortuitously revealed that US strategic nuclear weapons are deployed not somewhere deep down in a far-away corner of the Pacific but off the Japanese archipelago itself, where they are readily subject to mainland command, communication, and control (the three Cs) and have easy access to Soviet targets in case of a pre-emptive strike. Thus the position and function of the Japanese islands are commensurate with those of Norway in the sense that they serve as a command-communication-control base for Poseidon—soon Trident—submarines and other US nuclear weapons targeted on the Soviet Union.

In fact, it is now essential for the United States, in its new strategic posture in Asia, to deploy a Polaris arsenal in the vicinity of Japan and other parts of the Western Pacific so that the submarines, stationed in the Asian–Pacific region as theatre forces, can extend their nuclear umbrella over the immense expanse of Chinese territory. There are other signs that point to the integration of China in current US strategy. An array of anti-submarine 3C bases has been constructed in Japan, from Misawa in the far north to Yosami and as far south as Kesaji in Okinawa. During joint defence talks in Hawaii last June the United States demanded that Japan purchase no less than 125 P-3Cs, when the US itself has only 200 of these aircraft deployed through its entire global network of Anti-Submarine Warfare.

The second of the series of nuclear-related incidents was touched off by former US Ambassador to Japan Edwin Reischauer, when he revealed in an interview with *Mainichi Shimbun*, a leading Tokyo daily, that the Japanese government had approved the 'introduction' (or 'transit') of nuclear weapons on US ships and aircraft in Japan, by an 'oral understanding' given at the time of the 1960 revision of the Japan–US Security Treaty. Coming on the heels of the hit-and-run incident, this revelation created an uproar in Japan. This was a natural reaction in view of the overwhelming public support in this first and only nation to be a victim of atomic bombing for the three non-nuclear principles of 'not allowing the possession, production, or introduction of nuclear weapons'.

Successive Liberal Democratic governments have, to be sure, only given a most reluctant and perfunctory endorsement to the principles, while privately deriding anti-nuclear sentiment as 'nuclear allergy'. Their complicity in the introduction of US nuclear weapons, and the consequent violation in practice of the three principles, have long been suspected by knowledgeable observers and a sizeable section of the general public. All these qualifications notwithstanding, the non-nuclear principles have remained, officially at least, Japan's general consensus.

Many in Japan viewed the submarine incident and the Reischauer revelations as the outcome of a deliberate attempt by US authorities to turn Japan into a fully-fledged nuclear base against the USSR. I do not, however, share this interpretation. Anyone familiar with the dynamics of contemporary American politics since the Vietnam era—studded as it has been with a sequence of unexpected episodes such as the resignation of Johnson, the exposure of the Pentagon Papers, and the scandal of Watergate—should be aware that isolated fortuitous incidents are typically exploited with skill and resolution by groups in power or other forces behind the scenes to set in motion a major political drama, going well beyond the intentions or expectations of the protagonists initially involved in them. For our purposes here, we can thus disregard the question of how systematic an understanding of the strategic significance of transforming Japan into a nuclear base is possessed by politicians like Reischauer, Haig (reportedly irate over Reischauer's indiscretions) or Weinberger. What is decisive is not the insight or intention of individual leaders but the logic of the events now impending, as a US nuclear umbrella unfolds across East Asia.

What exactly is a nuclear umbrella? Few strategic concepts can match its ambiguity. In the early 1950s, when the two major powers already had nuclear bombs but not nuclear submarines or missiles deployed as delivery systems, there was no such concept as 'nuclear umbrella', although of course that of 'nuclear deterrence' already existed. No such term or idea can be found in Henry Kissinger's *Nuclear Weapons and American Foreign Policy*

(1956), C. Wright Mills's *The Causes of World War III* (1958), or Fred Cook's *A Warfare State* (1961). It was in the first half of the 1960s, probably towards 1962–63, that the nuclear umbrellas of both the United States and the Soviet Union began to take shape on a global scale, when medium and long-range ballistic missiles (either land-based or launched from surface ships or submarines) moved from experimental stages to actual deployment. If this is so, it would follow that the Japanese people were dragged under the US nuclear umbrella without realizing what was happening to them.

Reischauer, Weinberger and former Rear Admiral LaRocque all concur that Japan benefited from the US nuclear umbrella in these years because it was relieved of the onus of military spending and could thus enjoy an unblemished economic prosperity. As a factual statement, this assertion is at least partially correct. But it is no answer to the complaint of the Japanese people that they never sought shelter under such an umbrella in the first place. For them, the argument is at best gratuitous. In any event, it might be replied that the security arrangements between the two countries were not actually as one-sided as some Americans claim. Without Japan, the United States would not have been able to fight the Korean, much less the longer Vietnamese War, or to 'defend' South Korea, Taiwan, and the Philippines. Furthermore, the speed of economic growth has little correlation to the scale of defence spending, provided military outlays do not assume gigantic proportions. West Germany, for instance, achieved its own economic 'miracle' and far outdistanced Japan in building a welfare state, while standing in the front line of East–West confrontation from the start of the Cold War, reintroducing military conscription and sustaining a heavy military budget to support its own army and that of the NATO forces on its soil. Japan and West Germany differ greatly in their objective settings. But the rapid economic growth of the two countries is to be attributed not to a common exemption from the arms burden, but rather to a broad interplay of forces at work in the resurgence and development of world capitalism since the Second World War. A counter-hypothesis might even be that had the US imposed upon Japan massive rearmament and wholesale resumption of military production in the early years of the post-war epoch, Japanese capitalism would by now have made major inroads into the markets for such high value-added products as jet engines, airlines, large-scale computers, offshore oil drilling and heavy weaponry, presenting a threat to US industries far greater than that posed today in television, cameras or automobiles. Indeed, Japan might well have gone so far as to acquire its own nuclear arsenal and missile systems.[8]

In other words, it is plain that the argument lauding the 'benefits' of the nuclear umbrella to Japan is one that caters to the convenience of the United States. Japanese history could have taken many different directions in the three decades since the war. It is high time, therefore, that the Japanese people themselves let it be known to the United States what would suit their own 'convenience'. At the top of their list of priorities is the refusal to allow the introduction of nuclear weapons into Japan. The people of Japan have time and again reaffirmed Japanese identity as the 'sole nation to be a victim of nuclear weapons' and have upheld the three non-nuclear principles as a virtual national consensus, creating a public opinion that successive pro-American governments have had to reckon with. This total popular rejection of nuclear weapons remains intact even in the aftermath of a series of tumultuous incidents since the publication of the Reischauer interview. The United States may claim to have Japan—and now, with the emergence of the Reagan strategy, China as well—under its nuclear umbrella, but that is something that suits the United States, not Japan. If the Japanese are to define themselves to the whole world as the 'sole nation to be a victim of nuclear weapons', they logically ought also to define the United States government as the 'sole nuclear victimizer' for its wilful destruction of two major Japanese cities in 1945. They also ought to demand, as the 'sole victim nation', that the 'sole victimizer' strictly observe the three non-nuclear principles and refrain from introducing nuclear weapons into the victim nation.

It might be asked at this point, whether it is not contradictory to refuse the introduction of nuclear weapons into Japan while the country de facto remains under the US nuclear umbrella by virtue of the Japan–US Security Treaty, given that US forces in the Western Pacific are fully equipped with nuclear wepons. The present Liberal Democratic government, for one, takes refuge in this line of argument. The main thrust of the case advanced by Reischauer or Weinberger is very similar. But the contradiction is only real when viewed from the standpoint of US strategic doctrine. Looked at from an opposite point of view, the contradiction and lack of realism lie in the assumption by the US Defence Secretary and the chairman of the Joint Chiefs of Staff that Japan could emerge unscathed from a US attack on the Soviet Union, without anticipating retaliation. The true scenario envisaged by the American military must be to launch strategic nuclear attacks against the USSR on such a massive scale as to render any Soviet retaliation against the mainland United States impossible, while at the same time exposing Japan to the risk of being caught in missile crossfire and reduced to ruins.

Even if one supposed that the Russians were obsessed with the evil design of invading Japan, they would certainly then have to reckon with an all-out nuclear retaliation against their European heartland, and not just their Asian republics, for an attack on Japan, the largest industrial and commercial centre in the Asian–Pacific region, an economy which ranks second in the world in gross national product and consumes five million barrels of petroleum every day, would inevitably spell a global nuclear war threatening the very survival of the human race. In such a holocaust Japan—located in the front-line of US nuclear dispositions in Asia—would be doomed to annihilation.

It is thus evident that, contrary to prevailing opinion in the United States, the only logical and sensible choice if the Japanese are to ensure their national survival is to insist on the three non-nuclear principles. This is the position that addresses the circumstances of the Japanese, instead of the Americans.

A conventional response abroad is to dismiss as unrealistic egoism any call to exempt Japan from involvement in the global network of nuclear weapons systems of the two major powers, as a demand for the creation of an exceptional vacuum over the country. To be sure, if exemption from the nuclear-weapons network were limited to Japan alone and then caused an offsetting reinforcement of the network by the United States in the neighbouring countries and islands, the demand for such a limited exemption would prove not only egoistic but also altogether ineffective even for securing Japan's own safety. The demand for exemption from the nuclear-weapons network, therefore, should be extended from the initial Japanese refusal of nuclear weapons, to a general denuclearization of the entire Asian–Pacific region in solidarity with the peoples of the countries and islands of the area. Such a broadening of its scope is essential for the realization of the three non-nuclear principles in Japan itself, and for the ultimate security of the Japanese people. Those who dismiss a campaign for denuclearization as unrealistic are typically themselves adepts of the unrealities of nuclear war games, trifling with the fate of humanity and of the planet. It is they who represent the higher insanity of Strangelove and his coterie.

Conclusions

Indeed, it would be difficult to find more unrealistic arguments than those that have unleashed the recent discussion in Japan over emergency 'contingencies'. Few countries on earth are enmeshed as tightly as Japan in the intricate network of the international division of labour that makes up the fabric of the world economy. Fears of disruption in sources of energy or food supplies have been the two most popular themes raised in discussion of putative national security 'contingencies', but the problem is not confined to these two items. To import all its necessary resources, Japan needs to have access to a world market for its manufactured goods. A major international conflict, even one that occurred far away from Japan on the other side of the globe, would be certain to deal a serious blow to the Japanese economy by affecting either its raw material supplies or its export markets or both. Japanese capitalism, therefore, could not withstand the impact of a major conflagration anywhere in the world, even if Japan and the United States were to defend the 'sea lanes' for shipping oil from the Middle East successfully.

If Japan were seriously to prepare for 'contingencies' of this order, or to seek absolute national security while retaining the existing international division of labour, it would have to conquer the world. Once we accept that such a dream is neither possible nor permissible, it is clear that we have no other choice than to make an all-out effort—political, diplomatic, economic, and cultural—to preclude any 'contingency' of this kind ever arising. The alarmist politics of 'contingency planning' only serve to intensify all the real dangers. The record of successive Japanese governments here is one of shameful duplicity: they have unfailingly supported the nuclear strategy and deterrence doctrines of the USA with their votes in the United Nations and other disarmament conferences, while giving lip-service to the three non-nuclear principles at home.

Fortunately, however, popular opposition is growing to this stance in Japan itself. At the 1981 World Conference Against Atomic and Hydrogen Bombs held around Hiroshima and Nagasaki Days, about 150 overseas delegates from literally all over the world joined some 10,000 Japanese participants to pledge a common mobilization for the forthcoming Second UN Special Session on Disarmament, in favour of extending a non-nuclear umbrella around the world. The Japanese movement for nuclear disarmament appeared to have lost much of its initial vigour during the quarter-century since its inception in 1955; but it has now come back to life after the Polaris hit-and-run incident and the publication of the Reischauer interview. At the same time, the peoples of the Pacific islands, who have suffered from the after-effects of US, British, and French nuclear tests and protested against the proposed dumping of radioactive wastes by the Japanese government in the ocean, are intensifying their struggle for a nuclear-free Pacific in solidarity with similar movements in Japan, Australia, Hawaii, and the Philippines. The non-nuclear Constitution of the Republic of Belau (formerly Palau), the first of its kind in the world, was hailed by the entire conference as a common and exemplary goal.

Meanwhile, there could be nothing more contradictory than the position of the people and the governments of the NATO countries in Western

Europe with respect to the question of nuclear weapons. Although the NATO establishment has always been predicated on the possession and deployment of nuclear weapons, these did not become a major political issue until quite recently. The emergent movements against nuclear weapons in the countries of Western Europe, and the corresponding changes in the tone of governments, stem from an acute and pressing concern over their very survival as nations in the event of a nuclear exchange between the two major powers in the European theatre. Some sections of these movements are directing more attention to protest against the proposed deployment of new weapons such as the neutron bombs and Pershing II missiles than to a demand for the removal of nuclear weapons already deployed; and seem at least for the moment to stop short of making a frontal assault on the existence of NATO itself, which is predicated on the possession of a nuclear arsenal. Such a position may appear to be logically contradictory, but it is probably the way of all mass movements and politics in the real world to progress in disrespect of apparent logic.

The crucial novelty of these developments is that the European and American movements, which in the past had a relatively abstract knowledge of the disastrous consequences of nuclear war, have in recent years come to realize for the first time the true imminence and gravity of the danger confronting them. Because public opinion accepted the deployment of nuclear weapons early on, the movements in these countries had to start far behind the Japanese goal of the three non-nuclear principles. The Japanese efforts to realize these principles are thus of significance not only for Japan itself but also for the rest of the world, and can provide lessons for the European and American movements which got off to a later start, as well as to the non-aligned movement which seeks to establish a new international economic order in lieu of the arms race.

In conclusion, let us recall Bertolt Brecht once again. At the end of a statement he had prepared, but was not permitted by the chairman to read out, on the occasion of his subpoena to testify before the Committee on Un-American Activities of the US House of Representatives, in October 1947, Brecht noted: 'Great wars have been suffered, greater ones are imminent, we are told. One of them might well wipe out mankind as a whole. We might be the last generation of the specimen man on this earth.'[9] Four years later, in September 1951, in the midst of an intensifying cold war, he compared the fate of the whole human race to that of Carthage: 'The great Carthage conducted three wars. It was still powerful after the first, still inhabitable after the second. When the third war was over, it could be found nowhere.'

[1]Translated from a Japanese version of Brecht's notes on the performance in Los Angeles. See also Charles Higham, *Charles Laughton*, 1976, pp. 160 ff.

[2]Robert Oppenheimer's speech to members of the Association of Los Alamos Scientists, 2 November 1945, *The Bulletin of the Atomic Scientists*, June 1980, pp. 15–16.

[3]Victor F. Weisskopf, 'A Peril and a Hope', *The Bulletin of the Atomic Scientists,* January 1979, pp. 10–11.

[4]See my interview with Prof. Joseph Rotblat, *The Asahi Shimbun* (one of the largest-selling dailies in Japan), 5 August 1980.

[5]Henry L. Trewhitt, *McNamara: His Ordeal in the Pentagon*, 1971, pp. 114 ff.

[6]*Newsweek*, 24 August 1981.

[7]Sources in Tokyo recently claimed that the General Staff of the Chinese Liberation Army had asked the Japanese Self-Defence Forces to make a computer simulation of a projected second invasion of Vietnam. The Japanese response was reportedly that the invasion had to be in the dry season; that it was essential to send 1.5 to 2 million troops; that the expeditionary forces had to be better equipped than in 1979; and that it would still take four months to occupy Hanoi. The Chinese are said to have been forced to give up the plan at least for the time being.

[8]While military expenditure remains about only one per cent of GNP, Japan is already the seventh largest military power in the world, and the Japanese arms build-up, linked to a militarist ideological offensive, has been astonishingly rapid. Negotiations on the exchange of military technology between Japan and the United States are currently accelerating.

[9]From the text of a recording, *Bertolt Brecht vor dem Ausschuss für unamerikanische Tätigkeit*, Folkways Records, West Berlin 1963.

Nuclear Extermination and the National Security State

Marcus Raskin

In modern states, huge organizations enter daily into a series of activities which may not appear to be crimes or violations of anyone's rights. But once we remove the conceptual blinders from our eyes, the reality is that those actions are crimes in being. The armaments race, given the nature of the arms made and the war plans fashioned, is criminal when compared to laws of war or peace, the criminal laws of individual nations, or the standards of the Nuremberg and Asian trials.

The arms strategists' plans of 'taking out' millions of people either in first-strike or second-strike reprisal are surely not compatible with any internationally lawful system of defence. That we see nations and their leaders thoughtlessly reducing their actions to criminal activity hardly means that laws do not exist which directly contradict such behaviour. As the judges at Nuremberg said, 'after the policy to initiate and wage aggressive wars was formulated', a defendant was 'criminally responsible if he, being on the policy level, could have influenced such policy and failed to do so'.[1] Actions of a genocidal nature, once contemplated, are war crimes in being. The final act in a process which leads to a culminating event, in this case the signal for nuclear war, does not have to be completed for us to realize that the event is already in preparation. We need only to look at official arms budgets and strategic doctrines today to comprehend the criminal nature of the enterprise they embody. Government officials descend to the level of bureaucratic gangsterism as their political lives and practices fly directly in the face of Article 1 of the UN Charter and Declaration.

Once we grasp that we are living under imminent threat of a genocide which has not yet, thankfully, been played out as the final notes of civilization's Götterdämmerung, the entire spectrum of contemporary talks on arms control and disarmament appears in a somewhat different light. The participants in the current START talks in Geneva, now proceeding in the greatest secrecy, eschew essential moral, legal, and criminal questions when discussing armaments. There is a necrophiliac quality to the technical expertise which calculates one missile against another, as diplomats become brokers in charred bodies. When such negotiations are divorced from the fundamentally criminal nature of the weaponry or strategies under discussion, arms control talks are reduced to narrow quibbles between state representatives on the character and size of mutually genocidal forces. The result is that the START negotiations have once again helped to confer legitimacy on the entire range of weapons of mass destruction in the USA, creating the illusion among media and university elites, no less than the people as a whole, that such weapons are 'needed' and should be considered in the card catalogues of libraries and treasury accounts under the heading of 'Policy and Diplomacy' rather than 'Crime and Criminal Behaviour'. There can be no adequate comprehension of the real nature and gravity of nuclear weapons, or meaningful discussion of ways to limit and eliminate them, without a firm starting-point in the international legal principles governing acts of genocide and safety of populations, and in the Nuremberg criteria for personal accountability of public officials to national or international tribunals.

Arms strategists, scientists, governments, civil servants, defence ministries, and diplomats should be made acutely aware of the legally and morally exposed situation in which they now find themselves. For they continue to be responsible for the development of a type of weaponry and military technology which breaches every natural law and fundamental human right. Conventional arms control and disarmament discussions reason in epicycles: a clearheaded understanding of the dangers facing us must start from a quite different basis.

In the United States, the argument can sometimes be heard that a drive to mass extermination may be found in the unconscious, where the fears of man impel him to actions over which he has no control and small if any understanding. In this account, man is little more than a surfer on waves of violent urges he neither commands nor comprehends. Were this true, there would be little point in even discussing nuclear weapons. Humankind's conscious existence could be written off, as its unconscious life— exclusively ugly and destructive—propelled civilization into a black hole without recovery or escape.

Others advance much the same argument in somewhat less stark terms. They maintain that the arms race is an expression of unappeasable insecurity. Torn between Eros and Thanatos, societies bring about exactly what they seek to avoid. Caught in a series of self-fulfilling prophecies, they act in the conviction that our human 'natures' require defence of territory, retaliation against attack and more than a little aggression against potential enemies. In other words, militarism and bellicosity are part of human nature and it matters little that we are discussing a German, Chinese, African, Arab, Israeli, Latin American, Russian or American, for the fears and needs of human nature as mediated through the modern state are by and large the same. Accordingly, our weapons and the social system we have built around them are not causes but effects. The conclusions imposed by such a view leave us with a prognosis without hope. For it is only a matter of time before nuclear war explodes, out of the logic of human 'nature'.

Without ignoring any 'facts', it would be far better to start from an agnostic and pragmatic position on issues of this kind. We do not and perhaps cannot know the deepest springs of human actions. We may even accept the assumption that stirring inside the unconscious of all of us are many demons and destructive monsters. But it would still be only a fool who would deny the presence of conscious will and intention in history, of deliberately made and rationally constructed objects, actions and institutions which can thereafter be controlled, directed or changed. To deny this is to discount the very possibility of freedom.

It is because this is so that we can assign moral responsibility to those organizational processes and social systems which still appear to act from rational judgement, but in fact have stepped over the edge of madness. They are our Golem; to be pointed out, studied and destroyed. This is easier said than done, for in the United States there are many people who build this Golem and are made secure by it. US history points to the value of the Golem of war. If you are not Amerindian or Chicano, war has had its positive side for Americans.

Today our leaders generate, and people accept—internalized into their daily habits—a paradoxical version of military politics. They do not see that a behavioural goal of mass extermination is programmed as an eventuality by the state. Preparations for war are not preparations for war, but the way to guarantee the peace. To be fair, there are some who still see war as a positive good, or at the least, as a viable policy. Researchers at the Rand Corporation are expected to study nuclear conflict in a dispassionate, calculating perspective and to argue that it would not be catastrophic, at least for the United States. Economists often point out that except for the occupation of Vietnam, the US has gained from each of its wars. Even radicals have on occasion noted that slavery as a legal institution was abolished through the Civil War. Those who advocate war without necessarily saying so do not see it as a breakdown of civilization. Rather, they view it as a positive process of selection, much as the advanced nineteenth-century thinkers praised Darwinian natural selection as an important social principle. The state apparatus is merely the organized means of violence which carries out this exercise in selection. General George Patton, for example, is held to express the highest values of the state, cheered now in our film theatres as he would have surely been praised by Hegel.

The 'human' dimensions of warfare are often also extolled in these circles. It is said that feelings of warmth, love and honesty find their best expression in the adversity of war—where, supposedly, people can escape their humdrum existences to find transcendent purposes beyond themselves, which give meaning to their lives or endow them with new possibilities. This point of view is often identified with the right although versions of it can on occasion be found on the progressive side of the spectrum as well. The words may be different, but the melody is the same. In the United States, the creed of natural selection and the sentiments of existential camaraderie fuse in the nationalist fervour of flag and country. The result appears to be the embodiment of martial values.[2]

Yet in one sense there is little overt support in the United States for martial values as such; American society continues to pursue its ideological commitment to the transcendent ideals of life, liberty and the pursuit of happiness. This commitment, certified in the American Constitution, has often been manipulated in American politics and statecraft. Woodrow Wilson gained much political and ethical advantage in the world by flying the banner of the transcendent values of democracy and self-determination, even as he resegregated the federal government. Kennedy sought to unite transcendent ideals with martial virtues in a triumphalist doctrine that advocated resort to violence and war in the service of an ulterior 'good'. Such a spirit of triumphalism can be tapped for many different purposes.

During the Second World War this spirit was mobilized against Hitler's militarism. Nazi Germany sought to engage and annihilate bourgeois, socialist and humanist values. The purpose of the Third Reich was once and for all to replace transcendent values with martial codes, and to subordinate rationality and science to the service of an irrational destructive state. The Nazi goal was limitless domination, and the means used to achieve it were the considerable skill, resources and will of the German people. While martial values have always been important in the West, built into the bellicose armoury and structure of the state, it was only the Nazis who expressly proclaimed martial values to be ends unto themselves. The Nazi-dominated social system thrived on this purposiveness. For the great industrialists like the Krupps there was no contradiction between their slave labour camps, their profit sheets, their technological and managerial skill, their belief in martial values and their loyalties to the leadership principle. We will look hard and almost in vain through the war crimes records for doubts among either German industrialists, general staff or permanent bureaucracy about what, how and why they did what they did. But here the Germans are merely symbolic of the rest of us. *Until very recently*, I do not think one would have been able to find many doubts in the United States—or the Soviet Union—among those responsible for the employment and manufacture of nuclear weapons. Yet surely each of those weapons is nothing more or less than the equivalent of an instant Auschwitz, wrapped in bomb casings and held together by the protons and electrons of the martial and triumphal spirit. If nuclear weapons were used, one would no doubt look in vain at any future war crime trials for those who said, 'Stop, this is no different from preparing Auschwitzes'. But to look at nuclear weapons and the state that has generated them in this way requires a significant change in our ethical and cultural outlook.

In the American pantheon of technical accomplishments the decisions to make atomic bombs and to use them on Hiroshima and Nagasaki were thought of, mistakenly, as great and heroic organizational achievements which ended an old history and began a new one. First Christ, then the Anti-messiah of the Bomb. For Americans, 1945 was a time in which everything seemed permitted and possible—even good things. Members of Congress wanted the Manhattan Project to be used as a model for medical science in unravelling the secrets of cancer, stroke, and heart disease. After all, if organized science could be used so successfully to unlock the secrets of atomic nature, end a war and begin a new history, was it too much to believe that the old history of man's physical ills could also end, bringing humanity a long life free of pain and suffering? Thus was the National Institute of Health founded by Congress. But relatively benign initiatives such as this were little compared with the social deformations that the model of the Manhattan Project brought with it—the steady spread of official procedures of secrecy and security. These were to have an extraordinarily corrosive effect on American government.

The managers of the state had now learnt that they could keep secret from Congress and the people bureaucratic enterprises as mammoth in scope and purpose as the Manhattan Project, without interference or concern from a deluded public. Truman's Secretary of State James Byrnes told a group of objecting scientists that the atomic bomb had to be used because Congress would otherwise have wondered about the disposition of two billion dollars. But the real achievement was, of course, quite the opposite—the expenditure of huge sums of money on secret projects without alerting the world, a success not unlike that of the Nazis in concealing the concentration camps.

The decision to continue the development and manufacture of nuclear weapons and other implements of mass destruction after the Second World War, to a point where they threaten to become a social and economic way of life, was, of course, dictated by the logic of power politics. Highly advanced weapons have always historically been viewed as symbols of national supremacy. Battleships played this role in England and Germany throughout the first part of the twentieth century. Nuclear weapons have played it since the end of the Second World War, especially when integrated with a powerful missile system or air force. Americans thought that such weapons could diplomatically control the Russians. The continued and increased production of atomic bombs and then the development of hydrogen bombs became the basis of a new world order. They also generated a new state formation to contain and manage them—one that required stringent laws about secrecy, loyalty, conformity. Thus was the national security state created, as the inseparable framework for the production and deployment of thermonuclear weapons.

The American national security state essentially emerged at the end of the Second World War, although elements of it had been adopted in the First World War in emulation of the British Imperial Defence Council system. The purpose of this state was relatively simple and clear. American rulers were naturally hostile to both social democracy and socialism. Nor did they have any interest in embracing fascism. The former would have meant a redistribution of political and economic power to the base and middle of the social pyramid, with or without economic growth. The latter—a system once praised by the leaders of General Motors—would have meant a great increase in state-managed violence and authoritarian discipline, and would have discredited the transcendent ideology of democracy and justice which had mobilized popular support behind the American cause, against Germans and Japanese enemies. Fascism could be encouraged in the periphery of the American sphere of influence. It could not become an internal organizing principle of the American government itself. An uneasy compromise between external and domestic forms of domination was generated during 1945–50, while the national security state was hatched. Its managers assumed a world of continuous conflict, in which there would be neither war nor peace, where international organization would be a simple instrumentality of national power. This was a time when American leaders like Dean Acheson and George Marshall believed that the twilight conflict of the Cold War could be fought without damage to the internal life of the US nation, as they administered to the population purpose (anti-communism), well-being (defence planning to stimulate economic growth) and consensus (loyalty oaths and manipulation of assent).

The national security state acted as the ballast for empire. As such, it needed a bureaucratic organization that could simultaneously encompass the truncheons of torturers in the Third World where the United States funded and protected a series of client states, and the laboratories of the new scientific and technological elites which now dominated the universities and made them into handmaidens of research into nuclear, submarine and missile warfare. The Massachusetts Institute of Technology, to take only one example, received 92% of its funds from the Federal Government, most of it related to 'defence' projects. The new state structure set the framework for events which—in abstraction from the economic, social and political determinants of them—might otherwise be thought, mistakenly, accidental. Thus, some liberals believed the Indo-China war was an accident; others thought that the emergence of counterforce strategy was the accidental product of a mechanical bureaucratic imperative; others again have argued that war by miscalculation would be an accident, rather than the logical consequence of certain social structures that would render such a contingency hardly surprising. One might say that the only accident we have seen so far is that we have had only one nuclear war.

What then are the American determinants of the national security state and therefore of the US side of the arms race? Individually, they may appear to be parochial, but together the interests to which they summate can give the appearance to the outsider that the arms race and the state formation that promotes it are autonomous forces driving unstoppably towards war, not by accident but by choice. I do not accept this point of view.

The major groups that comprise the national security state and which bear directly on the drift to mass extermination are (a) the armed forces, including intelligence agencies; (b) specific elements of the business class which concentrate on defence; (c) labour unions; (d) scientists, strategists and technologists.

Armed Forces

The American military force of over two million uniformed personnel is not organized and trained for 'defence' in the way that word has had military meaning on the European continent. The United States does not count itself as having serious border problems with either Canada or Mexico, although in the latter case there are difficulties related to migrant labour. While Cuba has been a bone in the throat of American presidents since John F. Kennedy, it is no military threat to the United States. Instead of the conventional mission of frontier defence, American military forces are viewed—and employed accordingly—as endowed with global responsibilities which are statutorily indefinite. They extend in every direction geographically and are subject to no temporal limit. Their tasks are in principle continuous and can only grow in the future. Indeed, Dean Acheson at the beginning of the Cold War made it clear that the Monroe Doctrine extended to wherever and whenever American rulers believed freedom was endangered. In other words, there is an open-ended character to American military forces and the missions with which they are charged. They are designed to initiate or deter attack not only in defence of the United States but anywhere else in the world where American leaders conclude that an American interest exists.

The structure of the US armed forces is doctrinally and psychologically (if not in organizational reality) intended to give American leaders the capacity to escalate any given conflict in order—if possible—to win or *prevail*, as the phrase is used in the basic national security documents, at the next highest level of violence. The goal is to secure the basis of American political supremacy. US military leadership is in principle virulently anti-communist and anti-Soviet. But in fact American generals have proved quite flexible and willing to change enemies and friends as the need or situation arises. There is no revolt in the Pentagon against supplying arms to Communist China today.

An even more 'bizarre' example of Pentagon attitudes would surprise most American journalists. Not only Soviet, but US generals and diplomats secretly fear a rearmed, independent and united Germany more than they fear each other. Diplomatically, of course, there can be no even temporary resolution of the arms race which does not include a comprehensive settlement that allows Germany to escape the fate of being simultaneously hated and seduced. Would France and Britain, even if radical and humanist socialist parties were in power in either country, give up their nuclear weapons if a highly armed independent Germany existed, whether there was one or two of them?

It would thus be a mistake to reckon American military leadership to be either more audacious or more reckless than the general staffs of other lands. The average American general is quite cautious; the last of the derring-do types passed from the scene in an unsuccessful run for the Vice Presidency in 1968, General Curtis LeMay. Even he, a generation earlier, demanded that the orders to drop the atomic bombs on Japan be written and signed, to make clear the chain of responsibility for their use. In saying this, I do not mean to underplay belief among the higher ranks of the American armed forces in the 'inevitability of war with Russia', as one general on President Reagan's National Security Council Staff recently put it. (He has since been removed and returned to the Pentagon.) But I would judge the American military's views of the Soviet Union to be probably more sanguine than those of their communist counterparts in China. American officers are much more enamoured of new weapons than of fighting with them. They are less fixated with any particular enemy than with the process of war preparation as such. The Pentagon's interest is in military planning and the appearance of readiness to fight wars. As Mary Kaldor and others have shown, it puts enormous emphasis on weaponry which is extremely sophisticated, but whose consequences and conditions of use it only partially understands.

In general, the US attitude to weaponry is not dissimilar to that of the population to automobiles. Americans are enamoured of new gadgets and are eager to acquire new and more sophisticated home appliances and automobiles—if they can be brought on easy credit terms. It remains to be seen whether Congress and the American people will pay when the credit terms are not so easy. The assumption still persists in the military and in Congress that the United States is in a continuous race with the USSR, in which Americans have to be continuously first—especially in all matters of a military nature. The meaning of 'first' is usually defined in quantitative terms, although most military officers in the bureaucracy now admit to not knowing how to define 'ahead', or even retrospectively, in the arms race. As one might imagine, the great size of the armed forces, their call on the future industrial capacity, raw materials and resources of the economy, have the direct and intended effect of increasing the political power of the military interest *within* American society. The national security state, operating as an uneasy balance between various contending forces, is ultimately bounded by military perspectives and by a military establishment that may not act forcefully, but continues to enhance its corporate power.

The philosophy of American military leadership sees war as inherent in human nature. Consequently, it has only a rhetorical interest in disarmament. The Pentagon's interest in 'arms control' is merely in the service of rational and efficient planning. Thus, SALT II was favoured by American generals because it meant that the US and the Soviets would be able *jointly* to plan the next round of the arms race. There would be no surprises. The intelligence agencies are used to stimulate arms production and war planning. Of course, there is no interest in so-called unilateral disarmament by example. The military accepts and propagates the story that the United States unilaterally disarmed at the end of the Second World War. That the US demobilized its twelve million man armed forces at the end of the Second World War is true. The government then had no choice because there were riots in the armed forces by draftees refusing to stay under arms. But economic and political pressures from the American people to demobilize did not alter the fact that even after demobilization, the budgetary size of the US armed forces was approximately fourteen times larger than it had been on the eve of the Second World War.

Most important of all, US politicians and strategists took it for granted that the atomic bomb would not only be used by the military on the battle-field, but diplomatically as an *in terrorem* weapon in political negotiation. It was meant to take the place of a large standing armed force. In negotiations the US has repeatedly threatened the use of nuclear weapons, against both the Chinese and the Russians. In other words, it appropriated the atomic and hydrogen bombs as a diplomatic asset. At no point have the US military leaders ever thought of nuclear weaponry as a new phenomenon posing fundamentally different ethical and political problems from the conventional weaponry of the past. There was one short period in post-war American history where there was some rhetorical interest in cutting the armed forces because they were thought to be burdensome. This period spanned less than two years under Kennedy, who paradoxically caused a quantum leap in defence expenditures and embraced counterforce strategy. At the time, the American government felt it necessary to respond to Khrushchev's call at the United Nations for general and complete disarmament (GCD). The US tabled a GCD plan after agreement was reached between the Russian and American negotiators, John McCloy and Valerian Zorin, on the framework for such a disarmament arrangement. The final stages of the American plan were vague. Nevertheless, what began as a rhetorical ploy soon gained genuine advocates. This quixotic effort on the part of some of the more naive government planners of 1961–62 (this author included) was soon interrupted by the Vietnam War and disappeared under the overwhelming established consensus that disarmament itself would mean unravelling the modern security state. This attitude was not always the official American dogma.

At the beginning of the twentieth century the United States favoured disarmament. It successfully negotiated an arms limitation arrangement with Japan and Britain at the Washington Naval Conference of 1922. At that time, it was widely believed that armaments were inimical to capitalism and the market system, and that a large standing army would tend to generate a strong national state which would be bureaucratic and anti-capitalist. This view was most clearly spelled out by Herbert Hoover when he was President, and then again during the Second World War when he drafted a blueprint for peace. Earlier, a more idealistic view was taken by Woodrow Wilson's first secretary of state, the populist William Jennings Bryan, who spent much of his time before the First World War working out arrangements for mediation and arbitration between nations in the hope that an international system of adjudication could supersede war or revolution. American academics emphasized international rules of conduct in their writings and supported institutions and activities designed to enforce them. The various specialized agencies of the League of Nations which had this as their purpose were strongly supported within the United States. Those who did not support the League often did so on *radical* grounds. They held it to be an imperialist enterprise more likely to get the world into war again than to help it avoid a repetition of the catastrophe of the First World War.

In that epoch, American thinkers and philosophers spent much time looking for ways to outlaw war. John Dewey, America's foremost philosopher, criticized the Kellogg–Briand pact for its consecration of the right of self-defence. He also feared that any collective security arrangement of the kind envisaged by the League would merely lead to larger wars. The American tradition still favoured legal and political mechanisms for handling international disputes. Those government officials who believed in the use of military force to resolve them had to contend with Senator William Borah, the chairman of the Senate Foreign Relations Committee during the two world wars. Borah looked at war preparations and war planning as evidence of treason and conspiracy to commit war crimes. He even got the Senate to support a resolution to this effect.

Yet despite all this the American armed forces played an imperial role from the time of McKinley onwards. They were stationed in China and intervened many times in Latin America. But once the ideology of neither war nor peace was adopted, and the armed forces had first call on the resources of the society, it was clear that the old liberal and capitalist arguments had washed away.

The Business Class

From 1945 onward a major shift occurred in the American conservative attitude to armaments and the defence system. It is true that Senator Robert Taft and other Republicans sought to continue Hoover's legacy of low military budgets. They too believed that high defence spending would ruin a market economy. Taft had urged Eisenhower and his cabinet to reduce the defence budget at the end of the Korean War to ten billion dollars, but to no avail. He had also feared a shift in control from civilian to military leadership. But Taft's views were no longer the prevailing spirit of the Republican party. The Republicans, like the Democrats, and the business class that supported both of them, henceforward saw military expenditure as an essential stimulus to the economy. Employment and sales statistics seemed to support those who argued that without a continuous flow of government contracts many businesses in such fields as aerospace, chemicals and strategic metals would fail. It was taken for granted that high defence budgets were *not* inflationary. They were necessary. This Keynesian conviction continues to predominate among American political and business leaders. The present Secretary of Defence, Caspar Weinberger, has told the Senate Armed Services Committee that Reagan's defence budget will be used to revitalize American industry. The rhetoric of debate on military spending has now shifted so far that American liberals currently argue that the US is lagging economically behind its rivals because it spends too much on defence—thereby adopting the traditional conservative position that the American economy cannot afford the deficit spending that results from increased arms production. Indeed, one of the reasons the United States is now demanding larger defence expenditures from Western Europe and Japan is because of the inroads these nations are making into its commercial markets. The American insistence on increased military spending by allies and clients is intended to slow down their competitive advantage without the US itself having to take the *economic* risk of disarmament.

Periodic splits do occur within the business classes over the size and rate of growth of the military establishment. *However, such splits do not extend to the fundamental question of whether nuclear weapons should be used*. Conservative Republicans in the early years of the Cold War depended on the deterrent strategy of 'massive retaliation' as a way of proving American will to commit suicide and to impose it on other nations. This was seen as a cheaper strategy—'more bang for the buck', as Eisenhower's Secretary of Defence, Charles Wilson, who had been the head of General Motors, put it. But this strategy has long since been superseded, to the general agreement of the business and military classes. As noted above, nuclear strategy since the days of Kennedy (1961–63) has been founded on varying forms of counterforce.

As a result of the war in Indochina, the disposition of our armed forces and the utility of certain missiles or bombers have once again been questioned. Defeat by a 'fifth-rate military nation', as North Vietnam was called, gave many groups within the business classes pause. International corporations primarily interested in extensive non-military trade, for example IBM and Xerox, have tended to take one stance and those corporations mainly or solely dependent on military contracts another. Carter's Secretary of State, Cyrus Vance, represented the prudentialist position which sought trade, as well as an arms control arrangements with the Soviet Union in the first years of Carter's Presidency. Hectoring from the right and from conservative Democrats in and out of the Senate brought this strategy to grief. The Soviet invasion of Afghanistan weakened the position of those liberals and international corporations who had hoped to slow the growth of the defence budget through the provision of SALT II. The final defeat of the 'prudentialist' line occurred a year before Carter's term ended, when he accommodated to the position of those Senators who called for an increase in the arms budget of five per cent a year over and above inflation. These increases included massive new expenditures for nuclear weapons—a trend continued and deepened under the Reagan administration. The multiplication of nuclear weapons is now related to a renewed interest in *using* them in a so-called 'limited' way.

Organized Labour

Throughout the Cold War the labour unions, notably the AFL-CIO, have been an important pillar of the national security state in the USA. The reasons why American labour unions have played this role lie at once in the imperatives of anti-communism, popular perceptions of the American economy, and working-class patriotism. It is beyond the scope of this essay to rehearse the struggles within the American labour movement which ended in the wholesale suppression of communism and radicalism within its ranks. Suffice it to say that those struggles determined the official unions' attitude to the Cold War, of which they became ardent champions. Needless to say, this attitude carried over to the arms race. Labour leaders shared the belief in the need for a massive defence and intelligence apparatus. Such men as Jay Lovestone, a former leader of the CPUSA, continued his feud against his former colleagues as chief adviser to George Meany, the head of the AFL-CIO. Indeed, many of the ideological battlements of the national security state were supplied by former radicals, ex-Trotskyists or ex-Communists, who found economic and social refuge in the union bureaucracies, or the think tanks of the Rand Corporation and the CIA. From time to time labour unions were used, as were corporations, as instruments of the covert intelligence activity of the state. While certain leaders, like Walter Reuther of the UAW, regularly attacked the 'waste' of the arms race, this attitude never extended into a wide-ranging critique of the arms race as such, or the national security state; nor was support for disarmament deemed an important index of liberalism. By 1950, internal purges and application of the Taft–Hartley regulations requiring loyalty oaths from union officials had virtually destroyed all opposition to the Cold War within the American labour movement. The resultant purity and intensity of ideological anti-communism within the unions has ever since always thwarted—as it still does—any interest in serious disarmament or even arms limitation, since their leaders traditionally accept the view that arms are *not* the cause of tensions between adversaries but merely the consequence of them.

The second reason for labour's support of the arms race and the national security state is, of course, an economic one. Because there was little likelihood that the US economy would be centrally directed towards full employment for positive social purposes, labour union leaders had every reason to doubt that Congress would vote funds in a sustained way for housing, urban renewal, social welfare, or reindustrialization. The Marxist economists Magdoff and Sweezy have pointed out that before the United States entered the Second World War there was an 18% unemployment rate (in 1938–39). This devastating slump was ended only by the flow of military contracts in preparation for war. Since the 1960s, each recession within the United States has been a little deeper, lasted a little longer, and been more rapidly followed by another. The 1970–80 average unemployment rate in the United States was over 7%. At least 10% of the American economy is directly tied to military spending. If the arms race ceased, labour leaders and businessmen reason, there would be a terrifying depression in the United States. Ending the arms race without economic catastrophe requires state planning and direct government involvement in the productive process. But for that a sea-change in attitude would have to occur in the Democratic Party.

While a few unions, notably the International Association of Machinists, now favour a comprehensive reconversion plan, at no time since the beginning of the Cold War has such a plan had the backing either of substantial elements of labour, or of substantial (or insubstantial) numbers within the Democratic Party. Thus, without the political alternative of reconversion, the labour movement is locked into support of the general contours of the arms race. It does not matter that military spending creates fewer jobs than other civilian alternatives. (American arms production is not labour- but skill- and capital-intensive.) The likelihood of any other employment being created by the federal government, at least since the beginning of the Nixon period, has been very small. So the labour movement holds on to what it's got.

The third reason for labour's often uncritical support of the arms race is related to a fact too often overlooked by the left. Virtually all families of the American working class have had members who were in the armed forces at one time or another over the course of the last forty years. Material gains accrue from this identification, through veterans' benefits. Since the level of class consciousness in the US population is generally low, the predominant allegiance of American workers is not to other workers, three-quarters of whom are unorganized. It is to the nation. There is profound pride in the accomplishments of the United States as a nation; and it is taken for granted that other nations 'want what we have', as President Johnson put it to the troops in Vietnam. The assumption of workers is that strength and defence go hand in hand; that the United States is always turning the other cheek, and that 'we have been pushed around' over this past generation because of inept leadership, and inadequate attention to our defences. This does not make the American working class bellicose, but it does make it prey to those who identify national strength, patriotism and jobs as the three-legged stool upon which workers live their economic and psychological lives. There is no thought among this working class that there should be 'distributive national security' as well as 'distributive justice'.

Americans have often in their history fixed on a diabolical enemy to explain events. Russians have served well as this devil in the twentieth century, for the USSR has often acted foolishly and criminally—although it was the idealistic goals of Soviet ideology which caused fear among the business class, and only secondarily, criminal behaviour by the Soviet State. For the labour movement, it was the reverse.

It should be noted here that US perceptions of other nations can change bewilderingly quickly—a fact that can permit negative or positive shifts in foreign policy to occur very rapidly. Thus, at the end of the Second World War the Russians were perceived as friendly, before becoming inveterate foes; while vice versa, the Chinese were perceived as our undying enemies until Kissinger and Nixon paraded to Peking. Popular perceptions of US adversaries are constantly manipulated. At present the Russians and Cubans are rated our most dangerous antagonists. However, this does not mean that there is any great desire among the American people to go to war, let alone to fight a nuclear war. What remains critical is the working-class belief in nationalism, a creed which is emotionally more important to it than to the rich in the United States.

Scientists and Technologists

As with so much else in the national security order, the rise of the scientific and technological estate in the USA can be dated to the Second World

War. It was during the period 1945–50 that its influence on the direction of weaponry and the nature of the arms race first became strongly marked. During this period a few key scientists were able to buttress and shape the American arms drive because of the authority of their scientific feats. Thus, John Von Neumann, Edward Teller and Stan Ulam could yoke their own hatred and fear of communism, and their remarkable entrepreneurial skills, to their talents as physicists and mathematicians. It was during this period that scientists acquired their audience among men of political power. It was then too that scientists and technologists started to lobby for and to receive literally billions of dollars for the establishment of new laboratories, to test ideas which hitherto would have been thought crackpot or irrelevant, fantastic or just too expensive. Science and technology applied to military purposes were—still are—spared no funds by a Congress and bureaucracy enamoured of the nuclear age. In the process, the scientists who took part in the enterprise were changed, as was their science. On the one hand, they were now constrained by official secrecy. But this was a very small price to pay for being able to work on complex, 'sweet' scientific and engineering questions. To this day, if scientists in the US want to pursue exciting investigations on a pharaonic scale they know that the Defence Department will always be there to help them. That intercontinental missiles tipped with nuclear weapons and aimed at military or civilian targets ten thousand miles away are criminal or immoral does not alter the sense of exhilaration and accomplishment which scientists and engineers feel when they know their missiles 'work'. Today, the US has 26,000–30,000 nuclear weapons for its use. The technical problem of ridding ourselves of them would not be easy.

At the same time, the majority of those members of the scientific and engineering communities who are not integrally related to war work cannot be classified as outright opponents of the arms race. They generally adopt the arms control position. This stance allows the community as a whole to enjoy even greater political influence, as it is simultaneously involved in the arming and in the arms control process. There is also, of course, the economic ramification of military projects for the scientist and technologist. Scientists are no more criminally oriented than others, even if the way their science is practised typically limits the moral alternatives before them. But even the greatest and most ethically sensitive of scientists have on occasion succumbed to economic pressures without necessarily being aware of them. When Einstein wrote his famous letter to Roosevelt—a document drafted by Leo Szilard—he was not only informing the President of the possibility of German research into nuclear explosives, he was also trying to get a job for his friend and colleague

Szilard, a refugee whose summer grant at Columbia University had come to an end. Economic motivations of this type still form part of the stake that scientists and engineers have in the arms race. At present one-fifth of all American engineers are directly involved in defence work. Such collective investment in the war economy must be numbered among the obstacles to any rational reconversion of the current pattern of military expenditure.

Beyond economic security or opportunity for scientists, however, there is another problem involved here. Scientists and engineers are often consumed by wonder. They are playful. Too often this allows them to forget the consequences of what they do. The state and its bureaucracy customarily seek to take advantage of this capacity for intellectual play—to infantilize the scientist or engineer into divorcing ethical questions from the sweet proof or the demonic experiment. Any popular movement against nuclear war must address such scientists and engineers in their own terms, and convince them of the need for a *hippocratic oath* to forswear work on all weapons of mass destruction. The UN could be called on to administer such an oath, as well as our universities. Churches should be summoned to apply age-old sanctions to those who continue in the preparation and use of such weaponry.

Conclusion

To sum up, a people's strategy against nuclear war should be based on the following platform:

1. The American anti-war movement must put forward a 'no use of nuclear weapons, no surrender' position. That is to say, the United States would not surrender to an aggressor under any circumstance. But it would also under no circumstance use weapons of mass destruction.

2. The anti-war movement should encourage compacts of disarmament and peace between various regions of the United States and external areas, in the Soviet Union and elsewhere. Such compacts could then be presented to Congress for ratification, after having been pressed through state legislatures and city councils. A popular movement of this type would urge cities and states to 'buy' from the federal government the sort of defence they thought necessary for their particular region.

3. The world anti-war movement should encourage the UN Security Council to reconvene the military committee of the UN for the purpose of preparing a worldwide security plan, linked to comprehensive disarmament arrangements.

4. In the United States the anti-war movement should press Congress

and the President to adopt a ten-year overall disarmament strategy founded on the legal principles of Nuremberg and the philosophical conviction that nuclear war is the modern form of slavery, from which we must all free ourselves.

It is through a 'radical conventional' strategy of this kind that we might be able to survive to generate a world civilization whose existence is not built on the constant threat of mass extermination.

---

[1] *Trials of War Criminals Before the Nuremberg Military Tribunals Under Control Council Law 11*, Washington 1950, pp. 488–9. Quoted by Sanford Levinson, 'Responsibility for Crimes of War', Thomas Nagel, ed., *War and Moral Responsibility*. This is the lesson to be drawn from the trials of over 10,000 Germans found guilty of war crimes. Where actions were undertaken which by their nature were breaches of the code of war or of international law, and the official was in a position to stop or veto such policies but failed to do so, that person could be held criminally responsible.

[2] In 1977 a 115-nation conference signed an agreement against the use of weapons of mass destruction on innocent populations.

Strategic Arms, the Cold War and the Third World

Noam Chomsky

The meetings now being held throughout the United States are a domestic counterpart to the mass popular movement growing in Western Europe—a movement that reflects the deepening concern that we may be facing the final moments of our civilization, conceivably even the end of human existence. This is no idle concern. Any sane and rational person who considers the scale and character of contemporary military power, the current vast expansion of the arsenals of the superpowers, and the proliferation of armaments throughout the world, would surely have to conclude that the likelihood of a global catastrophe is not small.

One might argue, in fact, that it is a miracle that the catastrophe has not yet occurred. Between November 1946 and October 1973 there were nineteen incidents in which US strategic nuclear forces were involved (we do not have the record since, or the records for the USSR and other powers). That means, to put it plainly, that every US president has regarded the use of nuclear weapons as a live policy option. The examples are instructive. Here are a few:

1. The best known is the Cuban missile crisis of 1962. The Kennedy administration, according to memoirs of participants, estimated the probability of nuclear war at 1/3 to 1/2 at the peak of the crisis. Yet it was unwilling to accept a settlement that involved a complete withdrawal of Russian missiles from Cuba in exchange for the simultaneous withdrawal of US missiles from Turkey—even though the latter were obsolescent and an order to withdraw them had already been issued before the crisis erupted, since they were being replaced by Polaris submarines. This must surely be one of the low points in human history. Yet, significantly, it is generally regarded as a glorious episode.

2. In February 1947, bombers of the Strategic Air Command armed with nuclear weapons were sent to Uruguay in a show of force at the time of the inauguration of the President of Uruguay.

3. In May 1954, nuclear-armed SAC bombers were flown to Nicaragua as

part of the background for the successful CIA coup in Guatemala, which turned that country into a literal hell on earth to this day, with no end in sight.

4. In 1958, US strategic nuclear forces were involved in the US invasion of Lebanon. Furthermore, the invading US forces went ashore with atomic-armed rockets and the use of nuclear weapons was threatened if the Lebanese army attempted to resist the invasion.

We can learn a great deal by studying these nineteen cases in detail—and they are not the only ones when the use of nuclear weapons was seriously considered. Other powers have also issued nuclear threats: for example, the USSR at the time of the Israeli–French–British invasion of Egypt in 1956, and Israel in the early stages of the 1973 war, when Egypt and Syria attacked the Israeli occupying army in the Sinai and Golan Heights. Those who speak of the likelihood of nuclear war are hardly alarmists.

1. The Ideology and Reality of the Cold War

Why do the superpowers amass these huge systems of potential massacre and destruction? Each has an answer, and it is the same answer. Each superpower describes its system as 'defensive'. Each is concerned only to deter its violent opponent, whose aim is to take over the world. One is trying to defend itself while the other is trying to expand its power, in a kind of zero-sum game: what one gains, the other loses. The way the system is described by ideologists of the two superpowers is not totally false. Effective propaganda cannot be entirely false. But, on the other hand, the real truth of the system is quite different. If we hope to do more than protest impending destruction, if we hope to control and reverse the race towards mutual annihilation, if we hope to protect the actual as well as the potential victims, then we must come to understand the reality that lies behind the elaborate mythology of the Cold War. This is not very difficult, if we attend to the facts. The basic and crucial fact, which cannot be reiterated too often, is that the Cold War system is highly functional for the superpowers, which is why it persists, despite the likelihood of mutual annihilation if the system breaks down by accident, as sooner or later it will. The Cold War provides a framework within which each of the superpowers can use force and violence to control its own domains, against those who seek a degree of independence within the blocs themselves—by appealing to the threat of the superpower enemy to mobilize its own population and that of its allies.

In the case of Guatemala in 1954, for example, it would have been difficult—in fact, ludicrous—for the US government to claim that the United States was threatened with destruction when a moderate reformist government, with policies resembling those of the New Deal, attempted to expropriate unused lands of the United Fruit Company (offering as compensation exactly what United Fruit had claimed the lands were worth in a standard tax fraud, a proposal that aroused much indignation in Washington), to turn them over to miserable peasants. But matters appeared in a different light once the Eisenhower Administration announced that Guatemala was merely an outpost of International Communism, an advance base for a superpower aiming at global conquest, armed with nuclear weapons, with an ample record of brutality and atrocities. With the cooperation of the American press and other ideological institutions, this ridiculous claim was advanced, and believed, justifying US intervention to save the Free World from destruction by an enemy of Hitlerian proportions. When the USSR invaded Hungary two years later, it resorted to essentially the same rhetoric. The Soviet leaders did not even have the originality to change the record; the Khrushchev doctrine was merely a transposition of the Eisenhower doctrine devised to justify the imposition of the rule of sanguinary gangsters over Guatemala.

Similarly, the Johnson doctrine constructed to justify the US invasion of the Dominican Republic, in alleged defence against international communism, was reiterated in virtually the same terms in the Brezhnev doctrine formulated to legitimate the Soviet invasion of Czechoslovakia. Both were 'defensive interventions', undertaken to ward off the threat of the superpower enemy. The rhetoric accompanying the current US support for massacre in El Salvador and the Soviet invasion of Afghanistan is essentially the same. In Afghanistan the Russian leadership effectively exploits the Cold War conflict to provide a domestic justification, a way of rallying their population to support the invasion. The explanation that is presented to the Russian people is that they are entering Afghanistan to defend a legitimate government against attacks sponsored by the imperialist powers, who have designs on the USSR itself. Afghanistan is not a very plausible enemy for the Soviet Union nor for its population, but the United States and Western Europe are. The most effective means of winning the approval of the Russian people was to present the invasion as a defensive act against an aggressive major power.

It is precisely the same way, almost in the same words, that the American political leadership, American journalists and the American intellectual establishment present the Vietnam War to the American people. We were not invading South Vietnam, but responding to a request from the legitimate government for defence against an aggressor that was simply the puppet of the great superpower enemy. The documentary record shows that American planners understood very clearly from the late 1940s that they were fighting the nationalist movements of Indochina. They tried very hard to find links to international communism for propaganda purposes, but were never successful—not that it mattered. For it is instructive to see how most commentators continue to refer to the US invasion of South Vietnam in 1962, when the US Air Force undertook its defoliation and bombing missions against the rural population (about 80% of the people of South Vietnam at the time) in an effort to drive them into concentration camps ('strategic hamlets') where they could be controlled by the client regime the US had imposed. Twenty years later, after the expansion of this aggression to all of Indochina, it is still next to impossible to pronounce the dread words: 'US aggression', 'the US invasion of South Vietnam'—a record of subservience to state propaganda that any dictator could envy.

In short, the Cold War system has to a great extent served as the ideological framework for the state to mobilize its population for intervention and subversion. This ideological framework is necessary because the reality involves the application of very ugly measures which are morally difficult for people to accept. These measures may also be very costly in terms of life and material resources. The symmetry between the superpowers, however, is only a functional one. The United States has been doing this to a considerably greater extent than the Soviet Union, a reflection of the greater American power. In terms of degree of violence, number of countries subverted, numbers of bombs dropped, and number of troops overseas, there has by no means been an even balance.

2. The Break-Up of the Grand Area

This is the kind of system the Cold War has been. Today, we are clearly moving into another phase of it, what can be called the New Cold War. It is reasonable to suspect that there will be some fundamental differences, as well as similarities, between the two phases. Let us look at the differences first. The most fundamental—the one that is likely to be most significant in shaping the course of events—is that the New Cold War will probably prove a pretty lonely affair for the US political leadership. In that respect it will be very different from the earlier phase of the Cold War.

During the Second World War most of the industrial world was either severely damaged or totally destroyed. In contrast, the United States flourished during the war and industrial production soared. This led to a situation of extreme dominance of the United States over very large parts of the industrial world. As a Trilateral Commission report correctly states, the US was now 'the hegemonic power in a system of world order', and was to remain so for a quarter-century. In response to the situation that was developing, some high-level planning took place in the United States during the war. Most of the top-level State Department planners were involved and, of course, the Council for Foreign Relations, which is essentially the corporate input in the planning process. The planners understood that the United States was going to emerge from the war as the world's dominant power and they proceeded to determine how the world should be organized in such a way as to meet their interests. They devised the concept known as the Grand Area.

The Grand Area was to include at a minimum the Western hemisphere, the former British Empire, and the Far East. The maximum would be the limit—the universe—and somewhere between the two was to be the Grand Area. The Grand Area was to be organized in such a way as to serve the needs of the American economy, and that, of course, means the needs of those who own and manage the American economy—what is called 'the national interest' by political scientists. This was the plan to be adopted and implemented in the postwar period.

Within a few years after World War II the world was broken into two major blocs: the Soviet bloc, which at that time uneasily included China, and the US-dominated Grand Area bloc. In the course of construction of this system there were many conflicts internal to the major blocs themselves. For example, within the Grand Area there were conflicts during and after the Second World War between the United States and its major allies. There was a kind of mini-war going on during the Second World War between the United States and Great Britain. The United States intended that the Grand Area be constructed in such a way that it would be responsive to the needs of the American economy. That meant pushing the British out of their traditional markets in Latin America and removing them gently from such places as Saudi Arabia, where the oil was and is.

There were many devices used. One of them was manipulation of Lend-Lease Aid. Of course, Britain was on the front line, while the United States did not want to be the front-line power itself—too bloody. (Actually, of course, it was the Soviet Union that bore the brunt of the Nazi attack.) In order to keep Britain on the front line it was necessary to supply them with sufficient aid. In fact, the Lend-Lease Bill had a stipulation that British reserves should not go below $600,000,000, the level required to keep Britain fighting at the front line of the war against Germany. At the same time it was also stipulated that British reserves should not rise above a certain level, namely a billion dollars. The thinking behind that appears to have been that if Britain were in too strong a position it would be able to resist American penetration of British traditional markets and it would be able to maintain its position in the Middle East, and that wasn't the way the postwar world was supposed to be organized.

In Saudi Arabia, it was recognized that King Ibn Saud wanted to get on the take himself. It was decided that he must be bought off to follow Western interests properly. The first idea was that the British would pay him. However, this was decided to be too dangerous because the British might exploit the opportunity 'to diddle the US oil companies out of the concession', as Navy Undersecretary William Bullitt put it elegantly. For that reason, the United States should pay him off. This was a little tricky since the only device for doing this was the Lend-Lease Bill and according to law, lend-lease was to be given only to democratic allies who were fighting in the war against Hitler. It was a little difficult to interpret this in such a way as to apply to Ibn Saud. Putting the question of democracy aside (the USSR was receiving lend-lease aid), Saudi Arabia was in no way involved in the military conflict. But Roosevelt succeeded. In 1943, he announced that he hereby designated the Saudi Arabians as fighters for freedom and democratic allies. In this way, $100,000,000 in Lend-Lease aid was granted to Saudi Arabia. So it went in the post-war period, too. France was evicted from the Arabian peninsula in the late 1940s by some legal chicanery, and before long, control over Middle East oil—along with North American oil, of course—was fairly firmly in the hands of US-based corporations, closely linked to the state.

This history is pertinent to the Cold War today because it is important to understand the internal structure of a system that is coming apart. The fact that it is coming apart is very important for the future. In the early postwar period the United States acted so as to block the rise of national capitalism in Europe. It succeeded in forcing the French and the British out of the Middle East to a substantial extent, with the United States taking over most of the concessions. The theory behind it all was presented in terms of energy, which was then and is now the focus of considerable conflict within the blocs themselves.

The theory was expressed succinctly in a State Department memorandum on petroleum policy in 1944 which stated that the United States (American oil companies) should retain its absolute control in the Western hemisphere, while in the rest of the world there should be an open door to penetration by American enterprise. This is an intriguing interpretation of the open-door doctrine: we keep what we possess and the rest should be open to competition (in which we expect to do quite well, given the distribution of wealth and power). This is roughly the way things evolved for the early period of the Cold War.

There was a good deal of unity, or perhaps better, obedience. There was not much dissension within the alliance. There was some, however. For example, in 1956 the British and the French tried with Israeli aid to reinstate themselves as effective actors in the Middle East, though they were quickly pushed out.

There were other elements of conflict and tension, but on the whole, it was a unified Western front under US leadership. That was true of Europe and it was also true of Japan. Japan is now a major competitor of the United States but of course this is a relatively recent phenomenon. It is not true for the whole postwar period. In fact, as late as the early sixties the Kennedy administration was concerned about the viability of Japan's economy. It was thought that we might have to help them. In fact, it was not until the mid-1960s that the trade balance between the United States and Japan shifted in favour of Japan, a reflection in part of the Vietnam War. While the war was very costly to the United States by the late 1960s, the Japanese economy gained quite considerable benefits from their role as an off-shore procurement area backing up the war in Vietnam. One of the secrets of the Japanese miracle was to be in just the right place when the United States was fighting in Korea and Vietnam.

Up until the late sixties, in fact—until the cost of the Vietnam War began really to bleed the American economy significantly—the Grand Area alliance was a fairly obedient and unified bloc, in spite of some internal dissension. Now that situation is significantly different. First of all, Western Europe is moving toward a degree of independence in a slow but, I think, inexorable fashion. Every year there are further steps: the currency bloc, a parliament, the Euro–Arab dialogue, and other regular developments. It will presumably be a West European bloc largely under German dominance, with a subsidiary role played by France.

Another manifestation of Western European independence is resistance to the steps the United States has been urging towards a revival of a sharp Cold War confrontation. Germany, for example, has been refusing to break trade links with Eastern Europe or to undertake a massive armaments programme. However, these refusals are tempered. Sometimes the West Europeans agree and sometimes the agreements are very dangerous.

For example, in the fall of 1979, Western Europe agreed, under American pressure, to arrange for the installation of Pershing II land-based missiles and Cruise missiles which could hit the Soviet Union. This will include missiles placed in Germany. The flight time to Moscow is 5–6 minutes, and the Russians have memories concerning Germany. That may have been one of the factors, not a major factor, but one of the factors that led the Russians into military intervention in Afghanistan. Whether or not Europe will actually agree to have these missiles installed is not so obvious. It is highly possible that the agreement could collapse in the next few years.

Even though West European countries agreed to go along with the United States on the sanctions with respect to Iran, they were very explicit in saying that it was because they hoped that this would delay American military action and put off confrontation and perhaps the nuclear holocaust that might result if American action were to proceed. Then they were rewarded for that move with the hostage rescue attempt, to which Western Europe did not react with great enthusiasm, to put it mildly.

Though Western Europe is still acceding to American pressure to maintain or increase the level of confrontation, it is doing so very reluctantly, dragging its heels, unwilling to undertake the economic sanctions against the Soviet Union that the United States has been urging. There is also little doubt that Western Europe will simply move into the vacuum created by the US refusal to supply high technology to the Soviet Union, again exacerbating the conflicts that are increasingly developing between Europe and the United States.

Much the same is true with regard to Japan. The United States is trying to press Japan into large military expenditures just as it is trying to do with Europe. The Japanese too are dragging their feet. They are reluctant to enter the system of confrontation toward which the United States is trying to impel them. Here too sometimes the Japanese acquiesce and sometimes not. Meanwhile Europe and Japan are increasingly moving into areas of primary US concern, such as Saudi Arabia.

These tendencies seem to point in the direction of a breakup of the world into several more or less independent blocs, in particular a breakup of the Grand Area alliance into three monetary and political blocs. One would, in effect, be the European Economic Community, which with its European currency union and other institutions is slowly moving toward a German-dominated independent Western Europe. Another would be a US-dominated North American bloc—a dollar bloc, incorporating much of the Western hemisphere and other places, including most of the oil-producing regions of the Middle East. If it did not, there might be a major war because it is difficult to think the United States would give these regions up. Thirdly, a yen bloc which would perhaps increasingly resemble the 'New Order' which led to war in the Far East. In addition to these three blocs, there would be a Russian bloc, perhaps including some of the countries around the periphery of the Soviet empire.

A recent study of the OECD—the international organization of industrial capitalist powers—has discussed a set of possible scenarios for the future. Something like this was the one which they thought most likely to develop. This is the kind of situation which has led to war repeatedly in the past. This time it could lead us to the kind of war which civilization could not survive.

The other factor that differentiates the new phase of the Cold War from its predecessor is something really new in the history of industrial civilization. Throughout much of history there has been a fear of scarcity of resources. The fear has always been overcome either through the discovery of new resources or through improvements in technology. There may be a surprise again, but it does seem that the pressure on increasingly scarce resources has become qualitatively different from what it was in the past. Energy is the obvious case; but it is by no means the only one. Almost everywhere there is an actual or impending scarcity of resources, which means that conflicts among the economic units which are competing for them will become more harsh and exacerbated. This makes for an ominous situation. It has not gone without notice. There have been a number of recent statements by diplomats throughout the world saying that the current situation is reminiscent of the situation prior to World Wars I and II, when it was clear that events were drifting toward war. It wasn't entirely clear what kind of a war, or exactly what the alignments would be, but it was clear that the situation was getting out of control and heading dangerously toward war.

Although the Soviet Union is a military competitor of the United States, it is by no means an economic competitor. It is still a very backward economic unit. About all that the USSR produces effectively is armaments, and even that not too well, quite often. The GNP of the Soviet Union is roughly half that of the United States.

Western Europe, a highly advanced industrial unit, is a different story. It is slightly larger than the United States and operates at a very high level of technology, comparable to that of the United States. If the United States turns its production more toward the manufacture of waste (military production) and Europe does not, then disparities will develop. This is one of the reasons why the United States is trying to impel Europe and Japan to more military (that is, waste) production. However, it does not seem that either Europe or Japan is going to do this.

Some of these economic concerns were reflected in parts of the speech Henry Kissinger gave in 1973 when he announced the 'Year of Europe'. He stated that there were conflicts in the Atlantic alliance, problems between the United States and Western Europe. He went on to describe the conflicts. Among them was Europe's unwillingness to give the United States the support it needed.

Kissinger then described the way the world ought to be organized. He described the ideal arrangement as an alliance among the industrial capitalist nations and their clients with the United States managing the overall framework of order. In turn, other powers would have regional responsibilities within this overall framework of order.

However, Kissinger continued, there is now the possibility that Europe might move toward a closed trading bloc which would include the Middle East and North Africa and exclude the United States. In fact, if such a system did develop—trading blocs of the sort that Kissinger was warning against—the United States could become a second-class power with regional responsibilities with an overall framework of order for someone else to manage. This is not a picture of the world that American planners are very eager to contemplate. These possibilities are all very significant differences, which are likely to make the New Cold War system distinct from the old one.

3. Continuities

Let us now look at the essential continuities between the Old Cold War and the New one, which persist through these differences. Today, more than ever, a growing volume of military strategy and technology is designed by the superpowers not for war against each other, but for war against the weak, the defenceless people in underdeveloped countries who cannot strike back. This involves among other things helicopters, napalm, rapid deployment forces, and tactical nuclear weapons. These are not designed for wars against powerful nations. With them you would fight a war of total destruction to prevent them from destroying you. That would, of course, be impossible, but that is the only way a war like this could be fought—for a few days, that is.

These wars against the weak will continue to be conducted within the rubric of the Cold War system, that is, within the traditional pretence that we are somehow defending freedom from the onslaught of Russian imperialism. An accurate description of the Russian world power would look quite different. In a relative sense, Russian power probably peaked in the late 1950s and has since been slowly declining, as US power has. Though there are a few areas in which Russian power has advanced, there have been major defeats. The greatest defeat, undoubtedly, was the departure of China from the system of Soviet influence, which produced a major shift in the world power balance. The Russians have also suffered setbacks in Indonesia, Egypt, Somalia, Sudan, and Iraq, along with gains elsewhere.

It is very revealing to see how the American propaganda system responds to these changes. For example, when the Russians had dominant influence in Somalia, this was described as one of the major threats to world peace because Somalia dominated the Indian Ocean. Then when the Russians were expelled from Somalia and the United States moved in, suddenly it appeared that Somalia was not important at all. It is Ethiopia that counts—Ethiopia which controls the Indian Ocean. It did not have such importance when it was a US satellite.

If we look at US estimates of Russian military power we find similar chicanery in the ways it is estimated. There are countless articles and statements which allege that the Russians are enormously outstripping us in military expenditures. Occasionally a truthful analysis becomes available. There is a very good one by Frank Holtzman, an economist at Tufts whose specialty is the Russian economy.[1] He gives an account of how the CIA estimates Russian expenditures.

The CIA constructs what is called a dollar equivalent of the Soviet military effort. The question then becomes: what would it cost us to do what they do? Now the military system of the Russians is labour-intensive, while ours, of course, is capital-intensive. For us labour is expensive; for them it is cheap. For us capital is relatively cheap. For them it is expensive. This means that for us to duplicate what they do would be very expensive; in fact, for us it is relatively cheap to have a high-technology military force with a relatively small number of bodies. For them it is the other way around. Therefore, when we translate the costs for us to duplicate their system, it is very expensive. It would also be enormously expensive for us to duplicate the Soviet agricultural system, but we do not therefore conclude that we are far behind them in this area.

Now let us turn it around and construct a rouble equivalent to our military system. It turns out that the rouble equivalent is infinite—that is, there is no way for them to duplicate our system. They could spend every rouble they have and they simply could not construct our military system because the technology is too advanced for them to duplicate.

Holtzman also points out that there is a striking contradiction between the picture presented to the public and the information given to Congress in this field. On the one hand, when the military establishment addresses the public, it claims that the Russians are outspending us on defence; but on the other hand, when the Joint Chiefs of Staff testify to Congress, they always say that we are much stronger militarily than the Russians. Obviously, both of these statements cannot be true. Furthermore, NATO outspends the Warsaw pact by any measure, and much of the Soviet military effort is directed against China. Soviet military power is no doubt a major menace to the world, but there is much deception in the picture presented to the Western publics.

These are all parts of the strategy that is being used domestically to persuade the public to support the renewal of the Cold War system—a system which is going to be used as it has been used in the past, for war against the weak. This is why the peoples who are supposed to be defended by this system are often the most apprehensive of it. They do not want to be 'defended', because they know that it is pretence to justify American military intervention in their region. For example, the Kuwaiti press, which is quite conservative and anti-communist, makes a strong case against the dangers of American interventionism in its region, and even Saudi Arabia has warned against it, as has Mexico with regard to Central America.

In fact, it is very lucky for the world that the American hostage rescue attempt in Iran failed. If it had succeeded, in spite of the very sharp conflicts between the Arab states and Iran, the Arabs probably would have supported Iran against any measures taken by the United States. We might have seen a great political explosion in the oil-producing regions, one that might have brought industrial civilization to its knees.

The next time around, if the United States resorts to military action, that may happen. The Middle East remains a very unstable region. In Saudi Arabia, for example, there have been a series of coup attempts in the past years. There is a great deal of unrest in these countries, where a very small ruling elite controls extraordinarily rich economies, but where much of the general population lives in poverty. This is a very dangerous and unstable situation and may explode at any time.

Another respect in which the New Cold War is likely to be similar to the old one is in its focus on the Middle East. When the Truman Doctrine and the Marshall Plan were announced, the focus of attention was not really on Europe. There was a fear that the war in Greece and the instability of Turkey would spill over into the Middle East, the locus of the major resources of energy. This was the earliest version of the Domino Theory. Presently, concern over South-West Asia is also oriented towards the Middle East, which remains the major source of relatively cheap energy for the world. Any threat to US domination of the oil-producing areas could lead to an explosive international conflict. This is one of the most persistent and most dangerous continuities between the old Cold War and the new Cold War.

4. Nuclear Arms and Third World Oppression

Meanwhile, it is important to bear in mind that strategic nuclear forces and 'conventional forces' tend to grow in parallel. The Kennedy Administration set off the current arms race when it entered into a huge programme of military Keynesianism, justifying the strategic weapons build-up on the basis of a faked missile gap. At the same time it inaugurated the 'era of counterinsurgency', an epoch of subversion and outright aggression which brought death and misery to many millions of people throughout the world. We are in a very similar period today. When B-52s drop bombs in the Egyptian desert in Operation Bright Star, it is not the USSR that is under threat, but the people of the Middle East and Africa. When the US carries out naval manoeuvres in the Caribbean, as it did last summer, the target is not the Soviet Union, but Grenada, El Salvador, Nicaragua and Cuba. It is not very likely that tactical nuclear weapons will be used against the Russians, but they may well be used against opponents who are too weak to strike back. Similar comments apply quite generally to the doctrine of 'flexible response'. When we invade South Vietnam, then all of Indochina, as we did 20 years ago, it is a limited war for us but a total war for the victims—one that approached the dimensions of nuclear war, a fact that it is all too easy for us to ignore and to forget.

In this respect, the real function of 'our strategic nuclear capabilities' can sometimes be discerned even in the pronouncements of propagandists and planners. Consider, for example, the words of President Carter's Secretary of Defence Harold Brown, in his January 29, 1980 statement to Congress on the proposed military budget. 'Our strategic nuclear capabilities,' he said, 'provide the foundation on which our security rests.' Crucially, 'With them, our other forces become meaningful instruments of military and political power.' Very true, and the real point.

It is not at all unlikely that there will be a major nuclear war within the next few decades. It will not break out in Europe, but in some region of the Third World. Perhaps some state will resort to such weapons in a moment of desperation to protect what its leaders see as a vital interest, involving the superpowers as the conflict escalates. The Middle East, with its enormous reserves of relatively cheap and abundant energy, is the most likely candidate, though other possibilities can easily be envisaged: consider, for example, what might have happened had the USSR reacted to the Chinese invasion of Vietnam in 1979. If we are seriously concerned to prevent nuclear war, our primary attention should be directed to the role of the USA in maintaining or heightening conflict and oppression within the

236

domains of its influence and power, and to its tacit partnership with the superpower enemy in maintaining the Cold War system of confrontation for mutual advantage.

Our protest against the expansion of the nuclear arms race is vital, but we should remember that for a large part of the world it is only of secondary importance, or may even seem irrelevant. At this very moment, the Indonesian army is carrying out yet another major military campaign in Timor, this time threatening a Final Solution in a country where perhaps 1/4 or 1/5 of the population has been wiped out in the past few years with arms that the USA sent to Indonesia in the certain knowledge that they would be used for that purpose. Perhaps 5 years from now some crusading journalist will expose these facts. Four thousand Indians have already been murdered in Guatemala this year by a regime that we placed in power and have maintained in power with substantial doses of violence; meanwhile tens of thousands starve while most crops are exported for our benefit in a country where 80% of the workforce labours under conditions of semi-slavery. It is essential for us to mobilize against the dangers of nuclear holocaust today. But we ought also to think about the permanent costs of these systems of repression. They are sometimes harder to grasp than the danger of a terminal nuclear exchange. But they are the real meaning of the Cold War. We should not forget them when we turn our attention to the danger that this system of massacre and oppression may ultimately engulf us as well.

---

[1]Frank Holtzman, 'Are the Soviets Really Outspending the US on Defence?', *International Security*, Spring 1980.

Perverse Politics and the Cold War

Alan Wolfe

Why do policymakers in both the Soviet Union and the United States spend a disproportionate amount of time contemplating each other's extermination? More remarkable than that, why is that, after having devised apparently foolproof methods of achieving such an objective, planners on both sides not only continue their work but intensify its seriousness? If we cannot answer questions like these soon, we may never be able to answer them at all.

E. P. Thompson worries that the Cold War is irrational, a product of mass inertia.[1] I have a worse fear. The Cold War, in my view, is not only rational, but it represents the end product, admittedly in the form of an Aristotelean degeneration, of the two greatest popular forces unleashed in the modern world: socialism and democracy. A perverse democracy like the United States and a perverse socialism like the Soviet Union confront each other in the Cold War, each fueled by the idealism of ideological tradition, each, in the process, striving to deform and stultify that very idealism. True, without democracy and socialism the technology for mass destruction would still exist. True, one cannot deny an economic motive for the constant manufacture of weapons. Yet if we really wish to comprehend the deep structure of the Cold War—or in Thompson's terms, the logic of exterminism—we must look as well to the political forces that organize that logic and give it life.

To blame bureaucracy, to substitute a vulgar Weberianism for a simplified Marxism, does not take us far. Not abstract bureaucracies but concrete states are the actors in the Cold War. The United States and the Soviet Union are both superpowers; if I may be literal for the moment, this means that they have accumulated super amounts of power, more than any other countries in the world. The accumulation of that power is their special mark and their unique burden. An understanding of the Cold War begins with an appreciation of how America and Russia accumulated their power and then proceeds to an examination of what they have done with it.

The Accumulation of Power

States gather power in order to carry out, within a spatially or otherwise delimited arena, tasks that the individuals composing that arena cannot carry out themselves. Individuals can do many things that states have difficulty accomplishing, like producing art or innovating—hence, in the West, the praise of individualism and the distrust of government. Yet, bourgeois ideology to the contrary, there are also tasks which states carry out that individuals would only botch—hence, in the East, the reification of the state and the denigration of the person. Marxism and liberalism, each in its own way, have focused on the accumulation of capital, by and large an affair of private persons or groups. Such understanding must be complemented with a focus on the accumulation of power, by and large an affair of public agencies.

Of all the forms of collective action, two have characterized the modern world and have formed the character of the modern state. One is economic growth, the other the preparation for war. Neither can be accomplished by individual effort alone, though both require individual acts. To sponsor growth and protect national security, states have developed extraordinary powers to steer or direct collective action toward the accomplishment of collectively defined ends.

Growth is a phenomenon so ubiquitous that, once introduced into economic life, there seems to be no stopping its force. In the name of growth, capitalism was given a free hand, socialism consolidated its power, and development became the highest priority of the under-developed. There is no society where the allure of growth has been contained, none, at least in the modern world, where greater material prosperity has been deliberately and consciously rejected as costing more than it is worth. States differ, sometimes violently, over how to achieve growth; they vary not at all over whether to achieve it. To be modern is to want more.

While capital accumulation requires individual effort, growth, understood as an overall process, demands collective planning. Socialist bloc countries and Third World economies, short of time, understand this implicitly and proceed toward the objective of growth with blunt instruments, including terror and forced collectivization. Yet even the capitalist road, while praising the individual, requires planning to achieve the objective of growth. In some cases this planning is undertaken by 'private' corporations so large, integrated, and authoritative that they assume the character of states. In other cases the way is paved by indicative planning and efforts to convince individual actors to mesh their objectives into common ends. In no case is the pursuit of growth left to unplanned acts fashioned by an impersonal process called the market. A growing society, whatever it calls itself, will be one that consolidates unprecedented political power for the sake of encouraging that growth.

When they are not sponsoring expansion, modern states spend the bulk of their remaining time (and budget) preparing for war. No state in the modern world avoids planning for war. Militarism has been transformed from a somewhat sporadic affair of the aristocracy to an integral feature of political life affecting all. Tolstoy's ability to separate completely the action in the field from the conversation in the parlours is as irrelevant to the way the Soviet Union plans for war as James Fenimore Cooper's isolation of military virtues to the wilderness is to the United States. A modern state always contemplates violence, all the time. Some states have been able to contain the military and to limit its influence within specific sectors of society. Other have become what Harold D. Lasswell prophetically called 'garrison states,' bending all other social objectives to accord with militarist considerations.[2] It matters greatly whether society controls or is controlled by its military component, but it is a measure of how much the modern state plans for war that no society can escape the problem. In a century of total war, total planning for war becomes a bureaucratic routine.

More than growth, war has become, as Randolph Bourne understood, the health of the state.[3] World War I, the focus of Bourne's attention, had more to do with the building of the modern state than any other event. 'Neither race had won, nor could win, the War,' the British poet Edmund Blunden wrote. 'The War had won, and would go on winning.'[4] In the West, the war won by transforming the political economy of production. Corporate liberalism, centralized finance, the recognition of working class demands, the welfare state, economic concentration—advanced capitalism, in a word—were the product, not only of class struggle, but also of war.[5] At the same time, the war simultaneously weakened international socialism and substituted socialism in one country; advanced socialism was as much a product of the war as advanced capitalism. After this war, and to the present day, neither democracy nor socialism would ever be the same. Lincoln Steffens thought he saw in the Russian Revolution our fate. One war later, General Cummings, in Norman Mailer's *The Naked and the Dead*, saw it more clearly. 'You can consider the Army, Robert,' he told Lt. Hearn, 'as a preview of the future.'[6]

Sponsoring growth and planning for war intersect with each other at all points. A growing society is one that has more resources to be turned into war preparation, while a militarized society is one that, at some level, seeks to channel its garrison industries into growth. Those states which can accumulate the greatest amount of power are those that can expand their economies and increase their armaments. America and Russia have accumulated super power, in part, because both have married the intangible factor of ideology to the tangible reality of state machinery. The United States, the most 'democratic' of the societies of the West, harnessed fantastic mass energy for assembling power to accomplish its objectives. The Soviet Union, the most 'socialist' of the societies of the East, possessed the manpower and bureaucracy for assembling state power to achieve its objectives. The Cold War exists between two mobilized peoples, one mobilized behind the most progressive ideology of the nineteenth century, the other behind the most advanced ideology of the twentieth.

Democracy and socialism were instrumental in helping the United States and the Soviet Union grow and prepare for war. Yet in the process of building state power, both democracy and socialism would be transformed into something entirely new. In the United States, the dictates of growth and war mutilated democracy into something that Thomas Jefferson would never recognize, though Alexander Hamilton would. In the Soviet Union, socialism as an instrument of war and growth created a form of state power not only unrecognizable in Marx, but in fundamental ways counter to him. Democracy, at least that variety now practised in the United States, has become a major cause for the perpetuation of the Cold War; any elite fraction wishing to pursue a policy of militarization finds it relatively easy to fan the flames of popular discontent behind an arms build-up. Socialism, at least that variety now practised in the Soviet Union, is also responsible for the permanence of the Cold War; socialism is both the official ideology of the Russian empire and the organizing logic of its mode of war production. To discover how and why the two most liberating doctrines of the modern world were turned into support for Cold War proclivities is the purpose of the remainder of this essay.

Perverse Democracy

Democracy is a process, a noun that needs an adjective to complete the thought. In the United States, two conceptions of democracy have competed with each other since the Articles of Confederation, one based upon the notion of a republic, the other seeking to harness democratic energies for modernist expansion.

A republican form of government, as envisioned by its eighteenth century advocates, would be small-scale, localist (even agrarian), pacifistic, virtuous, and elitist. Rooted in antiquity, republicans sought in democracy a model by which proper middle-class citizens would decide, hopefully through face to face contract, their common fate. A democratic republic, in short, would be thoughtful, deliberate, and stable, incompatible either with rapid industrialization or with preparations for war. Modernizing elites, at least since Hamilton, sought, on the contrary, a nationalistic, bellicose, growing, dynamic polity, one that would use the state for the purpose of industrial and military expansion. Continuously blocked at the local level, and in the halls of legislative institutions that gave disproportionate power to regional interests, nationalists needed a device to overcome republican resistance to their dreams of modernization. As I argue elsewhere, a mass mobilizing conception of democracy enabled modernizing elites to fashion an alliance with a plebiscitary mass, squeezing out the localists in the middle.[7] When democratic energies were linked to modernizing tendencies, a new form of democracy was created: popular, short-tempered, easily manipulable, demagogic. Perverse democracy was a product of the need for modernizing elites to sponsor war and growth in the face of local resistance.

As Walter Karp has argued, the key turning point in the defeat of the republican alternative was the period between the Spanish American War and the outbreak of World War I.[8] During these years, modernizing leaders like Theodore Roosevelt and Woodrow Wilson learned the art of mobilizing popular passion in order to achieve concrete politico-economic changes in the American state. War, in short, has been an essential ingredient in transforming democratic republicanism into perverse democracy.

The spread of war and the growth of perverse democracy have proceeded in tandem. Each step in the advancement of the suffrage, and each expansion of the scope of state activity, has been paved by a war about to be fought or rewarded for a war just concluded. No other single factor in this century has contributed as much to the expansion of political participation as the need to assemble vast numbers of working-class and farm youth, from every corner of the state, for the purpose of sacrificing their lives in combat. War and perverse democracy reenforce each other. 'The organization of enthusiasm',[9] Elie Halevy's term for the manipulation unleashed by war, has become a model of public opinion dynamics in modern democracy. At the same time, war itself has spread the equalizing, uniformity-inducing features that constitute the criteria of citizenship in perverse democracy. 'The military tent where they all sleep side by side,' noted Theodore Roosevelt, 'will rank next to the public school among the great agents of democratization.'[10]

Democracy promised to the dispossessed a utopia in which the oppression of daily life would yield to the comradeship, dignity, honour, and equality of all people. To a much greater degree than is generally realized, war has come closer, if in a distorted way, to the realization of that ideal than anything experienced in peacetime. (The sense of fraternity, as its name implies, was, of course, exclusively male). War is the *civitas* of modernity, the classical ideal of a polity in which men put aside their private interests for the sake of a common good. As Marc Ferro has written about the Great War, 'far from being an ordeal, the war liberated men's energies. It was enthusiastically received by most men of military age'.[11] World War I was the culmination of the nineteenth-century impulse toward equality, bent out of shape to be certain, but there for all to see. Compared to the modern corporation, also a product of this period, war offered greater democratic gratification.

When working-class demands for access to political power confronted business and governmental elites after World War I, they could no longer be ignored. After a relatively brief Republican interregnum in the United States, the force of reform became a tidal wave that threatened to make extinct Republican complacency. Searching for a metaphor to make palatable the reforms of the New Deal, Frankling D. Roosevelt employed the power of wartime imagery. As the new president said in his inaugural address of 4 March 1933, 'I shall ask the Congress for the one remaining instrument to meet the crisis—broad executive power to wage a war against the emergency, as great as the power that would be given to me if we were invaded by a foreign foe.' As William E. Leuchtenberg noted, 'The war provided a precedent for the concentration of executive authority, for the responsibility of government, for the state of the economy, and for the role of Washington as the arbiter among social groups.'[12] War, which had both accepted and perverted democratic demands, would also provide the model to incorporate those demands administratively into the modern state.

When the demands of growth were added to the requirements of war, perverse democracy was advanced even further. Economic growth has not only been compatible with democracy as understood in the United States; to a significant degree, economic growth *is* democracy. For most people most of the time, democracy came to mean, not the practice of freedoms they barely understood, nor a right to vote increasingly unexercised, but the notion that material prosperity would continue to exist. The modern crisis of democracy is really a crisis of growth; in America, the extension of political rights and the provision of social entitlements had become so closely tied to growth that when the latter no longer existed, no one knew how to preserve the former. An expanding economy has meant far more to the realization of democratic desires than the Bill of Rights.

The democratic state that emerged out of a half-century of unprecedented war and fabulous economic expansion bore little resemblance to the one that entered it. Considered in a plebiscitary sense, war and growth broadened democracy enormously. More people were protected against the market than ever before. The state provided benefits unheard of fifty years earlier. Women, followed by other disenfranchised groups, were given the right to vote. A sense of belonging to a national society, of participating in an integrated realm, replaced a tradition of ad hoc regional and class divisions. The quantitative scope of democracy, symbolized by rising GNP and increasing expenditures on security, was unquestionably enhanced.

Quantity, as it so often does, came at the expense of quality. Democracy, understood in the republican sense as a healthy and vibrant public life that matures and enlightens the private self, rapidly deteriorated under the imperatives of growth and war. Controversy, education, information, participation, dissent, truth—none of the subtleties of enlightened political thought could survive the crass materialism of economic expansion and the crass conformity of militarization. The modern democratic state was as broad in base as it was narrow in purpose. Rather than democratic demands fashioning the character of the state, the tasks of the state determined the permissibility of democratic demands. Public life was to be about war and growth and democracy would have to fashion itself around that. Democracy did. Indeed, a mass society composed of generally unthinking, often ignorant, complacently privatized individuals expressing their will upon decontextualized, fragmented, and impotent public agencies in an ahistorical and often contradictory manner was hardly an obstacle to the realization of growth and war, but even seemed to many the most perfect imaginable system for realizing those ends.

By the time the Cold War arrived, in other words, democracy had been completely transformed from a republican vision into a modernized *re*vision, one perfectly adjusted to the state's war fighting and expanding tasks. Republicans had claimed that an enlightened public realm would prevent irresponsible acts. No longer. The Cold War solidified Hamilton's victory over Jefferson, as America's major contemporary neo-Hamiltonian has argued.[13] Instead of checking war and aggrandizement, democracy, in its new form, would contribute to it. The marriage between war and perverse democracy was solidified by the promise of a permanent state of international tension which would, to the delight of perverse democrats, make permanent those plebiscitary features of perverse democracy which had heretofore been temporary.

Some sense of the impact that the Cold War had on perverse democracy can be gleaned by looking at the special cabinet meeting called by Harry Truman on 21 September 1945 to discuss whether to share atomic technology with the Soviets. No other decision, one can say in retrospect, would be more important to future generations. (This writer was three years old at the time.) Had the US been realistic and recognized that there would be no national barriers to science, the entire Cold War might have been avoided and the nuclear arms race brought under control before it began. How did this most 'democratic' of societies proceed with this most momentous of decisions? One member of the cabinet, Henry Wallace, rambled on about Mongolian animal diseases. Two others, Fred Vinson and James Forrestal, said that the Russians could not be trusted because they had an Oriental mentality. Apparently the meeting was unable to focus. 'The discussion was unworthy of the subject,' Dean Acheson wrote. 'No one had a chance to prepare for its complexities.' If the elite was confused, the general public was schizoid. Over 80% of the population, in a poll taken at the same time as the cabinet meeting, recognized that the US monopoly on atomic secrets was about to end, most of them concluding that the Russians would soon have the bomb. Nonetheless, 70% of the population (and 90% of the Congressmen) were opposed to cooperation with the Soviet Union.[14]

The discovery of nuclear technology revealed a tremendous gap between the technical and scientific maturity of the United States and the staggering immaturity of its political system. Such combined and uneven development has continued to make the United States one of the main perpetuators of the nuclear terror that frightens the world. If the technology were a bit less perfect, or the political system a jot more sophisticated, matters would not be as scary as they are. But when unprecedented technological brilliance is so closely married to unprecedented political ignorance, trouble can only result.

In three specific ways does the deformity of democracy as practised in the United States contribute to the global impasse that is the Cold War. One is the trick that nuclear technology has played on democracy, a second concerns the monopoly of security possessed by the state, and the third involves the resulting lowest common denominator problem when foreign policy conflicts with public opinion.

Nuclear weapons have played a tremendous, and not especially funny, joke on democratic expectations. War and perverse democracy in the twentieth century have been intimately linked, each pushing the other beyond its limits. Democratic demands, unrealized within the confines of class society, have, in the past, achieved a modest, if distorted, fulfilment in the excitement of battle. Yet with the discovery of nuclear weapons, democratic wars of any sort can no longer happen. Observers like Raymond Williams are correct to point out that nuclear weapons do act as a deterrent;[15] there has not been, and there cannot be, a repeat of the World War II experience.[16] Nuclear weapons have made long-enduring, labour-intensive, mass-mobilizing wars obsolete. From this point forward, only two kinds of wars are possible. One is the sort of limited (though incredibly destructive) engagement symbolized by Vietnam, an elite war with little of the enthusiasm and tension-relieving sublimation of earlier efforts. The other is a nuclear engagement, guaranteeing a certain equality of death, but in no other way satisfying democratic desires.

America, in other words, is in a position where war is still capable of generating a nostalgic enthusiasm for a world that has been lost, yet actual war can never satisfy the nostalgia. Sandwiched between democratic memories and high tech realities, Americans are given to the fetish of what can be called abstract belligerence—bloodthirsty in general, almost pacifistic in the particular. All polls show the same configuration; huge rhetorical support for more weapons; confrontation politics; anti-Soviet hyperbole; very little, if any, support for specific interventions, loss of life, blood sacrifice. The result is an inevitable frustration, encouraging a rampant desire for a kind of security that can never again be achieved. American democracy has not caught up with what American technology has produced.' In the popular mind, war still has something to do with honour and dignity; in the technological nightmare, war is the end of everything.

Although war may be a democratic memory, the technology of nuclear war demands a secrecy and elitism totally at odds even with perverse democratic dreams. Called on to participate, but at the same time prevented from engaging in public action, the American people become spectators to the activities of their own government, bearing the same active/passive relationship to the Cold War as they do to a football game. (Indeed, the arms race is pictured in the American press as a kind of sport, one side ahead in offence, the other concentrating on defence.) Unable to achieve the democratic satisfaction that war promises due to the inhibitions of nuclear weapons, Americans are ripe for the kind of routinized demagoguy that passes for campaign discussion every four years. Inevitable, increasing frustration is the—forgive the expression—fall-out from the tension between an elitist technology and a perverse democratic vision.

To a significant degree, the frustrations of American democracy, in the postwar years, were channelled into growth. If war could not serve as an outlet for democracy, then expansion could. Energy that once went into combat found itself diverted into increasing GNP. When the energy gave out, the frustration doubled. If the major tasks of the modern state are to encourage growth and to prepare for war, what is one to do when growth has stopped and war is impossible? The rapid increase in Cold War sentiment since the middle of the Carter administration can be directly traced to the sense of anger and disappointment in the United States caused by a democratic system that demands war and growth but cannot provide either.

These difficulties would be difficult to resolve in any case, for they demand an honest self-examination that few societies have willingly carried out. But they are rendered even more difficult due to the state's monopoly of the means of security. National security is like no other issue in American politics, there to be manipulated at will, lied about with perfect sincerity, and changed as the situation demands. (Most presidents underestimate their own country's strength in order to obtain office, only to revise their estimates once they discover what the operationalization of their campaign rhetoric would cost.) When it concerns the nation's military forces, all the rules of pluralistic democracy are off. The media cooperate. Labour unions become participants. Both parties claim the militarist mantle. With a remarkably straight face, those who condemn government call upon it to perform Herculean tasks. Balanced budgets are sacrificed, inflation tolerated, and trade deficits accepted—all for the sake of national security. The chances of sponsoring a thorough and convincing programme for smaller military budgets and a less cumbersome imperial apparatus through the electoral system stands close to zero chance of succeeding.

Over the past two hundred years, as capital has become concentrated in ever more centralized forms, the means of violence have also become concentrated to a degree never before experienced. On the frontier, one always had one's rifle. In the nineteenth century, states played a considerable role in organizing the American armed forces. Even in the twentieth century, World War II was fought with weapons that are laughable from the perspective of the 1980s. Yet between the start of World War II and its end, a remarkable change had come over the administration of war. 'Out of this first war of both the mass and the machine,' Walter Millis wrote, 'this first truly global conflict, one salient and shocking fact was to emerge: the almost unbelievable power of the modern centralized, managerial and nationalistic state to drain the whole physical, intellectual, economic, emotional and moral resources of its citizens to the single end of military victory.'[17] Capitalists may extract surplus-value; the state extracts surplus security. Having given over to the state control over their destiny, people are unlikely to gamble with how the state uses that control. They have, after all, no other way to 'protect' themselves.

With so much at stake, it is little wonder that the rules of ordinary politics are suspended when insecurity becomes rife. As the American–Iranian hostage crisis indicated, security, once it becomes an issue in an election debate, plunges quickly down to the lowest common denominator of discourse. Not having fought a war on its own turf for one hundred and twenty years, America is myopic on the subject to begin with. When combined with the state's monopolization of the means of security, hopes for rational debate and clear understanding on matters of war and peace evaporate. European societies can still, to some degree, conduct meaningful discussion of these issues within the confines of the electoral system; America apparently, cannot.

Perverse democracy has become an obstacle to peace. Political perversion has never been stronger than in the age of Reagan; the same goes for the threat of war. One of the prime tasks of the Wall Street, corporate liberal, financial Establishment in the United States has been to keep people like Reagan from entering the White House. So long as American foreign policy was made by an exclusive, undemocratic elite, it was always *somewhat*—there is Vietnam—under control. Now that the elite has been discredited, foreign policy is once again made through perverse democracy, and Reaganism in the result. Under a demagogic president, with fabulous ability to orchestrate fears and insecurity, perverse democracy has taken its place as a major contributor to the continuing arms race.

I am not arguing that perverse democracy 'caused' the cold war. Obviously one cannot dismiss the fact that a capitalist democracy and a socialist polity would engage in rivalry, whether either were perverted or not. Moreover, big-power rivalry has been a feature of world politics since the advent of the modern state and would exist independently of the internal organization of the participating states. Finally, war and its demands need not be linked to democracy; fascism proved to be as fully compatible, if not more so, with war-making requirements as perverse democracy. My point is simply that long historical trends which transformed democracy from a republican concern with virtue and propriety into an expanded, more participatory, but also more manipulable form, prepared the groundwork for participation in the Cold War. Raising questions about the Cold War necessarily raises questions about democracy as currently practised. From an American perspective, the Cold War continues because, at some level and no matter how distorted, the American people have become convinced that they need it.

Perverse Socialism

The Cold War has another side. If perverse democracy developed through war and consolidated through growth, the socialist state, again in practice if not in theory, developed to encourage growth and was solidifed through war. In the East as well as the West, the perversion of one of the most humanistic and progressive traditions of the modern world bears substantial responsibility for the perpetuation of the Cold War.

Socialism Russian style, like democracy American style, originated in the trenches of World War I. It has been persuasively argued that the Russian Revolution took place at a time when international events unforeseen by the Bolsheviks (or by anyone else) so weakened the internal authority of the old regime that systemic transformation become possible.[13] World War I simultaneously destroyed the old socialist ideal of international solidarity and enhanced the new socialist ideal of the seizure of state power. If advanced capitalism was a product of the way America entered World War I, advanced socialism was an end result of the way Russia left it. Just as the war thoroughly changed the meaning of democracy, broadening it and narrowing it at the same time, the war changed the meaning of socialism, making it both more possible but also more problematic.

Unlike Americans, who, in the words of David Kennedy, 'disproportionately used their profits from the war years to fuel a spectacular expansion of the home economy,'[19] the Russians came out of the war devastated and disunified. Socialism's first real challenge was whether it could grow, not whether it could fight. Who could imagine, reading the great nineteenth-century classics of socialist thought, that the main selling point of the idea in the twentieth century would be its ability to organize economic growth? Yet the crucial turning point for advanced socialism was the resolution of the debates in the 1920s over economic growth, symbolized by the defeat of Bukharin and the emergence of the Stalinist form of primitive accumulation. Bukharin's notions of balanced growth, attempting to reconcile the obvious need to expand with a recognition of the peasant character of Russia, was the last chance for Soviet socialism to avoid the perversions of modernity. Once the goal become industrial catch-up, socialism had as much chance to be faithful to its ideological origins as democracy did to its.

Stalinism was a strategy of economic growth; one, to be sure, filled with irrationality and terror beyond the human imagination, yet one also relentlessly single-minded in its pursuit of modernity. By transforming the countryside through its liquidation, Stalin prepared the groundwork for the emergence of a modern proletariat. When World War II ended, two-thirds of the Soviet population lived off the land; in 1979, the figure was down to 38%. 'The Russian muzhik,' Daniel Singer writes, 'is historically on his way out in the same way as the peasant has been vanishing in the western world.'[20] Moreover, by promoting socialism in one country and sponsoring a nationalistic programme, Stalin unified the nation state, weakening the autonomous republics and concentrating political and economic power in the hands of a centralized elite.[21] The net result was to enhance the Soviet state's capacity to carry out the two fundamental political tasks of modernity: industrial expansion and the ability to fight war.

By the 1940s, the Soviet state was, for the first time in Russian history, capable of meeting the West on its own terms. No consumer society had been created, but the level of heavy industrialization could not be denied. Both the industrial potential of the Soviet Union and its somewhat more urbanized and proletarianized working class contributed to the Soviet success in World War II. Especially when compared to the humiliation of the Japanese War of 1905 and the disastrous peace terms signed at Brest-Litovsk, the Russians have taken their socialist revolution and, in the name of Stalin, transformed it into a state machinery capable of acting on twentieth-century terms.

To ask whether Bukharinism would have been a 'better' alternative to the Soviet Union is like asking whether Jeffersonianism is more appropriate to modern America than Hamiltonianism. Modernity does not allow such choices. Clearly, the pursuit of a Bukharinite strategy would have made the Soviets weaker in an age of war and growth. Without rapid and heavy industrialization, not only might the Russians have lost World War II, but Hitlerian fascism could have been the future for postwar Europe. Stalin's accomplishment in Russia, like those of the state builders in the United States, was to revise a progressive and humanistic ideology to make it compatible with the tasks of the modern state. Socialism might not have survived without Stalin. It did survive, but it barely resembled socialism.

At some level, the Soviet Union is still 'socialist', just as, at some level, the United States is still 'democratic'. In the Soviet Union the means of production are not in private hands, planning is the most prominent feature of economic life, there has been a marked tendency toward greater equality, and from time to time the Soviets act in support of socialist revolutions around the world. (Sometimes they do not, and in at least one case, the Ethiopian, they switched sides in the middle.) None of these advances, and advances they are, would have been possible without the consolidation of political power to expand economically and the consolidation of military power to ward off a threat to those gains. Yet the price paid for these accomplishments has been as great as the price paid in the United States to obtain women's suffrage, greater participation, and extensions of the welfare state—all products of the need to broaden the public realm in an age of perverse democracy. Perverse socialism is marked by top-down hierarchical decision-making, a controlled press and distrust of dissent, racial and ethnic chauvinism, industrial priorities, the militarization of society, and, most significant in the context of this essay, a commitment to 'keeping up' with the West that has, in its own fashion, contributed to the Cold War.

The Cold War has become intertwined with perverse socialism in the Soviet Union much as perverse democracy deforms the interventional behaviour of the United States. Stalinism may have been a path, however monstrous, to primitive industrialization, but it was not in accord with the more bureaucratic and impersonal second phase of growth that followed World War II. As Seweryn Bialer has written about the Soviet elite: 'They had been brought up in the midst of Stalin's barbarism; they were its willing participants; but now they yearned for a different, what they would consider a deserved and more stable, political lifestyle, for material progress, respectability, enjoyment. This in the deepest sense was the key reason why the system of mature Stalinism could not survive its creator. The leadership as a whole, and the elites, as a whole, wanted a new deal.[22] Growth rates flattened out after World War II, but they never stopped increasing; during the 1970s, a period of economic downturn, Soviet growth rates were still higher than American.[13] Having successfully launched Soviet society into the growth era, the Soviet state become responsible for the management of growth. Despite numerous economic problems, it has managed growth as well as can be expected for a society that so recently emerged into modernity.

In a similar fashion, Stalinism, appropriate for the kind of mass-mobilizing, labour-intensive war that World War II became, was highly counter-productive to the science-based, high technology, bureaucratic caution that emerged in the Cold War. Nuclear weapons played as much of a trick on Stalinism as they did on democracy. 'World War II,' Bialer writes, 'can be seen as the turning point, when the almost miraculous victory upon the brink of total disaster made credible the attribution of nearly magical powers to Stalin, and his identification with this great patriotic achievement evoked widespread, genuine admiration.'[24] The Great Patriotic War, indeed, required massive sacrifice, positive participation, mobilization—all the very features of a political system that nuclear weapons deny. A cult of personality is intolerable when personalities can push buttons which would blow up the world. Trends toward the collectivization of war making and military decisions, already well under way, were given an added impetus when science and technology were so devastatingly unleashed.

The Soviets, like the Americans, have a collective memory of war, but their recollections are different. War to the Russians means devastation so vast that it must, if possible, be avoided. To a significant degree the fact that the Soviets have generally taken the lead in arms control negotiations is a reflection of their more recent experience, at home, of the meaning of modern war. Yet fear of war, in a modernized state, does not lead to pacifism but its opposite. Precisely because the Russian people are horrified at the prospect of another devastation, they tacitly yield extraordinary power to their leaders to prevent it and their leaders use that power to build ever more weapons. The Soviet state is responsible both for making war and for insuring that it not be fought, a paradox that strengthens bureaucratic and impersonal tendencies in the military sector.

Socialism, then, was indispensible in transforming Russia from a feudal, underdeveloped monarchy into a modern state capable of expanding and defending itself. It would be difficult to imagine, even if the course of history could, by some act of intellectual curiosity, be changed, that a moderate bourgeois regime emerging after World War I could have had such profound, and rapid, modernizing characteristics. Yet to achieve these extraordinary results, socialism increasingly been divorced from its intellectual origins, perverted into a new doctrine that would make its contribution to the Cold War. The deformities of the Soviet system have been endlessly catalogued, more, I am sure, than the ills of any other social system in human history, so not much time need be spent on the subject. Nonetheless, it is worth reiterating the effect that such perversions as hierarchy, nationalism, and empire have had on the course of the first socialist revolution of the twentieth century.

Socialism, like democracy, has diverse, even contradictory, roots. Economic justice or more efficient planning—that was the question. Competition from the West answered it. 'The dilemma of Soviet economic policy,' Rudolf Bahro has written, 'is reminiscent of the children's tale of the hare and the tortoise, where the tortoise bends the rules of the game. Each time the Soviet economy pauses for breath after a bout of exertion it hears a voice from the end of the course shout: "I'm already here." '[25] Once the decision was taken to play catch-up with the West, hierarchy became inevitable. Growth, as the Reagan administration has happily announced, requires a certain injustice; in the Soviet version of growth politics, a willingness to tolerate inequality became the price to be paid, not especially reluctantly, to expand the domestic economy. Military competition with the West reenforced that conclusion as strongly as economic competition initiated it, for war, and its preparation, requires hierarchy as fully as growth. A growth-oriented economy linked to a war machine is not likely to be a vehicle of social justice. Ironically, the Soviet leaders were not successful in matching the West economically. But they did achieve a certain equality in nuclear weapons, thereby legitimating the domestic inequities among the population.

War economies and growth economies have striking similarities. Studies of Third World regimes, for example, have demonstrated that military elites promote industrial values more consistently than they do values of equity, thereby accepting as given and unalterable international capitalist relationships.[26] In the Soviet case, perverse socialism became a mechanism for achieving growth and war planning simultaneously. At first, centralized economic planning possessed the sure advantage of channelling investment into war production without the cumbersome system of incentives and pay-offs characteristic of the West. The entire Soviet economy, as Oskar Lange once pointed out, began to look like a Western war economy, organized to achieve a specific objective.[27] Yet if socialism paved the way to fight war, over time the fighting of war began to serve as a model for the organization of socialism. Since World War II, and especially since the decision of the Soviet elite after the Cuban missile crisis to play serious military catch-up with the West, the defence sector establishes the goals and the economy is altered to meet them, not the other way around.[28] Socialism was once the end, and the strengthening of the state the means to reach it. Now enhancing the state is the goal, and socialism tailored to achieve that.

If liberalism is the ideology of the market, nationalism is the world-view of the state. Democracy in the West, originally hostile to liberalism, made its accommodations with it in the interests of growth. Socialism in the East, originally antithetical to nationalism, has transformed itself in its image for *raisons d'état*. Growth and war are the concrete embodiments of the national spirit. Engaged in a grotesque competition to bring itself down to the level of America—though, in fairness, American under Reagan seems determined to bring itself down to the level of the Soviet Union—the Russians have married the ideology of socialism to the interests of nationalism. The defence of socialism becomes the defence of the Soviet Union, and militarism and preparations for exterminism are clothed in the language of progressive humanism. Like E. P. Thompson, I have heard people speak of socialist and capitalist nuclear weapons and, like him, I am flabbergasted. The arms race is an affair of nation states, and all ideology is secondary to that.

The ultimate deformity of socialism in the Soviet Union was reached with the Polish worker rebellions of 1980. Not only had socialism come to stand for hierarchy and national power, now it posed itself as a bulwark against—socialism. Americans who watched their government suppress democratic movements in Latin America in the name of democracy could only force a wan smile as they heard Soviet and Polish Communists denounce a workers' revolution. In both cases the reason was the same: the protection of an empire rationalized by an originally anti-imperialist ideology. For the Russians to view events in Poland as an attack on socialism is to confuse an economic vision and the arms race imperatives of the Soviet state.

Socialism, once again in practice, not in theory, has emerged as a major contributor to the Cold War. Perverse socialism is as strongly embedded in the Kremlin as perverse democracy is in the White House. Moroever, there is every reason to expect an increase in perversion as events conspire against the Soviet elite. As state builders, the Kremlin leaders have come to depend, like all state builders, on growth and security. 'If there is any single value that dominates the minds and thoughts of the Soviet establishment from the highest to the lowest level,' Bialer writes, 'it is the value of order; if there is any single fear that outweighs all the others, it is the fear of disorder, chaos, fragmentation, loss of control.'[29] States bring order, and growth and war are the health of the state. Without them, disorder threatens. In the 1980s, threats of an economic crisis at home have combined with the limitations of empire abroad to frustrate and puzzle the Soviet leadership. America's response to disorder has been to choose a nostalgic Reaganism. Russia's occurs at a time when the entire Soviet elite faces a period of transition. Without a willingness to explore alternative sources of order, the two superpowers seem destined to strengthen the very features of their society that once gave them life, but now threaten them with extinction.

Cold War Politics

In the American literature on totalitarianism, recently revived with the published thoughts of Ambassador Kirkpatrick,[30] an unbreakable link is said to exist between the oppressive internal character of the Soviet Union and its expansionist external behaviour. In the Soviet literature on imperialism, as Jerry Hough has demonstrated, the exact mirror image is reflected: capitalist societies are said to expand because of their flawed internal organization.[31] Cold War scholarship conveniently blames, not only the other side, but the other side's *system*, for the perpetuation of the

Cold War. With bad scholarship so bipartisanly consensual, one is tempted to conclude that both are wrong and that internal structure has little to do with external behaviour. But that oversimplifies. Perverse democracy and perverse socialism are very much connected to the behaviour of the states that embody them, if in different, and important, ways.

Contrary to the theory of totalitarianism, there is substantial evidence that the more open a society, the greater is its proclivity to practise an aggressive foreign policy. America, for example, has developed a more active and belligerent foreign policy precisely during those periods when its domestic political system was most open to controversy and dissent. In another place, I argue that there have been three identifiable periods since the end of World War II when Cold War politics dominated American domestic life.[32] These are:

1. *The formation of the Cold War (1947–51)*. During this period, perceptions of the Soviet threat were used to rally support for the Marshall Plan, to adopt the basic outline of containment strategy as contained in the top-secret memo NSC-68, and to force through a sharp increase in military spending. The period crested with the Korean War, which unleashed all those military forces in American life that were frustrated when World War II ended.

2. *The Kennedy round (1960–68)*. Campaigning against Eisenhower, John F. Kennedy made the extraordinary, and completely false, claim that the US was behind the Russians in missiles. As a result of the hysteria that followed, a crash programme of new military spending was begun, domestic American life was significantly militarized, and counter-insurgency plans were developed that generated, a few years later, the invasion of the Dominican Republic and the Vietnam War. It took the election of a Republican named Nixon to bring about detente and the first SALT treaty.

3. *Cold War III (1978–present)*. Two years into the Carter administration, the American mood suddenly turned sharply to the right. SALT II was held up, calls for new military spending were ubiquitous, and plans to 'unleash' the CIA were put under way. The hostage crisis in Iran and the Soviet invasion of Afghanistan accelerated the momentum of this process, but its tragic direction was set well before these Middle Eastern catalysts occurred. Ronald Reagan has continued the Cold War course begun by Carter. At the time of this writing, no one can tell when the new round of hysteria will end, but economic constraints may cut into it soon, if they have not already.

Those who seek to understand US foreign policy as a result of Soviet actions fail to grasp the domestic dynamics behind each wave of aggressive foreign policy in the United States. In the final analysis, I would argue that perverse democracy is more responsible for fanning the flames of anti-Soviet hysteria in Washington than any actions taken in Moscow. Each period of Cold War mania, I have argued, has in common the following five characteristics:

1. All of them began under Democratic Presidents, especially those who saw in the Soviet threat a way of overcoming domestic opposition to their economic and social policies.

2. All took place at a time when relations between Congress and the President significantly deteriorated. The first two periods were marked by attempts on the part of Presidents to regain authority at the expense of Congress. The last one is more Congressionally inspired, especially in its origins, but Ronald Reagan has certainly picked up the Presidential momentum.

3. The waxing and waning of the Cold War can be directly related to inter-service rivalry. When there are insufficient public funds to support all the favourite projects of all three armed services, the losing service will generally discover a previously underplayed Soviet threat in order to prevent itself from declining relative to the other two.

4. Periods of Cold War hostility in the United States occur at times when the foreign policy establishment is internally divided, generally after a major crisis (the Chinese revolution, Sputnik, Vietnam) has broken down a previously existing equilibrium. Perceptions of a Soviet threat are indispensable in attempts to redirect American foreign policy, from Asia to Europe, for example, or from Europe to the Third World, or from China to the Soviet Union.

5. There is a definite link between the Cold War and economic stimulation, but it is not a simple attempt to 'fine-tune' the economy through reflationary arms spending, in part because the lead-time is so great. Rather each phase in the Cold War coincides with the emergence of a 'growth coalition,' a constellation of interests unified around a long-term growth strategy, regardless of whether it calls itself supply-side or demand-side.

In short, the United States invariably turns to a more aggressive foreign policy stance when its domestic politics are fractured and broken. Periods of relative harmony and consensus, when issues are not especially salient and when there is little democratic excitement and mobilization, are periods when detente or international relaxation find themselves more popular. Throughout most of the postwar period, splits in the majority coalition, which was the Democratic Party, tended to be resolved through rediscovery of the Soviet threat. Now matters have shifted, although the same underlying dialectic is at work. Republicans are becoming the majority party, and part of the formula for their success is that they have adopted the same programmes of economic growth and military superiority that once beguiled their opponents.[33] (In the 1940s and 1950, when the Democrats called for more spending on arms, the Republicans advocated restraint and were given to isolationism). Any majority party in America is a divided coalition. For the Republicans in the present, as for the Democrats in the past, the Cold War is a force for unification. Ronald Reagan's domestic economic programme, already in trouble on Wall Street, will exacerbate the differences in his party between orthodox monetarists and supply-side expansionists. Under such conditions, one would be foolish to discount the possibility of military adventurism somewhere around the globe. Given the state of the economy, however, Reagan will have to find a way to pursue Cold War foreign policies without spending as much on the military as the Democrats did in the past.

Soviet expansionism has entirely different roots. Russia has had a long history of imperial dreams, and the consolidation of state power under a socialist regime has enabled those dreams to be realized in more systematic fashion than the periodic skirmishes of the tsars. States with the power to expand will expand. It is neither the economy of a society, nor its ideology, that compels aggressive behaviour in the international system. The state itself, as the Weberian and Schumpeterian position holds, seeks the opportunity to consolidate its power, both at home and abroad. Economic and ideological factors shape *how* that power is consolidated. The importance of perverse socialism is that it affects the behaviour of the Soviet state in the Cold War, just as perverse democracy affects the behaviour of the United States. The asymmetry in the Cold War is due to the fact that the behaviour induced by each perversion is distinct.

As a highly centralized, authoritarian state, the Soviet Union practises a quite different kind of imperial politics from that of the United States. The absence of competing political parties, combined with the lack of freedom of thought and expression, ironically removes one of the pressures toward inconsistent imperial behaviour. Whereas the United States *politicizes* its path toward empire, the Soviet Union approaches its hegemony *managerially*. The Russians are far more interested in fashioning agreed-upon rules for imperial conduct than the United States.

Dictatorships seem so much more compatible with the smooth management of empire than democracies—surely a major reason why imperialists in the United States continuously seek restrictions on a free press and on popular inquiry. Soviet leaders need not fear that the agreements they make in the international system will be distorted and ridiculed in the emotions of an election campaign. Nor need they worry that secrets will be 'leaked' in a fashion requiring them to disown them. There is less of a gap in the Soviet Union between the demands of empire abroad and the management of empire at home.

This is not to suggest an absence of pluralistic pressures. There are interest groups in Soviet politics, and splits within the elite over relations with the United States are very real. Moreover the Soviet Union at the moment is in the throes of a generational transition more significant than any in its history. In 1980 the average age of the full members of the Politburo was 70.1, compared to 61.0 in 1964 and 55.4 in 1952. Andrei Gromyko first came to Washington when Roosevelt was president. Boris Ponomarev, Central Committee Secretary, was named to the executive committee of the Comintern when Jimmy Carter was twelve and Edward Kennedy four.[34] (Ronald Reagan, however, was a ripe twenty-five.) The Russians not only have the oldest elite in the world, it is one that has served together longest because the Stalinist purges removed an entire generation from office. Such a massive transition in leadership as the Russians will soon experience may make the smooth management of empire more difficult, perhaps leading to the kinds of unpredictable actions that characterize the United States.

Nonetheless, just as perverse democracy shapes the character of America's foreign affairs, perverse socialism acts to colour the Russian approach. The Russians approach their empire the way an *oblast* manager approaches his region. Planning, only moderately successful at home, is inevitably extended abroad. Kremlinology is more of an exact science than Americanology. They always seem puzzled at what we do; we are rarely puzzled at what they do. Sometimes the Russians find in Washington a planner like Kissinger who shares their urgency about imperial management. Just when they think they have cut a deal, a new administration comes to power—there have been five American presidents between 1968 and 1981—determined to repudiate his predecessor's policies. A Reagan or a Haig, when he denounces the Russians, objects to the existence of the Soviet empire. Soviet abusive rhetoric, as in the Gromyko speech of September 1981 to the United Nations, denounces the fact that the Americans have an empire less than their refusal to share it.

From the standpoint of preventing nuclear war, managerialism is preferable to politicization. The uncertainty and immaturity coming from Washington continuously upset whatever momentum toward arms control is established, while the Russians, who are second to none in their pursuit of national self-interest, are more likely to see that self-interest realized through big-power agreements. When perverse politics interconnect with the Cold War, a drastic irony results. That party to the Cold War which has a far preferable domestic system has the more dangerous foreign policy, while the party that has a horrendous internal organization acts with greater external restraint at a time when primitive impulses are impossible to contemplate. The very lack of anything resembling democracy in the Soviet Union places restraints on its behaviour abroad. The very presence of democracy in the United States, especially of the perverse type, undermines its ability to act as a mature power. Sceptics might ask themselves whether at the height of the Iranian—American hostage crisis, they would have been willing to put the question of the use of tactical nuclear weapons in Iran on the ballot, at a time when 'Nuke the Ayatollah' bumper stickers were proliferating.

Yet while managerial predictability is certainly preferable to political instability, to have to choose between the two would be like the kind of option a condemned prisoner might make between the hangman's noose and the gas chamber. Soviet nuclear weapons are as dangerous to the world, by their very existence, as American nuclear weapons. One side may indicate more willingness to establish rules for the arms race, but neither is serious about bringing it to an end. Relief from the madness of the arms race will have to come from somewhere beyond both perverse democracy *and* perverse socialism. The US and the Soviet Union are too locked into their mutual *danse macabre* to offer the peace movement much hope.

Yet there is, nonetheless, hope for peace. Within the peripheries of perverse democracy and perverse socialism there has been discovered, of all things, democracy and socialism. Demonstrators in Western Europe have been campaigning against nuclear weapons and, in the process, reminding the world that democracy is possible in a democracy. Workers in Poland have been campaigning against Soviet perversions and, in the process, informing us that socialism is possible under socialism. What ultimately gives perverse democracy and perverse socialism their mobilizing power is also what makes democracy and socialism too important to be left to those who speak in their name. So long as human beings value life, the original radical impulses in both doctrines will constantly come to the surface, in the process saving, not only the doctrines, but perhaps the world as well.

[1]E. P. Thompson, 'Notes on Exterminism, The Last Stage of Civilization,' *New Left Review* 121, May–June 1980: now in this volume.

[2]Harold D. Lasswell, *National Security and Individual Freedom*, New York 1950, pp. 23–49.

[3]Randolph Bourne, *The Radical Will: Selected Writings, 1911–1918*, New York 1977.

[4]Quoted in Paul Fussell, *The Great War and Modern Memory*, New York 1975, p. 13.

[5]See Robert D. Cuff, *The War Industries Board*, Baltimore 1973.

[6]Quoted in Fussell, p. 320.

[7]Alan Wolfe, 'Presidential Power and the Crisis of Modernization,' *Democracy*, Vol. I, Number 2, April 1981, 10–32.

[8]Walter Karp, *The Politics of War*, New York 1979.

[9]Cited in Raymond Aron, *The Century of Total War*, Boston 1954, p. 89.

[10]Quoted in David Kennedy, *Over Here: The First World War and American Society*, New York 1980, p. 17.

[11]Marc Ferro, *The Great War, 1914–1918*, London 1973, p. 8.

[12]William E. Leuchtenberg, 'The New Deal and the Analogue of War' in John Braeman et al, *Change and Continuity in Twentieth Century America*, Columbus, Ohio 1964, pp. 105, 125.

[13]'Yet today America can learn more from West Point than West Point from America. Upon the soldiers, the defenders of order, rests a heavy responsibility. The greatest service they can render is to remain true to themselves, to serve with silence and courage in the military way. If they abjure the military spirit, they destroy themselves first and their nation ultimately. If the civilians permit the soldiers to adhere to the military standard, the nations themselves may eventually find redemption and security in making that standard their own.' Samuel P. Huntington, *The Soldier and the State*, New York 1964, p. 466.

[14]This paragraph is based on the material in Gregg Herken, *The Winning Weapon: The Atomic Bomb in the Cold War, 1945–1950*, New York 1981, p. 30–31.

[15]Raymond Williams, 'The Politics of Nuclear Disarmament, *New Left Review* 124, November–December, 1980: now in this volume.

[16]A persuasive case that nuclear weapons have acted as a deterrent is made by Michael Mandelbaum, *The Nuclear Question: The United States and Nuclear Weapons, 1964–1976*, Cambridge 1979.

[17]Walter Millis, *Arms and Men*, New York 1956, p. 265.

[18]Theda Skocpol, *States and Social Revolutions*, Cambridge 1979.

[19]Kennedy, p. 346.

[20]Daniel Singer, *The Road to Gdansk*, New York 1981, p. 93.

[21]See Alvin Gouldner, 'Stalinism: A Study of Internal Colonialism,' *Telos*, 34, winter 1978.

[22]Seweryn Bialer, *Stalin's Successors*, Cambridge 1980, p. 46.

[23]Jerry Hough, *Soviet Leadership in Transition*, Washington 1980, p. 131. Bialer agrees: 'The major conclusion that emerges from our presentation of Soviet performance in the Brezhnev era is that the Soviet regime has by and large been able to deliver the goods; it has generally been able to satisfy popular expectations for higher standards of living.' Bialer, p. 154.

[24]Bialer, p. 30.

[25]Rudolf Bahro, *The Alternative in Eastern Europe*, London 1978, p. 134.

[26]See, for example, R. N. Tannahill, 'The Performance of Military and Civilian Governments in South America, 1948–67,' *Journal of Political and Military Sociology*, Vol. 4, No. 2, Fall 1976; Eric A. Nordlinger, 'Soldiers in Mufti: The Impact of Military Rule upon Economic and Social Change in the Non-Western States.' *American Political Science Review*, Vol. LXIV, No. 4, December 1970 and the similar literature cited in Mary Kaldor, *The Baroque Arsenal*, New York 1981, pp. 157–162.

[27]Oskar Lange, *Essays in Capitalism and Socialism*, Oxford 1970, cited in Kaldor, p. 113.

[28]Kaldor, pp. 99–129.

[29]Bialer, p. 145.

[30]Jeane Kirkpatrick, 'Dictatorships and Double Standards', *Commentary*, November 1979, and U.S. Security and Latin America,' *Commentary*, January 1981.

[31]Jerry Hough, *The Soviet Union and Social Science Theory*, Cambridge, Mass. 1977.

[32]Alan Wolfe, *The Rise and Fall of the 'Soviet Threat'*, Washington 1979.

[33]For considerably more detail on this point, see Alan Wolfe, *America's Impasse*, New York 1981.

[34]Hough, *Soviet Leadership in Transition*, passim.

Warfare and Capitalism

Mary Kaldor

War belongs not to the province of Arts and Science but to the province of social life. It is a conflict of great interests which is settled by bloodshed . . . It would be better, instead of comparing it with any Art, to liken it to business competition, which is also a conflict of human interests and activities; and it is still more like State policy, which again, on its part, may be looked upon as a kind of business competition on a great scale. Besides, State policy is the womb in which war is developed, in which its outlines lie hidden in a rudimentary state, like the qualities of living creatures in their germs.

The essential difference consists in this, that war is no activity of the will, which exerts itself upon inanimate matter like the mechanical Arts; or upon a living but still passive and yielding subject, like the human mind and the human feelings in the ideal Arts, but against a living and reacting force.

CARL VON CLAUSEWITZ

'The Bomb is a Thing', says Edward Thompson, and how does one analyse a thing? In chapter 1 of *Capital*, Marx sets out to analyse the commodity. He describes its two-fold character; as a use-value, an object of consumption, a quality, and as an exchange value, an object of production, a quantity of resources, of human effort required for its manufacture. He places great emphasis on the contradiction between these two properties of the commodity—the constant struggle to increase use-value and reduce exchange-value. This contradiction is daily resolved in the market place where society, in the form of individual buyers and sellers of commodities, daily makes its judgement of 'How much is enough?' about the appropriate social division of labour to produce the appropriate mix of use-values.

The Bomb has a use-value, its destructiveness, and it requires resources—workers, scientists, laboratories, factories—for its manufacture. But it does not enter the market place. There exists another form of commensuration for armaments: war. Battle, says Clausewitz, or 'the decision by arms' is 'for all operations in war, great and small, what cash payment is in bill transaction'.[1] But what if war is very infrequent, if the Bomb is too destructive to be used? How does the contradiction between the Bomb as object of consumption and the Bomb as object of production ever get resolved? How is the question 'How much is enough?' ever answered? The possibility of allocating more and more resources for increasingly otiose ends can become a reality. The manufacture of warfare can overtake the society which it theoretically serves. And the pressure to resolve the contradiction between the use-value of the Bomb and its requirements for labour can itself become a cause of war.

In his essay in this volume, Edward Thompson has put forward the notion of exterminism, the idea of the bomb as the object of a new social order which has shaped and structured the societies out of which it grew, thrusting them inexorably towards extermination. Raymond Williams has criticized the notion on the grounds of technological determinism. He points out that nuclear weapons were 'consciously sought and developed . . . for known and foreseeable ends'. Their debate is part of a wider debate about the nature of the arms race. It is generally assumed that explanations which focus on the utility of armaments—balance of power theories or accounts of imperialism—are incompatible with explanations which focus on the manufacture of armaments—military-industrial-complex theories or arms economy theories, which argue that the capitalist economy needs armaments. But the idea of the dual nature of armaments, as objects of consumption *and* objects of production, suggests a way in which the debate might be reconciled. We could indeed build upon the contradictions between the different explanations to find a new analysis of the present crisis.

Armaments are the means of warfare. As objects of consumption, they are the instruments of a particular form of coercion. If, in the abstract, we can define a given class-based social formation in terms of its property relations, i.e. the appropriation of factors of production or labour time (dead and living) and forms of coercion through which this appropriation is carried out, then warfare can be seen as one form of coercion—one element in the reproduction of property relations. This is, in a sense, the orthodox interpretation of warfare—the emphasis on armaments to further the projects of the ruling class.

In this essay, however, I want to argue that the historical development of particular forms of coercion can only be understood through an analysis of how these forms are themselves produced and reproduced on the basis of a given set of property relations, i.e. how labour time is extracted in order to carry out particular forms of coercion. Without such an analysis, the notion of warfare as coercion degenerates into functionalism; it presupposes a ruling class, peculiarly free of the social relations within which it is defined, able to act subjectively in its own interests in a way that would be impossible in the sphere of production. Indeed, it might also imply that crises could be resolved through resort to warfare. The aim of the essay is not to offer the analysis. Rather the aim is to set out a new approach and raise the questions that need to be answered.

In order to develop the argument, I want to put forward the concept of a mode of warfare. Before doing so, a brief preliminary discussion of the place of warfare in the forms of coercion that characterize modern capitalism is required.

Warfare as Coercion

Warfare is socially organized physical coercion against a similarly socially organized opponent. In this, it can be distinguished from violent crime— individual acts of physical coercion—or repressive activity—socially organized physical coercion against individuals.

Under capitalism, warfare has become an aspect of state activity. This is true even of civil wars where the insurgent forces are generally organized as a form of proto-state power. Any attempt to analyse the role of warfare has to deal with the role of the state. In earlier modes of production, warfare played a direct role in the reproduction of property relations. Under feudalism, warfare was primarily aimed at the acquisition of land. In antiquity, it was through warfare that slaves (and land) were acquired. Under capitalism, the acquisition of control of factors of production and the appropriation of surplus value is carried on through purely economic means, through the exchange of equal values. For the first time, warfare plays an *indirect* role in the reproduction of property relations, through creating the conditions in which the exchange of equal values can take place. This separation of warfare from the mode of production is part of a general separation or specialization of state activity which occurs under capitalism. I do not want, here, to enter the great debate about the nature of the state. Rather I take, as a starting point, the notion of the state not as an institution, a centralized politico–legal apparatus, but as a form of social relations. In particular, the state comprises those non-economic forms of coercion which have, as it were, been removed from the process of production, and yet are required for the functioning of capitalism. According to Picciotto and Holloway: 'The form which exploitation takes under capitalism does not depend on the direct use of force but primarily on the dull compulsion of uncomprehended laws of reproduction. Indeed, the form of the appropriation of the surplus product in capitalism requires that relations of force should be abstracted from the immediate process of production and located in an instance standing apart from the direct producers. Thus, both logically and historically, the establishment of the capitalist process of production is accompanied by the abstraction of relations of force from the immediate process of production, thus constituting discrete "political" and "economic" spheres.'[2]

The notion of militarism is itself capitalist. It emerges with the distinction between warriors and entrepreneurs in place of the feudal lord. Many liberal writers—Victor Hugo, Herbert Spencer, Schumpeter—conceived of warfare as something antithetical to capitalism, a remnant of pre-capitalist societies or as a some inexplicable exogeneous phenomenon. Even today, prevailing ideology would hold that Western armaments are a response to external events, to the non-capitalist militarism of the Soviet Union, or the pre-capitalist behaviour of the Arabs.

In one sense, of course, warfare *is* antithetical to capitalism, in that it stands apart from the process of production, in that it constitutes a potential interruption to the commodity production essential for the exchange of equal values—the possibility of interfering with the free flow of resources—labour, goods, money. Yet warfare, like other forms of non-economic coercion, is needed to prevent such interruptions. These interruptions are not so much historical remnants or random occurrences, in my view they are an inevitable consequence of the working out of capitalism.

It is certainly true that, historically and even today in some parts of the Third World, warfare or state activity generally was required to 'free' the labourer from paternalistic, pre-capitalist relations of dependency so that he could sell his labour in the market place, to eliminate monopolies and tariffs of various kinds which protected pre-capitalist enclaves and prevented the free movement of commodities, and to establish the political primacy of the middle classes (the Third World 'modernizers'). But more important is the response to the fundamental *uneveness* of capitalism. At the heart of the capital relation is the exploitation and subordination of the worker. And the spread of capital, the accumulation of surplus-value, is necessarily a dynamic Darwinian process, absorbing and simultaneously expelling workers, and bringing about the rise and fall of companies, technologies, industries, regions, and nations. It would be surprising if the victims of this process did not respond, if they did not organize their own form of interference to the process.

State activity provides a social and political framework for uneven development. Legal, ideological and other forms of coercion—or even consent—are required to repress or mollify victims of the process. And this framework may gradually materialize in social institutions—research and education, for instance—and industrial structures. One might, for example, link the historical development of the British State with a techno-material infrastructure that traces its origin to the primacy of heavy engineering and shipbuilding, the craft-based labour relations as well as the physical reliance on coal, railways, etc. in the mid-nineteenth century.

Warfare is the State's last resort. It could be said to arise from precisely the separateness of state activity and capitalist development—the fact that each evolves at its own pace. At certain times, the framework of State activity, including the technico—material infrastructure, may not facilitate accumulation and may indeed become a fetter on the further development of capitalism. State activities, the various forms of coercion, are resisted and consequently shift through what one might describe as a continuum of forms of coercion, from political legitimacy (consent) through ideology and law up to the more extreme physical activities of repression and war. A particular problem arises from the territorial basis of the state activity and the global scope of accumulation. Votes are canvassed, soldiers are recruited, taxes are collected from within the geographical boundaries of the nation. Warfare and other forms of state activity are reproduced within the territorial confines of the state. Capitalism knows no such limitations. The capitalist state is caught between the global requirements of capital and the need for its own reproduction. Hence, the continual pressure for a world organization, which could be peaceful—e.g. the EEC or the UN—or violent, e.g. imperialism or inter-imperialist wars. World government, as has often been pointed out, is the utopia of the modern multinational corporation.

As Meszaros has put it: 'The effective establishment of capitalism as an economically interlocking world system greatly contributes to the erosion and disintegration of the traditional historically formed and locally varying, partial structures of social and political stratification and control, without being able to produce a unified system of control on a world-wide scale. . . . The "crisis of hegemony, or crisis of the state in all spheres" (Gramsci) has become a truly international phenomenon.'[3] War can be seen as a last-ditch attempt to reorder these 'historically formed and locally varying, partial structures' both domestically and on an inter-

266

national scale. It can be seen as an international form of class struggle whose outcome is determined by the ways in which particular classes are organized for war. It can be a kind of forced development of particular social formations through a dynamic and destructive interchange. But it is an interchange that can only be understood in the context of an analysis of the mode of warfare, whether one is discussing a war between different social formations, as in civil wars or, to some extent, in the Napoleonic wars, or inter-imperialist wars like the two world wars. In other words, the way in which war can resolve, albeit temporarily, the contradictions of state and capital depends to a large extent on how particular states adapt themselves for war. This is considered further below.

In my view (and it would take another essay to expound this properly), the present crisis stems from the erosion, both internally and internationally, of the state system that emerged from the Second World War. It was a system in which the American state became the guarantor of global accumulation—through dollars, grain, military alliances, etc.—in much the same way as Britain had done in the mid-nineteenth century. As the geographical pole of capitalist accumulation shifted from America to Europe and Japan, as political, scientific, or educational institutions materialized that were no longer appropriate to the new industries, labour processes and patterns of consumption, so the particular set of class alliances and political forces that made this possible has broken down. The American state has increasingly, albeit falteringly and contradictorily, began to act on behalf of decaying American capitalism instead of on behalf of global accumulation. It has begun, as it were, to *interrupt* the 'natural' tendencies of capitalism rather to facilitate them.*

Continued preparations for war can be viewed as a kind of restatement of the resolution of the last war. It is, I would argue, designed to impress European and Third World states as much as the Soviet Union. In the post-war period, there has developed a disjunction between inter-imperialist, i.e. economic, competition (between the US, Europe and Japan) and military competition (between the US and the Soviet Union). As domestic US capital and labour suffer the effects of imperialist competition, undermining both the fiscal basis and legitimacy of the American state, the enemy seems somehow to get displaced and blame is

*One can see this in various international events, like the rise in food prices (from the dismantling of grain reserves to the end of the food aid), the rise in oil prices (which the US allowed to happen), the devaluation of the dollar, the deliberate increase in interest rates, and, subsequently, the attempt to assert military control both in the Third World and within NATO, as well as in a certain domestic bias towards certain industries and certain segments of society.

accorded to the Soviet Union. Deterrence can be viewed as a kind of imaginary replay of World War II, in which the Soviet Union plays the role of Nazi Germany and the United States 'saves' Europe. It is a way of reiterating the fact that European lives are dependent on American goodwill. In much the same way British warship-building of the late nineteenth century was sustained by the memory of Trafalgar. This was not simply the most appropriate form of propagating an ideology of military power. It has to do as we shall see with the nature of the mode of warfare. Because of the static nature of military institutions in peacetime, perceptions of military power and the environment which nurtures them tend to be shaped by some dominant military experience. For obvious reasons, the lessons of actual military engagements—for instance, the role of machine guns in the Boer War—were better understood by those who were concerned to challenge British power. As we shall see, the two World Wars created a new military experience on which to base the criteria for military power. The modern aircraft, tank, and submarine, even the intercontinental missile (a version of wartime strategic bombers) are symbols of the fact that the United States could engage in and perhaps win an even more terrible war in the future. But because these have not been used, no-one knows whether this is really true.

As consent breaks down and other forms of coercion—economic, political or legal—falter, so the replay of World War II is given more and more emphasis. In previous epochs such displays of military memory could have been put to the test. This is now the central problem of our time. Is there any way in which outmoded state structures—structures which fetter the development *both* of capitalist accumulation and of alternative visions for society—can be defeated short of war?

To quote Meszaros again: 'The blind "natural law" of the market mechanism carries with it that the grave social problems necessarily associated with capital production and concentration are never *solved*, only *postponed* and indeed—since postponement cannot work indefinitely— transferred to the *military* plane . . . The capitalist system of our times, however, has been decapitated through the removal of its ultimate sanc- tion—an all-out war on its real and potential adversaries . . . For the first time in history capitalism is globally confronted with its own problems which cannot be "postponed" much longer, nor indeed can they be trans- ferred to the military plane in order to be "exported" in the form of an all- out war.'[4] In effect, capitalism's problems are 'exported' in the form of a simulation of war-deterrence. The new emphasis on nuclear war-fighting can be seen as a desperate attempt to make that simulation more con- vincing. What happens next? Is deterrence to be squeezed into a suicidal attempt to prove itself? Or can we dismantle the war simulation machine from within?

The Mode of Warfare—The Military-Industrial Complex

Warfare can *never* reproduce itself. Armaments are means of destruction, they can *never* re-enter the production process as means of production or consumption. In any society warfare is parasitical, dependent upon the productive possibilities of society as a whole. The most that warfare can do is to create the conditions for its own reproduction. Under feudalism and antiquity, this was achieved, as we have seen, directly through the acquisition of land or slaves. Under capitalism, warfare has only an indirect role to play. The possibility that warfare might *not* increase the productiveness of capitalism, that it might grow unchecked, introduces the possibility of warfare as a cancerous growth within capitalism.

To put it another way, so long as warfare is 'progressive', that is to say, exercised on behalf of global accumulation, then it can create the conditions for its own reproduction. Militarism may extend the province of accumulation, as Rosa Luxemburg suggested, by colonial expansion, by eliminating pre-capitalist modes of production and drawing peasants into the money economy. Militarism, as we have seen, may prevent nationalist barriers to the free flow of resources, provide 'stability' for investment, etc. But if warfare is used for regressive ends, as an interruption to global accumulation for the purposes of competitive nationalism, or to defend an outmoded political system, the problem of reproducing warfare arises.

In the rare instances where Marxists have written about the mode of warfare, they have tended to assume that modes of warfare 'reflect' modes of production. Bukharin says, vis-à-vis the army: 'Here we want to mention incidentally that the entire social structure is characterized by a peculiar monism of its architecture: all of its parts have one and the same "style". Just as in production relationships men are arranged according to a specific hierarchical scale, corresponding to class groupings, so in the state apparatus itself and in the army particularly this social hierarchy is reflected.'[5] The same kind of assumption is apparent in Engel's very illuminating text on the subject, where he talks about skirmishing as a reflection of the American revolution and the late nineteenth century battleship as a 'floating factory'.[6]

The point is not that modes of warfare 'reflect' modes of production but rather that warfare can only be produced on the basis of a given mode of production. This fact may account for the 'monism' of style but it is important to make the distinction. The mode of warfare can *never* exactly reflect the mode of production because of its essentially parasitical nature, and because war as a form of commensuration differs from all other forms of commensuration. (Of course, war can be viewed as a form of commensuration for society as a whole. Precisely because of its parasitical nature, it represents a kind of test for the society which produces it; this was especially important for pre-capitalist modes of production.)

In this one could draw a parallel with analyses of the family. The bourgeois family is typically a product of capitalism. Yet the ties of bondage which characterize the mode of housework in no way reflect the relation between worker and entrepreneur that we are accustomed to think of as typical of capitalism. Likewise, the bastard societies that are to be found in large parts of the underdeveloped world in which pre-capitalist modes of production have been dragooned into production for the world market are also essential components of the global social formation we call capitalism.

The distinction between the mode of production and the mode of warfare is important for two reasons. First, it means that warfare can never be a more or less 'neutral' instrument of the ruling class, neither more or less 'advanced' than the society it serves. Neither the loyalty of those who participate in the warfare sector nor the victory of 'progressive' causes can be counted upon. Armaments are only 'consciously sought' to the extent that they are consonant with established military structures. Or to put it in the language of orthodox strategic analysts the 'rational actor' model only applied in so far as it is recognized that his views of what is 'rational' are shaped and/or constrained by his own situation within the decision-making apparatus. Why deterrence, for instance, and why the extraordinarily lavish elaborations of deterrence rather than, say, the newest conventional forms of defence, based on the revolution in electronics?

Secondly, many socialists have tended to assume that a guerrilla army or a citizen's militia could represent a socialist mode of warfare; somehow, these organizations look a bit like a socialist society might look. It may be, however, that a guerrilla army is simply insurgent, rather than socialist, an appropriate way of countering established armies, whatever the nature of the insurgency from which it has emerged. It may be that a socialist mode of warfare is a contradiction in terms: that the consequence of any social interchange at the point of warfare is to pollute the course of revolution. These questions can only be resolved—and they have to be resolved if we are to develop a coherent 'defence' strategy for the left—through a separate analysis of modes of production and modes of warfare. This is an issue to which we shall return.

What are the characteristics of the mode of warfare in the present epoch? We could borrow the terminology used to analyse modes of production and look separately at the means of warfare and the relations of warfare. The means of warfare are the weapons and the way they are used. The relations of warfare are the organization of men, the nature of the military hierarchy, the way men are drawn into the armed forces. The means of warfare are at once the product of a particular level of technology in society and the appropriate tool for a particular set of military relations. The relations of warfare are those most convenient for organizing a body of men in a given society and most liable to generate loyalty, to gain assent for the role of warfare and the unenviable risk of fighting wars.

A characteristic of the modern army, in which it shares the style of capitalist production, is the apparent dominance of the means of warfare. Modern armies are very capital-intensive. The procurement of hardware accounts for about half the modern military budget and the ratio of direct combat personnel (pilots, gunners, tank crews, etc.) to support personnel (electricians, repair men, administrators, cooks, etc.) has declined dramatically over the last hundred years. This growing capital-intensity is not simply numerical; it has a social significance as well. Elsewhere, I have described the concept of the weapon system. The weapon system, in hardware terms, combines the weapon platform—tank, ship or aircraft, the weapon—gun, missile, or torpedo, and the means of command and communication. As a concept, thought up by the US Air Force, it serves to unify the cast of people—scientists, designers, workers, bureaucrats, technicians, soldiers, sailors or airmen—involved in its design, development, production and acquisition. Continuing the analogy with the commodity, there is a kind of weapon system fetishism in which the weapon system as a piece of separate independent hardware, a thing, appears to dictate its own patterns of consumption and production and to weld together the military and industrial components of the mode of warfare. It could be that our own awe of the Bomb makes us victim of this fetishism, unable to identify a meaning in the social system that produces it and therefore apparently helpless in the headlong momentum of modern militarism.

The Means of Warfare

Western armaments are largely designed, developed and produced by capitalist enterprise. Even where arms companies are nationalized, they operate as sovereign entities, on the principle of independent viability.

They can retain their viability only through constant striving for new customers. Like other capitalist enterprises, they compete against each other to maintain or increase their share of the market. This entails a constant struggle for technical 'improvement', as defined by the customer.

Interestingly, this type of arms producer is relatively recent. Private manufacturers entered the arms business in Britain and Western Europe in the late nineteenth century and, in the United States, around 1940. Prior to this, arms were produced in State arsenals—the Royal Dockyards or the Royal Ordnance Factories for instance—which often dated back several hundred years. The existence of these arsenals was and is guaranteed by the state. Even today, provision for financing excess capacity of the Royal Ordnance Factories is a regular item in the defence budget. To some extent, state arsenals, where they co-exist with capitalist enterprise, have been drawn into the competition for orders. Nevertheless, the lack of interest in innovation, the technological conservatism of state arsenals has been widely documented. To some extent, as we shall see below, these state arsenals are very similar to both military and civil industrial enterprises in the Soviet Union.

The arms companies in Britain, France, Sweden or the United States are specialist companies dependent on military orders for their survival. This is, by and large, not true of arms manufacturers in West Germany and Japan; in these countries, arms are generally a small proportion of the output of the arms manufacturers and, therefore, competitive efforts may be directed elsewhere.

The arms manufacturers are capitalist in the sense that they are dependent for survival on profit, that is to say, on the difference between the price of what they sell and the cost of production. But it should be stressed that this is a paper profit. It does not reflect the relative efficiency or inefficiency of the individual enterprise. Because there is no orthodox market for them, armaments do not have a value; that is to say, there is no way in which society can judge what is socially useful labour. Clearly more labour goes into the production of arms than the wage-equivalent paid to those who perform the labour; but this is not reflected in the profit, since the price of armaments is an arbitrary political decision. Even in the international market, except possibly the small arms trade, the price is largely determined by a process of *political* bargaining between government. When people talk about the profitability of armaments production, about the comparative advantage of military sectors they are commenting on nothing more than a set of political priorities—a decision by the state or a foreign government to offer a 'reasonable mark-up'.

In this, there is a strong parallel with the Soviet Union where prices are the outcome of bureaucratic bargaining and hence do not represent a value. But, as we shall see below, there is also a difference with the Soviet Union in that Soviet armament enterprises are not dependent on profit (even politically determined profit); thus they do not exhibit the same degree of competitiveness and do not constitute an autonomous dynamic within the armament sector. The absence of value stems from the fact of the state as a purchaser. But the absence of commensuration—a process otherwise necessary in all class societies where producers are alienated from the products of their work—stems from the distance from consumption. In the case of other state-purchased products, it stems from the separation of state and society—a relevant consideration for the Soviet Union. This method of 'cost accounting' represents a distortion within the capitalist system as a whole, with as we shall see, serious implications for the current crisis.

Finally, we should draw a clear distinction between the fact that armaments do not have a value and the fact that they are paid for out of surplus. Because armaments do not re-enter the production process, the entire cost of armaments—cost of production plus mark-up—represents a *deduction* from surplus-value earned elsewhere in the economy. This is irrespective of whether military spending contributes indirectly to the growth of surplus value, as we shall discuss below. But this is a separate point. Luxury consumption goods may have a value but they too are a deduction from surplus value, a tax on potential accumulation.

The arms manufacturers are divided into prime contractors and subcontractors. The prime contractors are, by and large, the manufacturers of weapon platforms—ships, aircraft, tanks. The manufacturers of engines, weapons, and command and communication equipment (electronics companies) act as subcontractors. (In West Germany and Japan, electronics companies are prime contractors.) Because of the way in which price is determined, technological 'improvement' takes the form of product improvement, i.e. attempts to increase the utility of the product as defined by the customer, rather than attempts to cheapen the product.

The state determines the utility of armaments. In the absence of war, this determination is based on a collusion between the producers, the arms companies, the armed forces and the bureaucrats. It depends on a set of state structures, which, in part, are historically given and, in part, are shaped by their own internal logic. War preparations, the simulation of war, as we have seen, depends to a large extent on the memory of past wars: the institutions of warfare, the social relations within them (described below), were born out of the actual experience of past wars. The consequence is a deep-rooted conservatism, an idea of military utility that is dictated by the simulation of warfare (based on the memory of past wars) and the relations of warfare (based on the experience of past wars)—consequently an idea which is almost impervious to actual military contingencies, as the war in Vietnam showed.

So the imperative of the armourers, the drive for technological 'improvement', is confined within the routines and traditions of the armed forces and the bureaucrats. The criteria of technical 'improvement' that seemed important in World War II continue to be emphasized—speed, range, payload or protection. As the routines and traditions get more rigid and institutionalized, these improvements get harder and harder to make. The result is huge increases in complexity and sophistication, in the labour required to make armaments, for diminishing utility, even as utility is defined by the state. The mind boggles at the billions of dollars poured into the Tridents, the MXs, the nuclear powered aircraft carriers. The absolute level of destructiveness is, of course, increased; yet military utility, not as defined by the state, but as defined by the role of warfare in particular situations, although evidently unmeasurable, may actually be declining. Many of the criteria which are emphasized—speed, for instance—may become irrelevant as vulnerability of all types of weapons systems increase. Complexity, sophistication and cost may prove military handicaps—modern weapon systems go wrong; they require spare parts that are never available; they require expensive training, practice, and ammunition which can never be afforded; and they are prime targets.

This then is the basis of the permanent arms race: competitive pressure from the armourers for technological 'improvement' which involves ever greater resources for ever diminishing utility.

It should be stressed, at this point, that to say that the utility of armaments is tested in war is not at all the same thing as to say that utility is measurable. One of the achievements of capitalism was the attribution of numbers to commodities, numbers which measured not utility but socially necessary labour time. Previous societies had forms of commensuration by which the social utility of labour could be assessed, although not with numerical precision. War, likewise, provides a test of whether the labour going into the manufacture of weapons has a utility in terms of victory or defeat. The permanent arms race has no mechanism for determining the match between resources and utility, only a subjective collusion between armourers and militarists.

This general interpretation of the permanent arms race clearly distinguishes it from Clausewitz's notion of Absolute War which provides a theoretical underpinning for action–reaction interpretations of the arms race. For Clausewitz, war always tends to the extreme. It is 'an act of violence pushed to its utmost bounds, as one side dictates the law to the other, there arises a sort of reciprocal action, which logically must lead to an extreme'.[7] Real war departs from ideal Absolute War on account of friction—time, logistics, mistakes, etc.—and political constraints. Some have seen the permanent arms race as a continuation of the tendency towards Absolute War in peacetime, i.e. a competitive struggle between nations, a continuation which has reached the point of nearly eliminating friction so that actual war could approximate Absolute War. In fact, however, this notion is misleading. It is certainly true that the creative forces released by the emergence of capitalism have over a long historical period dramatically increased destructiveness and brought the ideal concept of Absolute War closer to reality; eliminating technical if not political 'friction'. But the permanent arms race, at least on the Western side, is a different phenomenon because it can be explained entirely without reference to an opponent. The notion of Absolute War is only relevant insofar as the experience of World War II institutionalized the idea of perpetual technical change within the structure of the American state.

In theory the tendency for expansion of the means of warfare is unlimited. In the absence of war, of any objective test of the utility of armaments, the only constraint is that imposed by the relations of warfare.

Relations of Warfare

Mass armies emerged with capitalism. Whether or not this was the consequence of the 'free' status of the exploited classes under capitalism or merely the long-term historical tendency towards Absolute War, it was only within the last two hundred years that widespread involvement in wars, both as victims and participants, became the norm.

The relations of warfare can be viewed from two aspects; the general problem of how the working class as a whole is persuaded or coerced to part with labour for the purpose of fighting or producing armaments and the particular problem of how the individual within the armed forces is persuaded and persuaded again to kill or risk getting killed. This distinction corresponds to the distinction between the concept of exploitation and the concept of subordination, which is often used in discussions of the relations of production.[8] Exploitation is the general problem of coercion, of persuading workers to produce more than they receive for their own reproduction; under capitalism, this is an economic form of coercion—the wage relation. Subordination is the particular problem of maintaining control in the factory; it is the specific form of an abstract relation just as use-values are a specific form of the general abstract notion of value.

One might expect that, under capitalism, the relations of warfare, in general, would be based on economic coercion. The state would buy soldiers and munitions workers out of surplus-value. To some extent, this is what happened in countries like Britain and the United States, where there are volunteer armies. But there are definite limits to this form of coercion. In wartime, because of the tendency to Absolute War, the surplus-value available to society is never sufficiently large. The state therefore resorts to forms of non-economic coercion, physical and ideological coercion—conscription and the appeal to ideas like patriotism and loyalty.

In a society which has developed beyond non-economic forms of coercion, where the exploited classes enjoy a measure of political and physical freedom, such forms of coercion are not always possible, particularly when the working class is coerced to fight bloody capitalist wars or when the purpose of such wars is clearly regressive. Before World War I, few socialist writers believed that capitalism could survive a war.[9] In fact, the two world wars were fought through an important element of consent. That is to say, the participation of the working class in the wars was obtained through major concessions—redistribution of income, trade union power and, particularly in Britain, the role of shop stewards, the welfare state. Indeed World War II, at least in Europe, was fought by an alliance of progressive capital and the working class against fascism. This element of consent is so important that it is often treated as one of the ways in which anticipations of socialism may emerge in capitalist society. Alternatively one might say that it is one of the major ways of rebuilding political alliances and state structures so as to overcome capitalist crisis. It was the failure of the American state to obtain consent for the Vietnam war that led to its defeat.

In peacetime, the extent to which the state can afford to 'buy' soldiers and munition workers depends on the extent to which militarism can create the conditions for its own reproduction through facilitating accumulation. Ross Luxemburg argued that militarism increased the rate of exploitation, thus, in a sense, 'paying for itself', because taxation was levied on the working class.[10] In effect, military spending, in her view, was financed by depressing the real wage. Militarism may have had some limited effect of this sort as a consequence of ideological coercion, the appeal to patriotic sacrifice. But there are clear limits, imposed by the resistance of the working class, to any significant lowering of the real wage. The constancy in the share of private and public consumption testifies to this fact.[11]

Robert Rowthorn, in his interpretation of Rosa Luxemburg, suggests that militarism may increase the rate of exploitation through increasing productiveness. He says that 'militarism could cause beneficial changes within the capitalist sector itself. It creates a secure and growing market for arms producers and their suppliers, and the presence of such a secure and dynamic group of industries acts as both a stabilizer and an engine of growth for the capitalist sector as a whole.'[12]

The argument that military spending stimulates demand, thus avoiding capitalist crisis, and promotes innovation was the subject of much writing on the arms economy during the 1950s and 1960s.[13] This writing was based on the experience of World War II and the immediate post-war period and owed its intellectual origins to Marxist theories of underconsumption and to Keynes. The 1930s depression was viewed as a crisis of underconsumption that was resolved by a massive injection of 'waste' spending—a resolution that could equally well have been achieved by digging holes or building churches. It might be more pertinent, in the light of current experience, to treat the underconsumption of the 1930s as a manifestation of a more fundamental contradiction between the needs of global accumulation, at that time materialized in new patterns of consumption, Fordist production methods, associated with the automobile, electricity and chemical industries in the United States, and the European state system, largely established in the nineteenth century and only partially undermined by World War I, and associated with older and less 'progressive' forms of accumulation. In other words, it could be described as a disproportionality between different branches of industry brought about by the failure of the social and political framework of capitalism to develop at the same pace as capital.

World War II brought about a decisive shift in the international state system, in domestic class alliances, as well as massive physical destruction of existing European industry. In particular, the mode of warfare underwent an incredible transformation (which was begun at the end of World War I) from a system which combined the products of late nineteenth century industry—heavy engineering and shipbuilding—with the military relations of an even earlier era,[14] to a system which built upon and speeded up the techniques of mass production, the technology of the internal combustion engine, and the growing application of science to industry, that were emerging in the immediate pre-war period. Thus the outcome of World War II was the release of accumulation from the limits imposed by an earlier era, so that any increase in demand merely served to absorb the excess capacity which developed in the 1920s and 1930s. World War II also involved a process of military innovation that subsequently helped to boost technology in the civilian sphere.

Today, it can be argued, as we have done above, that the very same state system that was so progressive at the end of World War II has now, itself, become a fetter on global accumulation which is developing in new branches of production, electronics, and new areas of the world. No amount of 'reflation' whether through military spending or other forms of spending could do more than alleviate the conditions of the present crisis. The very rigidity of the mode of warfare and its development along linear lines has become a distortion within the capitalist system. As military technology becomes conservative, complex and costly, it becomes more and more removed from civil technology—if anything, a degenerate influence on the latter. The continued survival and growth of declining industries, like automobiles and aircraft, and indeed the subordination of newer industries like electronics in the military sector, represents an interruption to the process of rapid change that is necessary for continued accumulation. The practice of cost-accounting, of awarding fictional profits to the military industries, artificially reverses the priorities of capital by shifting resources from productive to non-productive branches of industry instead of the other way round. In other words, it entrenches and does not overcome the disproportionality between different branches of production that lies at the heart of the present crisis.

Another way of putting it might be in terms of declining rates of profit in particular branches of industry. Although a proper discussion of this subject is outside the scope of this article, one could argue that at a certain stage in the development of particular industries or families of industries, social relations get embodied in particular techno-material infrastructures and this in turn limits the creativeness of human beings, confining workers within established hierarchies inside physical structures of brick and steel inherited from the past. It is this social domination of dead over living labour, rather than a numerical domination of dead over living labour expressed in a rising value composition of capital, that explains the tendency for what orthodox economists describe as 'decreasing returns'—a decline in the rate of growth of productivity. In an era of increasing returns, such as occurred during and after World War II, when new industries and technologies are established, military spending can indeed help to speed up accumulation. But in the current situation, military spending merely reinforces the domination of dead labour, caught as it is in its own inheritance from the past, and at the same time artificially increases the rate of profit in those same industries which might otherwise be shown to be decreasingly productive.

If the simulation of war cannot 'pay for itself', if indeed the very process of accumulation is slowed down, then the state subjected to the expansionist pressure of the permanent arms race must seek new ways of co-opting labour—conscription, bigger military budgets, etc. It is precisely the difficulty of carrying out such measures, despite the manufacture of anti-Soviet hysteria, that has led to a series of crises within the military sector. Nott's recent defence review in Britain is an example—we can expect similar reviews in the United States in the future. This is discussed further below.

The same kind of contradiction is apparent at the level of individual subordination within the armed forces. During the 1950s and 1960s, it was fashionable for bourgeois military sociologists to argue that, in modern managerial society, traditional techniques of military command—discipline, ideological coercion, etc.—were outdated.[15] The weapon system was thought to impose its own form of command, through a rigid technical division of labour. The soldier appears to be the instrument of the weapon system, a component part of team which services and operates the system. The fighter pilot, who is often viewed as the modern hero of individual combat, is, in reality, part of a team which averages 70 people. Furthermore, the weapon systems are themselves ranked and subdivided: from the aircraft carrier, with aircraft to operate from its deck, to destroyers, submarines and frigates to defend it, and finally supply ships to replenish it. The bomber and the battle tank have a similar function for the airforce army. Linked to all these are communications and logistics.

The military sociologists of the 1950s argued that the individual was committed to the technical success of the team undertaking and this was what 'motivated' him. By and large, the rank of the individual is defined by his technical specialization. However, technical pride turned out to be sadly inadequate as a motivation in Vietnam, particularly when the utility and role of the weapon system was so questionable. Indeed the fact that the technical requirements of modern weapon systems had led to a swelling in middle-ranking technical officers, who were based at comfortable rear camps and who did not risk death, contributed to breakdowns in military command in Vietnam—'fragging' (killing officers with hand grenades), massive combat refusals, desertion, drug and alcohol addiction. Today, bourgeois military sociologists are arguing for a return to the 'gladiatorial' concept of soldiery.[16] Yet their predecessors were correct in pointing out that capitalism had gone beyond such concepts.

Now, there is a new pressure for military unions and even, in some countries like Holland, for the democratization of the armed forces, with election of officers, for instance. Yet is this compatible with a capitalist role for warfare, or indeed warfare at all? What are the projects that such armies would be willing to carry out?

Before we consider these questions, a detour might be useful to see whether any of the argument about the mode of warfare in capitalism is applicable to the Soviet Union.

The Soviet Union

So far I have entirely ignored the question of the Soviet Union. Certainly, it is possible to explain the permanent arms race without reference to an opponent, in terms of the domestic characteristics of the Western mode of warfare. Yet the Soviet Union is a very suitable opponent. An opponent which responds and builds upon every new level in the arms race provides the ideal justification for the armourers, the generals and the bureaucrats. Given the increasingly 'irrational' nature of American armament—that is the growing commitment of resources for rapidly diminishing utility—how do we explain the 'irrational' Soviet response—if indeed it is a response and not a separate autonomous drive? Certainly, as Roy and Zhores Medvedev point out in these pages, the United States led the way in every new military technology—nuclear weapons, MIRVs, guided cruise missiles, etc. But why has the Soviet Union felt it necessary to follow the American example? Why, in an era of overkill, does the USSR need to match the number of nuclear weapons on the other side? Why, when complex sophisticated weapon systems are so vulnerable and unreliable, do Soviet designers push their own technical 'improvements' in the same direction—albeit at a much slower rate? Khrushchev asked these questions and this was one of the reasons for his downfall.

The analysis so far suggests a new way in which we might begin to understand the Soviet system. It was a system which emerged in opposition to capitalism and from its inception was involved in warfare to defend itself against the latter—first, to fend off the Entente interventions of 1918–1920, and then through the five-year plans directed towards preparing a military capability against the expected attack by Nazi Germany, which duly occurred in World War II. A number of commentators have described the Soviet system as a 'war economy' in the sense that it resembles the organization of capitalist economies during war-time, with tight centralized control directed in the first instance towards the achievement of war aims.[17] Could we not describe the USSR then as not so much a socialist system, but a system that embodies the antithesis to capitalism represented by warfare?

In a capitalist system, needs and resources are matched in the marketplace. Decisions about the allocation of labour, goods and investment are taken by individual entrepreneurs for the purposes of private profit. Rudimentary democracy in the West means that there is some form of slow, rather inefficient commensuration for non-military state activity. Through political parties, elections, criticisms in the media, dissatisfaction with the health service, education, gas or electricity can filter through to the state machinery. In a truly democratically planned society, needs and resources would be determined directly through organized contacts between consumers and producers. In the Soviet Union, decisions about the allocation of resources are taken centrally by the state on the basis of a set of official priorities. In a system where dissatisfaction can scarcely be voiced, these priorities are very resistant to external demands. Rather, they are in turn shaped by the structures of the state which were largely created out of the experience of war. All commentators on Soviet affairs have noted the priority accorded to the warfare sector—not only in terms of resources, but in special privileges for its workers, in the ability to commandeer scarce materials, to cut through red tape, and so on. [18] It was the need to raise the level of productiveness in order to fight the Germans that was the overriding objective of the first five year plans. The imperatives of intense military competition in both the 1930s and 1940s provided an extraordinary impetus for industrialization—something which has only been matched by capitalist societies in wartime.

It would be wrong to confuse the priority of war preparations with a tendency to wage war, to confuse militarism with imperialist expansion. The Soviet system was developed in *opposition* to capitalism and that is its raison d'être. The role of warfare is *defensive*, against capitalism. In the West, warfare has a role which is defined by the purpose of capitalism. Where warfare has been deployed in the East, in Hungary, Czechoslavakia or Afghanistan, the aim has been to secure buffer states.

Nor does the mode of warfare contain inherent dynamic properties, precisely because it lacks the creative tension with a capitalist mode of production that is characteristic of Western society. Indeed, there is no clear distinction between the mode of warfare and the mode of production because both are aspects of the same state activity. Although there is an ostensible wage relation, there is no free market for labour, and relations of production are based on a form of conscription and ideological coercion—appeals to patriotism, Soviet-style socialism, etc. The element of consent is probably much less important than in the Western warfare sector because Soviet workers have never experienced prolonged periods of 'freedom' from non-economic forms of coercion. In the West, during war time, the capitalist dynamism of enterprise is by and large subordinated to the aims of war. This is always true in the Soviet Union. Unlike in the West where means of warfare are produced by capitalist enterprise and represent the immediate link between the mode of warfare and the mode of production, both means of warfare and civil production in the Soviet Union are produced in state enterprises, with guaranteed employment, much like the state arsenals of the West. Hence, the dominant tendency in the internal organization of the Soviet system is conservatism. Left to its own devices, one might expect the Soviet system to produce the same mix of armaments and other products in the same quantities, year after year. Those who received the dominant share of resources last year are the most powerful in determining plan allocations this year and therefore receive the dominant share of the resources next year. War preparations represent an important priority because they have always been important in the past. Put simply, there is in such a system neither a dynamic tendency for military expansion nor yet an autonomous interest in reducing allocations to armaments—in favour of consumption, say. Roy and Zhores Medvedev emphasize the combination of subordination and conservatism that characterizes the military sector in the Soviet Union.

But the Soviet Union is not left to its own devices. War is one of the few forms of commensuration that exists outside of the State. The form of commensuration, the tendency to compare against an external enemy, is then internalized and continued in peace-time. The desperate wartime struggle which so dominated its whole development is transformed into the convenient rivalry of the permanent arms race. War is not the discontinuity it represents for capitalism. The military planners whose notions of military utility have always been assessed externally with reference to an opponent, shift from the life-and-death exigencies of war to the symbols of the arms race. The Soviet state is designed to react, albeit conservatively and heavily as befits its military organizations. Indeed the very fact that the military–industrial institutions in both the United States and the Soviet Union were shaped by the same experience, World War II, lends the concepts of military utility, which emerge from the permanent arms race, a peculiar plausibility.* It might be much more difficult to react to a different opponent, one armed with the products of progressive capital—say cheap and simple electronic devices.

In other words, the Soviet system as a whole exhibits the characteristics of the warfare sector in the West. This is not just because there is no clear separation between the mode of production and the mode of warfare. It is also because, historically, warfare as defence against capitalism has been one of the most important priorities of the system—a purpose of production, like profit in the West—and because war and the permanent arms race

---

*Interestingly, the differences between the Soviet and American concepts of military utility, as well as the similarities, can be traced back to the experience of World War II. For example, American nuclear weapons thinking was grafted onto the experience of strategic bombing. The Soviet Union never had a strategic bombing role in World War II; for Soviet military thinkers, nuclear weapons were an extension of artillery, something on which Stalin placed great emphasis.

represent one of the few mechanisms for commensuration which can impart dynamism to an otherwise conservative order.

But what are the consequences for the Soviet system as a whole? If the permanent arms race has indeed dragged the Western mode of warfare in the direction of degeneracy, away from military and economic realities, then surely it becomes much harder to mobilize production in general on the basis of the requirements of military technology. The idea that military technology is a forcing house for civil technology appears to be widely accepted by Soviet leaders. Techniques of systems management, for instance, developed for managing major weapons programmes in the United States, continue to be applied in the civil sector. If growing cost and diminishing utility are the characteristics of Western armaments, then these characteristics are increasingly shared by all types of products in the Soviet Union. If continued armament production maintains and extends declining industrial sectors in Western countries, then this is likely to be true of Soviet industry as a whole. This may well be the explanation for the low productivity growth the Soviet Union has experienced in recent years. Given the enormous share of production for which the warfare sector accounts (approximately 25% of manufacturing) the central problem for the Soviet state is: whether the mode of production can continue to reproduce the mode of warfare.

There may, of course, be certain solutions. One question that needs to be asked is about the consequences of importing Western civil technology. Can this raise productiveness? Could it be assimilated by Soviet institutions? Could it promote changes in the division of labour which might undermine current relations of production? Is detente consistent with the role of the military sector in the Soviet Union?

These are questions that need answers. For our purposes however, if we can sustain the idea of the Soviet Union as a system shaped by warfare which only exists in opposition to capitalism, then this could have great significance for a socialist anti-militarist strategy in the West. For it suggests that what we do and what we succeed in achieving could indeed have profound implications for the Soviet and East European peoples.

Against Warfare

Warfare is, then, located at the centre of capitalist crisis. Capitalism needs the state, needs non-economic forms of coercion, and, as long as states are divided by geography, needs warfare. Yet the state, in general, and warfare, in particular, represent an a priori burden on and a potential interruption to the process of capitalist accumulation. This tension between warfare and capitalism explodes periodically in war.

This is the situation we face today. The capitalist world has outgrown the American era. The breakdown of consent and the failure of non-violent forms of coercion to resolve the current international crisis have led to increasing reliance by the United States on the threat to employ the state's last resort—warfare. At the same time the American mode of warfare has developed in grotesque directions into a simulation of World War III, as an elaborate, extraordinary, expensive and destructive replay of World War II. It has diverted resources in such a way as to constrain and distort accumulation and so accentuates the underlying causes of the crisis. As the memory of World War II fades, and the knowledge of nuclear weapons increases, so the message that is supposed to be conveyed by deterrence (whether to Third World revolutionaries or to European statesmen inclined to challenge the level of US interest rates) is ignored.

War, the ultimate form of commensuration, has, in the past, provided a resolution to such situations, imposing a more 'rational' division of labour on the mode of warfare and defeating regressive uses of warfare. As accumulation slows, as tensions between the different poles of accumulation—US, Europe and Japan—grow, as the military dominance of the US is challenged, the pressure for such a resolution mounts. In the Soviet Union, the need to renew the creative wartime dynamic also constitutes a pressure for war. War is an act of desperation. In the early post-war years, it may have been possible to have the arms race without war, conveniently encapsulated in the ideology of deterrence. As ruling military—industrial interests are squeezed on either side, the need to 'test' the efficacy of armament increases even though the consequences of such a test are likely to be quite different from what the proponents envisage. For those whose lives and positions are vested in the warfare state, both West and East, war may be the only possible outcome.

Yet war is extermination. To prevent war must be the overriding aim not only of socialists but of all humanity. This analysis contains certain implications for an anti-war strategy.

First, our aim must be to secure the collapse of the mode of warfare. The contradictions I have described—between the utility of armaments and the resources required for their manufacture and between the relations and means of warfare—affect the warfare sector itself. This is apparent in both the arms industry and the armed forces.

As we have noted, it becomes harder and harder to pay for armaments as the growth of costs come up against budgetary limitations—hence Nott's defence review in Britain. As weapon systems are pared and cancelled, the impact of the defence industry is very uneven. Some companies are overworked, short of supplies, unable to meet performance targets and time schedules. Others face bankruptcy and massive redundancy. The insecurity of defence employment has led many defence trades unions in Europe and America to press for the conversion of arms industries to socially useful production.

As the utility of armaments declines and their destructiveness increases, as the technical division of labour swells the officer ranks, as pay and conditions are squeezed by the cost of armaments, disaffection grows within the armed forces. This is expressed in growing criticism of defence policy, in rapid turnover, high rates of AWOL, low rates of re-enlistment, in alcohol and drug addiction, in unwillingness to fight, pressure for unionization and greater democracy in military organization. [19]

These demands for the transformation of the arms industry and the democratization of the armed forces would need to be central components of an anti-war strategy—a way of mobilizing soldiers and defence workers and undermining the mode of warfare.

Secondly, an anti-war strategy needs to comprise a broad *international* coalition of political groupings. Warfare arises from the geographical division of capitalism into nation states. The confusion of nationalism with the struggle against the consequences of capitalism has, historically, proved self-defeating and indeed has led to war; the Soviet Union represents an extreme example of such confusion.

Would such an international coalition include 'progressive' international capital? This is a question which those on the left in the anti-war movement must consider seriously. Accumulation has proceeded in Germany and Japan in the post-war period almost in the absence of militarism. Non-economic forms of coercion were carried out on their behalf outside their territories by the United States. Now that American power is being abused in American interests, these states might be expected to respond with their own military build-up, based on what might be considered more progressive forms of military technology. To some extent, this has already occurred and bears ominous implications. Both West Germany and Japan have increased their military budgets and both are at the forefront of the development of what might be considered more 'cost-effective' armaments—Precision Guided Munitions, based on electronics technology, simpler and cheaper types of weapon platforms. But the world does learn from experience. The dangers *both* of interrupting global accumulation and unleashing economic warfare between the main capitalist blocs *and* of increasing the risk of war are widely acknowledged. One of the most important legacies of the Second World War was the widespread anti-militarist sentiment among the defeated powers. An effective strategy for peace needs to be able to constrain the development of militarism in these two countries through the development of popular movements.

Could such a strategy involve an alliance with those ruling economic and political groups that currently identify their interests as war avoidance and the defeat of the military machines of the superpowers? Would such a strategy be compatible with the survival of capitalism? If socialists ally with progressive capital, who would emerge as the dominant partner? The Second World War was based on a similar alliance, and capitalism survived—though not without significant material advances for socialists. The Second World War changed the nature of capitalism and greatly improved the economic and political position of the working class within it. It may be that because capitalism is fundamentally based on coercion and conflict, it is impossible to imagine a capitalist society which did not rely on socially organized physical violence as a form of coercion and conflict 'resolution'. Warfare has been so central to the history of capitalism and the nation state system. Could one imagine a coercive society, a class society, in which warfare was eliminated? Would this necessitate the creation of a world state? Is there indeed yet another stage in the development of class society? Capitalism might be said to represent 'progress' in relation to previous societies because it eliminated forms of individual physical coercion and, by separating out and specializing different forms of coercion, exposed the brutality of socially organized physical coercion. If so, could one envisage a class society which imposed constraints on warfare? In other words, does 'progress' represent a continual narrowing of the arena of coercion? Or is class society ultimately always pushed to the extreme, to the last resort? At Auschwitz, after all, slavery was reintroduced.

Thirdly, a strategy for peace must be aimed at the warfare sector in both East and West. If the Soviet Union is to be viewed as the creation of capitalist war and the permanent arms race, then the struggle against the political system as a whole in the East, the movement for civil rights, is actually the *same* as the anti-war movement in the West. The success of the one is dependent on the other. What comes after the warfare system is intimately linked with what comes after capitalism.

Finally, what about socialism? What would be a socialist defence policy? A socialist mode of production would presumably be one in which the worker was not alienated from the products of his labour and in which production and consumption were a single collective process. In such a system, there would be neither commensuration nor coercion (or consent). It is difficult to envisage such a society, but there are certain questions that its possibility raises. Is there space for physical coercion in the transition to such a system? Or for non-democratic forms of commensuration like war? The idea that it is possible to create a socialist mode of warfare through the abolition of ranks misses the point about how warfare is used. Or indeed, how the means of warfare are acquired. And the idea that physical coercion can be used to achieve socialism neglects the problem of how warfare is reproduced and whether its reproduction is compatible with a socialist mode of production.[20]

An anti-war strategy is an act of faith. For it presupposes the possibility that class society does not degenerate into barbarism at the point of most acute conflict. But it is not simply an appeal, in the tradition of Russell and Einstein, for loyalty to humanity instead of class or nation. If one accepts, as I do, the difficulty, at least for the Establishment, of breaking free from class conditioning, then the only hope lies in objective constraints on warlike behaviour. This might be achieved through the collapse of the warmaking machinery.

A strategy for socialism would have to build upon contradictions that already exist within the mode of warfare, rather than counterposing a more 'advanced' mode of warfare in war or revolution. Such a strategy might include an alternative defence policy. Clearly, the destructiveness of all modern armaments is such that war would be catastrophic whether the armaments used are based on 'progressive' or degenerate technology. Against an infinitely ruthless opponent, there is no defence. But there may be a case for arguing for some kind of defensive conventional posture which would be capable of inflicting a very high rate of attrition on an attacking force. The point would not be to withstand attack but to reinforce constraints against the use of military force among those who would have to carry out such an attack, to expose the irrationality of such an attack so that enemy soldiers would be less willing to participate. Such a posture should be sharply distinguished from proposals for guerrilla-type resistance which, in my view, could well be retrograde, leading to social remilitarization. Such a conventional force would need to be democratically organized and supported by armament producers which have *no* need for armaments either to guarantee employment or to secure expansion. The aim, to repeat, would be to build constraints on the use of warfare, both by ourselves and by opponents, as well as on the production of warfare—a first stage, to coin a phrase, in the withering away of warfare.

Is such a transitional mode of warfare conceivable without war? Or can one conceive of something less than an all-out nuclear war? Until now, armed struggle has been an essential component of human evolution and remains so today in many parts of the Third World. War, pushed to the extreme, now threatens human survival. Yet the absence of war has also, as it were, confined further evolution, caged and indeed nurtured the problems of the present epoch which now stalk around with little hope of escape.

In this essay, I have tried to offer a framework within which we might discuss the possible escape routes. Its main purpose has been to raise questions—no one can individually hope to answer them.

[1]Carl von Clausewitz, *On War* (Berlin 1832), London 1968, p. 133 (for the epigraph, see pp. 202–3).

[2]John Holloway and Sol Picciotto, eds., *State and Capital. A Marxist Debate*, London 1979, p. 24.

[3]Istvan Meszaros, *The Necessity of Social Control*, London 1971, p. 26.

[4]Ibid., pp. 46–7.

[5]Nikolai Bukharin, *Economics of the Transformation Period*, New York 1971, p. 28.

[6]'The Force Theory' in *Anti-Duhring*, London 1975, p. 238.

[7]*On War*, p. 103.

[8]Brighton Labour Process Group, 'The Labour Process', *Capital and Class*.

[9]See Citations in W. B. Gallio, *Philosophers of Peace and War*, Cambridge 1978, p. 93.

[10]Rosa Luxemburg, *The Accumulation of Capital*, London 1951, Chapter XXXII, 'Militarism as a Province of Accumulation'.

[11]See Ron Smith, 'Military Expenditure and Capitalism', *Cambridge Journal of Economics*, March 1977.

[12]Robert Rowthorn, 'Rosa Luxemburg and the Political Economy of Militarism', *Capitalism, Conflict and Inflation*, London 1981, p. 251.

[13]See for example, P. Baran and P. Sweezy, *Monopoly Capital*, London 1966 or M. Kidron, *Western Capitalism Since the War*, London 1967.

[14]See John Ellis. *The Social History of the Machine Gun*, New York.

[15]See Morris Janowitz, *The Professional Soldier*, New York 1960.

[16]See Richard Gabriel and Paul Savage, *Crisis in Command*, New York 1979.

[17]Oscar Lange, *Essays in Socialism and Capitalism*, Oxford 1970.

[18]See David Holloway, 'War Militarism and the Soviet State', in E. P. Thompson and Dan Smith, ed., *Protest and Survive*, London, 1980

[19]In a recent survey of four US army battalions more than 60%, excluding the elite rangers, were unwilling to fight in any circumstances other than foreign invasions of the United States. (Charles Brown and Charles Moskos Jnr., 'The Volunteer Soldier—Will He Fight?', *Military Review*, June 1976).

[20]See Martin Shaw, *Socialism and Militarism*, Bertrand Russell Peace Foundation, Nottingham 1980.

The Sources of the New Cold War

Fred Halliday

I

In the course of his essay 'Notes on Exterminism', Edward Thompson remarks that it is 'now beside the point' to investigate the historical responsibility of the main protagonists for the current arms race. 'To argue from origins,' he writes, 'is to take refuge from reality in moralism'. It is the great merit of Thompson's argument to bring home to every reader, forcefully and unforgettably, the urgency of political action now to fight against the danger of nuclear extermination. The injunction to dispense with investigation of origins derives its legitimacy in part from this over-riding call to a sense of immediate priority. Rejection of historical inquiry, however, also involves something more than this. For it underlies many of the very analytic themes upon which the category of exterminism rests—in particular, the view that the arms race now under way is essentially irrational, impermeable to the normal methods of historical investigation and the political judgements which may follow from this.

Yet it is precisely here that a problem arises: for the validity or otherwise of some of the main themes of the argument for exterminism must depend upon judgements about post-war world history. In this sense, far from being irrelevant, historical investigation may have a central place in our understanding of the present world crisis and in our framing of political programmes designed to check and overcome it. Thompson is right to warn us that such an investigation could become purely moralistic—an ascription of blame to one side, of innocence to another. But it *need* not be moralistic: it can rather be a study—as calm and measured as we can make it—of the responsibility, distributed and differentiated, of the two major world powers, as well as of other historical forces at work, in the emergence of the exceptionally perilous international situation in which we now live. In this perspective, the case for exterminism can be examined, confirmed or challenged, by an inquiry that seeks to use an analysis of recent international politics to inform the present direction of the peace movement. In the face of the possible end of modern history as we know it, the pertinence of historical investigation is particularly strong.

There are three themes in Thompson's essay which we should address: 1) that the nuclear arms race has acquired an autonomous dynamic in both domestic and international politics, one that is out of control, inertial, and irrational; 2) that it is this dynamic, the logic of exterminism, which constitutes or structures world politics by establishing itself as the field of force of all state-to-state relations; 3) that distinctions between the USSR and the USA are secondary compared to their common involvement in this exterminist logic, which generates an isomorphism of the two societies, born of their shared commitment to the nuclear arms race. Certain political conclusions are evident once these theses obtain explanatory force.

What follows here is an unashamed search for origins: our purpose will be precisely to see how far historical evidence bears out the themes of the case for exterminism. We must all accept that the world is threatened with annihilation and that it is an ethical and political imperative for every socialist to fight this possibility with all their might. But this is not the same thing as saying that this threat *constitutes* the overall structure of world politics today, or that the arms race defines the very nature of the societies of the major powers. In reply to Thompson, we will argue three alternative theses, matching the three arguments for exterminism set out above: (1) that whilst nuclear weapons introduce entirely new possibilities of civilizational destruction, their manufacture is no more inertial, escaping any human social or political control, than other state policies have been in past or present—but reflects identifiable processes of conscious agency and decision; (2) that the deepest structures of international politics are constituted by the conflicts between and within social systems—conflicts that are profoundly shaped, but not displaced, by the nuclear arms race; (3) that despite a common participation in the arms race, the Soviet Union and the United States are fundamentally asymmetrical societies, governed by different histories and political priorities, and with quite distinct responsibilities for the current escalation of tension in world politics. The recent past is not 'the irrational outcome of a collision of wills': nor, on the other hand, is it—any more than any other period of world history—the product of 'a single causative historical logic'. It is rather the product of the convergence of a *plurality* of historical processes, each involving deliberate human action and calculation, which have in their combination yielded us the dangers of the New Cold War.

The category of Cold War itself recurs in two key passages of Thompson's essay. On the first occasion he writes: 'What is known as the "Cold

War" is the central human fracture, the absolute pole of power, the fulcrum upon which power turns, in the world.' Later he remarks: 'No doubt
we will have one day a comprehensive analysis of the origins of the Cold
War, in which the motives of the agents appear as rational. But that Cold
War passed, long ago, into a self-generating condition of Cold War-ism
(exterminism).' The general direction of the essay, it might be said, is to
suggest that the Cold War can now be equated with the nuclear arms race,
in a single complex—exterminism—that has become the overarching principle of world politics. In his discussion of arms production and its
economic dimensions, Thompson later introduces a further element into
his argument by identifying all major military expenditure with exterminism. We therefore have a fourfold equation: Military Expenditure = Nuclear Arms Race = Cold War = Central Fracture in World Affairs. Yet
forceful as it is, this equation is questionable: the four elements cannot be
so easily elided.

First of all, the overwhelming bulk of military expenditure is today on
conventional, not nuclear, armaments: this is not a trivial point, since
much of the power of the argument for exterminism lies in its claim that
the nuclear component, as a pervasively irrational and annihilatory force,
has become the dominant principle of modern social and economic organization. Yet in both Russia and the USA most arms expenditure is for those
conventional purposes which are still regarded as comparatively rational in
intent and non-exterminist in effect.[1] Secondly, for all their death-dealing
potential, it is difficult to describe the confrontation of the two major
nuclear weapons systems as the central fracture in world affairs. It would be
more accurate, we would argue, to say that they at once dramatize and
endow with infinitely greater risk a conflict whose bases lie elsewhere—above all in the conflict between capitalist and post-capitalist
worlds. This constitutive conflict is in its turn overdetermined by at least
four others: the contrast between parliamentary democracies and
authoritarian bureaucracies, the struggle between imperialist states and
their former colonies, the contradictions internally dividing each type of
society, and finally the rivalry between different powers within capitalist
and post-capitalist worlds alike. The confrontation of capitalist and post-
capitalist systems became a *global* conflict for the first time in 1945. It was
a peculiar and largely accidental fate that this globalization coincided
historically with the first production and use of nuclear weapons, by one
side. It is perfectly possible to imagine a—far direr—history in which the
atomic bomb, if it had emerged a few years earlier, would have coincided
rather with *inter-capitalist* military conflict, in the hands of Hitler as much
as of Roosevelt. (Just as it is also possible, not only to imagine but to hope,

and struggle for, a time when there is no longer a coincidence between the break beyond capitalism and the entrenchment of an authoritarian post-revolutionary bureaucracy.) The analytic task presented to us by the history that has unfolded since 1945 is first and foremost to trace out the connections between globalized social conflict—in all the complexity of its several dimensions—on the one hand, and the nuclear arms race on the other, rather than to elide these two distinct processes into a single logic.

It is also debatable whether the term 'Cold War' is best used as a description of the whole of this period, since the social and political conflicts criss-crossing on an international scale have known periods of markedly greater and lesser intensity—phases that have had important and varied consequences for the arms race itself. The term 'Cold War' was orginally used to designate one, particularly acute, period of Soviet–US confrontation, distinct from hot war, but also from periods of greater collaboration, such as the war-time alliance or the detente of the early seventies. The first Cold War lasted from 1947 to 1954. In this sense Cold War is a phase or mode of globalized social conflict, rather than simply coextensive with it. Seen in this light, the Cold War of the late seventies, and the increased levels of military expenditure associated with it, mark a new phase of international conflict: rather than confirming an inexorable and irrational process, we shall argue that the renewed incidence of Cold War today raises questions of historical explanation as to why world politics deteriorated when and as they did. Any such explanation would have to give great emphasis to the nuclear arms race: but it could not reduce the New Cold War to that race, nor could it treat the arms race itself as an independent variable determining all other political developments. It is in the interaction of nuclear arms race with globalized social conflict that the roots of the New Cold War lie.

The late 1970s and early 1980s have been marked by a drastic heightening in the pitch of world politics, a much greater emphasis upon the need for military preparedness on all sides, more violent ideological campaigns against the respective evils of opposing camps. These changes have co-incided with renewed calls for unity within American and Soviet blocs alike and official intolerance of dissent. In other respects this New Cold War differs from the first: US–Soviet negotiations on arms limitation do continue, in contrast to the complete break in substantive diplomatic communications of the earlier period; the predominance of the USA vis-à-vis the USSR and vis-à-vis its capitalist allies is greatly reduced; the two major post-capitalist countries are divided; the Third World plays a much more prominent role. Yet despite these differences the two Cold Wars have common features and contain common risks of war.

The election of Reagan in November 1980 marks the full maturing of a New Cold War, but the shift in world politics predates that. By 1978, half way through the Carter Administration, the main elements of a New Cold War were already in place; while the tensions of this period have their root in the attempt by the USA in the early seventies to use SALT talks and trade as a means of controlling Soviet foreign and defence policy, and in the rebuffs which this attempt encountered—on the battlefields of Indochina and Angola, and in the continued enhancement of Soviet military capacity within the framework of the SALT-I agreement. In essence, the New Cold War is a response by the USA and its allies to the failure of detente as a means of waging globalized social conflict to their own advantage. Neither side abandoned its commitment to this conflict; the Russians have essentially pursued the same military and foreign policies as before, with somewhat improved means for doing so. It is this Soviet refusal to alter traditional policies which, from the mid-1970s onwards, produced a change of posture in the West and the ultimate abandonment of detente. The deterioration in East—West relations was therefore neither irrational nor inevitable: it was not irrational in that it reflected responses by conscious political agents in the United States to what they saw as a challenge to capitalist power, and it was not inevitable in that this New Cold War has been the product not of one inertial process but of several convergent developments in international politics, whose origins are distinct from each other and were not pre-programmed to coincide chronologically. It is the combination of these forces which explains the genesis of the New Cold War with its accompanying intensification of the arms race.

Within the context of the 1970s, there are five processes which appear to have played a major causal role in precipitating the New Cold War. Whilst they have operated on different time-scales and exercised different forms of influence, it is their combination and mutual reinforcement which essentially accounts for the termination of detente. These five causal determinants are: (1) the erosion of the US nuclear superiority by the USSR; (2) a new wave of Third World revolutions; (3) the rise of a new militarism in the USA; (4) the political involution of post-revolutionary states; (5) the sharpening of inter-capitalist contradictions.

1. The Erosion of the US Nuclear Superiority by the USSR

The leading theme of New Cold War advocates in the West has been the need to redress the shift in the East—West military balance. Allegedly, the USSR has drawn ahead and the West has to catch up: to 'rearm', 'rebuild our defences', 'restore the balance' and so forth. At one level, this argument is simply a myth: the West has not disarmed, so it cannot *re*arm, and the Soviet Union has not attained superiority, in either the nuclear or the conventional fields. Yet as with all ideology this apparent set of falsehoods conceals certain real changes, to which the rhetorical calls to rearm provide an encoded guide. For the past decade has seen a substantial improvement in the USSR's military potential, one that has reduced or—in certain limited fields—ended the overwhelming superiority which the West once enjoyed. What is now being called for is a new drive for superiority, an attempt to regain the margins of earlier decades, under the guise of redressing an imbalance supposedly in the Soviet Union's favour. The orchestration of public debate, on both military and political issues, is designed to facilitate such a process. Such orchestration is visible in current discussion of at least four dimensions of the East—West military competition: total arms expenditure, strategic nuclear weapons, theatre nuclear weapons, and Third World conventional capability. In the speeches of Weinberger, Thatcher and Mitterrand, changes in Soviet capacities and expenditures are adduced as, in themselves, reasons for an increased effort on the West's behalf: what this kind of argument demonstrates is how far earlier capitalist conceptions of detente rested upon an assumption of continued NATO superiority.

Three expenditure arguments are commonly made: that the Soviet Union spends a higher percentage of its GNP on defence than the USA, that it spends absolutely more than the USA, and that its rate of spending has increased substantially in recent years. The first of these is certainly true, if only because the USSR has a far smaller GNP than the United States. On the other hand, per capita expenditure is higher in the USA than in the USSR ($494 to $404 in 1980). The third allegation is quite false: Soviet military expenditure has been increasing at around three per cent per annum in real terms over the past decade, or somewhat less than the average increase in GNP. There is no evidence of a sudden spurt in military outlays.[2] Many attempts to compare total US and Soviet arms spending exist, but the figures provided by the one major independent source, SIPRI, indicate a US lead of $111 billion over $107 billion for 1980. This disparity is greatly compounded if the allies of both major powers are included. NATO outspends the WTO by $193 billion to $120 billion, and if China is factored in, the gap is much greater again: this can be done either by subtracting the percentage of Soviet expenditure deployed in the Far East (around 25%) or by adding the Chinese total to that of NATO (a further $40 billion).[3] Japanese military spending amounts to a further $9 billion. In total. the combined powers arrayed against the USSR spend exactly *double* the amount on their armed forces that the Soviet Union and its allies expended in 1980—or $240 billion. When Western politicians talk of an 'unprecedented level' of Soviet military expenditure they are technically accurate: the Soviet Union spends more than it used to on arms. But the implication that the USSR spends more than any other state, let alone the combination of major states ranged against it, is a false one.

In the field of strategic nuclear weapons the USSR has gradually lessened the distance between itself and the USA. In 1970 it had 1,800 strategic warheads to the USA's 4,000: in 1980 it had 6,000 to the USA's 9,200: i.e., from having less than half the number of warheads possessed by the USA it now has two-thirds the number. Over the past decade it has also introduced those changes earlier pioneered by the USA: transferring some missiles to the less vulnerable submarines and MIRVing what were previously single-warhead delivery systems. The Soviet Union now has a nominal lead in megatonnage and delivery systems, but these—far from being indices of superiority—reflect Soviet inferiority in the qualitative dimensions of MIRVing and accuracy.

Much US strategic debate focuses on a supposed Soviet advantage through the 1980s in first-strike capability—a 'window of opportunity' which would enable the Russians to destroy all US land-based ICBMs in a sudden unexpected attack. But, quite apart from the political assumptions contained in this window thesis, even in military terms it is unsustainable. For the USA possesses a completely invulnerable second-strike capability based on its Poseidon submarines—missile-launchers which the USSR is in no position to either detect or destroy. Moreover, even if the USSR were now able to launch a devastating first-strike against the USA—which it is not—by the same argument this is something which the USA has been in a position to do to the USSR for the past three decades. The USA could, however, do so far more effectively since it *can* detect and destroy the flotilla of sea-going Soviet missile-carrying submarines.[4] If a window of sudden attack has opened on the USA, that window has for twenty or more years been open on the USSR. The mythology of an apparent Soviet advantage distorts what is in fact no more than a diminution of a previous US superiority.

Nowhere is this distortion more evident than in the field of theatre nuclear weapons, the improperly called Euromissiles. Here the official Western claim is that the introduction of the SS-20 has upset the pre-existing balance, necessitating the introduction of Cruise and Pershing-II missiles into Europe by NATO as decided in December 1979. A little history may clarify this. Theatre nuclear weapons have in fact been present in Europe since the late 1950s, when the NATO countries deployed the Thor and the Jupiter, and the Russians deployed the SS-4 and SS-5. These were land-based and single-warhead missiles. During the 1960s and early 1970s, NATO improved its theatre missiles by two innovations: first, it made them less vulnerable by transferring them from land to sea, onto Polaris submarines; secondly, it made them more devastating by MIRVing them, replacing the single-warhead Polaris missiles by the ten-warhead Poseidons. Since NATO no longer needed the older, more vulnerable missiles, the Thors and Jupiters were withdrawn. By choice, NATO no longer had land-based theatre missiles; but it had a clear advantage. As these changes were introduced, the Russians tried to get theatre weapons included in negotiations with the USA. This was the main point at issue in the long talks over SALT-II which lasted from 1972 through to 1979. The Americans refused: first, under Nixon, Ford and Kissinger, and then under Carter. It is significant that the Russians continued to press for these negotiations until after the 1976 Presidential elections: but, once Carter too had shown his reluctance to negotiate, the Russians moved to redress their inferiority in theatre weapons. So, in 1977 the first SS-20s were deployed. Far from giving the Russians an advantage, they still constitute an inferior system. They are MIRVed and mobile: these are two refinements over the SS-4s and SS-5s. But their range is not significantly greater than the SS-5, their megatonnage is less, and they are not very accurate. Even their supposed invulnerability, a function of mobility, is debatable: their sites have to be prepared in advance, and they take many hours to make ready.[5] Far from redressing a Soviet advantage, the December 1979 NATO agreement was therefore, as with concurrent programmes of greater overall military expenditure and strategic 'modernization', a means of trying once again to achieve US superiority.

The dispute over conventional forces follows a similar pattern. The NATO countries maintain 4.9 million troops under arms; the WTO countries 4.8 million. If China is reckoned in, another 4.7 million troops are ranged against the Soviet Union, making a combined total double that of WTO strength. The USSR has enjoyed a geographical advantage over the USA in Europe since the end of World War II, by reason of the fact that it is itself a European power, which the United States is not. On the other hand, its control of the Eastern half of the continent is far weaker than that of America over the Western half in economic and political terms—necessitating a military deployment for repressive purposes that involves, among other things, large numbers of semi-obsolete battle tanks in the WTO countries. In the past NATO has always insisted on its ability to cope with these: its huge reserve of anti-tank weapons, the superior training of its crews, and the greater qualitative abilities of NATO armour do, in fact, quite adequately balance the numerical Soviet lead in tanks. The official justification for the neutron bomb, a battlefield radiation shell, is therefore without foundation: it is not needed to offset any Soviet tank advantages.

Further propagandist stress has in more recent years been laid upon Soviet military capabilities in the Third World. Here the USSR was previously not just at a disadvantage, but was virtually powerless in the epoch of Stalin, and not much advanced even as late as the crises in Congo and Cuba in the early sixties. It now has a certain capability, albeit a very limited one. What the USSR has done is to break a previous Western monopoly on military activity in the Third World. Yet in all dimensions the capacity of the USSR to intervene for any purpose—good or bad—in the Third World is far less than that of the West. Its expenditure on such deployment is 10% of its total military budget, compared to 25% for the USA; its naval presence in the major oceans is qualitatively and quantitatively far weaker. NATO currently deploys 460 larger warships (frigates and above), the WTO 195. The United States has produced three times the warship tonnage of the Soviet Union since 1960; it possesses 13 attack aircraft-carriers, the USSR none. Whereas the USA controls a vast chain of overseas military bases and installations, the USSR lacks any base network outside the WTO at all; its air transport forces are numerically much smaller and lack any in-flight refuelling capability.[6] The panic which recent Soviet military actions in Africa and Asia has unleashed arises from the USSR's ability to play a limited military role, where previously none was possible. This ability is not just a product of a new capacity for deployment in the South: it is also a reflection of the strategic protection which the USSR's recent nuclear advances afford it, and—far more important—of the emergence of a series of crises in the Third World where a Soviet military role was either directly solicited by local anti-imperialist forces or was deemed imperative by Moscow for its own reasons of state. Kissinger and Nixon had hoped that through detente they could impose their definitions of restraint and 'good behaviour' upon the USSR; this has proven to be a false expectation.

The current US drive for a new superiority in strategic nuclear, theatre nuclear and conventional weapons, as well as in space and in chemical and biological weapons, has an underlying political intention, even though, like all collective human endeavours, it does not express any single historical logic and may well not have the consequences which its executors rationally or consciously calculate. First of all, the American military build-up is symbolic of an overall political determination to pursue the globalized social conflict under way since 1945 more aggressively and intransigently than before, a signal clear to ally and foe alike that US hegemony will be reasserted over and against the Soviet adversary, European and Japanese allies, or Third World challenges. Secondly, the attempt to achieve nuclear superiority in both strategic and theatre terms makes military sense to those who do envisage a nuclear exchange: such people exist and it is their decisions, not some doomsday inertia, which typically motivate new runs of military production. Thirdly, the drive for paramountcy, disguised as the restoration of balance, benefits specific interests within US society, even if it involves costs for American capitalism as a whole, a point returned to below. Finally, it enables the USA, with the much stronger economy, to project through its arms buildup massive strains and pressures onto the opposite camp, where the USSR is materially in a far weaker position to follow suit. The ideology of Soviet superiority, then, does not reflect an uncontrolled incremental thrust: nor, as Thompson suggests, does the USA confront an equal. Rather, the ideology serves to legitimate an American quest for strategic ascendancy that is organized for conscious political ends.

2. A New Wave of Third World Revolutions

The contest between the two blocs has never been fought out in direct confrontation in the industrialized world since 1945. It has always been mediated through political and military conflicts in the Third World. It is here that during the 1970s an important shift in the correlation of international forces took place. The twin assumptions of the Western conception of detente proved in effect to be mistaken. The Third World could not be stabilized, and the USSR could not be dissuaded from providing assistance to unwelcome movements or states within it. Although often presented in a fused form, as a Soviet threat itself responsible for unpalatable changes in the Third World, the actual pattern of events has typically involved quite distinct elements: an autonomous maturing of social tensions in Third World countries, followed by a subsequent, separate, Soviet response to these.

The explosive impact of the new wave of Third World revolutions in the seventies can be gauged by looking back at the opposite pattern of the sixties. The major impetus of post-war decolonization had run its course when Algeria finally achieved its independence in 1962. For a decade thereafter, the anti-imperialist dynamic in the Third World seemed to have been defeated or contained. No revolutionary movement came to power anywhere in the three continents for more than ten years after 1962. On the contrary, Western—primarily American—imperialism was able to thwart or destroy one potential opponent after another, in a virtually uninterrupted series of victories over nationalist or communist forces. These were the years of the fall of Goulart in Brazil, the massacre of the PKI in

Indonesia, the elimination of Nkrumah in Ghana, the crushing of Mulelism in the Congo, the invasion of the Dominican Republic, the repression of the Bolivian guerrilla, the breaking of Nasser in Egypt, the maintenance of Rhodesian and Portuguese power in Southern Africa. The Indochinese revolutions alone struggled on without succumbing to defeat. With this major—but still undecided—exception, however, the Third World seemed to have been contained by a set of controls which were one of the preconditions of detente.

Then, in 1974, the dikes burst. A cascade of Third World revolutions, some socialist, some radically nationalist in orientation, broke out. In the space of six years some fourteen states witnessed seizures of power by insurrectionary movements. Above all, of course, the US was finally driven out of Vietnam: the victory of the Indochinese Revolutions, after the longest military struggle of the twentieth century, signalled a great change in the world balance of power, whose effects were soon visible on the other side of the world. In Africa, the Portuguese empire belatedly collapsed to left-nationalist movements of liberation in Angola and Mozambique. Meanwhile, the third most populous state of the continent, Ethiopia, saw the overthrow of an imperial regime by jacobinized military officers. In West Asia, America's major regional ally was uprooted by the Iranian Revolution, while a local communist movement seized power in Afghanistan. In Central America itself, the Sandinist guerrillas were able to achieve a classical Cuban-style revolution in Nicaragua. This chain of upheavals not only altered the objective relationship of forces in the Third World, it also had an—arguably even disproportionate—effect on the subjective psychology of Western strategists. The loss of Indochina was, of course, the most important in both regards; but the sheer scale of American defeat in Vietnam induced repression of its significance in the manifest discourses of US politics. Paradoxically, it was to be events of a much lesser nature—in particular the seizure of US hostages by Iranian students in November 1979—which were to unleash the latent mechanisms of a revanchist militarism and renewed readiness for Third World interventions that have since found expression in the Reagan Administration.

Beyond their own dynamics, however, the new wave of Third World revolutions occasioned a substantial and visible exercise of Soviet military power in support of them. The USSR supplied the heavy military armour needed for victory in Vietnam; it provided the airlift and strategic equipment for Cuban forces in Angola and Ethiopia; and it directly deployed Soviet forces themselves in Afghanistan. Even where there was no Soviet military involvement as such, states allied to the USSR or revolutionary movements in conflict with the West were in some measure protected by the fact that the new strategic potential of the USSR stayed the hands of US officials who might otherwise have envisaged direct intervention, as in Iran. At the same time, the chain of Third World revolutions in the seventies coincided with a major shift in the organization of the world capitalist economy, which endowed the South with a quite new importance: as supplier of raw materials, particularly oil, as a market for exports, and as debtor. These changes are discussed in the context of inter-capitalist conflict below. Irrespective of revolutionary movements or of Soviet initiatives, they would have galvanized a new sense of urgency amongst strategic planners in the West, as its long-term dependence on the South threatened to become more and more pronounced. The result of the combination of these factors is that the Third World has now come to occupy a central place in the anxieties of NATO councils and constitutes one of the major spurs for the unleashing of a New Cold War in the West. The fomenting of an alarmist political atmosphere in the advanced capitalist countries has been essential to the call for increased military expenditure: Kissinger ceased to use the word detente after the Cuban mission had saved the Angolan Revolution in 1975. Brzezinski said that the Soviet–Cuban role in Ethiopia buried detente in 1978. Later amplifications and reiterations have put similar emphasis upon Iran and Afghanistan, where the upheavals came long after the onset of the New Cold War but then certainly intensified it.

In this context, it is important to distinguish different elements in the military build-up now underway in the USA. For contrary to the conventional image, the great bulk of the new disbursements are for conventional military forces that can be used for counter-revolutionary interventions in the Third World. These expenditures are also those which will take effect soonest—in the course of the present US Administration. Even some of the nuclear developments formally presented as designed for the 'central'—i.e. European—front are justified informally as destined for Third World arenas, and in particular for regions where the USA feels it might be difficult to deploy sufficient conventional forces for its purposes, such as the Persian Gulf. Both the neutron bomb and the Cruise missile have been discussed in this list, on the assumption that their use against targets located outside the territory of the USSR and against non-European populations would not lead to a full-scale nuclear confrontation. Here in particular the political logic of the current US drive towards military aggrandizement becomes evident: very concrete and material economic interests are at stake, ones whose traditional safeguards appear to have been eroded or threatened by the spate of revolutions in the 1974–80 period. The New Cold War is a response at all levels to what is perceived as this danger: the ideology it purveys mobilizes domestic populations behind the prospect of new interventions in the Third World, blames all subversive changes in the South on the USSR, and legitimates increased expenditure on rapid deployment forces to reimpose traditional imperial controls.

3. The Rise of a New Militarism in the USA

If the two immediately dynamic determinants of the present international crisis lie in the historical processes just discussed, these cannot on their own account for its full configuration. For the New Cold War to emerge, the proximate causes in the arms race and in the Third World had to be complemented by reinforcing conditions within the Great Powers themselves. In fact, developments in both the USA and the USSR independently provided such a concomitance in the past decade. The third major determinant of the New Cold War must be located within the world's major capitalist state. Whatever the importance of the reduction in Western nuclear superiority or the advance of Third World revolutions in this period, these needed translation into American domestic politics in order to produce the changes that culminated in the Reagan Presidency. Here, once again, no single synchronized logic was at work. For the forces within US society which eventually triumphed with the electoral victory of Reagan in 1980, and are now bidding to change the political economy of American capitalism, have been largely independent of wider movements in the outside world, just as their gradual ascent long *predates* the international convulsions of the late seventies.

The roots of the militantly conservative coalition that dominates the US political scene today seem to lie in a steady geological shift within the American social formation. The past twenty years has seen the cumulative decline of the older centres of North-Eastern industry, the traditional heartlands of US capitalism, and the rise of a more dynamic and less trammelled entrepreneurship in the West and South. This change has been a gradual and far from uniform or complete one. Most of the greatest corporations and financial houses still remain the household names of the East Coast. But the relative shift in the balance of wealth and growth between the major regions of the USA has nevertheless by historical standards been very pronounced since the sixties. Today, the bulk of the US population lives West of the Mississippi for the first time in the history of the Republic. The newer capitalism of California, Colorado or Texas has a number of characteristics that differentiate it from that of the Atlantic Coast and old Mid-West, apart from its higher levels of profit and faster rates of accumulation (although not unrelated to these). Two have been of particular political importance. These are the persistence and vitality of non-corporate, personally-controlled capital, much of it speculative—such as that which figures so prominently among financial backers of Reagan's candidature itself; and the weakness or outright non-existence of organized labour unions. These conditions have given rise to a style of unbridled laissez-faire ideology and unreconstructed political reaction closer to the outlook of nineteenth-century business than to the institutionalized welfare and corporate liberalism of the older industrial zones of the East. The conflict between these two wings of American capitalism first achieved symbolic expression in the successful capture of the Republican nomination by Goldwater in 1964. His defeat of Rockefeller in that year revealed the second major asset that Western-format capital would deploy in the years to come: a capacity to mobilize a large layer of devoted cadres from the ranks of the petty bourgeoisie across the country, fervent with far right values—something that his New York opponent entirely lacked. This was not enough, however, to win the contest for the Presidency, where Johnson submerged Goldwater in an electoral avalanche.

For the US right to gather the mass weight and further strength necessary to conquer the White House itself, two major changes had to occur in the seventies. The first was, of course, economic. Johnson's victory in 1964 coincided with the most buoyant period in post-war American history—the apparent apogee of the Keynesian success on which the Democratic Coalition had been founded since the New Deal. A decade later, an acute economic recession was hitting the United States. Throughout the later seventies, popular living standards stagnated while inflation accelerated and unemployment slowly spread. The result was increasing dissatisfaction in the traditional Democratic constituencies themselves, above all the white working class. In the same period, the moral and cultural homogeneity of American society—founded in the main on the Protestant work ethic, centrality of the family and exaltation of the nation—started to disintegrate. Large marginal populations dependent on welfare rather than jobs emerged at one end of the social scale, while growing fixation on consumption rather than production developed at the other. The rise of a women's movement, partly a reflection of changes in occupational pattern, challenged traditional family structures. Moral codes were further unsettled by militant homosexual movements. Black insurgency shook myths of national unity at home, while defeat in Vietnam destroyed illusions of patriotic invincibility abroad. This generalized rending of the fabric of customary ways of life included much that was liberating for previously oppressed groups in US society. But intersecting with industrial decline and urban hopelessness in the cities, it also coincided with increased levels of crime and violence threatening all sectors of the population, especially exposed working-class areas. It was finally this combination of economic deterioration and cultural disorientation that swung a large section of the US proletariat itself to the programme of the ascendant right.

In 1980 the Republican Party was able to forge an electoral bloc dominated by wild-cat Western capital, fielding droves of petty-bourgeois activists, and rallying over half the members of the trade union movement, to gain a comfortable majority. The cross-currents of the sixties had given way to a tide of popular right-wing sentiment that swept Reagan easily into power.

None of these developments, quietly brewing within the American economy and society over two decades, was directly connected to the international scene, save for US humiliation in Vietnam. Nevertheless, the primary *focus* of the ideological constellation in which Reagan won power was not any problem internal to the USA, but in the hallowed manner of psychological displacement, was cathected upon an external entity—namely the USSR. In the doctrines of the New Right, Russia was blamed for the worst of America's woes from Vietnam onwards, with Third World 'terrorism' playing a subsidiary role. The solution it advocated was to achieve a new military superiority that would prevent the Soviet Union from gaining ground as it had done for a decade or more, and would deter further defiance by outlaw nations like Iran or Libya, responsibility for whose conduct could be laid directly at Russia's door. In this discourse, the Soviet threat became not just a military or political menace, but a comprehensive ideological construct enshrouding virtually all of America's problems and the combating of which would introduce a new era.

The advent of the Reagan administration, meanwhile, had been in a significant measure prepared by the evolution of the Carter Presidency before it. Although Carter had been elected in 1976 on a platform of national retrenchment and non-confrontation, and for two years officially at least more or less adhered to this, there were early signs during his tenure that winds were blowing in a different direction. Legitimate emphasis on human rights in the conduct of foreign policy was soon made a mockery by lavish praise and support for the Shah of Iran, revealing it as primarily a tactical campaign against the USSR; military expenditure, which had temporarily fallen with the end of the Vietnam war in 1973, started to rise again; Cruise technology was set in motion. But it was from 1978 onwards that Carter moved sharply to the right, at once of his own volition and under pressure from other forces on the American political scene. A Republican Party which had narrowly failed to nominate Reagan as its candidate against the incumbent Ford was in no mood to show mercy to a Democratic

President, who sought in vain to meet its demands for a more belligerent global stance. The neo-conservatives of the Democratic Party itself were for their part increasingly hostile to the USSR and found Carter, as even Nixon and Ford who preceded him, too friendly to Moscow. It was they who had put the most effective spoke in the wheels of detente in the early seventies, with the Jackson Amendment. The New Right movements, organizing on the basis of single issues like abortion and gun control, propagated a myth of American weakness expressed all the way from alleged capitulation at SALT talks to the dangers of surrendering the Panama Canal. This political force, as we have seen, was already formed by the end of the sixties and was in place, with its institutions, finances and grievances, by the middle of the seventies. US strategic nuclear superiority was an article of faith for it.[7] Besieged by this range of lobbies, Carter constantly gave ground, calling for escalating levels of military spending in 1978 and demanding the deployment of Cruise and Pershing II in Europe. Well before the Soviet invasion of Afghanistan and the seizure of US hostages in Iran at the end of 1979, a determined coalition had stymied the SALT-II treaty in Congress. Carter's proclamation of a Rapid Deployment Force for the Gulf and attempt to organize an Olympic boycott were of no avail in capturing the leadership of this New Cold War momentum. The basis of Reagan's victory in 1980 was already now laid.

The conjunctural forces building towards a renascent American militarism in this period were, of course, powerfully assisted by the constant lobbies in US political life operating to increase military spending—what have sometimes been called the sectional 'iron triangle' in Congress, the Pentagon and the arms manufacturers. The focus of their efforts is the annual summer hearings on military appropriations, prior to the financial year that begins on 1 October. These sectional interests played a major part in fomenting a New Cold War, from which they could expect to drive very material benefits—federal investments in home constituencies, further cornucopias of ultra-modern technology, and vast cost-plus contracts, respectively. Orchestrating a resentful jingoism after the defeats in Vietnam and Angola into determined pressures to expand arms production, they were instrumental in securing far larger budgetary allocations for the Defence Department from 1979 onwards. In doing so, the 'iron triangle' was able to argue that increased military expenditure would alleviate a US economy plunged in recession. Whilst considerable doubt can be thrown on the macroeconomic effects of outlays on arms in a period of inflation, and on their consequences for the international competitive position of US capitalism, specific industries unquestionably do benefit from them, including such vital sectors as motor manufacturing and aerospace that have been suffering from sluggish demand and low rates of profit. The permanent and professional component of US militarism, temporarily driven into abeyance in the wake of American withdrawal from Vietnam, could thus reemerge more forcefully and effectively than ever in the later Carter years, and now sits virtually unchallenged on Capitol Hill under Reagan. These interests must be counted among the key mediators of the history of the seventies: far from budget allocations in the US being the result of some unthinking inertia, they were planned and premeditated objectives of some of the most tenacious and single-minded lobbies in world politics. Their contribution to the unfolding of the New Cold War should not be underestimated, even if today the superior initiative in launching the huge American armaments programme has passed to the White House itself.

4. The Political Involution of the Post-Revolutionary States

Internal political changes in the USA, autonomously engendered within its continental economy and society, have thus had a formative impact on the turn towards a New Cold War in the last few years. Developments within Europe and Japan provided no adequate counter-weight to the trend towards a new belligerence in Washington. But the ability of the Western powers to mobilize popular support and credibility for a confrontation with the USSR required certain objective preconditions within the adversary camp. The fact that the depiction of Soviet policy by Reagan and Haig is false does not mean that the USSR and other post-revolutionary states have played no part in generating the New Cold War. For if US denunciations of Soviet military 'superiority' or 'violations' of detente in the Third World are ideological, there have been several respects in which the evolution of the USSR—not to speak of China—over the past decade or more has indeed contributed to the present dangerous international situation.

We noted at the outset that the original Cold War was not just a conflict between capitalist and post-capitalist states—that is, societies defined respectively by private ownership of the means of production, and the abolition of that ownership. It also involved a confrontation between parliamentary and bureaucratic political systems within the industrialized world, as well as a struggle between imperial and colonized societies in the underdeveloped world. In the latter, the moral advantage always lay—as it does to this day—with the communist states, as objective allies of national liberation movements against colonial and neo-colonial exploitation by the Western powers (if in practice the degree of subjective aid provided has always varied). In the former, however, the moral advantage has since 1945 rested with the richer Western states, which have represented regimes of capitalist democracy in marked contrast with the absence of socialist democracy in their poorer communist adversaries. It is this contrast of course, which, forms the exclusive staple of official Western interpretations of the Cold War, as an epic conflict between the 'Free World' and 'totalitarianism'. This ideological construction, based as it is on a real and material difference between OECD and Comecon states, has nevertheless had an uneven history of success in capturing popular imaginations in the West (even more so, obviously, in the East). Paradoxically, at the height of post-war Stalinist terror in the USSR and Eastern Europe—the late forties and early fifties—large sectors of the labour movement in the West refused to enroll behind the banners of the crusade against 'totalitarianism'. These included not only the mass communist movements, which were imbued with illusions in the nature of CPSU rule at the time, but also large numbers of working people and socialists who were not—but who were aware of the huge disparities in wealth and war-time suffering between the West and Russia, and looked forward to a humanization of conditions in the post-revolutionary states in better times to come. The end of the first Cold War appeared to promise just such a change. In the epoch of 'peaceful coexistence' proclaimed by Khrushchev, many of the worst crimes of Stalinism were denounced, the bulk of the apparatus of police terror was dismantled, prison camps were dissolved, and a freer cultural and political climate started to develop in the USSR. Hopes of a progressive transition from liberalization to real democratization within the Soviet bloc were widespread, inside and outside the Communist movement of the time.

It was these expectations that the fall of Khrushchev and the stabilization of a lengthy period of further bureaucratic rule under Brezhnev disappointed. The nearly twenty years that have now elapsed since the end of Khrushchevism have not been experienced as disastrous by the populations of the USSR themselves. By the standards of previous Russian history, the Brezhnev epoch has been one of steady economic and cultural improvement in the conditions of life of the mass of the people, modest enlargement of their domestic rights (abolition of the internal passport), and growing security in their private lives. Overall, there is little doubt that most Soviet citizens are far better off today than they were under Khrushchev, let alone Stalin. Even the public emergence of a small dissident movement is in part a measure of the long-term relaxation that has occurred in the USSR. Its treatment by the ruling authorities is repugnant by any socialist standards; but it has been less ruthless than the fate meted out to all past opposition. This may be partly because there is little sign that the majority of the Soviet population wavers from a now inherited loyalty to the state created by the October Revolution.

On the other hand, in the relatively more developed societies of Central and Eastern Europe, popular pressures for genuine political liberties within the post-capitalist order have mounted relentlessly, in an area where Brezhnevite consolidation has no natural national basis. Soviet responses here have been uniformly repressive. The greatest crime of the Russian leadership in this period was the coordinated invasion of Czechoslovakia in 1968, to preempt the Prague experiment in a democratized Communism. The mass revolt against bureaucratic misrule by Polish workers in 1980–81 has likewise been met with a ruthless coercive clamp-down, if on this occasion so far by the Polish army and party itself. Both Czech and Polish movements represented much more sustained collective aspirations towards a freer socialism than could the short-lived and elemental Hungarian revolt of the fifties. Yet while the latter was the object of far bloodier repression, the thwarting of the promise of the former has had much graver consequences for the credit of world communism as a whole, in a period when world capitalism has been able to expand the area of parliamentary democracy in its South-European tier—Portugal, Spain and Greece.

The record of the USSR at home and on its marches in Eastern Europe cannot be regarded as an active cause of the New Cold War in its own right, in the same sense as the rise of Reaganism in the USA. For the capitalist states were perfectly willing to pursue detente with the Soviet Union even through the blackest episode of Brezhnevism, the invasion of Czechoslovakia—described by President Johnson as no more than a 'traffic accident' on the road to mutual understanding between the Great Powers. Moreover, the USA found no difficulty in forging a close alliance with Maoist China a few years later, at a time when mass purges and wholesale persecutions were raging on a scale greater even than the Stalinist terror of the late forties—just as Washington today patronizes Pol Pot's forces in South-East Asia. But once the Western powers had decided, for quite other reasons, to unleash the New Cold War with a full-scale ideological offensive against the Soviet Union, they had to hand the necessary materials to do so. The well-worn themes of 'totalitarianism' and 'gulagism' could now find a relatively fresh resonance within the ranks of labour movements that had been deeply demoralized by the frustration of the hopes raised after the death of Stalin for genuine democratization in the East. The result of the political involution of the post-revolutionary states of the Comecon bloc has thus been to embolden the enemies of socialism, and to divide and discourage the forces favouring socialism in the West itself. The New Cold War would not have been so easy to launch had the USSR been making any visible progress towards a more democratic Communism in the past decade.

The domestic involution of the Soviet Union and the Eastern European states has, meanwhile, been accompanied by a noticeable shift in Russian policy on issues of war and peace. Prior to the 1970s, the Soviet Union was manifestly far weaker than the West and its disarmament positions rested on precise and positive bases: a ban on all nuclear weapons, the ending of all foreign bases, and the simultaneous dissolution of NATO and WTO. These policies were maintained up to and through the 24th Congress of the CPSU in 1971. But with the development of detente, the Soviet leadership started imperceptibly to cease reiteration of these positions and by the time of the 25th Congress in 1976, Soviet proposals were of a much more short-term and technical nature, formulated like those of the USA in terms of the details of SALT negotiations.[8] This shift in disarmament policy, combined with a real increase in Soviet military strength, has greatly reduced the moral advantage which the USSR enjoyed in the past when it alone called for worldwide and complete nuclear disarmament. Thus even though the Soviet Union has continued to press far more consistently and seriously for arms control than the USA (as befits the heavier burden of military spending on its economy), this change of emphasis has lent more credence to Western propaganda portraying Russia as an arch-militarist power than it would otherwise have had.

This image has in turn been tinted in lurid colours in the depiction by Western governments and media of the more active Soviet role in the Third World in the seventies. In reality, the record of the USSR in the South has remained, as before, deeply ambiguous: but on balance it has if anything marked a political improvement over Russian performance in either the Khrushchev or Stalin periods. In the past, the main single criticism socialists always made of Soviet foreign policy in the capitalist world was its refusal to provide adequate—often indeed any—moral or material aid to revolutionary movements abroad; a refusal motivated by the determination to seek collaboration with the dominant imperialist powers for the sake of narrowly national and bureaucratic interests. Stalin's sacrifice of the Spanish Republic and the Greek Revolution, his hostility to the Chinese Revolution, are notorious in this regard. Khrushchev made an isolated break with this tradition when the USSR sustained the Cuban Revolution with substantial aid against the US blockade. At this time the Soviet Union also started to provide economic assistance to national bourgeoisies in countries like India or Egypt as well. But in other respects, Khushchevism continued along the essential lines of Stalinist egoism—imposing the Geneva agreements on the Vietnamese Revolution in the fifties, and starving it of equipment in the sixties; not to speak of its gratuitous rupture with China in the same period. By contrast, the Brezhnev epoch has seen a new Soviet willingness to help or shield revolutionary or national liberation movements across the Third World, with or without any hope of immediate material returns. Thus, as we have seen, the victories of the Vietnamese, Angolan and Ethiopian Revolutions would have been impossible without large-scale Soviet military aid. Even the Egyptian and Syrian semi-successes against Israel in the Yom Kippur War, which led directly to the emancipation of OPEC, were feasible only because of the availability to Arab forces of modern Russian equipment. Meanwhile, economic assistance extended to the Third World has—contrary to much received opinion—increased substantially under Brezhnev, from $3.8 billion to non-Communist countries in 1954–65, to $7 billion in 1966–75.[9] In all these respects the USSR has represented a more active and progressive influence in the Third World than before.

At the same time, however, the greater assurance of Soviet policy in the Third World has by no means led to the disappearance of its traditional regressive features either. These encompass a range of practices. Although aid or intervention on the side of generally emancipatory forces has been the predominant pattern in the seventies, it has not been a uniform or consistent one. In some regions, the USSR has given far too little assistance to national liberation forces, diplomatically or materially: Southern Africa is a recent case in point. In others, it has cultivated friendly relations with viciously reactionary tyrannies, for petty local advantages—Idi Amin's Uganda or General Videla's Argentina. More lasting damage has been done by the transposition to the newer revolutionary states in the Third World of Soviet models of ideology, party building and state organization, replete with the police controls and negations of socialist democracy to be found in the USSR itself. South Yemen—for all the positive contrast it makes with the corrupt feudal states surrounding it in the Arabian peninsula—has been a representative example of this process. In Ethiopia, the formal principles of Soviet-style nationalities policy have found particularly repressive implementation in Eritrea. In Afghanistan, the Russian decision to rescue a brutal and isolated Communist regime has encouraged the rallying of large sections of the population to the banners of clerical counter-revolution. As in the more developed post-capitalist societies of Europe, so too in the newer revolutionary states of Asia and Africa, the political character of the Soviet model has served to reinforce the image of socialism as a system that limits rather than extends the freedoms exercised in advanced capitalist societies.

Yet it must also be said that the USSR has not been the main or direct pressure behind the worst episodes of privation or repression that have scarred the new states created in the turbulence of the seventies. Soviet advice has on the whole sought to moderate economic policies whose radicalism was calculated to disrupt production and to generate major refugee problems, as in Cuba or Vietnam, as well as in Afghanistan. Likewise, it has tried to restrain the reigns of terror unleashed at different times in Kabul or Addis Ababa—just as it has also tried to compose, rather than aggravate, regional conflicts in the Horn of Africa. But the USSR has usually possessed neither the economic resources, nor the degree of political leverage, to alter these trains of events. The endogenous dynamic of most of these revolutions, in conditions of cultural backwardness and economic penury far more drastic than those of the Soviet Union in the twenties, has driven them on their own towards political systems recalling some of the most sombre features of pre-war Russia. The result has been that the multiplication of newer revolutionary states in the later seventies has often been accompanied by the repetition of institutional processes reminiscent of those which discredited the Soviet regime in the thirties.

Finally, it is clear that the USSR has typically sought to extract strategic advantages from its interventions in the Third World, whether or not these were in the interest of the countries concerned themselves. In most cases, its objectives have not gone much beyond refuelling facilities for its naval forces and fishing fleets, or landing rights for its aircraft. There is no doubt that its world-wide intelligence and tracking capacities have been enlarged in the wake of its increased military assistance to the Third World revolutions in the past decade. But no permanent overseas bases have been set up by the Soviet Union anywhere outside the WTO itself. This record of relative caution may, however, yet be broken in Afghanistan. There for the first time outside Eastern Europe the Red Army itself has been deployed in support of a local Communist regime that would otherwise have been overthrown by its domestic opponents. The primary blame for this sequence of events must be put on the Afghan Communist movement itself, whose brutal and fractricidal rule jeopardized its own progressive reforms and rapidly isolated the PDA regime in 1978–79. The Soviet decision to rescue it from collapse cannot be compared with the invasion of Hungary or Czechoslovakia, where Russian troops were used to crush a popular movement towards a more democratic socialism. The guerilla forces threatening to seize power in Afghanistan were feudal and clerical in ideology, fighting for a return to social conditions that have kept the Afghan people crouched in untold backwardness and misery. Nevertheless Russian intervention inevitably provoked nationalist reaction and widened the scope of the civil war into a long-drawn-out and bloody struggle. No short-term gain, whether political or strategic, could compensate for the international crisis detonated by this action. The Soviet march into Afghanistan was not an offensive move, either against the West or the local state, but a defensive operation of the type traditional in Eastern Europe: the forcible maintenance in power of an already established Communist regime in a bordering country—in this case established by internal rather than external forces, unlike most of Eastern Europe. It was guided by the constant spirit of post-war Soviet foreign policy: what we have we hold. But the scale of national resistance, and of international alarm, it was bound to arouse was very different; even if it held an Islamic Vendée at bay in Afghanistan, it has done substantial harm to the wider cause of peace and socialism.

Meanwhile China, the other major Communist power, has played its part in diffusing the image of socialism as a project subject to moral entropy in the past decade. Once the frustration of the reforming impetus of Khrushchev's Russia became evident in the sixties, Mao's China came to be viewed by wide sections of the left in the capitalist world—developed and underdeveloped—as the main hope for a better and freer variant of Communism, one more open and egalitarian at home, and more principled and disinterested abroad. The destruction of these hopes was to be the second great blow to the moral heritage left to the post-war world by the Third International. It can now be seen that the record of Maoist China after 1958 was in nearly all major respects one of virtually unrelieved reaction and failure. At home, the reckless economic and demographic adventurism inaugurated with the Great Leap Forward led to nearly two decades of relative stagnation, leaving behind huge numbers of unemployed in towns and countryside alike. Politically, the Cultural Revolution, proclaimed as a mass movement of spontaneous revolt and liberation, in fact came to combine chaotic factionalism and ruthless regimentation: great waves of repression broke over the country, in which thousands died and many millions were persecuted. Abroad, the breach with the USSR originally provoked by Khrushchev's arrogant termination of aid was solidified and compounded by a foreign policy systematically aimed against the Soviet Union, far surpassing in anti-Russian motifs earlier anti-Chinese themes in the propaganda of the USSR—even extending to vast territorial claims dating back to the time of the Manchus. Eventually, the logic of this obsessional hostility led Peking to form a full-scale, if informal, alliance with Washington itself, even while the USA continued to control and protect the KMT regime in Taiwan; and to woo virtually all the world's most right-wing regimes, from Pinochet's Chile to Mobutu's Zaire to the Shah's Iran.

The death of Mao has permitted the relative amelioration of a Chinese version of Khruschevism to emerge at home, albeit one much more dependent on imperialist investment from Japan and the West than was Russia in the fifties. But it has produced no improvement—rather the reverse—in

Chinese foreign policy. Collusion with Nixon and Kissinger to thwart the victory of the Vietnamese Revolution was scarcely veiled from 1973 onwards. Once the US was driven out of Indochina, in defiance of Mao's counsels to Hanoi, China proceeded to patronize and arm the demented Pol Pot regime in Cambodia—a government in a category of its own for mass killings—as a weapon against Vietnam, encouraging border provocations and ideological vituperations alike. The result was a Vietnamese invasion to overthrow the Cambodian regime—unleashing the fatal prospect of a cycle of wars between post-revolutionary states. The Vietnamese had at least a tangible political goal, and appear to have been greeted with initial relief by wide sections of the Cambodian population, whatever their other feelings. The Chinese attack on Vietnam that followed it was, on the other hand, a senseless act of vindictive aggression serving only to demonstrate Peking's utility to Washington in South-East Asia. More than involution, the trajectory of the post-revolutionary states reached a nadir of degradation in this 'inter-socialist' war visited upon Vietnam by China, only four years after the withdrawal of the United States.

In all, the responsibility of the Chinese state for the onset of the New Cold War must be reckoned a heavy one—greater certainly than that of the Soviet state. This is not because its domestic record has been worse, as it has—Western governments and media have paid little attention to political repression inside China, which forms no part of the ideological arsenal of world capitalism. It is rather for two other reasons. Firstly, China has itself been a prime fount of some of the most virulent and inaccurate anti-Soviet propaganda of the past decade, diffusing it through much of the Western left, as well as the Third World. In that sense it has been a co-author of the New Cold War in the realm of ideas and attitudes. Secondly, however, its hardening option for a full-scale alliance with the United States has more than any other single factor contributed to the new strategic confidence with which the latter has embarked on a course of confrontation with the USSR. The 'China card' has greatly emboldened the New Cold War planners in Washington, and introduced a quite new dimension of insecurity in Moscow. We are unlikely yet to have seen the worst of the tension that this alignment of the most populous post-capitalist state with the most powerful imperialist state will generate on the international scene. The tragedy of this development can be seen all too clearly if we compare the diplomatic and political role—on the whole constructive, pacific, mediatory—played by the first Communist state to rebel against Soviet domination, Yugoslavia, with that of the truculent and cynical China of these years.

5. The Sharpening of Inter-Capitalist Contradictions

The four major elements of the New Cold war so far discussed all have their precedents in the original Cold War itself. Their combination today inevitably brings echoes of the past. In the period from 1947 to 1954, Western capitals rang with alarm at the speed with which the USSR first produced an atomic and then hydrogen bomb, while remaining greatly inferior in overall military technology. Anti-colonial revolutions with socialist or radical nationalist leaderships menaced imperial rule in Vietnam or the Philippines, Malaya or Guatemala. McCarthyism was sweeping the United States. In the Soviet bloc Stalinism was implacably repressive; the postrevolutionary states split when Tito was expelled from the ranks of the Cominform. The long and variegated history that stretches from the First to the Second Cold War is thus not without its own continuity, although each of the elements that made up the original constellation of 1947–54 have undergone far-reaching transformation today. The fifth component of the contemporary phase of Cold War, however, is qualitatively new. Inter-capitalist contradictions have reemerged to play a major role in the world politics of the seventies and eighties.

These contradictions are not so much *active determinants* of the New Cold War (like the relative decline of Western nuclear superiority or the new wave of Third World revolutions), or *positive or negative conditions* of it (like the rise of the new militarism in the USA, or the involution of the USSR, respectively), as what can be termed its *complicating context*. The contradictions themselves are complex ones. They involve not only a revival of traditional inter-imperialist tensions, in new forms and within new limits, but also conflicts between industrial and less industrial—that is, imperial and former colonial—states within a common capitalist world, and finally antagonisms between the former colonial states themselves. The emergence of this skein of contradictions is still very recent; and the consequences of each of them for the future of world peace remain hard to foresee. But there can be little doubt that so far their net effect has been to increase rather than decrease the dangers inherent in the build-up of the New Cold War.

Throughout the first half of the twentieth century, inter-imperialist competition was the main constituent of international tension and the major cause of war. The Second World War saw the culmination of these conflicts. The result of it was to leave one power, the United States, absolutely predominant within the advanced capitalist world—economically, politically and militarily. Former enemies and allies alike were henceforward subordinate states, coordinated within an American monetary, diplomatic and strategic system constructed on a world scale. The First

Cold War had the subsidiary effect, or function, of enforcing US hegemony over the European colonial powers—in the name of a common defence of the 'Free World'—and allowing Washington to break into domains previously reserved to them: first in the Middle East, then in the Far East and other areas. But in the succeeding twenty years, Western Europe and Japan grew much more rapidly than the US, reestablishing rival centres of economic power of a greater dynamism than that of America itself, and threatening to displace it from markets and supplies across the globe, as well as conquering sectors of US demand at home. Unlike the pre-war situation, however, the reemergence of a number of fiercely competing industrial economies has not been accompanied by any comparable multiplication of military power. In this domain, US paramountcy remains virtually as great as ever.

The result has been to give inter-imperialist conflicts a new twist in the present period. On the one hand, there is no sign of any danger of major inter-imperialist wars: not only is the disparity of military strength too great for this, but—even more important—all are united in ultimate solidarity against the leading post-capitalist state, Russia. On the other hand, this very fact has actually accelerated the speed with which US financial and economic hegemony—burdened with the costs of overall defence of the capitalist bloc—has been eroded. The central issues here are trade and currency rates, the former as much as the latter pitching the USA against both the EEC and Japan. The USA has a trade surplus with Europe, but has sought to improve its position further by limiting European exports such as steel, whilst trying to force open European markets for larger volumes of US agricultural products. By contrast Japan enjoys a huge trade surplus with America, which has been the subject of even greater conflict and popular irritation in the USA. On the financial front, the abandonment of the Bretton Woods system of fixed exchange rates by Nixon in 1973 has created a whole new arena of negotiation and friction between the advanced capitalist countries. The USA, facing a payments deficit originally swollen by the Vietnam War, has sought to recoup its position by nationalist policies—first devaluation under Nixon and Carter, then high interest rates under Reagan—in the monetary field, and growing protectionism in trade relations. Neither response has so far yielded appreciable results.

It is in this context that some US strategists have argued that an increase in international tensions vis-à-vis the USSR must encourage, if not oblige, the Europeans and Japanese to be more accommodating in the economic field, if only because Washington will have reminded them who it is that, in the last instance, guarantees their military protection. In other words, there is an economic motivation to the ever more insistent calls for Atlantic (and Pacific unity) against the Soviet Union that now resound from America. Moreover, at the same time the United States can press—again, in the name of exigencies of the New Cold War—increased military outlays on the European powers and Japan. Without in any way weakening US strategic superiority over its allies, higher rates of arms expenditure by (especially) West Germany and Japan would be calculated to ease the pressure of these states on the US economy, as resources were unproductively diverted into the kind of military research and development that has proved to be such a structural fetter on American capitalism. The United States thus has a dual interest in promoting a New Cold War climate of a militarist type, in relation to its allies. One of the major domestic sources of the chauvinism of US public opinion in the late 1970s has been the generic sense of a lost power, in which the visibly increased economic and diplomatic freedom of action of the EEC and Japan has played its part. All-round confrontation with the USSR serves to create conditions of quasi-emergency in which the USA can reassert its suzerainty over the other advanced capitalist countries.

Meanwhile, the developed capitalist world as a whole has faced a number of quite new challenges from the developing capitalist states of the Third World. The most spectacular of these has been the ascent of the OPEC states since 1973. Whilst price rises of oil were neither the precipitating nor principal cause of the accelerating inflation in the advanced capitalist countries of the past decades, they have certainly been perceived as such by official and much public opinion in the West, where the producers' cartel has engendered a double response. At the state level it has generated wide-ranging American plans for military intervention in the Persian Gulf in the event of any move by local states to block oil exports in the future, or any takeover of a Persian Gulf state by anti-imperialist or revolutionary forces. These projects have played a major role in ensuring a continuum of interventionist planning in the USA: the very year in which US military forces withdrew from East Asia, in 1973, was the one in which the Joint Chiefs of Staff began preparing for the rise of a new challenge in West Asia. This governmental response has been accompanied by a general hardening of popular attitudes in the West against the oil producers, the effects of whose actions are directly felt at the garage pump and in the domestic energy bill. Indeed OPEC price increases, fused with the detention by Iranians of US hostages, turned the Arab and Persian inhabitants of the Middle East into the symbolic objects of imperialist revenge *par excellence* in the United States at the end of the seventies, far more than the Indochinese or Latin Americans whose gains have in social terms been more threatening to American interests. Rendered simultaneously responsible for the ravages of the recession and the weakening of the USA's international position, they furnished the pretext for a tide of chauvinist sentiment that has notably served to assist the revival of US militarism.

Western and Japanese dependence on raw material imports from the Third World is, moreover, by no means confined to petroleum. The strategic minerals essential to military production are also mainly extracted from underdeveloped areas—in this case, above all, Southern Africa. The tougher attitude of the Reagan Administration towards the advance of national liberation forces in this region finds part of its explanation in Washington's resolve to keep a firm protective grip on these minerals, whether cobalt (Zaire), chromium (Zimbabwe), uranium (Namibia), or manganese (Gabon, South Africa): not to speak of the gold mines of the Rand itself. The general propagandist concern with key primary commodities has raised the spectre of 'resource wars', the denial to the USA or its allies of access to vital resources by enemies—whether the USSR or local states. The possibility of any such action is, in reality, very remote. The conjuring up of the contingency, however, serves to occlude the fact that it is the USA, with its incessant boycotts and trade limitations, which has been waging a 'resource war' against the Soviet Union since 1917, not to speak of subsequent blockades against China, Cuba and Vietnam.

Meanwhile, the growth in the leverage of OPEC has been accompanied by other shifts in North–South relations, as the rise of a limited number of New Industrializing Countries has challenged traditional market shares in some goods within the advanced capitalist nations, fuelling demands for protectionism. The potential of this competition for generating international tension should not be underestimated, if the OECD recession of the seventies persists and deepens. But for the moment it is overshadowed by the danger to the global financial order latent in the top-heavy accumulation of Third World debts, for the most part concentrated in brittle military dictatorships that are deemed vital to US strategic interests, such as South Korea, Turkey or Brazil. The combustible material being stored up for the future by these chains of two-way speculative dependence is obvious. It is not difficult to imagine scenarios in the next decades analogous to the creditors' ultimatums of the nineteenth century, delivered by naval flotillas against the Khedivate in Egypt, Mexico or Venezuela.

Finally, and perhaps most gravely, as the independence of the postcolonial states has been consolidated, and their bargaining strength in the international capitalist economy has improved, conflicts *within* the Third World have tended to multiply. Here lies one of the newest and most unpredictable of all the political developments of recent years. There now seems to be every prospect of Third World nationalism repeating much the

same cycle of military adventures and aggression that took European
nationalism from the romantic liberalism of the early nineteenth century to
the strident chauvinism—in some cases eventually fascism—of the early
twentieth century. If inter-capitalist wars of the classic type still remain
virtually unthinkable between the developed countries, they are becoming
ever more practicable—and put into practice—among the developing
countries. There the ideology of national unity has generally ceased to be an
integrating force welding together different strata or ethnic groups in a
genuine common front against imperialism, since independence was established. Economic problems and pressures have multiplied, and with them
internal class struggles have come to the fore. Productive forces have
developed remarkably in some Third World capitalist states, but even in
these huge disparities of wealth and privilege exist—far wider than any in
the advanced capitalist countries themselves; while vast other regions are
the sites of terrible malnutrition and hunger, where a sixth of the world's
population lives on the edge of starvation. In these precarious conditions,
projection of social tensions outwards by dictatorial or demagogic regimes
onto neighbouring states, as the source of grievances or ills within the
nation, has become increasingly frequent. The anti-imperialist nationalism
of earlier periods is widely degenerating into an introverted obscurantism
and official chauvinism pitting one Third World state against another.

The result has been a steady increase in the number of border conflicts
and outright wars within the Third World. In recent years heavy fighting
has erupted between Pakistan and India, Libya and Egypt, Algeria and
Morocco, Honduras and El Salvador, Ethiopia and Somalia, Iran and Iraq.
The protracted Arab–Israeli dispute, while not reducible to it because of
the Palestinian question, partakes of much the same character. All of these
conflicts had endogenous roots, and cannot simply be ascribed to the
machinations of outside powers. But it is also true that the capacity of
Third World states to wage modern warfare is dependent on the levels of
military equipment they receive from the industrial economies—capitalist
or post-capitalist. The militarization of the Third World has been proceeding apace over the past decade, and provides one of the major mechanisms
interlocking the developed and developing economies together. Arms form
the major export industry, for example, of French capitalism. Longer and
bloodier wars must lie ahead if this trend continues. The possibilities of
greater power being drawn into conflict with each other via their role as
suppliers of local combatants has already been demonstrated in the Middle
East and the Horn of Africa. Even though both the USA and the USSR
have shown themselves to be aware of the dangers of this contingency, and
have so far on each occasion limited these conflicts from 'above', there is no

guarantee that such reciprocal controls will continue to operate indefinitely. Worst of all, a wide range of the more advanced states in the Third
World are now on the verge of achieving nuclear capability—in every case
exclusively because of Western aid. These include, besides Israel, some of
the most sinister despotisms to be found anywhere on the globe: Argentina, Brazil, South Africa, Pakistan, Taiwan and soon no doubt South
Korea among them. It is here, in the tricontinental Balkans of the modern
world, that the greatest dangers of nuclear exchange and world war may in
future lie.

III

Such, we would argue, have been the main developments that have given
rise to the New Cold War. If unchecked, their momentum could lead
towards a Third World War that would realize the exterminist potential of
the present arms race. With this, we return to the question posed at the
outset of this essay: namely, the relevance of historical investigation to the
political orientation and practical action of the peace movement, in a
context of gathering dangers of nuclear annihilation.

A historical analysis suggests, as we have seen, that it is not the arms
race alone which constitutes the basis of the contemporary international
crisis, or indeed provides the over-arching unity of the postwar world. The
stockpiling of nuclear weapons has always inter-related with other constitutive dimensions of world history since 1945, of which the most important
so far has been the globalized social conflict of capitalist and post-capitalist
states. International politics form an arena of social forces that are, albeit
diverse, quite identifiable and, as much as any historical agencies, intelligible. Even the arms race itself is not a wholly inertial process. However
instinctively difficult to do, it is necessary to distinguish between the
horrendous *effects* of a nuclear war, which would be beyond reason for all
those engaged in it, and the *causes* that could potentially generate one,
which are rationally discoverable. Edward Thompson rightly abjures
explanation of the present danger in terms of a 'single causative historical
logic'. But his own presentation of the relentless thrust of exterminism
itself tends at times to suggest such a logic—in which exterminism
becomes a modern version of the doomsday machine, both source and
consequence of an annihilationist demiurge. The reason, surely, is that the
alternative he proposes to us is a misleading one—either a 'single historical
logic' or a 'messy inertia'. If these are the only possibilities, the latter can
all too easily become another, inverted variant of the former. In reality,
human history and agency, individual or collective, typically form a world

intermediate between the two, where rational intention and control are thwarted or deflected by antagonistic conflicts of interest, pressures of unconscious desires, or constraints of natural necessity, without ever being finally cancelled by them. The current critical condition of world politics contains the danger of nuclear war. But this danger is less a result of the inertial push of exterminism, than the consequence of a combination of international and national conflicts, within which competition in nuclear weapons—manipulated and managed for conscious purposes—forms the most incendiary component.

Does this component dictate the crystallization of essentially similar political formations in the two great powers, mediated by the reciprocity of their antagonism? The foregoing historical analysis lends little support to the thesis of an isomorphism of the USSR and USA, or of post-capitalist and capitalist societies generally. Nor is the oft-repeated claim that centrally planned economies and war economies are effectively equivalent a persuasive one: it has to be asked under what conditions these were created, what purposes central control fulfils, what the mode of reproduction or internationalization of these systems is. It would be as relevant to compare a monastery to a regiment on the grounds that both involve pledges of obedience, male exclusivity and a sense of corporate identity. In the case of the USA and USSR such a comparison is particularly inapposite, given the totally different experiences of modern war that these two societies have had. The USA is, indeed, a vivid example of how centrally planned economic organization is not necessary for high levels of militarization. If we look at the historical character of the Soviet Union and the United States as societies, or at the respective roles they play in the world at large, there is not so much an isomorphism as an asymmetry of internal structure and international consequence.

The record of the past decade is, in this respect, clear enough. The two world powers do not have an equal responsibility for the current Cold War, or for the arms race that is accompanying it. The deterioration in the international climate in the latter part of the 1970s has been essentially precipitated by changes in the global posture of one state, namely the USA. No such change can be detected in the USSR: it has not engaged in a sudden expansion of its military forces, it has not seen a quite new leadership emerge after a ferocious internal political debate, and it has not introduced new conditions into US–Soviet negotiations, let alone abandoned the explicit pursuit of detente. This is not to say, as we have stressed, that the USSR bears no responsibility for bringing the present crisis upon us. In a longer-term sense its political involution has helped to render it possible at all. But this responsibility is different in kind from that of the USA. Lest this judgement appear unduly one-sided, it should be noted that such an interpretation is one with which the American protagonists of the New Cold War effectively agree. Their argument is that the USA has had to change policy in the face of the continuity of Soviet designs, a continuity which it had earlier been hoped the USA could rupture by the enticements of detente. All the issues around which the New Cold War is mobilized are issues upon which the USSR has maintained constant positions through the nearly two decades of the Brezhnev epoch: steady increase in military capability, cautious support for Third World revolutions, persistence of bureaucratic dictatorship. The New Cold war is a response to this consistency, an expression of the refusal of the capitalist world to accept it.

What are the implications of this analysis for the new European peace movement that has arisen since 1979, and to which Thompson's appeals are so forcefully directed? This movement exists in, has indeed been provoked into existence by, a determinate historical context; and this context has shaped its potentiality by both opening and restricting its opportunities for action. For if we are to be realistic, the movement is confronted with what is at first sight an encumbering paradox: that if the political responsibility for the New Cold War is disproportionately attributable to the USA and its allies, the room for political mobilization against the New Cold War is disproportionately restricted within the USSR and its associated states, to the point where it is not yet in any meaningful sense capable of independent articulation in them. The ideology of the European peace movement has on the whole rested upon a formal claim of symmetry on both counts—equal responsibility for the New Cold War in general, and for the European missile confrontation in particular, and equal possibilities of that popular internationalist opposition to the dangers of a nuclear conflagration of which Thompson speaks. Yet in fact neither parity obtains. Far from encumbering the movement, however, the two *dis*parities may, in their combination, point the way to an avenue of real political advance, attainable through mass mobilization in the 1980s.

We can perhaps see this most clearly if we consider the central political slogan of END itself: the call for a 'nuclear-free Europe from Portugal to Poland'. The demand is an even-handed one, aimed at East and West alike. But in practice its effect is likely to be differential. For there is no hard evidence that there are nuclear weapons in WTO territory outside the USSR itself. The Soviet Union, unlike the United States, does not have missile bases outside its own frontiers today. Some battlefield warheads may be stockpiled in Eastern Europe; or if not, could be moved there at very short notice. But the main Soviet instruments of nuclear weaponry are located in the western regions of the USSR itself. The principal END demand is thus one that is much more likely to be acceptable to the Soviet Union than to the United States. Indeed, it was precisely this asymmetry between the two great powers which led to the failure of the Rapacki Plan in the fifties—the most hopeful forerunner of contemporary projects for nuclear-free zones in Europe. NATO flatly refused to envisage the denu-clearization of Central Europe, because this would have meant the with-drawal of US nuclear bases in West Germany. Today, if there were any international dynamic towards a general European peace, the USSR would not have to respond to a call for denuclearizing Europe from Portugal to Poland by any major withdrawal on its part. What the USSR would have to do is what it has time and again committed itself to doing, namely imple-ment its declared policy of not targeting nuclear weapons on countries that renounce the possession or deployment of these on their national territories. That commitment would, of course, involve the dismantling of the SS-20s and comparable missiles, whose range is specifically European. But such action would plainly represent a change of a quite different order from that involved for the strategic dispositions of the United States, with its myriad nuclear bases and installations in Western Europe, if it were to respond to the same END call.

The disparity here is one that goes back to the very genesis of the Cold War itself. The US was the first power to build nuclear weapons, and is so far the only power to have dropped them. It has also from the start refused to make any commitment against their *first use* in any future conflict. NATO strategy is based, to this day, on the principle of possible first use of weapons of mass destruction in Europe. The USSR, on the other hand has always pledged itself never to use such weapons first, and has sought—in vain—a reciprocal declaration to this effect from the USA. The moral and political distance between these two positions is inescapable, and helps to explain why the immediate demands of the peace movement should press closer on one side than the other. Edward Thompson, for all his insistence at one level on the isomorphism of the two great powers, at another level has himself pointed out as clearly as anyone this historical difference. While emphasizing all the repressive weight of the Soviet state at home and in Eastern Europe, he comments that 'the basic postures of the Soviet Union' seem to be still 'those of siege and aggressive defence', while the United States seems 'to be more dangerous and provocative in its general military and diplomatic strategies'.[10] More recently, he has written of the way in which the causes of 'peace' and 'freedom' were divided respectively between East and West by the Cold War, in Europe the most enduring suppressions of the latter coming from the USSR, the most ominous threats to the former coming from the USA.[11]

If this is so, the strategic objectives of the European peace movement must now be two-fold—the disengagement of the Western half of the continent from the military system that represents the major seat of potential war, and the Eastern half from the political system that represents the major negation of civil liberties. These two tasks are inter-related, but they are not identical. For the moment, independent mobilization remains, beyond a few individuals, impossible in Eastern Europe. The peace movement is thus of necessity largely confined at present to Western Europe. it is here that the first *initiatives* for that larger 'repair of Europe', which Thompson so eloquently evokes, must realistically be taken. The immediate priority is, of course, to stop the installation of Cruise and Pershing II. The ultimate goal, towards which every step should be directed, is the termination of the Atlantic bond that ties Western Europe to the USA, and the creation in its stead of a denuclearized, neutral and independent bloc of states in the advanced industrial economies of the Old World.

Under what conditions could such a bloc emerge? Are there any organized forces within the present West European political order that could—under popular pressures—contemplate such a prospect in the eighties? In a longer-term economic perspective, as we have seen, European capitalism is gaining an ever-increasing independent strength vis-à-vis American capitalism. Already, the GNPs of the EEC and USA are more or less comparable. Should not then military and political subordination pass away, once economic inferiority—the huge discrepancy in wealth and resources that gave birth to NATO and the Marshall Plan in the first instance—has disappeared? To ask this question is to register another paradox. There have been two principal actors on the West European scene since the foundation of NATO: the European bourgeoisies proper and European social democracy, each represented through their respective party organizations. Of these two, it has typically been the *former*, not the latter, that has shown most capacity to resist or challenge US interests. De Gaulle's defiant regime in France was the most dramatic expression of this contrast. But even after his death, the rule held: Giscard's foreign policy was manifestly more independent of Washington than Mitterrand's has (so far) been. In England, too, with its more heteronomous post-war traditions, it has been Conservative governments that have on occasion risked American displeasure, not Labour ones: whether under Churchill (Geneva), Eden (Suez) or Heath (EEC). Temptations to European independence have thus been associated more with the political right than the left. In consequence, these have at the same time customarily gone together with emphasis on European nuclear armaments—whether De Gaulle's *force de frappe* or Macmillan's shadow of it after the collapse of Blue Streak. On the other hand, if

European social democracy has traditionally been more subservient to American foreign policy, it has also (by the same token) been less inclined to pursue nuclear autonomy—even though, of course, after late conversions neither Wilson nor Mitterrand were to break with their predecessors' legacies.

It is thus possible to envisage a common movement towards capitalist independence from the US in the European capitals in the next decade— one that would, of course, be actively encouraged by the USSR, in a Soviet counterpart of America's China policy. But such a Europe would not renounce nuclear weapons, it would retain its own. This would not be a mere reproduction of the status quo under a new guise, for a European nuclear deterrent would in all likelihood be a minimal rather than a maximal force, since it could not seriously entertain the ambition of replacing American military supremacy on a global scale. Some critics of the present arms race, like Zuckerman, see merit in prospect like this, as an alternative strategic model that could influence the two great powers back to more rational levels of stock-piling. In practice, however, the emergence of an integrated European nuclear command seems very improbable. Not only have the European bourgeoisies shown decreasing momentum towards any federal unification within the EEC over the past decade. But above all there remains the virtually insuperable stumbling-block of West Germany —the most powerful capitalist state in the continent, yet the one that cannot be granted control of nuclear weapons without simultaneously threatening France and the USSR. For this reason, if for no other, a continental Gaullism still appears unlikely to emerge.

What then, on the other hand, are the prospects of European social democracy losing its traditional allegiance to the United States? Historically, there have been two main reasons for its pronounced Atlanticism. The first lies in the political psychology of social democracy as such. Defined domestically by its structural subordination to capitalism, it has always had a deeply engrained mentality of deference to the dominant classes whose social order it has sought to administer for the benefit of the dominated. This familiar lack of class confidence or strategic elan at home has naturally been translated into diplomatic and military subservience abroad, to the far more powerful dominion of US capital. The temerity or vigour of a De Gaulle or Churchill, representative of ancient ruling classes, has been quite alien to it. Moreover, the Atlantic pact has also brought social democracy important material advantages. For the US military shield has kept defence costs relatively lower in Europe, and so facilitated the construction of the welfare systems that have been the most distinctive social-democratic achievement there. The fiscal burden of European nuclear independence, and (even more) matching conventional forces, would have been much greater. These determinants continue to apply today. But they have become relatively weaker over the past decade. In particular, West German social democracy—unlike French, British or Italian—showed itself capable of a genuine measure of foreign policy autonomy in the early seventies, when Brandt launched his *Ostpolitik*: the most hopeful single development in the European state system since the onset of the Cold War. Even in the later seventies, the turn of the Socialist International—under SPD influence—away from US imperialism in Latin America, towards qualified aid to national liberation movements and the concerns of the Brandt Report, indicate a potential for new directions in the next decade.

The peace movement must do everything in its power to encourage similar signs of a break with a discredited past in Europe itself. The willingness of the major social-democratic parties to move, under the pressure of broad popular demands, towards European disengagement cannot be predicted in advance. Every allowance should be made for the possibility of a progressive evolution by them, of the sort projected by Tony Benn in the Labour Party.[12] But at the same time, the objective obstacles to such a development would be underestimated by the peace movement at its peril. In principle, a capitalist Western Europe independent of the United States, with *neither* American troops *nor* nuclear weapons of any sort, is perfectly conceivable. Sweden today presents a local example of such a position: highly defended, prosperous and neutral. Switzerland, under a succession of right-wing coalitions, provides another. However, it is clear in practice that the strategic importance of Western Europe as a whole to the United States renders any dismantling of NATO a very different proposition from these, as American discussion has always made clear. Even the prospect of failure to install Cruise and Pershing II has produced threats of stringent US reaction. Here, a genuinely independent Western Europe could and should call American bluff on the issue—recently raised again—of 'de-coupling': far from capitulating to US pressure for the stationing of Cruise missiles on the grounds that otherwise US public opinion will insist on the withdrawal of the 330,000 troops stationed in Europe and so 'de-couple' the USA from the NATO alliance, the European peace movement should state calmly but without qualification that this is a desirable goal in which the European left and the American right can collaborate. This would, of course, soon bring reality to the fore: the USA has no intention of loosening its military grip on Europe, and would attempt to resort to the full panoply of destabilization, from press vilification to economic pressure to outright coercion, in order to preserve its beachheads on the old continent.

It is here that the limits of social-democracy would be fatally encountered. To sustain and master the deep *political crisis* that would ensue from any real rupture with the Atlantic pact, only a mass socialist movement would be adequate. Over twenty years ago, Edward Thompson rightly insisted that just such a scenario would amount to nothing less than a revolutionary challenge to the capitalist order, in any allied country.[13] At what he called this 'river of fire', a popular movement could only prevail by following the logic of that challenge through to a socialist society on the other shore. The moral confidence and political determination necessary to confront the structures of Atlanticism could never be credibly divorced from the historical ability to imagine a qualitatively freer and more equal social order, and the capacity to fight effectively for it. A century of social democracy has shown that, whatever its other gifts, it cannot be expected to demonstrate these.

The same logic holds true for the second essential task of the peace movement in Western Europe—the defence and promotion of political liberties in Eastern Europe. Here too, social democracy has often in the past played a counter-productive role, stoking up the crudest passions of anti-communism more even than many of its bourgeois counterparts. The line that descends from Ernest Bevin and Jules Moch is by no means extinct today, as figures like Soares or Craxi remind us. But equally it would be wrong to neglect the positive and effective influence of the policies pursued in recent years by Brandt or Kreisky, in helping to further conditions for liberalization in Eastern Europe. The peace movement has every motive to support and develop the initiatives of those trends in the Second International that seek to combine diplomatic conciliation with political pressure for greater civil rights, in their relations with the Soviet bloc. Yet here again, there exists a limit beyond which it is not plausible to imagine that the impact of European social democracy could go. For what the states of Eastern Europe lack is something that it has itself signally failed to achieve, namely *socialist* democracy. In the long-run, the only *transformative* aid that the Western labour movements could bring to the societies of the East would be the creation of a freer socialism in their own countries, based on higher levels of wealth and longer traditions of civic association.

But for that the precondition is the overthrow of capitalism—in other words, precisely the revolutionary change which social democracy has always refused to contemplate. Its own accommodation to the rule of capital, and torpid administration of bourgeois society, morally incapacitate it from any full challenge to the Communist states in the East—which, whatever their other manifold defects, have historically passed beyond capitalism. The mere counterposition of bourgeois parliaments to bureaucratic polit-bureaux will never help to resolve the complex problems of a producers' democracy on the other side of the private ownership of the means of production. The Western labour movement—now not only in its social democratic, but increasingly also Eurocommunist formations—has undergone its own form of political involution since 1945, steadily losing combativity or capacity to project any other future than the most mediocre stewardship of capitalism—whether with welfare and full employment yesterday, or with austerity and unemployment today. It is only when it finally earns its great historical privileges in the effort and risk of actually building an advanced, emancipated socialism—rather than complacently celebrating the benefits bestowed on it by capitalism—that it will provide a real source of inspiration, or exercise a major power of attraction, in the post-capitalist states. In the field of 'freedom' as much as of 'peace', the deadlock of the Cold War can in the long run only be broken by progress towards this third term.

But once real movement was made towards it, the effects would not be confined to the Old World. An independent Western Europe, capable of rejecting the world of *both* nuclear missiles and multinational corporations, would not only transform the perspectives for Eastern Europe and the Soviet Union. It would also decisively alter the balance of forces in the Third World, by providing an alternative source of economic, political and strategic aid for countries now crushed in the conflict between East and West. At present, every hopeful revolt in the ex-colonial countries risks being polarized into the magnetic pattern of the Cold War, as the USA opposes or the USSR sustains it. The consequences of this polarization have already been seen: they threaten both international peace and the construction of any non-repressive socialism in the South. It is the logic of this interaction that could be reversed by an active and militant European foreign policy, which took an independent stance in support of Third World peoples and states, dissolving the present rigidity of alignments and supplying insurgent movements and societies with the substantial material and moral assistance they desperately need, in their own fight against hunger, penury and oppression.

Such a prospect would, it goes without saying, involve an enormous change in world politics. But it would still leave the two great powers confronting each other with their own lethal arsenals. What hope, it may be asked, is there for any basic change in the American and Russian strongholds of overkill themselves, where no peace movements of a scale comparable to those of Western Europe are yet in sight? If the immediate dangers of the present international situation are contained, however, there exist some grounds to look forward to an alleviation of the New Cold War by the mid eighties. The fortunes of the Reagan Administration seem likely to repeat the trajectory of the Thatcher government at home—relentless deflation, rising unemployment, falling rates of profit and of output. Despite the greater economic reserves of US capitalism, and the more aggressive resilience of its Western sectors, there is every chance that this regime of callous reaction will provoke a wide popular repudiation at the next Presidential election. The result would probably be to usher in a neo-liberal Democratic administration, in a climate in which the militarism of the New Right had fallen into some discredit along with its monetarism. By then, too, the Brezhnev epoch will surely be over in the USSR, as age takes its toll of the Soviet leader and his closest colleagues. In such circumstances—a concurrent political change in the USA and USSR—conditions would doubtless improve for a fresh start in disarmament negotiations.

The underlying reality, however, that could then finally force the arms race into reverse is the nuclear parity of the two great powers themselves. For, as we have seen, it has never been true that the arms race was a competition between equals—its history is that of the constant US efforts to maintain or improve its military superiority over the USSR. The current recrudescence of the Cold War is directly related to the narrowing of the gap between them, as Washington strives to retain a vanishing supremacy. Once the irreversible fact of Soviet strategic equality is accepted in the United States, however, the mainspring of the nuclear arms race may be broken. It is still too early to foresee when American opinion will resign itself to the end of the epoch of US global hegemony, inaugurated at Los Alamos. But once it does, the conclusion that nuclear stock-piling is literally senseless—even for the most cold-blooded of ruling classes—may at last be drawn. If that were to be so, the New Cold War might yet be seen in retrospect as a drama of catharsis which, however racking while it lasted, assisted the passage to an era of lesser international tension.

But that passage will open only if there is conscious and collective resistance to the dangers of war now. That resistance has already begun in Europe. The peace movement there grows from a concern about the survival of contemporary civilization itself and includes many who are not socialist. That breadth of the movement is now its greatest strength, and must be preserved as such. But within it socialists will argue that peace can in the end only be secured by a political process that extends beyond the avoidance of war itself. The New Cold War that threatens us all is the distorted product of the conflict between a militaristic capitalism and an involuted and bureaucratic socialism. It can only be transcended by a socialism that, whilst not equating these two international forces, seeks to be a historical alternative to both.

[1]Of US military expenditure for Fiscal Year 1982, 7.8% is for strategic nuclear forces, i.e. $17.4 billion out of $222 billion (*Department of Defense News Release*, 4 March 1981). Out of a British defence bill in 1981 of £12.3 billion, £300 million or 2.4% is for nuclear weapons (*Sunday Times*, 24 May 1981).

[2]Arthur Macy Cox, *International Herald Tribune*,12 August 1980. For an excellent overall survey of the US–Soviet balance see Fred Kaplan, *Dubious Specter: A Skeptical Look at the Soviet Nuclear Threat*, Institute for Policy Studies, Washington 1980.

[3]*World Armaments and Disarmament, SIPRI Yearbook 1981*, London, p. 156. All figures are in constant 1978 prices.

[4]'Though the Soviets have more submarines, the US can easily detect where they are—whereas the Soviets, so far as is known, have never tracked even one of the 2,000 voyages that US missile-firing submarines have made, some of them very close to the USSR's shores', *Time*, 27 July 1981. The 'modernization' of the US strategic nuclear forces decreed by Reagan places particular emphasis upon new systems of communications with submerged missile-carrying submarines.

[5]The CEP—circular error probability—of an SS-20 is reckoned by Pentagon sources to be 1,500 feet, compared to 600 feet for the most advanced Minuteman missiles, and 250 feet for the Cruise and Pershing. On the SS-20 see Andrew Cockburn in *The Nation*, 28 November 1981.

[6]Michael Klare, *Beyond the 'Vietnam Syndrome'*, Washington 1981.

[7]See Frances Fitzgerald, 'The Triumphs of the New Right', *New York Review of Books*, 19 November 1981.

[8]For the 24th Congress, see *Keesings Contemporary Archives*, 12 June 1971: for the 25th Congress, see ibid. 21 May 1976.

[9]US Central Intelligence Agency, *Communist Aid to Less Developed Countries of the Free World, 1975*, July 1976, p. 5.

[10]Edward Thompson and Dan Smith eds, *Protest and Service,* London 1980, p. 49.

[12]See his creative 'Lisbon Address', *Arguments for Democracy*, London 1981, pp. 196–210.

[13]'Revolution', *New Left Review*, 3, May–June 1960, p. 9. It is interesting to recall the detail of his scenario: 'Should the protest in Britain gain sufficient strength to force our country out of NATO, consequences will follow in rapid succession.The Americans might reply with economic sanctions. Britain would be faced with the alternative of compliance or of a far-reaching reorientation of trade. The dilemma would agitate the consciousness of the whole people, not as an abstract theory of revolution but as an actual and immediate political choice, debated in the factories, offices and streets. People would become aware of the historic choice presented to our country, as they became aware during the Second World War. Ideological and political antagonisms would sharpen. Non-compliance with America would entail winning the active, informed support of the majority of the people for policies which might bring with them dislocation and hardship. Hardship would involve the fair distribution of resources. The dogmas of the sterling area would fall. Stringent controls would have to be imposed on the banks and finance-houses. Curragh-like intrigues by members of the military ruling caste might raise the question of "smashing" the military-bureaucratic institutions. One choice would disclose another, and with each decision a revolutionary conclusion might become more inescapable. Events themselves would disclose to people the possibility of the socialist alternative; and if events were seconded by the agitation and initiatives of thousands of convinced socialists in every area of life, the socialist revolution would be carried through.'

Europe, the Weak Link in the Cold War

Edward Thompson

The editors have suggested that I might add a comment on the essays in this volume, since some of them commenced in the form of comments upon my own 'Notes on Exterminism'. A review of the whole would be out of place, not only because my own opinions on many points are less weighty than those of the contributors but also because any review would suggest some kind of summation—and, in effect, closure—of the discussion.

But what is remarkable about this volume is the openness of tone and of terms, the reach for international discourse, the common pursuit of convergent analysis and strategies. It would be quite sufficient if I simply added a note to say this: I am heartened by this volume, an international discourse of a new kind has been opened, and this must go on.

If I add some further comments, it is in the hope that these will help this process along. I allowed my 'Notes on Exterminism' to stand without revision, since several of the contributors to this volume had taken these as a text for criticism. But clearly some judgements have been overtaken by events: the MX missile system has now been modified in response to domestic opposition in the USA, the Soviet Union—according to SIPRI figures—has now taken a greatly enlarged share of the world's arms trade, and so on. And there have been larger shifts of scene than that: above all, the emergence of mass peace movements in Europe, the Far East, and now in the United States itself—movements which already perform an uncertain yet significant international role.

My 'Notes' were written in May 1980, in the aftermath of the NATO 'modernization' decision and of the Soviet invasion of Afghanistan (both in December 1979), and against the background of the US failure to ratify SALT II and of a bellicose and seemingly 'consensual' all-party militarist hullabaloo in Britain (*Protect and Survive* and so on). There was then no effective peace movement in Europe—something in Holland and in Norway, a first stirring of the new movement in Britain, but as yet very little in West Germany or Italy. The peace movement in the Far East was also quiescent. And Solidarity did not yet know its own name.

The times favoured intellectual pessimism. I can accept the reproof of Raymond Williams and of those other contributors who detect some sentences in my 'Notes' that could support a determinism according to which the rival weapons systems, by themselves, and by their reciprocal logic, must bring us to extermination. I ought to have known better than to have gestured at Marx's suggestive image of the hand-mill and the steam-mill. Yet the 'Notes' did not only suggest that: there was also, already, in the European Nuclear Disarmament Appeal, the outlines of a strategy of resistance, and my essay concluded with a conspectus of this alternative—a conspectus which has taken on flesh in the past two years, in the realities of the peace movements.

If the times are not quite as dark today, they are still dark enough. And I am unwilling to abandon the category of 'exterminism' without at least a tentative defence. The term itself does not matter: it is ugly and over-rhetorical. What matters is the problem that it points towards. There remains something, in the inertial thrust and the reciprocal logic of the opposed weapons systems—and the configuration of material, political, ideological and security interests attendant upon them—which cannot be explained within the categories of 'imperialism' or 'international class struggle'. This volume, rich in several forms of political reflection, is thinner on analysis of the material and ideological bases of the new militarism. And there are some plain misunderstandings of my argument.

Thus Roy and Zhores Medvedev challenge my view that 'a situation could ever reach the point in the Soviet Union when "hair-trigger military technology annihilated the very moment of 'politics' " '. And they argue, in response, that 'the Soviet system is too conservative and densely bureaucratized for this to happen'. If the Party exercises comprehensive control of most sensitive aspects of intellectual and social life, 'how can one imagine that those military experts who manage the Soviet Union's ICBMs could possibly launch them in an emergency without collective decisions at the highest levels of the Party and state?' And the Medvedevs conclude that 'strict and comprehensive safeguards exist against any possibility of either a mistaken or deliberate initiative by any level of the military hierarchy alone'.

That may be so, if we stress *initiative*, although even here there is room for little accidents which perhaps do not receive Politbureau sanction, such as the episode of the Soviet submarine in sensitive Swedish waters. But if we accept the Medvedev's arguments in a literal sense, then we can only conclude that the Soviet Union is doomed by its bureaucratic and conservative procedures to be the loser in any nuclear exchange. For military-technological considerations have already shrunk the time in which any collective decisions of Party or state can be made. Nuclear weapons are so devastating that response to an attack—or pre-emption of an anticipated attack—must be almost instantaneous. And the whole absurd theory of 'deterrence' demands that such near-instantaneous capabilities can be displayed. In one example, the Pershing II is advertised as a highly accurate and swift weapon: if sited, as planned, in West Germany it will be seen as a potential weapon of first strike, capable of taking out Soviet ICBMs and command and communication centres in the western Soviet Union in a few minutes of flight. In the view of one well-informed American authority, Arthur Macy Cox, such a threat could be met by the Soviet military only by the introduction of LOW (Launch-On-Warning) automated systems, which would despatch a nuclear counter-strike on the trigger of an electronic alert signal. The collective decisions of Party and state would then be pre-empted within the circuits of a computer. And an influential lobby for LOW systems exists in the USA as well. Where would be the moment of 'politics' then?

We have not yet reached the point of automated response, and this terminus may be averted. But nuclear weapons technology is undoubtedly devaluing the moment of politics. Several of the contributors to this volume, in reasserting the primacy of politics, may have neglected to give to the modernized weapons systems (and to the influential software attendant upon them) sufficient weight as independent variables whether autonomous of the political process or interactive with it.

This question ought to remain open for analysis a little longer. New contributions on this question, some of them coming from positions rather far from those of the traditional 'left'—notably Jonathan Schell's *The Fate of the Earth*—will ensure that it will not be tidied away. Schell is asking whether advanced civilization may not be falling subject to a tendency towards its own self-extinction—a tendency which, if not reversed within a decade or so, might become irreversible? That is much the same question as is proposed in my 'Notes'. What name, then, are we to give to such a tendency? And what *is* a 'tendency'? Is this moment simply the product of an accidental coincidence—the coincidental invention of an appalling new military technology superimposed upon a particular episode of world-wide political confrontation? Or can we speak of entering—at some point after 1945—into a distinct historical epoch (perhaps a terminal one), with distinct characteristics governed by the reciprocal non-dialectical contradiction between two military blocs whose competition, at every stage, reinforces their mutal hostility and their exterminist resources—an epoch which requires a new category for its analysis?

I proposed the term 'exterminism' because, in my view, the second of these alternatives may be correct. I have rehearsed the argument recently, but without recourse to the term, in my lecture *Beyond the Cold War*:

'What is the Cold war now about? It is about itself. . . .

The Cold War may be seen as a show which was put, by two rival entrepreneurs, upon the road in 1946 or 1947. The show has grown bigger and bigger; the entrepreneurs have lost control of it, as it has thrown up its own managers, administrators, producers and a huge supporting cast; these have a direct interest in its continuance, in its enlargement. Whatever happens, the show must go on.

The Cold War has become a habit, an addiction. But it is a habit supported by very powerful material interests in each bloc: the military-industrial and research establishments of both sides, the security services and intelligence operations, and the political servants of these interests. These interests command a large (and growing) allocation of the skills and resources of each society; they influence the direction of each society's economic and social development; and it is in the interest *of* those interests to increase that allocation and to influence this direction even more.

I don't mean to argue for an *identity* of process in the United States and the Soviet Union, nor for a perfect symmetry of forms. There are major divergencies, not only in political forms and controls, but also as between the steady expansionism of bureaucracy and the avarice of private capital. I mean to stress, rather, the *reciprocal* and interactive character of the process. It is in the very nature of this Cold War show that there must be two adversaries: and each move by one must be matched by the other. This is the inner dynamic of the Cold War which determines that its military and security establishments are *self-reproducing*. Their missiles summon forward our missiles which summon forward their missiles in turn. NATO's hawks feed the hawks of the Warsaw bloc.

For the ideology of the Cold War is self-reproducing also. That is, the military and the security service and their political servants *need* the Cold War. They have a direct interest in its continuance.'

I do not consider that this volume has settled this matter, one way or the other. If we do require a new category to define this distinct epoch of nuclear-confrontational history, yet it goes without saying that this does not, by some gesture of a wand, mean that all previous categories are dispensed with or all prior historical forces cease to be operative. That may also be a misunderstanding which my 'Notes' invited upon themselves. Imperialisms and class struggles, nationalisms and confrontations between publics and bureaucracies, will all operate with their customary vigour; they may continue to dominate this historical episode or that. It will mean, rather, that a new, featureless and threatening, figure has joined the *dramatis personae* of history, a figure which throws a more abrupt and darker shadow than any other. And that we are, as Schell and I have argued, already within the shadow of that extreme danger. For as the shadow falls upon us, we are impelled to take on the role of that character ourselves.

The USSR: the Consequences of 'Reaction'

Roy and Zhores Medvedev turn away from this mode of analysis. As Soviet patriots (albeit 'dissident' ones) they react rather strongly against any notion of co-responsibility by the superpowers for the current crisis or of 'symmetry' of any structural kind induced in the rival powers by three decades of confrontation. They offer a different analysis, of a historical character, in which Soviet militarization is shown to be in reaction (sometimes *over*-reaction) to the military threat of NATO, and especially the USA.

I found their contribution to be in every respect illuminating, as well as positive and encouraging. I welcome especially the sense of solidarity with which they write, and the patience with which they explore disagreements. If I explore these disagreements further (and from the weak position of a greatly inferior knowledge of Soviet history and reality) it is because of the extreme importance of the issues, and the urgency with which the European and American peace movements await a discourse of genuine internationalism with wider sections of the Soviet public. And for this to take place we must first remove certain road-blocks and controls which the Medvedevs scarcely mention.

I learned much from the Medvedevs' essay and have few and insignificant disagreements with it. Yet it leaves much unsaid, and in doing so it could close off some lines of inquiry prematurely. The Medvedevs are viewing history as rational *causation*, whereas I am viewing the contemporary opposed militarist structures as historical *consequences*; so that some of our arguments are flying past each others' ears. Everything the Medvedevs say about the prior responsibility of 'the West' for militaristic pace-making may be true; yet the consequence of three decades of Soviet response to that may have been to enstructure militarism deeply in Soviet society also.

The Medvedevs argue that the Soviet Union has militarized itself reluctantly, defensively, that the Party remains in control of all organs of the state. Yet history is full of examples of the way in which deeper processes can override or coopt such controls and intentions. It simply is not possible for a major economy to be inflected towards military priorities for some three decades (and more) without profound consequences in social, political and ideological life.

The Medvedevs argue that 'military-industrial-research interests in the Soviet Union. . . do not constitute a "state within the state" as they do in the United States, but remain a subordinate part of the state'. I am surprised they can argue with such confidence, in view of the opacity of Soviet state structures and the paucity of published information—which they are the first to acknowledge. 'Subordinate', in any case, to what? To a Party which itself must in some part represent these interests (to which some 15% of the GNP is allocated) and some of whose leading executives are recruited from the military-industrial-security areas? There are some scraps of evidence known to me (many more weighty evidences must be known to the Medvedevs) which suggest that 'isomorphic' replication of militarist priorities is not unknown in Soviet life. Thus 'Boris Komarov', the Soviet ecologist, refers repeatedly to the ways in which 'defence' priorities can always over-rule the well-intended environmental regulations of Soviet authorities. The sad story of the pollution of Lake Baikal commenced when 'the Ministry of Defence needed new durable cord for heavy bomber tyres. Such things are referred to tersely as "strategic interests of the country" and are not subject for discussion even within the Council of Ministers. The immunity of the Baikal projects to any criticism is explained by these "strategic interests".' And recounting the story of the poisoning of wild life by PCB (polychlorinated biphenyls) he concludes that 'the secret of PCB, as might have been expected, was buried in one of the defence ministries. PCB was required for extra-strong insulation for military equipment: its composition and hazards were concealed for reasons of military secrecy: 'Here too "strategic interests" prevailed. In the most literal sense strategic interests pervade our whole being whether we want them or not'. And to all this 'Komarov' provides some lighter footnotes. He describes the wholesale slaughter of wild life by high- (and even low-) placed military, overriding every protective regulation: 'eagles, hobbies, kites, and other birds of prey are wiped out from military helicopters just for practice;. Marshal Chuikov has even been known to sweep through whole areas with a column of all-terrain vehicles, field kitchens, etcetera, slaughtering every bird and beast in sight; polar bears have been hunted by helicopter; and so on.[1] It is all reminiscent of the safaris of British officers in Kenya or in the Indian princedoms, thirty or fifty years ago.

The Medvedevs will understand that I do not introduce this evidence with 'anti-Soviet' intent. I am simply insisting that one cannot divert huge resources to secretive and protected military areas without incurring huge social consequences; that the same consequences which are felt here in Britain at Stornoway or at West Wycombe[2] are felt there at Baikal or at Kyzyl-Agach. When 'strategic interests of the country' are not even subject for discussion within the Council of Ministers, in what sense are these then 'a subordinate part of the state'? Is this not only too familiar to us in 'the free West'?

If polychlorinated biphenyls, protected by 'strategic interests', can poison the water and grass of the Soviet Union, I would think it probable also that similar toxic ideological compounds, also protected by 'strategic interests', will be poisoning or confusing the minds of the Soviet people, just as these poison minds in the West. The ideological PCBs commonly found on this side are those which offer partisan, alarmist, or directly nationalistic descriptions of reality—which justify each and every measure of militarization in the name of 'deterrence' and the threat of the Other—which directly inhibit genuine international discourse, and which repress or inhibit critical reflection and discussion as threats to the 'security' of the state. One need not read very far in the literature on contemporary Soviet reality to learn that such toxic compounds are widely dispersed, on that side as on this.

This does not mean that we should look for structural symmetries in the opposed superpowers. I have argued, not for this, but for reciprocal and interactive modes of strategic and ideological confrontation. If symmetry now, in the 1980s, begins to appear, this is consequence and not causation. We are entering upon extremely uneasy times, and we ought not to refuse consideration of the possibility that one of the options still open for a resolution of the political problems of the Soviet Union is a military one. It is already apparent that some sections of the ruling establishment there are displaying anxiety lest the peace movement should infect Soviet youth, but in a form critical of Soviet reality. In the past few months there has been an assault upon 'pacifist' tendencies weakening the 'heroic-patriotic' faith of Soviet youth. Boris Pastukhov, a leader of the Comsomol, has called for 'Undertaking with yet greater clarity of purpose the military-patriotic upbringing, the moral, political, psychological and technical preparation of youth for service in the ranks of the armed forces, to instil in young people courage, the will and readiness to perform heroic deeds. . .'[3]. This is the moralistic and nationalist claptrap of all armed states. But even if it is argued that these necessary ideological measures are imposed upon Soviet authorities by the aggressive postures of the West in association with China, the consequence must be nationalistic and militaristic indoctrination. And behind this claptrap, is it not possible to distinguish the features of a distinct militarist lobby? Marshal Ogarkov, the Soviet Chief of Staff, has recently published a book, *Always Ready to Defend the Fatherland*, which advocates the demands of the military in an unusually open way. He advocates, like his NATO analogues, not only a massive programme of weapons 'modernization', but also advanced preparations for switching 'the entire economy to a war footing': 'In order to increase the military preparedness of the country, today as never before it is necessary to coordinate mobilization and deployment of the armed forces and the entire economy . . . .'. To achieve these objectives 'is not possible without a stable centralized system of leadership of the country and the armed forces . . . an even greater concentration of management'.[4]

This centralized management, this stable and concentrated system of leadership of the-country-and the-armed-forces, looks rather like some kind of military junta to me. Because Marshal Ogarkov has given a thought to this possibility it does not mean that it will come about. But we have seen already, in Poland, a military junta displace the Party in power: and while this was a Polish solution arising from Polish conditions, it establishes a new precedent nonetheless. For the radical political weakness of the Soviet Union and of every Warsaw Pact state is to be found in the weakness of civil society; it is sixty-five years on from the Revolution, and yet civil society in the Soviet Union has a sparse and insecure presence, existing within the controls and by the permission of the Party and the security police; and it is precisely where civil society is weak that the military (in alliance with other interests) can most swiftly enter in. It is not just a question of force: it is a question of legitimacy. Where no form of power is legitimated by civil accountability and due and open process, then one form of power might just as well give way to another. Each is as legitimate or as illegitimate as the other.

As the Medvedevs will know, speculations as to the line of political succession when Brezhnev departs are not confined to the sensational articles of Western Kremlinologists. People in Eastern Europe are watching and holding their breath, within the state apparatuses as well as without. No doubt this is true in the Soviet Union as well: why else is that ailing old man clinging on for so long? If Brezhnev should suddenly depart at a moment when Reagan, Haig and Thatcher are working out their infantile aggressive fantasies, then it is probable that the Politbureau will look around for a Marshal or two to answer them; or the Marshals themselves may enter the room without knocking. And we might argue then how far the West was co-responsible for this outcome—an outcome in which Western rulers, by their own provocative actions, had summoned into reality the 'worst case' of their own inflamed imaginations.[5]

I hope, profoundly, that the Medvedevs are right and that my own fantasy is wrong. Yet for it to be proved wrong may at the least require that the possibility be steadily faced, so that action may be taken to prevent it. And what disturbed me most about the Medvedevs' brilliant essay was a sense that the accumulation of absences and silences amounted even to complacency. This is so far out of character in these two indomitable and uncomplacent authors that I must be wrong. Yet the sense lingered with me, especially at the article's conclusion—in the section sub-headed 'The Responsibility of the Peace Movement'. And it turned out here that this responsibility fell wholly, and without qualification, upon the peace movements of NATO and of Western European nations. The solution to the immediate crisis will (it seems) be met by the pressure 'for unilateral nuclear disarmament in Europe' but for 'Europe' it seems that we should read 'Western Europe' and nothing whatsoever is said about the need for any peace movement, or even reciprocal strategy of agitation, in the East. So that while the Medvedevs' analysis is very much more rich and flexible than any from apologists of the Soviet state, yet their conclusions are pat and even orthodox.

The Ideological Blockade

Now this is a matter which, for our very survival, must be honestly faced and openly argued out. For the Medvedevs, in the first pages of their essay, suggest an immense Soviet audience—an ordinary Soviet public, and also partisans of socialist democracy like themselves, Soviet citizens who attend to the work of the Western peace movement and who share its concerns. Let us trust that this is so. It may even be so. Yet something, somehow, has become skewed. For one of the most remarkable facts of the past two-and-a-half years has been the Soviet *absence* from the European peace movement. What Soviet citizens have taken part in its discourse, or been willing to engage, upon equal terms, in its councils? A handful of doctors: Roy and Zhores Medvedev; that is all.

No doubt a host of other Soviet citizens might wish to do so but are inhibited by bureaucratic constraints. These constraints are not—or are not often—those imposed by the West. They belong to the long-standing ideological self-blockade, by Communist states, of their own citizenry: the Communist international default. To examine, as rational causation, the history of this default might give us a very different historical answer to the question of co-responsibility for the Cold War than does a history confined to the arms race, A history of the arms race can be offered, as the Medvedevs offer it, in terms of NATO action and Warsaw Pact reaction: this tends then to the complacent conclusion that if NATO should halt its provocative actions the Warsaw Pact will instantly cease to react, and the peace-loving intentions of the Soviet Union will then become plain to all mankind (except, perhaps, to some Afghan tribesmen). But a history of the ideological confrontation of the two blocks, which has contributed as much as military measures to the adversary posture underpinning the Cold War, must result in more ambiguous conclusions. It has to be said, again and again, and in terms which demand a Soviet response, that the repression of the Prague Spring (1968) was as much the action of irresponsible warmongers as was the NATO 'modernization' decision of 12 December 1979. And if it is the responsibility of the Western peace movement to contest with every resource the latter decision, it is the responsibility of the Soviet people also to contest the ideological and security structures which poison the political discourse of Europe, enforce its division into 'two camps', and legitimate the Communist international default.

I will not attempt to sketch this alternative ideological history here, although I have gestured towards it in *Beyond the Cold War*. But the presence of this history, as consequence, is manifest in Europe today. By 'Communist international default' I mean the refusal of the Communist apparatuses of the Soviet Union and of the Warsaw bloc to permit direct international discourse between citizens or groups, unregulated by their own security and ideological controls; their insistence that all exchange, even between peace movements, takes place upon their own favoured ideological terrain; the radical insecurity which inhibits any manifestation within the Warsaw bloc which might express a critical view of any aspect of Soviet reality; and the very damaging attempts to manipulate, or to divide, Western democratic movements, including Western Communist parties, trade unions and peace movements themselves, in order to subordinate them to the diplomacies of the Soviet state.

All this has a complex and bitter history. After 1945 there was the severance of ten thousand strands of international discourse, each severance causing confusion and pain. I can recall that moment, when the frame-up of the Hungarian Communist leader Laszlo Rajk was announced, and when we opened our papers in surprise to discover that Konni Zilliacus (the Labour Party's leading internationalist MP, expelled from the PLP for his stubborn work for peace), Basil Davidson and Claud Cockburn (two of the most able, internationally expert journalists of the British left) had all been 'unmasked' as imperialist agents. And so it has gone on. Frame-ups and the unmasking of imperialist agents are less in fashion now. But the same arrogant authoritarianism, the same bureaucratic manipulation, and the same fear of any East-West discourse taking place outside the authorized forums and the permitted ideological terrain—all these remain in force.

The World Peace Council congeals some of that history and protracts it into the present. I am aware that many younger members of the European peace movement cannot understand the distaste with which some of us grey-headed ones regard that mendacious bureaucratic organization and its national subsidiaries: these quasi-official state 'Peace Committees' appear to them as plausible places for international communication; and their efficiency as travel agents for visiting delegations eliminates many of the difficulties and costs of less structured exchanges. I will only say that some of us still active in the peace movement have had twenty-five or thirty years of experience of the WPC's manipulations and bad faith—a Council which, in all that time, has never found fault with a single Soviet action—and that the subject has become merely boring.[5] It is an organization whose function is to structure authorized East-West exchanges and to blockade all others. It is a satire upon any authentic internationalist discourse. The son of the traduced and executed Laszlo Rajk now runs a *samizdat* bookshop in Budapest. Any honest East-West discourse must hold a place open for him.

Let us propose this in a more positive way. The conditions which threaten us today—which throw the shadow of extermination upon us all—are military, political and ideological. For more than two years an influential peace movement has been developing, in Western Europe, Japan, Australia, the United States, from the spontaneous and democratic initiatives of the public. This has been contesting, in the first place, the menacing military and political dispositions of the NATO powers. What might give to this movement truly impressive strength—what might even bring some victory within reach—would be a junction between the Western peace movement and some congruent movement of opinion in the Soviet Union and in Eastern Europe.

This cannot come from travel and conference-promoting agencies subordinate to the *realpolitik* of the Warsaw Pact states. The present position is absurd. The orthodox Communist media, in the East, welcome and publicize the manifestations of the Western peace movements while at the same time censoring their demands and inhibiting an equivalent discourse in their own nations. This book will not be published in the Soviet Union, and if the articles or pamphlets of Bahro or Magri or Chomsky or my own *Beyond the Cold War* appear in Eastern Europe they will appear in *samizdat* and at the publishers' risk.

The Soviet state may not have co-equal responsibility for the thirty years of arms race, but it does have—and at this moment it has—co-responsibility for the continued ideological division of Europe, the Cold War. Europeans await, with increasing anxiety, the return of Soviet citizens to an international discourse: youth must be able to travel, writers to publish, peace movements to confer and to canvas alternative strategies, without attending upon some Office of Orthodoxy. It is not good enough that the gifted citizens of one of the greatest nations of the earth should cower secretively behind security barricades, and excuse themselves from all responsibility for this predicament with apologetic histories which always place the blame upon the shoulders of others.

We accept this blame: we in the West are contesting the policies of our own states. We ask the Soviet people to accept their responsibilities also: only their initiatives can begin to dismantle their own security and ideological barricades and repair the Communist international default. And the matter is urgent: the peace movement in the West, which anxiously awaits their response, cannot guarantee the continued vitality of its presence if that response fails to come. One cannot maintain the morale of a movement so inchoate and so moody without some signs of success; and one can imagine more than one scenario (a deterioration of the situation in Poland, a NATO adventure in Libya or the Middle East, a show trial of Czech 'dissidents' or a submarine disaster off Stornoway or in the Black Sea) which would check it or throw it into reverse.

Peace depends now and in the immediate future upon the élan and the continual enlargement of the democratic internationalism of the non-aligned peace movement. It depends upon the forging of a new internationalism, unmediated by state structures, between the citizenry West and East. The opportunity is open, now, and the response from Soviet citizens must begin to show itself before the end of 1982. We must find ways to signal this urgently to the Soviet public in the coming months. There is no need, of course, to signal this to Roy and Zhores Medvedev: they are themselves evidence of the internationalism of Soviet citizens, and pledges that the junction between autonomous movements for peace and for socialist democracy, East and West, can still take place.

The Problem of Historical Explanation

I am chided by several contributors, including Mike Davis and Fred Halliday, for my seeming disregard for historical analysis. I ought to explain this treason to my own historical trade.

Contemporary history is always a weak and provisional exercise, not only for the obvious technical reasons (the insubstantial and unvalidated nature of some crucial evidence) but also because we are not yet at a sufficient distance from the full process to know what are the most significant questions to be proposed. We carry over into the present the questions proposed, not by the present (whose shape and outcome we cannot yet know), but those proposed by the past. Hence what is offered as analysis very often turns out subsequently to have been only a descriptive phenomenology arranged in a certain order by the conventional wisdom (or one of the alternative conventional wisdoms) of the times. I find some passages of Davis's essay suggestive; but in sum it seems to me to be a description of events, selected and tied together by a conventional Leninist wisdom of a self-confirming kind.

I have already drawn a distinction between 'history' as causation and as consequence. Eventuation is incessant and without seams; yet there are moments of qualitative change, when new social or political configurations appear, new ideologies become dominant, old hegemonies are challenged and new hegemonies arise: and at such moments of change new questions must be proposed. We prefer always to cling to older categories of analysis derived from the past, even when these are wearing down into misleading stereotypes which we recognize only because we have come to expect them. Yet something, at some point, has changed. The Third Reich, as state power or as Nazi ideology, cannot be explained by assembling the causative forces that brought Hitler to power; and the Cold War today, in its military and ideological emplacements and ritual confrontations, cannot be explained by returning again and again to its origins and allocating blame. Mike Davis confronts me triumphantly with a seeming 'contradiction' in my imagery in *Beyond the Cold War*: at one point I employ the fluid metaphor of a river of change, at another I refer to a political culture struck, at the onset of the Cold War, into 'glaciated stasis' and to an intellectual culture struck with 'an ideological permafrost'. Which is it to be, asks Davis—'Fixed or fluid? The inconsistency condenses the paradoxes of Thompson's general sketch of exterminism: the supreme humanist become arch structuralist, the moralist turned clinician, the historian rejecting history'.

Aha, he must have me there! Yet I think he does not. For the contrast between the fluidity of the course of real socio-economic change and the fixity of Cold War ideology and categories is at the heart of my argument. The Cold War, as ideology, is stuck for ever in the rehearsal of its origins, and of the apparent intentions of its actors; but the reality has long moved on. To identify that changed reality we may have to show a provisional treason to the historical method. We may have to hold back for a little attempts at a totalizing historical explanation and look as directly as we can at contemporary evidences: the historians may then set to work, with greater effect, when they know what is new and what is significant—what they must explain.

The histories proposed by Halliday and by Davis are well-informed and suggestive. I assent most often to Halliday's account, not because anything is proved, but because his selection and ordering of significancies conforms most closely to what my own common sense approves. But I am wary of the way in which Davis offers to tidy up thirty years of history, and package it into categories which, on inspection, are rhetorical or descriptive rather than analytical. 'The dominant level of world politics', he assures us with confidence, 'is the process of *permanent revolution* arising out of uneven and combined development of global capitalism'. I wonder what this means? That the poor of the world continue to resent and to resist the rich, and they do so with enlarged expectations and self-confidence in the post-colonial era? The 'uneven and combined development of global capitalism' suggests something more precise and grander than this. And this is sometimes supported by organicist metaphors and by the attribution of goals and intentions to social classes of a kind which I have long found to be at enmity with historical materialism. When Halliday speaks of 'a period when world capitalism has been able to expand the area of parliamentary democracy in its South European tier—Portugal, Spain and Greece', I wonder what Supremo of 'world capitalism' thought up this clever mystifying tactic and by which agents it was set in motion? When Davis announces that the opposed blocs may annihilate each other soon, not through any surge of militarist irrationalities, but in consequence of 'the recurrent historical phenomenon of class *error*' in mistaking their own rational class interests, then he must know himself that he has reduced his own explanatory method to the absurd.

'Class error' supposes a platonic paradigm of 'true' class interests to which history *ought* to conform: the real history is chided—or would be chided if there was any Leninist intellect left in the void to award marks for error—because it does not match the metaphysic. Such exercises have a hypnotic compulsion as we move in seven-league strides through five continents and three decades, finding that every event and phenomenon is rationally interconnected and that 'the dynamic of class struggle on a world scale' is the mainspring of all. No doubt it is. And so it was also in the days of my youth, when I and my generation were addicted to Palme Dutt's 'Notes of the Month' in *Labour Monthly* in which the same compelling rationality of global class struggle could always be found at work. Yet in particulars and in predictions Palme Dutt turned out so often to be wrong that the compulsion of the hypnosis began to fade, until we fell, alas, victims of the heresy of William Blake: 'To Generalize is to be an Idiot. To Particularize is the Alone Distinction of Merit. General Knowledges are those Knowledges that Idiots possess'.[6] Blake's heresy is absurd, and no one writing in this volume is an Idiot. We are generalizing, every one of us, and until we have sketched in some provisional historical chart we cannot select the 'minute particulars' which merit more scrupulous attention. I am not taking refuge in an irrational refusal of historical explanation. Yet Blake's expostulation still carries force. Davis offers many shrewd observations: yet when he seeks to sew these all together, in a seamless explanatory whole, as a totalizing history of the 'Cold War', too many minute particulars—and among these some of the most significant—wriggle out of the large mesh of the generalizing net. Do the categories of 'class struggle on a world scale' really explain to us the course of the Iranian revolution? The degeneration of the regime of Pol Pot? The adversary relations of China and the USSR? The generational shifts in political consciousness in Europe, East and West, associated with the peace movement and the movement for civil rights? Or the imperial atavism of the British government's response to the Falklands crisis? By attempting to explain it all in one global mouthful we end up with everything left to be explained.

Moreover, if we presume that the explanatory schema of global capitalist crisis will be adequate to every occasion, then we can certainly sketch out logical lines of connection between every event (the world market is universal and money is always making mayhem everywhere) and these will look plausible on the page. But these schemata may be deployed to the exclusion of other matters which, when we consider minute particulars, may have greater relevance—demographic pressures, resurgent nationalisms, tenacious cultural traditions, military-industrial lobbies, ideological crisis. In preempting the schema we preempt also the permissible questions. From the standpoint of the future will the significant question be how Third World nations came to have 'revolutions', or will it concern the nature of the societies to which these revolutions gave rise—how post-revolutionary societies became militarized, how internecine rivalries developed between them, or, again, as Bahro might insist, how the course of development was diverted into the blind alleys of monoculture or of inapposite industrialisms?

I find in this month's newspapers that very foul things are going on in the Indian Himalayas, with the unprecedented destruction of vast forest areas, with consequent soil erosion, and that this menaces the North Indian plains and the densely populated Ganges delta with far-reaching ecological changes—silting of channels, alternate flooding and droughts perhaps even changes in the monsoon pattern. It is not difficult to blame world capitalism for this (and for the famines that may follow on), through the local agency of avaricious contractors and corrupt local officials.[7] Yet I learn also that an identical deforestation is going on in the Tibetan Himalayas, without benefit of capitalist contractors or (for all I know) of corrupt officials. Here also 'whole hillsides have been devastated and day and night rivers are full of logs being sent down river to China'.[8]

My point, which is a commonplace one, is that what may be seen from one aspect as a crisis of global class struggle may be seen from another as a crisis of modernization. What is taking place, across the globe, is a rupture of subsistence economies, of customary norms and demographic patterns, and with the shattering of custom there is an unprecedented uprush of expectations. Of course this is intensified by exploitation: of course it gives rise to class struggles. But have we always got the exploiters and the class alignments right? What are offered as Marxisms, in some parts of the Third World, turn out on inspection to be ideologies of educated, recently urbanized modernizing élites, some of them displaced, unemployed, hostile to their rural origins, and in search of employment in the lower levels of urban bureaucracies—ideologies which can bear very hard (as they did in Afghanistan) upon the urban poor and the rural population as a whole. I cannot go all the way with Bahro and see our troubles as derived, *tout court*, from 'industrialism'. That seems to be to be an argument, rooted in both Germany and Britain in a long-distant moment of Romantic protest, composed of contradictory, negative as well as positive, elements. But I cannot refuse the questions which Bahro proposes either. That bastard offspring of utilitarianism and of capitalist market economics, 'modernization theory', with its hatred of custom and its indifference to culture, has an uncomfortable affinity with certain theories and strategies derivative (or purportedly derivative) from Marx. Marxists of the old, Stalinist, school, in some parts of the developing world, understood Western modernization theorists only too well. What makes one anxious is not the points at which 'global class struggle' are announced but the points where the adversaries become indistinguishable. In their single-minded pursuit of the goal of economic 'growth', in their arrogant assumption of their right to recycle cultural norms, some modernizers and some Marxists have found a common identity.

If we were to ask these questions, then we would have to ask them also of the history. I can offer no answers. But I ask them sharply of Mike Davis, because I find his recourse to existing categories over-confident and insufficiently curious about the need for new. It insists that we encompass the present within categories derived from the past and that no others are required: 'the strategic arms race must be conceived as a complex, regulative instance of the global class struggle'. And if it *must* be conceived so, then examples can be deployed to make the conception plausible. But inconvenient evidence quietly falls away. The 'dynamic of the Cold War' is presented with one highly visible protagonist—an insatiably aggressive capitalism pre-programmed to limitless expansion—and a dimly perceived reactive protagonist, the Soviet Union, which is threatened and contained. And as Davis crosses and recrosses the globe in his seven-league boots ('then came Luanda, Managua and Teheran'), identifying tectonic plates and huge geo-political formations, it is possible to overlook the fact that his is a highly selective, self-conforming vision. One episode that escapes his vision altogether is Gdansk: that is, the astonishing sixteen-month life-cycle of Polish Solidarity.

Solidarity's life-cycle is one of the most remarkable and authentic examples of self-activity in history, and without doubt the most massive and purposive working-class movement in any advanced society since the Second World War. To be sure, it had certain features which might wrinkle the nose of a purist: it was nationalist, Catholic, predominantly male, and in its last months over-confident. Its internationalist perspectives were confined and confused. But my point, at this moment, is that an analysis of the contemporary crisis in terms of the global class struggle which cannot find any place for this astonishing episode of class struggle has somehow lost its way. Can the struggle have been between the wrong classes and in the wrong part of the globe? And, if so, should we not ask whether not the history but our own categories and political perspectives may not be wrong? For Solidarity's insurgence (and it may yet prove to be only the first stage of a continuing episode) has signalled that there are extreme tensions—and perhaps possibilities of transformation—over there, on that side, which have the most direct bearing on the Cold War and its history. Things over there may now get worse; they may get better; but, after Solidarity, neither ideological controls nor state structures, over there, can remain the same.

Europe and the Third World

This brings us back, by a circuitous route, to relations between the Cold War, Europe, and the Third World. I have been criticized by several contributors for awarding such preeminence in my analysis to the fracture of power and of ideology through the heart of Europe as 'the central locus of the opposed exterminist thrusts': the place of origin of the Cold War and the place where its adversary postures are continually regenerated and refreshed. I am persuaded that I must take the criticism into account. I welcome especially the forceful correction of Kugai. It is not so much that I find my proposal to be wrong as that I am now unclear as to the proposal's status: I do not know what evidence would be required either to support it or to refute it.

It would be better if I stood the proposal on its head: *Europe, in the 1980s, is the weak link in the Cold War*. The contributions to this volume which evoke my warmest response are those of Europeans—Bahro, Magri, the final pages of Halliday, the generous comments of Balibar. Each of these explain, with eloquence, why the weak link lies there. Their contributions speak for themselves. The question now is not whether Europe is the locus which generates the Cold War but whether Europe may not be the continent on which, as Erhard Eppler has said, the 'chain of armaments' might be struck through. Europe is now the locus of opportunity; and for this reason Europeans now carry a responsibility to the rest of the world—to the Third World in particular—to realize whatever opportunity allows.

Certainly Europe is menaced by particular military dispositions, by a density of weaponry, and by strategies which threaten a limited theatre war. But that is not all that has brought the new peace movements into being, as some North American observers may have supposed. There are also particular political and ideological conditions peculiar to Europe which make the fracture of its political culture seem increasingly arbitrary and insupportable. As direct conflicts of interest between the confronting blocs recede into insignificance in the heart of the continent, so congruent economic and cultural interests assert themselves. No 'global class struggle' divides the workers of Gdansk from those in Newcastle, or the peasantries of Hungary and Greece. The old ideological compulsions of the Cold War are losing their hold upon the rising generation. As impulses for socialist democracy or for civil rights find expression in the East so these can meet with a response in the peace and labour movements of the West. Increasingly it appears, in common-sense political perception, that the adversary structures of the armed blocs are all that are holding this confluence back. All this is a theme of my *Beyond the Cold War*.

To say that the Cold War is now perpetuated by its own self-reproducing inertia—that it is about itself—is perhaps a European perception. It is small comfort to those in El Salvador, Afghanistan, or Namibia. Yet it may be, within Europe's own context and conditions, true—as a perception which is challenging rather than complacent or Eurocentric. It is here that the chain might be struck through: but it is here also that new transformations, of the most radical and affirmative import for the rest of the world, might commence.

I am unwilling to predict what form these transformations might take, if the best case came about. I would predict only that we would have to devise new categories to explain them. In a general and loose sense I would agree with Halliday: socialist democracy, in some sense, might be the vocabulary of change in both worlds. But it would have to be more sharply anti-statist and libertarian than anything in the dominant Communist or Social Democratic traditions, or in Marxist theoretical orthodoxy: nothing less will be tough enough to meet the opposition, and maybe repression, of the opposed militarized states. It is likely also that (following Bahro) it will be informed by an alert ecological consciousness since the congruent struggles, West and East, will be founded upon the human ecological imperative. That being so, it will shatter or transform or transcend the ritualized and long-inert categories of 'Communism' and of 'Social Democracy', whatever historical legacy or detritus is left in the institutions and forms of particular nations. It is not that the Second International will make it up and enter a marriage with the Third. New forces and new forms will replace them both.

That is the best case, and the worst case remains at least as probable. This best case is argued eloquently by Lucio Magri, with whom I express my solidarity and accord. I welcome most especially his definition of the possible relationship between the European peace movement and the Third World. Success of the European best case might open up the possibility of wholly new kinds of relationship between the advanced and the underdeveloped worlds. His definition of the matter is superb and I urge readers to return to it again and again: 'Any new relationship with the Third World presupposes a qualitative change in our own type of development. Such a change would have to involve a reorientation of the European economies away from the quantitative multiplication of goods for consumption and export, and the wastage of natural resources that goes with it, towards another style of development: one that was sober in its consumption, exported technology and knowledge rather than commodities, sought a reduction in labour-time performed, gave priority to improvements in the quality of living.'

The arms race is a theft of resources from the Third World. The export of arms, military infrastructures, and of militarist ideologies (some of them disguised as Marxisms) from the advanced world to the Third World is a way of distorting social process, of aborting revolutions or of stifling their potential at birth. This is not only an era of permanent revolution but an era in which every revolution is screwed up as every nation is dragged into the polarities of the Cold War. If Europeans could strike through the chain of armaments—and the diplomacies and ideologists that go with it—and find a third way then in that moment the possibility would open up of a new non-exploitative relationship with the Third World, bringing mater- ial and cultural reinforcements to the strategy of non-alignment and afford- ing more space to Third World nations to pilot their own course of development independently of either bloc.

This is the European opportunity. It is also the European responsibility to the world. I see no refusal of international solidarities in this. I do not know what Davis means when he warns the peace movement not to 'pine nostalgically for the restoration of a lost European or Northern civilization'. I do not know that European civilization is yet lost, and I do not know that in all its manifestations it has been disgraceful. It is not disreputable to hope that living generations will survive. If we suppose (as Davis seems to do) that 'the hopes of socialism in the Northern hemisphere' are dependent 'upon the desperate and courageous battles' being waged in the Third World, then this could be an excuse for giving any action up, falling into the role of observers, or nourishing an enlarged sense of unproductive guilt. We have to act where we are and to seize the opportunities within our reach. However much we are moved by Davis's peroration, few of us will take a gun to El Salvador or join the Chipko movement hugging trees in the Himalayas. Too large a sense of guilt disables the will.

I end with a confession of uncertainty. I will not fight for the category of 'exterminism' provided that the problem it indicates is not tidied away. We are at the end of an epoch, when every old category begins to have a hollow sound, and when we are groping in the dusk to discover the new. Some of us must be content to offer unfinished 'Notes', or may risk (as Bahro sometimes does) provocations and prophecies. I distrust only those who (after Cambodia, after Solidarity and Polish martial law) are satisfied with the old categories and who offer to explain overmuch.

We are engaged in an international discourse of extraordinary complexity. We are trying to construct, out of the collapse of earlier traditions, a new internationalist constituency and one capable of acting urgently and with effect. We cannot write our recipes at leisure in the drawing-room and pass them on to the servants' hall (although some try to do that still): we must improvise our recipes as we sweat before the kitchen fires. Even in Europe, to assemble that internationalist constituency into a common peace movement—from so many nations, traditions, and from two adversary blocs hung around with misrecognitions—requires extraordinary skills. Intellectuals and communicators have particular responsibilities and roles in putting that internationalism together in these early stages. They are the couriers who must take the first messages across the frontiers of ideologies. And they must be self-mobilized; they must find their own routes; they cannot wait upon any High Command of party or of peace movement to tell them what to do. It is in this spirit that the editors and contributors to this volume have acted, and I salute their work.

April 1982

---

[1]'Boris Komarov', *The Destruction of Nature in the Soviet Union*, London 1980, pp. 7, 33–4, 77, 87–9.

[2]I mention West Wycombe because it is a village adjacent to the site of a new twelve-acre underground bunker in the Chilterns to be constructed for NATO air strike command by the Ministry of Defence on property owned by the National Trust, whose officers have readily agreed. The National Trust! Perhaps the Soviet Politbureau is a 'National Trust' of the same kind? (See *Guardian*, 21 April 1982).

[3]*Christian Science Monitor*, 11 March 1982.

[4]*Guardian*, 12 April 1982.

[5]Can I mention just *one*, small episode of that old history to explain one's contempt for the WPC? In the 1950s, during the Korean War and the contest around German rearmament, a number of prominent members of Yorkshire Labour Parties were expelled for their activity in the West Yorkshire Federation of Peace Organizations, of which I was then Secretary: their offence was to work in the same organization as Communists, and to support the campaigns and conferences of the World Peace Council. Dorothy Greenald, a West Riding magistrate and county councillor, who was one of the expelled, became a member of the World Peace Council and was indefatigable in attendance at Council executive meetings from Helsinki to Colombo. In 1956, at the time of the Hungarian insurrection, it must have come to the notice of some WPC bureaucrat that Dorothy Greenald was sharply critical of Soviet actions, and was an associate of 'revisionists' like my wife and myself. Her name disappeared without explanation from the list of Council members and she was struck from the mailing list. She has still, after twenty-six years, received not a line of explanation or apology. She is still of course, active in the movement for peace. But it is not possible to have serious political relations with a Council which manipulates people like that.

[6]From Blake's 'Annotations to Reynolds'.

[7]*The Times*, 7 April 1982.

[8]*Tibet News Review*, winter 1980–81.

Index

354